EASTBOURNE SCHOOL, DARLINGTON

The Growth, Success, and Failure of a Secondary School

An example of the development, organisation and provision of secondary education 1936–2007

Eastbourne School, Darlington

The Growth, Success, and Failure of a Secondary School

An example of the development, organisation and
provision of secondary education 1936–2007

R. V. Bryant

JANUS PUBLISHING COMPANY LTD
Cambridge, England

First published in Great Britain 2015
by Janus Publishing Company Ltd,
The Studio
High Green
Great Shelford
Cambridge CB22 5EG

www.januspublishing.co.uk

British Library Cataloguing-in-Publication Data
A catalogue record for this book is available from the British Library

ISBN 978-1-85756-833-2

Cover Design: Pictures supplied by the author

Printed and bound in the UK by PublishPoint
from KnowledgePoint Limited, Reading

Contents

Introduction

Eastbourne School, Darlington, opened as the Eastbourne Senior Mixed School in August 1936 in new purpose-built, although incomplete, premises. In 1939 it became two single-sex schools; and after the 1939–45 war, as a result of legislation introduced in the Education Act of 1944, it evolved into girls' and boys' secondary modern schools. Finally the schools combined again in 1968 to become the Eastbourne Mixed Comprehensive School.

Passing through these stages of development it is a practical, real-life example of the growth of English secondary school education from the 1930s to the present day.

As a senior school and then as two secondary modern schools, Eastbourne evolved as a relatively uncomplicated system providing a high standard of education in numeracy, literacy, music, speech, drama, general knowledge and physical activities, combined with a sense of order and discipline, to young people destined to take their places in the world of adult employment at 14, later 15, years of age.

It may also be seen as an example of an eventual failure of the education system, for by 2007, and after various attempts to right its declared shortcomings, Eastbourne School was finally closed.

As the head teacher of the comprehensive school from January 1973 to August 1986, I have been saddened by its demise and dismayed by the effect this must have had on generations of young people who had been educated there, and on the many teachers who have worked with such enthusiasm and great loyalty to produce many, often unnoticed, very significant successes.

In this attempt to outline the history of the Eastbourne secondary school I hope to record something of the spirit of each stage in its development, its successes and frustrations, and attempt to analyse why it was eventually labelled by the local newspaper, the *Northern Echo* (2006), as 'The Worst School in the Country', a label that should never be given to any educational establishment which, for reasons beyond its control, may seem to merit it.

The education system from 1800 to the 1930s

For those whose memories or experience do not stretch back that far, a description of the education system as it was before and by 1936 is significant, in appreciating both the nature of the new Eastbourne Senior School and what has happened since. A very significant aspect of the growth of the education system is the concept of compulsory education for all and the ongoing raising of the leaving age for children and young people.

Before 1800, education was provided by fee-charging private schools, church charity schools and grammar schools. The latter were established by various foundations to provide teaching in classical languages and evolved to become the traditional grammar and public schools. The first true education system was provided by the church and based on the monitorial system: a plan in which one teacher instructed a number of pupil teachers, or monitors, who then delivered the lessons to smaller groups of pupils. The founders, Andrew Bell and Joseph Lancaster, established the Anglican National Schools Society and non-conformist British and Foreign Schools Society for this purpose. The first government involvement was in 1839 when a committee was set up to administer the allocation of a small grant to these societies.

The next significant development came in 1870 when the Elementary Education Act created the School Boards, giving them authority to raise money on the rates in order to fund new schools which would supplement the church system. This was the birth of elementary education and elementary schools. The charging of school fees continued and whether or not attendance was compulsory was left to the discretion of the individual boards.

It was little more than 100 years ago, in 1888, that the county council system of local government was introduced and ten years after that they were given authority to raise money on the rates in order to pay for deserving elementary school children to attend grammar schools. This was not for all children and was not entirely free. It was an education for those academically able children not already in fee-charging grammar and public schools but whose parents could afford to support them.

Although the 1899 Education Act established the Board of Education, it was not until 1902 (the Balfour Education Act) that local education authorities (LEAs) were set up, national regulations introduced for elementary and secondary schools, school examinations rationalised and a handbook produced for teachers. Even then it was expected that the government would not provide much more than 50 per cent of the cost.

Further encouragement was given to the notion that able children should continue in school when in 1907 local authority secondary schools became eligible for a grant if they made 25 per cent or more of their places free. In 1932 the Special Places Scheme was introduced whereby parents of children selected for secondary education were charged according to their ability to pay.

In 1911 a compulsory school-leaving age of 13 was established but the opportunity to remain at school until the age of 14 depended on where you lived, the better-off local authorities providing places while others could not afford to do so. It was also in this year that the Board of Education called for the provision of more practical and vocational work in the secondary curriculum, for science and art examinations to be reformed in order to encourage the teaching of new subjects, and for more teachers with industrial experience to be employed. Was this a genuine desire to educate a realistic workforce, to provide an education according to the needs of the young, or a means of maintaining the class system? Unfortunately, practical and vocational courses came to be seen as inferior to, rather than merely different from, the academic courses provided in the grammar schools. Yet what is education for if it ignores the realistic requirements of industry and commerce and the realistic ambition of young people to earn their living?

Grammar schools required pupils to attend until the age of 16 and followed a clearly defined academic curriculum leading to the Schools Certificate Examination introduced in 1917, with, of course, compulsory games, largely rugby, football, cricket and athletics.

Although there were undoubtedly children from less-well-off families who had the intellectual ability to benefit from an academic education, the poor could not afford the fees required. Even if the fees were paid by means of a scholarship, the cost of keeping a growing youngster in school was prohibitive: they had to work in order to provide the necessary income to help feed and clothe both themselves and other members of the family. In addition, there was a psychological factor which acted against some youngsters being allowed to continue with their education. Some parents could not accept that their children should be allowed to follow what they regarded as an easy life in school when they should be out in the real world earning their keep!

In 1918 a further Education Act raised the compulsory school-leaving age to 14 and required LEAs to provide advanced instruction for older or more intelligent children, including provision beyond the statutory leaving age. Fees for elementary education were abolished, playing fields and swimming pools were to be provided, plans were advanced for nursery education, and an intention to introduce part-time education for 14- to 18-year-olds established. The Act encouraged LEAs to experiment with different types of provision, leading to the introduction of Junior Technical, Commercial and Art schools in some parts of the country. Other authorities introduced higher elementary schools; some had similar establishments which they called central schools, and others senior schools.

Secondary schools in Darlington before 1936

Most children in Darlington in the 1930s attended elementary schools until they reached the age of 14 years and then left to seek employment. The brightest could go to one of three secondary schools if they reached the required entry standards and their parents could afford to keep them for the extra two years, the leaving age for them being 16 years.

The Darlington Queen Elizabeth Boys' Grammar School

In 1897 Darlington Grammar School had 133 scholars of which 13 were boarders; in 1910 it was known to be administered by a board of governors; and the school existing in 1934 had been opened in 1911. When the Darlington local authority, the Corporation, took control in 1917 the number on roll was still only 217.

In the summer of 1933 it was decided that the school should be enlarged and in October the total number of pupils was 567. Although the figure for 1935 is given as only 570, the total quoted by the speaker at the Old Boys' annual dinner in 1936 was 600. The school was clearly well established by the time the Education Committee were considering the provision of what would eventually be the Eastbourne secondary schools.

The Darlington High School for Girls

For girls taking up a secondary school education there was the High School, in 1897 a small school of eighty-seven girls occupying the building known as Claremont in Trinity Road. The new school, as it was in the 1930s, was opened in Cleveland Avenue in 1911 when there were 145 pupils on the roll. In the early 1900s, when it was taken over by the Darlington Corporation, numbers had risen to 298, of which 79 were 'free place holders' and 219 fee paying

There is a record of the school playing fields being extended in 1933 to some five acres and in the same year the building was also extended by the addition of two classrooms and a practical room. In October that year the roll had grown to 485 of which 331 were 'free and special place' pupils and 154 fee paying.

Central Commercial School

It may seem that secondary schools in Darlington were all single-sex schools, but there was in 1932 a third secondary school for boys and girls known as Central School.

In March 1932, Alderman Leach, the councillor who had a long association with the development of Darlington education, is quoted as saying that Central School could be converted into an elementary school for boys coming from the south-east of the town. The point of this remark was that there would, consequent on such a change, be no need to build a new school in this part of Darlington.

Numbers on roll at this time were about 149 boys and 116 girls although it was said that some 91 had entered at the start of the new school year and this was a greater number than would normally be accommodated.

The headmaster, Mr W. G. Bainbridge, at the school's annual Speech Day on 6 February 1932, stressed that Central School was not then five years old, when speaking of the small number of pupils taking the School Certificate Examination; thirteen had been entered in 1931 but only eight gained certificates, although three were described as passing with honours. He also pointed out that pupils entering the school before 1928 were entitled to leave at the statutory school-leaving age of 12 and not obliged to remain until 16 as expected in secondary schools.

There was opposition from those who saw great benefit in the keeping of three secondary schools, not least from the parents of pupils who valued the provision of education from Central School. A 'large employer' of young people is said to have commented that he found pupils from the school to be superior to those from the grammar schools for entry into industry, and it would appear that the school probably orientated its teaching styles towards more vocational learning than the traditional academic teaching of the grammar schools.

Nevertheless, with the driving energy of Alderman Leach behind the scheme to change the purpose of Central School, the approval of the Board of Education was achieved in 1933 and pupils moved to the grammar and high schools. It was reported in 1935 that boys from Gladstone Street School had been transferred to the grammar school.

Other schools known to have existed in Darlington in the 1930s

Alderman Leach School

The Alderman Leach Primary School was opened in the 1930s and named after the founder of the Darlington School Board and long-serving member of the Education Committee. The Darlington School Board was formed in 1897.

Albert Road School

Albert Road School was opened as a British School (by the British and Foreign Schools Society) in 1866 and at the time of the 1902 Education Act it became a Darlington elementary school, with 885 pupils on roll. In May 1933 the school team defeated St John's School in the Pike Pease Cup football competition and at the start of the 1936 autumn term, a small number of boys were transferred to the new Eastbourne School.

On the Ordnance Survey (OS) map dated 1923 a school building is shown situated on the south side of Albert Road, at the junction with Pease Street. Another school building is situated on the north side of Albert Street near a church. To the east, on the far side of the River Skerne, is the site of the Darlington Forge.

The Art School

The Art School was opened as a voluntary school in 1857, in a room next to the Chapel in Union Street. In 1891 the Technical Instruction Committee took over the management of the school, which was housed in the Mechanics Institute, and in 1897 the Art School opened as a department in the Technical College.

Beaumont Street School

Beaumont Street School was situated in the centre of Darlington, school buildings being shown on the 1923 OS map situated on the north side of Beaumont Street and at the centre of a closely built-up area bounded by Victoria Road, Feethams, Houndgate and Grange Road. It was one of the Darlington elementary schools in 1902 with 792 pupils on roll.

At the time of the reorganisation of Darlington schools in 1933 it was proposed that the Beaumont Street premises, then occupied by both senior boys and girls, be used as a senior girls' school.

At the start of the 1936 autumn term, 194 boys and 115 girls transferred to the Eastbourne School because the senior departments at Beaumont Street were being closed.

Bondgate School

Bondgate School was situated on another centre-of-town site, on the south side of Bondgate between Larchfield Street and Barnard Street. It was reported as serving the West End of Darlington and a school building is shown on the site on the map for 1968. There was, however, a report in 1933 that the school was expecting to be closed but in 1935 the trustees of the Bondgate School building were requested by the local authority to extend the lease for another year, and at the start of the 1936 autumn term the junior department was still able to send six 11-plus girls to Eastbourne.

Borough Road School

Premises situated on the corner site between Brunswick and Borough roads were built by the Brunswick Street Board in about 1885 and in 1936 the school was still able to send eighteen 11-plus pupils, twelve girls and six boys, to the new Eastbourne School.

Corporation Road School

In 1902 Corporation Road School was one of the Darlington elementary schools and then had 436 pupils on its roll. Three blocks of buildings are shown on the 1923 OS map between Bartlett Street and Wilkes Street, fronting Corporation Road and clearly marked 'schools'.

A report of a significant reorganisation of the schools in July 1933 explains something of the departments existing and links them with

Reid Street School. The junior boys were to be accommodated in the premises of the 'present junior mixed school'; the junior girls were to occupy the senior girls' premises; and the senior girls from Corporation Road School were to be transferred to premises 'at present used by Reid Street Senior Boys and Junior Mixed Schools'. The purpose of the changes was to replace two junior mixed schools by two separate units, one for boys and one for girls.

The need for separate schools for boys and girls seems to have been a significant aspect of the thinking of at least some people during this period.

Reid Street School

Reid Street School, clearly marked on the 1923 map, is just under half a mile by road from the Corporation Road site. In a report to the Education Committee on 25 October 1934, Corporation Road and Reid Street junior schools are linked with reference to numbers of pupils on roll. Reid Street Senior Girls School was said to have spaces for 520 pupils but only 385 on roll and there is also a decrease in numbers of pupils shown attending the joint infant and junior departments of Reid Street and Corporation Road.

Gladstone Street School

The 1923 map shows the Technical College on the corner site between Northgate and Gladstone Street and behind the college premises is the school building. In the reorganisation of 1933 it was said that the Gladstone Street premises would be used as a senior school for boys from the south-eastern part of the town and in December the headmaster, Mr W. Coates, in his speech at the annual prize-giving, commented that the school had benefited from the transfer of pupils from Reid Street in the previous summer, particularly in practical work. He also reported that a prefect system had been introduced at the start of the term.

Kendrew Street School

Kendrew Street leads off Northgate parallel to and south of Gladstone Street and a school building was located on its southern side. It was one of Darlington's elementary schools and in 1902 had 367 pupils, but by 1932 there were plans for its closure.

Gurney Pease School

The Gurney Pease School was built in about 1885 by the Gurney Pease Memorial Board and had 294 pupils in 1902 but only sent two girls and two boys at the 11-plus stage to the new Eastbourne School in 1936.

Harrowgate Hill School

Harrowgate Hill School opened as a Board School at about the same time as Gurney Pease and in 1902 was an elementary school with 342 pupils. There are school buildings shown on the OS map of 1923 on the corner of Thompson Street West and Bowman Street, and they were still there in 1968. The only part of Harrowgate Hill built up in 1923 was that situated within the triangle bounded by Honeypot Lane, Thompson Street West and the Durham or North Road. To the east and north-east were open fields, with more open countryside north-west of Honeypot Lane (now known as Longfield Road).

Haughton School

In 1923 the Haughton School was situated at the corner of the Haughton village between Haughton Road and Salters Lane, close by the church. Open fields separated the village from Darlington.

Immaculate Conception School

The Immaculate Conception School was the Catholic school for girls recognised by the Board of Education in 1904 when it had approximately 48 pupils on roll.

Junior Technical School

The education authority reported in 1932 that they had had problems with the Junior Technical School arising out of a Board of Education regulation allowing only a two-year course rather than one for four years. Also, with the existence of the Central School, it was claimed that it was difficult to find enough boys of appropriate ability to fill the Junior Technical School.

The school was consequently closed following the reorganisation of Darlington schools in 1933.

North Road Senior Girls' school

In about 1968, school buildings were shown on Pendleton Road between it and North Road, near Rise Carr, so was this a replacement for Rise Carr or the same school (see below)?

On 11 May 1933 the girls won the Darlington Elementary Schools netball tournament. At the start of the 1936 autumn term a small number of senior girls were transferred to Eastbourne.

The Ragged School

The Ragged School in Darlington was referred to as the Leadyard School which, for 68 years up to 1933, held a service for poor children every Sunday evening and, before the introduction of elementary education, also taught lessons. A bequest of Mr Arthur Pease had given the school the use of the premises rent free but in 1935, with the redevelopment of this part of the town taking place and the building being just outside the slum demolition area, it was expected that it would be demolished during the next year or so. There was no offer of alternative accommodation so it was expected and soon proved to be the end of the Ragged School. However, in July 1935 the school held its twelfth annual children's outing to Redcar. At 9 a.m., 650 children congregated in the Market Place and subsequently moved to Bank Top Station, fearing that it would be for the last time.

Rise Carr

St Paul's National School opened in Westmoreland Street in the late 1860s with the first purpose-built accommodation being erected circa 1869. By 1902 it was an elementary school with 348 pupils.

There are school buildings marked on the OS map of 1923 by North End recreation ground on Hammer Street, and they were still shown at the same location on the Darlington Street map circa 1968. There was no school in Westmoreland Street around that time.

St John's Church of England School

St John's Church of England School opened as a National School in 1859 and by 1902 was an elementary school with 648 pupils. The 1923 OS map shows a school building on Yarm Road west of Louisa Street.

At the Education Committee meeting held on 27 January 1933, the facilities were said to be inadequate for senior pupils and the suggestion made that the school should close the senior department. Earlier, in 1932, it had been said that senior pupils would be transferred to Gladstone Street, involving a considerable walk to and from school for the pupils, particularly at dinner time. A final decision was awaiting the opening of a new school east of the railway and at the start of the 1936 autumn term, 111 boys and 112 girls were transferred to the new Eastbourne School.

St Mary's Boys' Roman Catholic Grammar School, Hummersknott

St Mary's boys' school open in 1924 with a roll of approximately 59, and by 1933 catered for about 155 pupils. It was reported that the school produced an operetta on 20 April that year.

The reorganisation of Darlington schools in 1933

On the last day of March 1932, at a special meeting of the Education Committee, the chairman, Alderman C. H. Leach, announced proposals to reorganise Darlington schools, based upon a report made by the CEO, Mr H. Whalley, which some described as 'revolutionary'. A significant aspect of the changes was the closure of Central Secondary School, which was described as 'deficient', for instance, having no biology laboratory. A comment made by Alderman Leach also raises another interesting insight into educational thinking of the times: referring to separate boys' and girls' schools, he said this 'is not a desirable state of affairs'.

Commenting on the objections to the closure of the school, particularly those from the parents' committee at Central School, in what appears to be his usual confident style, the Alderman said: 'I can only assume that the rumours arise from their not knowing exactly what we propose.'

Other arguments in favour of the changes included the necessary taking out of use of older premises, the already planned increase in accommodation at the boys' grammar school and the enlargement of the high school, which, with the new use for the Gladstone Street premises, would avoid a much greater expenditure on a completely new school in the south-east of the town.

Another factor leading to the conclusion that it was not necessary to build new schools was the fall in the birth rate from 1,723 in 1920 to 1,116 in 1931.

If these recommendations had been acted upon in full there would never have been an Eastbourne School. For instance, in 1932 it was proposed that boys from the Dodmire School catchment area should go to Gladstone Street, councillors hoping to arrange for some reduction of fares on the trolley buses. Alderman Crooks pointed out that there would be a need for an extension to bus routes along Geneva Road first.

The plans were adopted by the local authority on 7 April 1932.

The Bridge Street slum clearance

An example of this change is given in the *Northern Despatch* of Wednesday 25 September 1935, when it was reported that the Minister of Health had agreed to the local authority's Bridge Street Compulsory Purchase Order for the purposes of demolishing some ninety-two houses and eighteen shops; workshops and warehouses; the Wheatsheaf Inn, in Bridge Street, and the Robin Hood Inn, in Park Street; an old school building in Bridge Street, the property of St Cuthbert's church; and the Methodist Mission in the area of Chapel Street and Park Street.

The scheme involved the rehousing of 520 people with the building of 12 houses having three bedrooms, a living room and parlour; 64 with three bedrooms and a living room; and 30 with two bedrooms and a living room. The locations of the properties were to be in Harris Street, Geneva Road, Yarm Road, Freeman's Place and Harrowgate Hill; a large proportion therefore being in the developing south-east of the town. Semi-detached council houses were already being built in Hundens Lane in 1933.

A change in the education policy

Subsequent to the planned closure of the Central secondary school, among some considerable controversy and the claim of savings because no new school need be built, there was mooted a plan for a new school at Bank Top, east of the main-line railway.

On Friday 10 August 1934 the Education Committee agreed to the building of a new elementary school for 520 pupils at Hundens, with access from Yarm Road via the Fairway, the contactors to be R. Blackett and Son of Darlington, with Dunhouses Quarry at Staindrop supplying stone. There was some debate about a possible reduction in the estimated cost of £24.500 because the Board of Education had rejected the proposal for a gymnasium at the school. As there was no gymnasium in any of the other Darlington schools, and for reasons of economy, it was considered unwise to pursue the matter.

At this date the school was to be built on two floors, with eleven classrooms; an assembly hall with balcony and stage; and science, art and staff rooms. Woodwork and metalwork rooms were also included in the plan, as was a domestic block with a model flat. A library and medical room were to be situated above the main entrance.

And so the Eastbourne Schools were born!

A New Purpose-Built School 1936–1939

In Darlington, in the north-east of England, in 1934, resulting in part from the need created by the growth in population and from the local authority's intent to update its education service, it was announced that a new school was to be built at Hundens, an area of open countryside immediately to the east of and within easy walking distance of the town centre, where a small new residential estate was being built. Semi-detached houses with front and back gardens opened onto narrow paved and tree-lined roads with names like The Fairway, The Broadway, The Mead, The Stray and The Causeway: a modern spacious development contrasting greatly with the older closely built terraces of houses built for workers in the town's heavy industry, where front doors opened directly onto pavements and small back yards accommodated outside toilets.

The site on the Ordnance Survey map of the mid 1920s shows only one of these roads complete, The Mead, with the isolated Hundens Farm, the smallpox hospital, the hospital for infectious diseases, a curling pond and brickworks all separated from each other by fields. The school was to be built on an area south-west of the pond with access from Yarm Road via The Fairway. Located close to the Eastbourne area of the town, it was to be called the Eastbourne Senior Mixed School, Darlington.

The significance of this development lies in its being a purpose-built school according to the most modern design of the time: an exciting and innovative project.

The building

Constructed of a dark-red brick, with two storeys straddling a central archway, it was typical of the style of a new surge in school building in the late 1920s and early 1930s. But it was also at the forefront of this development. Mr Oliver Stanley, President of the Board of Education, who had been invited to officially declare the school open, said that it was one of the finest he had seen anywhere in the country.

The first part to be completed was eventually to be the girls' school, situated to the left of the central arch, and it was in this part of the premises that the mixed school opened in 1936. It was described in the *Northern Echo* of Tuesday 29 September 1936 as 'Darlington's Super School at Eastbourne'. As well the main block at the front of the school and its partner, a range built at right angles to it, there was the domestic science unit at the north-west corner, which included a fully furnished flat, or bungalow. As both boys and girls were to be accommodated, a workshop block had been built at the north-eastern extremity.

It is necessary to understand that the progressive thinking of the time did not perceive girls and boys to be the same in their aspirations for adult life. In general girls would be destined for a short spell of employment before marriage, when they would become full-time housewives and mothers, and boys were seen to be the family money earners working in industry and commerce. They would need different skills and the provision for the development of these skills could clearly be seen in the layout and structure of the building.

The cost of the new school, reported to have been in the region of £25,000, seems, by today's standards, ridiculously small and is a pointed reminder that inflation, or the devaluation of money, has always been with us. When complete the accommodation was to be for 1,100 pupils and the description of its specialist rooms does not seem by any means out of place by today's standards.

Approaching the school from the main gate at the end of The Fairway, the visitor could not help being impressed by the extensive south-facing frontage broken by the lines of rectangular-framed sash windows, each divided into smaller panes, aligning both storeys of the main teaching blocks.

The entrances

The entrances to both of the schools, boys' and girls', were enhanced by substantial brick-columned porches that extended outwards from the main building line. Originally, passing through the double swing doors, the visitor entered a modest lobby, its lower walls tiled in a pleasant green, the head teacher's room being situated to one side. Ahead, crossing the lower-floor corridor, were more double doors leading into the assembly halls, with oak-panelled walls rising to the full height of the two-storey building, and brightly lit by daylight streaming in through the high windows. This style of window, using small sheets of glass rather than the large panes of later years, was a feature of schools being built at the time and, with the break-up of the walls by the lines of bricks and mortar, gave the buildings an attractive appearance lacking in the uniformly plain structures of the latter half of the twentieth century.

The school halls

Each hall had a balcony at its rear and in front a broad, deep stage framed by a rectangular proscenium arch. There was a large storage area beneath each stage and dressing rooms behind. Projection rooms in the roof, above the balcony, and a large roll-down screen at the back of each stage transformed the hall into a cinema. Seating was provided in the form of units of six wooden seats, each folding back to allow people to stand comfortably. A total of 500 people could be accommodated in each hall.

At the opening in 1936 there were already in place facilities for physical education, science, art, woodwork and metalwork and domestic subjects. The gymnasium was situated behind the hall so that the behind-stage dressing rooms were also available for sports changing. Showers were also provided. Measured against the facilities seen in today's sports halls, the provision would seem small and old fashioned but it must be emphasised that it was remarkably advanced in the 1930s. The walls were lined with wall bars, ladder-like structures attached to the walls. Beams and ropes could be lowered from the ceiling and other equipment included the springboard and vaulting horse, a box-like structure with a padded leather top, for gymnastics.

A similar set-up was built into the boys' school, a mirror image of the girls' department, between 1936 and 1939.

3

Leaving the assembly hall and immediately turning right along the corridor, people would have seen three general-purpose classrooms, a science room (a laboratory) and a science-lecture theatre. On the floor above were seven classrooms, an art room and library. The latter was another innovative feature of the new school, the reading of books to be encouraged.

The woodwork and metalwork shops must have been isolated, beyond the site for the boys' classroom blocks, near the curling pond, which, many years later, was filled in and surfaced, to be known as the shale area.

Perhaps, the showpiece of the time was the provision for domestic subjects: four teaching rooms and the flat. The flat was a modern bungalow, with sitting room, bedroom, and kitchen, and would have been envied by many of the parents and other visitors to the school on that Monday in September, many of whom would have lived in the smaller terraced houses of the town. The teaching rooms had up-to-date electric and gas cookers, sinks, work tables and ironing boards.

The completion of the building took another three years and the head teacher made several references to work continuing on the site. On the day the school opened workmen were still finishing the handicraft rooms (the workshops) and the science room. In May 1938 there is mention of the 'new extension', the CEO and Education Committee visiting the school and the head teacher attending the Education Office to discuss the project; and in January 1939 the head attended the meeting of the subcommittee dealing with the matter at the Town Hall. The CEO and HMIs (His Majesty's Inspectorate of Schools) visited the school. On 17 July 1939 four rooms in the new extension were occupied for the first time. At the end of August that year, at the start of the new term, when the mixed school was reorganised into separate boys' and girls' departments, the new extensions were not complete. It was reported that 'three boys' classes were accommodated in the science room, the library and a classroom of the Senior Girls' Department. The hall of the Senior Girls' School was shared'.

The first day at the new school

The school opened for pupils for the first time on 18 August 1936 when the head teacher, Mr George Welford, recorded the event on the first page of the school log book.

Eastbourne Senior Mixed School Log Book 18ᵗʰ August 1936, page 1:

On Tuesday, the Eighteenth Day of August, Nineteen Hundred and Thirty-six, this school, the Eastbourne Senior Mixed, Darlington opened for the first time at 9 am. The number of scholars enrolled was 633. Boys numbered 347 and girls 286. The majority of the scholars came from Beaumont Street Senior Boys' School and Beaumont Street Senior Girls' School and St John's Church of England School. All the senior boys and girls from St John's School, who were eleven years of age on or before the first of August 1936, were transferred to this School; and since Beaumont Street Senior Boys' School was closed as a Senior School most of its pupils were transferred here. Beaumont Street Senior Girls' School is ultimately to close as a Senior School and as accommodation was not available for all its pupils, only so many were transferred, the rest remaining at Beaumont Street Senior Girls' School until building operations on this site are completed.

There are two things worthy of note relating to the first school assembly: the first is that it was opened with the saying of the Lord's Prayer, reminding us of the significance of the Christian faith in the education system at the time; and the other is the attendance of representatives from Darlington's education service: the Chairman of the Education Committee, Alderman C. H. Leach MA, OBE.; the CEO, Mr H. Whalley BSc; and the Deputy Education Officer, Mr W. G. Bainbridge BA, BSc. Their attendance demonstrated the importance attached to the occasion and that being given to the place of the new school in the forward-looking education system of Darlington.

The Programme for Official Opening Ceremony

Chairman The Worshipful The Mayor of Darlington Councillor T. E. Hudson

The Scholar's hymn – Land of Our Birth (Rudyard Kipling – Tune Arizona).

Prayer by the Rev. J. Scott B. D. Mayor's Chaplain

The Worshipful the Mayor

The Chairman of the Education Committee (Alderman C. H. Leach MBE., MA)

The President of the Board of Education (The right Honourable Oliver S. G. Stanley MC, MP)

Vote of Thanks to the President of the Board of Education

Proposed by C. H. Peat Esq. MP for Darlington

Seconded by Councillor R. Luck Vice Chairman of the Education Committee

Vote of Thanks to the Worshipful the Mayor

Proposed by Alderman C. H. Leach MBE, MA.

Seconded by Alderman T. Crooks

The National Anthem

The formal proceedings were followed by Tea and the Inspection of the Buildings and it was noted

'The President of the Board, kindly gave permission
for the School House System to include one House to
be known as the Stanley House'

The official opening of the new school 26 September 1936

The nature of the official opening ceremony, on 26 September 1936, is further evidence of the significance given to the project, The Right Honourable Oliver Stanley MC, MP, President of the Board of Education attending.

During the evening the school was open to the public between 6 and 8 p.m. when some 5,000 visitors attended, very clearly demonstrating the interest shown in the new project by the people of Darlington. The headmaster noted: 'It was 8.45 p.m. before the last of the General Public left the premises. The whole of the Staff was on duty.'

The staff

The first head teacher of Eastbourne School was George William Welford, who retired from the boys' school in December 1959 after serving for approximately twenty-three years. When appointed he must

6

have been about 40 years of age and had some twenty years' experience of working in schools.

A rough guide to salaries of head teachers in the late 1930s

Schools were graded I to V according to size:

I	average attendance not more than 100
II	over 101 to 200
III	201 to 350
IV	351 to 500
V	over 500

The salary scale for head teachers was then obtained by adding to his or her salary as an assistant teacher a promotion increment of £24 per grade for a man and £18 per grade for a woman, and subsequently five annual increments of £12 for a man and £9 for a woman – in each case, one annual addition (presumably the first) being slightly lower than the remainder.

Teachers' annual salaries at this time were determined according to the Burnham Scales listed below:

Men
Uncertificated
£108 by £7.10s to £174 (if appointed before 1.4.1914 to £222)
Certificated college trained 2 years
£180 by £12 to £366

Women
Uncertificated
£99 by £6 to £153 (if appointed before 1.4.1914 to £174)
Certificated college trained 2 years
£162 by £9 to £288

There were no graded posts or posts of special responsibility at this time, all teachers except the head being known as assistant teachers, of which there were 22 (12 men, one of whom was part-time, completing only six out of the ten sessions, and 10 women) which suggests an approximate pupil–teacher ratio of 29:1 and classes of something like thirty pupils, but as great emphasis was placed on the teaching of practical subjects and classes using practical rooms would be smaller, general teaching groups were considerably larger.

Additional notes on teachers' salaries

- Assistant teachers with less than two years' college training – the minimum was less than above by one increment although there was no difference in the upper limit

- For four years' continuous training there was an addition of one increment at the lower but there was no difference at the upper limit

- A university graduate commenced at point two on the scale (with an additional increment), with no difference to the upper limit.

- A graduate with four years' continuous training commenced at point three (with two additional increments)

The most obvious observations on the above are the apparent smallness of the salaries and the significant differences between the remuneration of men and women. The devaluation of money is always with us and in the 1930s, with the 1920s–30s spread of suburban residential development, one of the millions of houses with two to three bedrooms, two reception rooms, a kitchen and bathroom would have cost something like £300 to £400. Another significant factor is the apparent expectation that no school would have more than 650 pupils, a small number when compared with the development of the comprehensive schools in the 1950s and subsequent years.

Something of the qualifications and teaching experience of the assistant staff employed at the new Eastbourne School can be obtained from the summary of data extracted from entries in the school log book. Two of the men and two of the women were specialists in the practical subjects. Only one of the men was a graduate and only three of

8

the women studied at a university. The majority were qualified teachers who had completed courses at specialist teacher-training colleges.

Most had several years of teaching experience and were in the early to mid years of their teaching careers. Only one was apparently newly qualified. The significance of this is that the staff were mature rather than young but not approaching retirement. In addition, at the time the women were all unmarried, it being a condition of service that they resigned when they married, with the result that some devoted their lives to their vocations, even remaining in the same school for all or a large part of their careers.

Teachers at Eastbourne in 1936

Men

John Robert Farrage, aged 45, 1st Class City and Guilds Metalwork, 1st Class City and Guilds Woodwork

Percy Longstaff, aged 35, Westminster College, promoted to head of Beaumont St. Junior & Infants School 31 August 1943

Percy Hardy Moss, Involved in PE

Robert Newton, aged 21, Birmingham University, involved in PE & left to the RAF 25 June 1940

John Peacock, aged 33, 1st Class City and Guilds Woodwork, 2nd Class City and Guilds Metalwork

William Robinson Richardson, aged 44, Sunderland College, Died 22 November 1946

Arthur John Rottenbury, part-time woodwork and metalwork, left to a post in Hereford 30 August 1937

John Willy Scott, aged 32, Bede College, promoted to the headship of Barnard Street School 6 September 1940

George Frederick Smith, aged 31, Chester College, to North Road School as youth warden 19 July 1946

Thomas Tranter, aged 30, Sheffield City, to Gladstone Street Boys' School as youth warden 19 July 1946

Thomas Arthur Tweddle, aged 31, Westminster College, Science, To Gladstone Street School headship 26 July 1940

Henry Musgrave Wilson, aged 49

Women

Elizabeth Wormald Dover, aged 25, Northern Counties Training College of Cookery and Domestic Science

Nora Fenby, aged 38, Goldsmith's College, University of London, became long-serving head of the girls' school

Merla Horn, trained certificated teacher, left on marriage 31 March 1939

Ida Mary Maughan, aged 47, St Elphin's Warrington, retired on health grounds 17 December 1943

Jane Owen, aged 34, Bangor University BA

Mary Blanche Reed, aged 53, Northern Counties Training College of Domestic Science, retired 30 April 1946

Edith Alice Richardson BA, aged 29, Durham University

Nellie Soper, aged 26, Neville's Cross Training College, became part-time 31 December 1945

Winifred Storer, aged 44, Avery Hill College, London, PE, became youth warden & part-time teacher 31 August 1945

Isobel Thompson, aged 37, City of Leeds Training College, resigned and moved to Reading 20 December 1951

Staff changes between 1936 and 1939

Changes in staff during the period August 1936 to August 1939 were few but temporary teachers were used from time to time. For instance, three teachers were absent on a physical training course at Scarborough during the first week of the term in August 1936, not an ideal way to start a new school, and two temporary teachers covered their absence. As two of the teachers on the course were male and the two replacements female, that surely prevented the commencement of a routine timetable.

Only two teachers appear to have resigned from the staff of the school during its first three years: Mr Rottenbury, the part-time instructor teaching woodwork and metalwork, who obtained a post in Hereford in August 1937, and Miss Horn who left at the end of March 1939 when she was about to marry.

Five teachers joined the staff during this period: Mr G. Spence arrived in February 1937, Mr J. Goynes and Miss O. Hannan in August

1937, Miss V. Welbourne, newly qualified, in August 1938, and Miss R. Cape replaced Miss Horn in March 1939.

As far as can be ascertained from the school log book for the period, the staff only increased by three. If temporary teachers are discounted and as the school roll had risen to 863 by February 1939, the pupil–teacher ratio was then about 35:1.

The *Darlington Education Handbook* for 1938 gives a number of conditions relating to the duties of assistant teachers. For instance, they 'shall at all times act under the direction of the Head Teacher'. It was felt necessary to state that assistant teachers should attend regularly and punctually, give every assistance to the head teacher in 'the conducting and managing' of the school and 'diligently' teach the classes allocated to their care. The careful keeping of the school attendance registers was emphasised and it is recorded in the school log books that these were examined and checked regularly by a senior official from the Education Department, usually the Deputy Education Officer.

All appointments were subject to a probationary period of one year and it was stated that the appointment should be terminated unless reports on the probationary period were shown to be satisfactory by the LEA.

Two paragraphs in the head teacher's copy of the regulations for Eastbourne were found to be underlined in red ink, as though there had been a need to emphasise them. The first relates to the time of arrival of teachers and says that they 'shall be in their places at least ten minutes before the time appointed for the opening of the school'. The second states: 'Assistant Teachers shall undertake, in accordance with the Head Teacher's allocation, the supervision of children in the playground during playtime, for 10 minutes before and for a reasonable time after each school session.' These particular regulations were understood, accepted and remained unquestioned for many years.

The pupils

The school's first pupils came largely from the Beaumont Street Senior Schools which were situated north and parallel to that part of Victoria Road, now a part of the Inner Ring Road, where the senior departments were being closed. There were 194 boys but only 115 girls, being a part of those due to be transferred, because the buildings at Eastbourne were not ready. Mr Welford reported construction work was continuing in the handicraft and science rooms as well as in the grounds.

The second largest group of pupils came from St John's Church of England School, all boys and girls aged 11 on or before 1 August 1936, 111 boys and 112 girls being transferred.

A small number of other senior pupils came from the Albert Road Senior Boys', Gladstone Street Senior Boys', and North Road Senior Girls' schools.

In addition there was an intake of 55 girls and 37 boys from primary schools and a number of others, making a total intake of 347 boys and 286 girls – quite a large school for that time.

Eastbourne School's first intake from primary schools

School	Girls	Boys
Dodmire Junior	35	29
Borough Road Junior	12	6
Bondgate Junior	6	
Gurney Pease Junior	2	2

The School Size
August 1936–February 1939

School Roll	Total	Boys	Girls
August 1936	633	347	286
August 1937	781	402	379
February 1938	805	396	409
August 1938	812	374	438

The school-leaving age

At the time of the opening of the Eastbourne Senior School, the leaving age was 14: the pupils were physically less mature then for their age when compared with their age group today. The pre-war and wartime teachers were working with children – a very significant factor when the changes in education over future years are considered.

During the next three years most of the pupils entering the school at the age of 11, transfers being made in February and August, came from five primary schools, the majority from Dodmire and St John's. Dodmire School is situated on the edge of an area of established dwellings, while St John's was in an old building east of St John's Church.

A word on discipline

In 1939 the Bishop of Durham, D. H. Hensley Henson, speaking at the annual meeting of the Darlington Training College, quoted the well-known saying 'spare the rod and spoil the child'. He agreed that the maxim sounded harsh but believed that experience suggested there was some truth in it, explaining further that if discipline is absent education is at risk.

In 1935, at the annual prize-giving of the Gladstone Street Boys' School, the head teacher, Mr W. Coates, appealed to parents to co-operate with the teachers by providing a proper supervision of their boys outside school. Do things ever change!

To punish children or not is a subject which tends to provoke an emotional response whenever it is raised and, as corporal punishment was thought to be appropriate in the pre-war and immediate post-war years, consideration of the Darlington Education Authority regulations concerning punishment is interesting.

Regulations on Corporal Punishment dated January 1938

(1) Head Teachers shall reduce all forms of punishment to the minimum compatible with the welfare of the children and the school, and shall not in any case inflict corporal punishment (save for grave moral offences) until other methods have been tried and failed.

(2) Head Teachers shall be responsible for all punishment, but they may delegate during pleasure the power to inflict slight punishment to such of their certificated assistants as they consider to be fit and proper persons to be entrusted with the power. Head Teachers who either give to or withdraw from their assistants the power to inflict slight punishment shall do so in writing and note the same at the time in the log book.

(3) In a mixed school under a master, any necessary corporal punishment of girls must be inflicted by an assistant mistress duly delegated by the Head Teacher.

(4) A cane, authorised by the Committee, is provided for each department. When an assistant entrusted with the power of inflicting punishment has need for exercising that power the assistant shall obtain from the Head Teacher the cane and the punishment book and immediately after inflicting the punishment, enter and sign a record of the same in the book. He must forthwith return both the cane and the book to the Head Teacher who must initial the entry. The Head Teacher, immediately after inflicting corporal punishment, shall enter a record thereof in the punishment book. In girls' and infants' departments it is left to the discretion of the Head Teachers to permit the use of the open hand instead of the cane, as an instrument of punishment, but such substituted punishment must be recorded in the punishment book.

(5) Corporal punishment with the cane must not be inflicted on children under the age of seven years of age.

(6) All irregular, cruel, and excessive corporal punishment is absolutely prohibited. Blows by the hands, cuffs, boxing the ear, striking on any part of the head, and shakings shall be deemed to be irregular punishments.

(7) All cases of cruel corporal punishment will entail dismissal.

(8) Head and Assistant Teachers shall exercise special caution in dealing with delicate and nervous children.

(9) If an Assistant Teacher breaks any of these rules the Head Teacher shall report the same to the CEO immediately.

The entry by Mr Welford in the school log book for 15 January 1937 demonstrates the use of corporal punishment was considered to be necessary and that a considerable number of the male staff were authorised to use it:

> Under Section 8 paragraph 2 of the Regulations for Public elementary schools I give Messrs W. K. Richardson, R. Newton,

J. W. Scott, T. Tranter, T. A. Tweddle, J. Peacock, R. Farrage, J. R. Rottenburg the power to inflict slight punishment.

> The punishment in each case is a stroke of the cane on the hand – sometimes more than one.

Extra details were entered into the punishment book in some instances:

Two 14-year-olds, with six aged 13, 'missed' assembly; how they came to miss this, the first event of the day after registration is not given!

The misbehaviour outside school was largely the raiding of orchards and stealing apples.

One 13 and another 12-year-old were punished for misusing library books.

Two 12-year-olds were punished for squirting water, using a water pistol, and drenching boys in the cloakroom. Another pair were caught splashing ink onto walls and another interfered with material on a science bench.

The entries show that the names of the vast majority of the boys do not appear at all; most of the names that do appear do so only once, but there is evidence that a few repeatedly get into trouble and are not deterred by the punishment.

The question is: did the discipline style of the time deter the majority from engaging in antisocial behaviour and a minority from drifting into crime?

Juvenile delinquency

When a child's misbehaviour is such that it comes to the attention of the police and the courts the young offender is described as a juvenile delinquent, but this is a relatively new concept and previously children were dealt with by adult courts. A very significant change came about with the introduction of the Children and Young Persons Act which came into force in November 1933, a piece of legislation that changed authority's attitude to the seriously misbehaving child and brought into focus the question of whether treatment rather than punishment is the best way to correct wrongdoing.

On 4 September 1933 an article appeared in the Darlington *Northern Despatch* by one Agnes Carruthers, who was involved in social work, giving some insight into the older reformatory system applied to young offenders and arguing for a change in the system. She cites the cases of three boys each sent to a reformatory for between 1 and 6 years, one of whom was only 9 years old.

Carruthers wonders at the severity of the sentences for what she sees as fairly trivial offences such as minor theft and mild violence, and refers back to times when boys were transported, flogged and hanged. Much of their behaviour she explains in terms of lack of parental control and claims that not one of them is born a criminal. Rather, she says, many children are turned into criminals by being imprisoned with characters far worse than themselves.

She also advances the concept often heard today of the appearance of many older delinquents as people who have been badly treated when they were young, bad treatment that she sees not only in the home but also being handed out in the harsh reformatories.

Such understanding resulted in the introduction of the Children and Young Persons Act.

The Children and Young Persons Act 1933

On 23 October 1933 the *Northern Despatch* published a review of the new Act, which they referred to as the Children's Charter, pointing to instruction in proper behaviour being more effective in bringing improvement than the birch (that is a flogging). The aim of instruction, it was said, was to restore a right balance of the mind.

Young offenders could still be removed from the home, being sent to the Home Office residential schools, known as Approved Schools, where the aims were to be the improvement of character and the generating of positive interests. An alternative, particularly for younger boys, was committal to the care of the local authority, where the child would be placed in the residential care of a suitable person. Another form of treatment, leaving the child in its home, was the probation order, placing the youngster under the supervision of a probation officer.

On 7 November 1933 Councillor J. D. Hinks became the first chairman of the juvenile court in Darlington. His appointment was to be permanent so that at least one magistrate would know the boys and girls, their cases and whether they had offended more than once. Other members of the panel were Councillor S. Hardwick, Councillor H. P. Bell, Mr W. Coates, Mrs C. H. Leach, Mrs Ferguson and Mrs J.

D. Sinclair. It was remarked that inclusion of women was a sign of the changing times. The magistrates were seen as people who had sympathy for children.

Instead of meeting in the intimidating environment of the adult court the panel would meet in a room in the Town Hall, with the magistrates seated on chairs used on special occasions by the mayor and alderman. There would be no dressing up as in the 'uniforms' of the adult courts and the police witnesses would give evidence in civilian clothes.

The organisation of the classes in the new school

The summer vacation at this time was of one month's duration in the senior elementary schools but seven weeks in the grammar schools, a situation which was to be changed with the enacting of the 1944 Education Act. The opening of the school in 1936 was at 9 a.m. on 18 August, some ten to fourteen days earlier than today. The school closed for the mid-term holiday on Friday 30 October at 4 p.m. and reopened at 9 a.m. on Thursday 5 November, a break of three working days (i.e. weekdays). The end of the Christmas term was at 4 p.m. on 23 December, the holiday lasting until 11 January 1937, the Christmas holiday lasting on average for two weeks each year. There was a three-day break of Monday, Shrove Tuesday and Ash Wednesday in mid February, term ending on 25 March with a break at Easter of seven working days, the summer term starting on Tuesday 6 April. The next holiday was the Whitsuntide closure lasting six working days, with the summer vacation starting with the closure of the school on Friday 16 July. In addition, Ascension Day was a holiday and it became the custom, in theory, for an extra day to be awarded at the annual prize-giving.

The autumn or Christmas term in 1937 started on 17 August and the school year ended on 29 July 1938.

The start of the school day was clearly defined:

> The door of the classroom shall be closed at 9 o'clock, and the roll called and prayers offered. Immediately after prayers the doors shall be reopened, and the children admitted who have assembled in the meantime; and from that time the Bible instruction, in all schools, shall be given. The roll shall be finally taken and closed by 9.40 a.m. (regulation 22, dated 1938).

A list of prayers considered to be appropriate was provided with the regulations in the Education Handbook.

It was also stated that a service should be held at the opening of each morning session and, in order for this to be possible and both of the above regulations to applied, prayers, Bible instruction and the service came together to be known as the daily school assembly.

The Education Act of 1870 is quoted as authority for these regulations and it is added that 'no attempt should be made to attach children to any particular denomination'. There was also provision, quoted from the Education Act of 1921, for children to be withdrawn from religious instruction and morning service at the request of parents. Children withdrawn were expected to be given instruction in secular subjects during the period of withdrawal, where practicable in a separate room.

An observation entered in the school log for 23 February 1938 indicates that the pupils were placed in classes according to their ability: an evening concert being arranged for 'leavers in year 3 and the A & B streams in year 2'. On 17 May 1938 an HMI visited the school with reference to the teaching of the C Stream, or least able, children.

The school catered for boys and girls aged between 11-plus and 14 in three year groups. In March 1938 there had been four classes in year 3, labelled 3.1, 3.2, 3.3 and 3.4 according to the ability of the pupils, but due to pupils leaving at Easter, these were subsequently reduced to three.

Later Miss Fenby introduced the concept of an upper and lower division of the year groups, for instance as in U4 and L4, where U and L stand for upper and lower teaching groups in year four; and, even more confusingly, U3.1 and L3.1, which appear to denote upper and lower divisions of year three, with the addition of the figure 1 representing the first stream. There remains a tantalising puzzle for a keen future researcher to solve!

Entries such as that for Thursday 7 July 1938, when 'the timetable for boys and years 2 and 3 for the girls was suspended for the Inter-House Musical Contest and Festival', suggest that classes were single sex, anticipating the intended division of the school into separate boys' and girls' departments.

It is also apparent that boys and girls were separated in relation to the house system; this is an entry in the school log for 3 February 1938: 'Time Table for the Boys suspended at 3.20 p.m. and a House Rally held in the Hall when the new boys were allocated to their respective Houses and the House System explained.'

Bearing in mind more recent developments, where house systems have embraced the pastoral care of the pupils, the arrangement in Eastbourne in 1938 was purely for competitive purposes. For instance, the first mention of the House Competitive Cross Country Run is in April 1938 when it took place after 3.10 p.m. when the timetable was suspended. In January 1939 'the boys held their Annual Inter-House Music Festival in the afternoon commencing at 3 p.m.' Once again, the question arises: were girls and boys being taught different things separately? On the other hand, there is the report of the school concert on 28 October 1937 when the timetable was suspended 'in order that the Singing, Choral Speech, Physical Training Displays & Dramatic Work associated with the School Concert could be presented educationally to the whole school assembled'.

The Local Authority Regulations state: 'No class shall exceed 50 on roll without written authority from the Chief Education Officer.'

The curriculum

The curriculum and timetable had to be approved by the Education Committee with the head teacher being given discretionary powers to determine the time allowance for each subject. A further requirement was for instruction in secular subjects to take two hours in the morning and two hours in the afternoon.

The importance applied to religious instruction has already been mentioned, and this was expected to be included daily in the timetable at the beginning and/or end of each session.

The school curriculum of the pre-war years was, in comparison with today's teaching programme, much simpler, containing a straightforward emphasis on English language and calculation, and with a clear division between workshop subjects for boys and domestic subjects for girls.

The simplicity and emphasis on basic skills and knowledge is illustrated by the subject headings given on the report forms, which were issued to parents twice yearly and included the internal examination results (of which more is reported later).

Subject headings used on the report form used in 1937:

> arithmetic, reading, writing, composition, English (grammar etc.), geography, history, dictation, art, algebra, geometry, science, manual instruction, needlecraft.

Subject headings used on the report form used in 1939:

> arithmetic, reading, music, composition, English (grammar etc.), geography, history, dictation, art and craft, algebra, geometry, science, woodwork instruction, metalwork instruction, domestic science, needlecraft.

There can be no doubt that the practical subjects were given great importance and the facilities at the school were first class, the workshops (for the boys) being used for a Board of Education refresher course for handicraft teachers for two years running, only the onset of war preventing a third in 1939.

The second course, held in September 1937, was attended by 107 handicraft teachers and staffed by HMIs: an inspector of schools from Rhodesia also took part in the course.

The two handicraft rooms, the art room and geography room were used and the gymnasium was used for providing tea at break times.

A 'public meeting' was held in the hall at 3 p.m. on 10 September, addressed by Mr Vaughan Taylor HMI, with Mr Tilley, the Director of Education for Durham, as chairman.

An exhibition of craftwork made by the students during the week was held in the gymnasium.

For girls, the purpose-built work rooms, the self-contained flat and the proportion of the timetable given to the subject, demonstrate the importance given to the teaching of housecraft (later called domestic science).

Out-of-school visits

Needless to say there was some disruption to the teaching of the pupils when it was stated that the timetable and specialisation were suspended for the week. Each class was set to work on a temporary syllabus – the objective being the strengthening of known weaknesses. The opportunity was also taken to take some pupils on out-of-school visits. Thirty-three boys in 3.1 visited the waterworks on the morning of 6 September and forty from class 3.2 in the afternoon. The following day thirty-nine boys in class 2.2 made the same visit in the morning with forty-four from 2.1 doing so in the afternoon. On 8 September forty-two boys from 3.1 and forty from 3.2 visited the *Northern Echo* buildings in the afternoon for one hour each. On 10 September thirty-eight boys from 2.1 visited the Cleveland Bridge Works in the morning and thirty-three from 3.1 in the afternoon. Each party was accompanied by two members of staff.

Such visits were to become an integral part of a subsequently developed careers education programme. There were further visits, such as that to Sherwood's Garage, where, for instance, boys were given a lecture on the petrol engine by Vauxhall lecturers.

Physical education and games

It may be supposed that the absence of physical education and games from the school report form illustrates a lack of significance given to this area of the curriculum but there is other evidence that shows the opposite to be the case. It was merely accepted that this aspect of a child's education was not examined and reported on in the biannual school testing programme.

National fitness was certainly seen as important, there being in existence at the time the National Fitness Council, and on 8 December 1938 thirty boys and twenty-four girls in the charge of Mr Moss and Miss Storer travelled to Newcastle to take part in a display organised by the council. The Darlington Authority Physical Training Organiser, Mr J. Hayfield, was responsible for the arrangements.

On both the 8th and 9th of the month, twenty-four girls took part in physical training displays at Hartlepool and Stockton. The school was actually closed on the afternoon of 10 December when a national fitness display was held in the Baths Hall. A boys' class and a girls' class took part in the display.

In May 1939 two male members of staff attended the first of a series of lectures and demonstrations relating to physical education organised by Mr Hayfield, and a similar course, led by Miss Potts, was attended by two female teachers. Once more a clear distinction between boys' and girls' education is illustrated.

The boys' annual school camp

The emphasis on physical and outdoor activities for boys is further demonstrated by the head teacher's development of and involvement in the annual school camp, which was initiated in 1937 and took place immediately following the closure of the school for the summer holidays. It soon became an outstanding event among the extra-curricular activities of the boys' school. It is first mentioned in the log book entry for 26 January 1938 when a party was held at 4.30 p.m. for the boys who had attended the camp at Saltburn in 1937. The following public figures all attended the function: Chairman of the Education Committee Councillor R. Luck, Councillor H. Bell, Alderman J. D. Hicks, Alderman W. Heslop, Alderman A. J. Best, Councillor B. Bodd, Councillor T. E. Hudson, Councillor Waters, Lady Starmer and the Deputy Education Officer, Mr W. G. Bainbridge BA, BSc. This is an indication of how things were done and significant in giving prestige and formality to events. Tea was served in the gymnasium and a film show given in the school hall afterwards.

Again, in February 1939, a party was held for the boys who had attended the camp at Saltburn in 1938. This was again supported by the attendance of Councillor R. Luck, Mrs Luck, Councillor H. Bell, Mrs Campbell and Mr H. Whalley, CEO.

The third annual camp was held at Eastgate in Weardale during the period 8–15 July 1939 when fifty-four boys, including four old boys, and ten masters attended.

Inter-schools athletics

The Darlington Schools' Athletic Association was founded in 1908 and in 1933 Mr John Paxton, headmaster of Albert Road Senior Boys' School, had just retired from the organising committee, being awarded a gold medal for his services. The chairman at the presentation, Miss Spenser, pointed out the introduction of the school sports day, the swimming gala, football, cricket and netball games, comparing these activities with the boring drill routines practised in her schooldays.

The Medical Officer had reported that the physique of children had improved, and Mr Paxton said that this was in part due to the introduction of the programme of exercise laid down by the Board of Education, but he also referred to the introduction through games of the competitive spirit.

Mr Paxton pointed to the complete lack of organised games in the girl's schools before the days of the Athletic Association and the encouragement given to them for the introduction of hockey.

The inter-schools athletics championship was well established by the time of the opening of the Eastbourne School, being held at Feethams in July each year, when the schools closed for the afternoon.

The log entry for 14 May 1937 confirms the existence of school football teams and their involvement in inter-schools tournaments: 'The School's Senior Football Team competed in the Final for the Pike Pease Cup and won the trophy by defeating Gladstone Street Senior Boys' School 3 goals to 2 after extra time.'

The significance here is firstly that the event merited entry into the school record, secondly the actual winning of the match was seen as important and thirdly that a physical activity was given prominence.

The 1938 season of swimming lessons for boys started on 3 May and for girls on 4 May. They took place at the Town Baths, each session lasting thirty minutes.

The academic curriculum

The academic aspect of the curriculum emphasises the elements of English language (reading, the writing of compositions or essays and grammar being tested by terminal examination) and calculation (arithmetic). The use of the library was practised during timetabled library periods and there is reference on 22 and 23 November 1938 to evening library sessions held between 6 and 7.30 p.m.

The library

The Education Handbook states quite clearly the Authority's expectations concerning the use of the school library and during the last six months of their school career: 'Organised lessons on how to use the Public Library shall be given at the Library, and each scholar given a Library ticket', indicating the intention that children should be given positive encouragement to read and use library books.

The operation of the school library mirrored that of the adult libraries, books being issued and allowed out on loan for one week, with the provision for extended loans so long as the book or books were brought back to the library for this purpose. All books were stamped with the return date.

The Clara Lucas Prize

Further encouragement to write essays was given to the girls through the Clara C. Lucas essay writing competition.

In November 1935 Miss Alice Lucas made a bequest of £500 to the LEA, to be invested in 'trustees securities' and the income to be used to provide prizes for a girls' essay competition. At the time £500 would have purchased a modern house comprising two bedrooms, two reception rooms, kitchen, bathroom and box room, and was therefore a considerable sum. It was said that prizes of an average value of 10 shillings (equivalent to 50 pence in today's coinage but not in value) should be awarded to girls in the Darlington elementary schools who produced the best essays on 'domestic subjects' in an annual competition.

The prizes were to be inscribed with the words 'In Memory of Clara C. Lucas'. Clara Lucas was the sister of Alice Lucas and had served on the town council.

These were the rules for the award of the Clara Lucas Prizes. Paragraph 38 in the Darlington County Borough Education Committee Regulations dated January 1938 (which refers to the Education Sub Committee 1935) states:

(1) The Clara C. Lucas Prizes shall be awarded on the results of an essay competition held once only in each year. The competition shall be open to girls of the Darlington elementary schools whose thirteenth birthday falls within the period 1st June to 31st May immediately preceding the competition, and who make written application to take part therein.

(2) All of the essays shall be written in school during a normal school session at times fixed for the purpose, and no girl shall submit more than one essay.

(3) The essay shall be on matters connected with domestic subjects and the subjects shall be chosen by a person or persons approved by the Education Committee.

(4) Essays worked in any school shall first be marked by the Head Teacher of the School, who shall assign to them numerical marks in accordance with a scheme of marking issued by the Chief Education Officer who shall determine the final order of merit for the school.

(5) Prizes shall be apportioned to the numbers of girls who compete.

(6) Each prize shall consist of suitable standard or classical literature of the approximate value of 10 shillings, and in each book shall be inscribed the words 'In memory of Clara C. Lucas'.

Other academic subjects

The teaching of other academic subjects was being developed at this time, as illustrated by the inclusion in the building of specialist teaching rooms. An HMI visited the school 'to meet specialists and to talk over their respective rooms as far as structure and equipment were concerned'. Other HMIs called in to discuss the schemes of work in geography and history for example. There were other visitors wishing to see the science room and its equipment.

In science, biology was being taught: students from the Darlington Teacher Training Course commenced group practice in biology with Class 3.1 and an HMI visited the students taking part in these lessons.

On 24 November 1937 the timetable for the third year was suspended and a special lesson on electricity given by Mr T. A. Tweddle, the science teacher, who also gave science lessons at teachers' refresher courses. Afterwards, two films lent by the Electrical Development Association were shown to the pupils.

Music

Music was to play an important part in the life of the school and this was already becoming clear in the pre-war years.

> 27th October 1937
> The timetable was suspended at 3 pm. in order that the dress rehearsal for the school concert could be completed and the Hall set out for the Public Performance in the evening.

> 28th October 1937
> The timetable was suspended at 2.30 pm. in order that the singing – Choral speech – Physical Training displays and Dramatic work associated with the School Concert could be presented educationally to the whole school.

The Darlington Schools Non-competitive Musical Festival

A report in the *Northern Despatch* dated 16 April 1935 has a paragraph headed 'First in the North of England' and refers to the Schools Non-competitive Musical Festival, which was expected to be held in the Baths Hall on Tuesday 8 October. It was to be the first of many such festivals held annually in Darlington, an event still taking place today although there is no longer the convenient Baths Hall available for the competitors.

Some 3,000 schoolchildren were expected to take part, every Darlington school being involved: thirteen infant, twenty junior and seventeen senior choirs were entered for the singing events.

It was the Darlington Teachers' Association, the local association of the National Union of Teachers (NUT), that organised the festival; Dr Geoffrey Shaw, the music adviser to the national Board of Education, acted as director; Mr T. Henderson was president; and Mr W. C. Leonard was chairman of the festival committee. The secretary was Mr E. J. North, who had been secretary of the Darlington Teachers' Association for the previous ten years and had taught at the Corporation Road, Reid Street and Gladstone Street schools. Clearly an active member in local education, he had been connected with the Darlington Schools Athletic Association for twenty-two years and took an active part in sport himself, playing cricket and football – he was captain of the Bishop Auckland team that played in the amateur cup final in 1921. During the Great War Mr North was a sergeant-major gymnastic instructor.

Members of the organising committee were Miss N. Brennan, Miss E. A. Hopper, Miss I. Maughan, Miss L. Lambert, Mr C. Bennett, Mr H. Craig, Mr G. Welford, Mr J. J. Clarke and Mr P. Longstaff. Miss Lambert, Mr Bennett and Mr Craig also served on the music selection committee, as did Miss Benjamin, Miss Birdsall, Miss D. Dowson, Miss L. Hogg, Mr R. Pawson and Mr R. Farrage.

Mr G. Welford became the long-serving head of the Eastbourne Boys' School. Mr P. Longstaff also served on the staff of the school (later becoming head teacher at Beaumont Street Infants and Junior Mixed School), and Mr Clarke served there as Chief Assistant Master before becoming head teacher at the Corporation Road Primary School. Mr Farrage was qualified in both metalwork and music, being responsible for the development of music in the boys' school for some 14 years.

Miss I. Maughan worked at the Eastbourne Girls' School before retiring due to ill health.

The energy and enthusiastic involvement of this group of teachers initiated and developed a tradition of participation in musical performances which has lasted to the present day, although, regrettably, now showing signs of declining interest.

Some examples of events taking place helps with the understanding of the importance awarded to music and drama. On 1 December 1937 there was a school holiday when the Darlington Schools Non-competitive Musical Festival was held in the Baths Hall. Auditions took place throughout the day and a public concert given by a massed children's choir took place in the evening. An end-of-term concert, which included musical and dramatic items, was held in the hall on 23 February 1938. The Salvation Army Band and the Lydian Male Voice Quartette performed musical items to an audience of school leavers in 1938 in year 3 and the A and B streams in year 2. Some 297 pupils and 82 parents attended.

These were the aims and objectives of the festival as set out by the organisers in 1935:

> To promote a love of music in schools; to give encouragement and assistance to teachers of music in schools; to create such a love of singing that boys and girls in later life will desire to join adult choirs and play a part in the musical life in the place in which they live; to hold an annual festival at which schools shall sing individually and massed, and at which both teachers and children will receive from the director of the festival helpful hints and criticism. In brief not to find which choir sings the best but to give help to all who need it and to sing for the joy of singing.

On 17 March 1938 the Darlington Amateur Orchestra, Miss Marjorie Farrage (soprano) and Miss Bessie King (contralto) gave a performance in front of leavers (1938) in year 3 and the A and B streams in year 2. The audience of 271 pupils and 163 parents and friends indicates that such a concert was suitable for both children and parents, and was well supported.

In March 1938 a group of singers associated with the International Opera Company gave a demonstration of operatic singing to pupils.

On 5 May 1938 Miss Maughan escorted children representing Darlington in the Non-Competitive Festival of Song to the Albert Hall, London. The two representatives from the Eastbourne were William Brown and Bella Brown. On the following day the timetable for third-year boys and girls was suspended at 2.40 p.m. for them to listen to the broadcast of the Musical Festival at 2.50 p.m.

27

School examinations and reports

The only examinations taken by Eastbourne pupils during the early years were the twice-yearly tests held in January and June. The log book informs us that on 28 June 1937 'Timetable suspended for the Terminal Examinations', and on 17 January 1938, 'Specialisation suspended, examinations commenced', lasting three days on each occasion.

From entries on the school reports for parents it is clear that each subject was awarded a total of 50 marks and the actual marks obtained by the pupils were recorded. These were totalled and a rank-order list of pupils in each class produced, and the position of each child in the class was entered on his or her report form. The significance of the marks and position in class was emphasised by the strict streaming system, with pupils being promoted or demoted according to their performances.

The school report also recorded the number of times the pupil was late and absent. Conduct was described briefly in a few words, as was progress made. Brief observations were also made by each subject teacher and in the final year of schooling comments brought together as a summary testimonial. The system is illustrated in the sample reports.

The Special Places in Secondary Schools Examination

In 1937 the Eastbourne School was a senior mixed council school, not a secondary school. The Darlington High School for Girls and the Queen Elizabeth Grammar School for Boys were the secondary schools and admission was to 'fee-bearing places' or 'special places', that is, by parents paying for their children to attend or by the children passing the appropriate level in the Special Places in Secondary Schools Examination. The working of the system was explained in the LEA handbook.

The annual Special Places in Secondary School Examinations were the only addition to the programme of internal tests and, for example, it was reported on 17 March 1937 that a Junior Scholarship Secondary School Examination was held during the morning when 148 pupils sat the examination – 70 boys and 78 girls. The term 'scholarship' is derived from the fact that the successful examination candidates had their fees paid by means of a grant, and on 24 August 1937 the head teacher recorded that the following had been successful:

Maurice Brown, Morris Kay, Alan Williams, Mavis Bean, Dorothy Bell, Marjorie Bennett, Joan Bramley, Joyce Dodds, Sheila Eckford, Careta

Griffiths, Joyce Moore, Christina L. Scott, Beryl Simpson, Florence Mary Stephenson, Audrey Tagley, Jean Whittam and Elizabeth Wright.

That is, 3 boys and 14 girls, a total of only 17 out of the 148 who were entered: about 11.5%.

On 9 March 1938 a secondary school entrance examination was held in the morning at Dodmire Junior School, and Miss Fenby, Miss Maughan and Mr J. W. Scott were invigilators. There was a further examination on 5 May 1938 when the second intelligence test was held at 10.15 a.m. This type of test, avoiding the use of language and calculation, was designed in an attempt to detect bright children who might otherwise fail the examination due to what was thought to be their social background, involving a lack of contact with reading and arithmetical materials. A local education authority regulation prevented practice in intelligence tests and other special coaching for these examinations being carried out in schools.

The involvement of parents in the life of the school

At the official opening

The first opportunity for parents and friends to visit the new school was on the occasion of its official opening and subsequently, on 27 July 1938, the school was open to parents from 2–4 p.m. and from 6–8 p.m. During the afternoon 372 parents saw the school following its normal timetable under working conditions, and in the evening 297 parents attended.

In association with celebrations for the Coronation

There was another occasion for parents and friends to visit the school in 1937, an unusual and special year due to the ceremony associated with the coronation of Their Majesties King George VI and Queen Elizabeth. The school closed on 12 May, the day of the coronation, and on 13 May there followed a day of celebration when the school assembled at 1 p.m. for a programme of sports lasting from 1.30 p.m. till 3.45 p.m. when rain disrupted the plans. Afterwards each class had tea in their classroom, each pupil being given a coronation mug and a new penny.

The school was visited by leading figures in the community: the Mayor and Mayoress of Darlington, Councillor and Mrs R. Luck, Lady Starmer, Councillor J. Hinks, Councillor T. E. Hudson and Mr T. Crooks (ex-alderman).

Formality and ceremony

Adding to the ethos of the school was the local and national attention given to formality and ceremony. In the day-to-day, month-to-month life of the school there was established an expected formality and constancy, providing security – young people knowing what they were supposed to do and how and when they were supposed to do it.

Life also included ceremony, occasions when things are turned from everyday normality into a fairyland pageant, and people seem to enjoy these occasions, even needing such events in their lives.

The awarding of prizes

The local Education Committee determined the procedures to be adopted for the awarding of prizes, expecting head teachers to submit to the committee their proposed arrangements for the distribution of the prizes and copies of any reports that were to be presented at the meeting.

The nature and cost of each prize was prescribed: 'Each Prize shall be a book suitably inscribed and of a cash value not exceeding 3s.6d.' There was to be one Special Place Prize, two Class Prizes for each class above the first year, and two Leaver's Prizes.

The nature of the prize-giving is illustrated by the head teacher's log entry for the first such occasion, held at 3 p.m. on Tuesday 3 November 1937. The Mayor, Councillor R Luck, presented the prizes and the following accompanied him on the platform: Lady Starmer, Mrs Whalley, Alderman J. L. Hinks, Councillor M. Gallagher, Mr C. H. Leach MA OBE (Chairman of the Education Committee and ex-alderman) and Miss Waters. The headmaster, Mr G. W. Welford, presided.

The second prize-giving was held at 3 p.m. on 25 January 1939, when Lady Starmer presented the prizes and the chairman of the Education Committee presided. Councillor H. Bell JP, vice chairman of the Education Committee, Councillor Chandlers, Councillor B. Dodd, Mrs Luck, Miss O. M. Stanton, principal of The Darlington Training College, and Mrs Whalley also attended.

A core of influential local people, a team, in a small authority observed the putting into practice of the council's regulations and supported their new school, giving leadership and an atmosphere of importance to the proceedings.

The celebration of special events

The first anniversary

On 18 August 1937 the flag was flown to commemorate the first anniversary of the opening of the school.

Armistice celebrations

On 11 November 1937 a special lesson on 'Peace' was given to all classes between 9.30 and 10.10 a.m. Similar procedures were followed in 1938 when the school was dismissed at 11.30 after Armistice Day celebrations.

Empire Day

Special lessons were arranged for each class on Empire Day, 24 May 1939.

The approach of war

The outbreak of the Second World War in September 1939 put a temporary stop to educational reforms, although even a superficial study of the Eastbourne Schools demonstrates that not all advancement was put on hold.

The raising of the school-leaving age was abandoned among the more pressing preparations for evacuation of schools from target areas, although welfare schemes were established to combat rising juvenile delinquency, which was thought to be the result of war time disruption to family life. But the spark of reform flourished to culminate in the Butler Education Act of 1944, devised and enacted by the wartime national government comprising a coalition of all political parties.

The school was due to be reorganised in 1939 into separate boys' and girls' schools but the country was about to be plunged into the turmoil of the Second World War with inevitable disruption and, although the separation did take place as scheduled, innovation must have suffered.

The first suggestion of war activities is the following entry for 27 June 1938 when Messrs G. W. Welford and P. H. Moss attended an Air Raid Precautions course from 11 a.m. to 12 noon and Miss N. Fenby from 3 to 4 p.m. The course continued throughout the week, with other members of staff attending similar courses in later weeks.

The Opening of the Eastbourne Senior Boys' and Girls' Schools August 1939

The Eastbourne Senior Mixed School was reorganised into separate girls' and boys' departments immediately before the start of the Second World War: a time of great uncertainty, only twenty-one years since the end of the Great War, memories of its devastation and loss of life still fresh in the minds of the adult population.

The girls' school log of 28 August 1939 stated: 'On Monday, the twenty-eighth day of August, nineteen hundred and thirty-nine, this school, "The Eastbourne Senior Girls' School", Darlington, opened for the first time at 9 a.m., the Eastbourne Senior Mixed School having been organised into two departments.'

The boys' school log for the same day stated: 'The Eastbourne Senior Mixed School was reorganised from today and became the Eastbourne Senior Boys' School; the girls, 381, were transferred to the Eastbourne Senior Girls' School. The number of scholars on roll was 417.'

The staff

At the changeover from mixed school to single-sex departments Mr Welford became headmaster of the boys' school and Miss Fenby the headmistress of the girls' school.

The new staff of the boys' school

> Head Teacher Mr George Welford
>
> J. J. Goynes, Bede College
>
> John Towers, age 23, Dudley Training College, from Gladstone Street

The new staff of the girls' school

> Head Teacher Miss Nora Fenby
>
> Mary Askew, aged 20, Hull Municipal Training College
>
> Olive Hunnam BSc, Armstrong College, Newcastle upon Tyne
>
> Lynda Maude Linford, Darlington Training College
>
> Margaret Winifred Thursfield, aged 21, became Mrs M. W. Brown, Leicester Domestic Science College
>
> Violet Anne Elizabeth Welborn, aged 22, City of Leeds Training College

There was therefore little change among the teachers and in some cases the continuation or commencement of what was to be a long period of service in one school, a factor of significance in the formation of a lengthy unchanging regime.

The pupils

There were 318 boys remaining on the roll of the new Eastbourne senior boys' school, and 381 girls had been transferred to the new Eastbourne senior girls' school. The former had a new intake from feeder primary schools of 99 boys and the latter 99 girls. The total on the roll of the boys' school was therefore 417 and that of the girls' school 480: two small schools compared with the size of today's much larger institutions and schools from which mere children would leave to take up employment when they attained the age of 14, a little after growing out of their thirteenth year, a very significant fact and one too frequently overlooked.

These children went out into the adult world of paid employment, where they would be a handful of youngsters among many grown-ups. Today they remain in a school environment, many young individuals among a handful of adults: the ratio of the immature to the mature has changed for most young people under the age of 18, and even for those under 21, and peer-group pressure during the years of adolescent development is now a far greater factor than it used to be.

The buildings

Although the Eastbourne Senior Mixed School was opened in 1936, it is clear that the buildings were still not complete by August 1939. In addition, as war approached, priority had to be given to the building of the air-raid shelters.

Boys' school log 28.8.39: 'The new extensions being incomplete, three Boys' classes were accommodated in the Science Room, the Library and a classroom of the Senior Girls' Department. The Hall of the Senior Girls' Department was shared.'

Girls' school log 28.8.39: 'Owing to the new extensions being incomplete the Senior Boys' School still occupied several classrooms, the Science Room and shared the Hall. Two Domestic Science Rooms, used previously as classrooms, were in the process of conversion for domestic science purposes, but were not available for use, the workmen still being engaged in structural alterations.'

The air-raid shelters

In November 1939 Miss Fenby reported ten 'shelters against Air Raid Bomb Explosions' were being built but were not complete. The three first-year classes and one second-year class were therefore not allowed to attend school until further notice. Five shelters 'along the north boundary, two between the Girls' and Boys' Cycle sheds, two behind the Domestic Science block and one on the Field' were ready for use. All of the shelters were in use by 27 November 1939 and the remaining classes attended. Each shelter was expected to accommodate fifty people.

As well as giving the location of shelters this entry makes it quite clear that the domestic science buildings were complete at this time. Two new domestic science rooms were 'ready for use' but being subjected to scrutiny with reference to making economies in the provision of equipment. And on 22 July 1940 a brief note states: 'Received 48 stools for Domestic Science Rooms from Reid Street Hut (formerly of Beaumont Street Domestic Science Centre).'

During the week of 18 October 1940 blackout shutters were fitted to the air-raid shelter ventilators and in November the floors were sprayed with 'sodium solicitate' to prevent dust getting into the air.

By June 1942 it was thought to be necessary to tar the shelter roofs as a protection against weathering.

Heating the building

It is clear from an entry in the school log book for November 1944, referring to the caretaker's duties, that the buildings were then heated by coal- or coke-fired boilers and during the war years the scarcity of fuel resulted in a cold school. The significance of boilers heated by coal or coke is that this type of fuel had to be loaded into carts and wheeled from the store to the two boiler rooms, manhandled down into the boiler rooms, which were situated below floor level, and then shovelled into the furnaces. Hard physical work and during a severe winter a very cold, unpleasant job.

The grave international situation

The years before the opening of the separate boys' and girls' schools were a period of increasing uncertainty, a dangerous, threatening uncertainty, due to the coming to power in Germany of the Nazi Party under the leadership of Adolf Hitler, and its militant threat, backed up by aggressive military action, designed to unite Europe under its dictatorial and inhumane regime. Children were not unaware of this threat; they could not help hearing of the invasions of other countries: Nazi air bombardments, jack-booted soldiers marching and tanks rumbling, grinding and grating their way into foreign cities.

The destructive bombing in April 1937 of civilians in Guernica, situated at the heart of the Spanish Basque region, by German bombers during the Spanish Civil War made quite clear the horror of attack from the air. The destruction of bricks and mortar by high-explosive bombs, the incineration of anything that would burn by incendiary devices and the mowing down of people by machine-gun fire left no doubt in the minds of anyone just what a Nazi attack could mean.

Children are adaptable, resilient and resourceful, being able to fit into new and changing circumstances, lacking the experience and understanding of true danger, and therefore would view much of the news with detachment and excitement. But even if they were too young to comprehend the seriousness of the situation, they would absorb the mood of impending gloom and doom from the adults around them.

It was in November 1937 that Parliament voted in favour of air-raid shelters being built in areas of dense population and arrangements were made to supply sandbags for building into protective walls at ground level in front of buildings.

In 1938 it was made a legal requirement for children to be given compulsory gas-mask drill.

In February 1939 it was decided to distribute air-raid shelters to people living in areas thought to be most at risk from air raids.

If these actions did not emphasise the deadly serious nature of what was going on, then surely the evacuation of children from towns and cities in August 1939 did so. Where parents wanted their children to be evacuated they were instructed to send them to school with a spare set of clothes, a toothbrush, a comb, a handkerchief and a bag of food for one day. The destination of the youngsters was unknown to the parents and the youngest children must have been completely bewildered, even if the older ones saw everything as a new adventure. But, of course, evacuation did not take place from Darlington. It was Darlington that received evacuees later in the war. In among all of this, only one week after the opening of the separate boys' and girls' schools, war had been declared. Wartime schooling had commenced.

A few telling entries from the schools' log books

30.8.39: The International Situation being grave, emergency precautions were taken to minimise risks in the event of an unexpected air raid. All pupils brought their gas masks to school and the masks were refitted and tested. Defective masks and misfits were reported to the Air Raid Precautions Officer.

31.8.39: Head Teachers' Conference at the Education Office at 11.30 a.m. Air Raid Precautions and Schools were discussed.

1.9.39: The Teachers Handicraft Course which was to be housed in the School 4.9.39 to 8.9.39 was cancelled.

1.9.39: At 5.30 p.m. the School assembled in the Hall and owing to Germany invading Poland, and Poland being Great Britain's ally, the gravity of the International situation was announced and explained to the children. They were instructed to watch in the local newspapers for an official notice, which would indicate whether the schools would be closed during the period of national emergency which would arise in the event of war.

4.9.39: Monday. England and France declared a state of war on Germany on Sunday September 3rd 1939. England at 11 a.m. and France at 5 p.m. In consequence a period of national emergency existed and the schools were closed as from today for an indefinite period.

13.11.39: Monday. The Boys' School reopened for 4 Third Year classes only – adequate air-raid shelters only available for 4 classes – shelters in course of construction for the remainder of the school.

20.11.39: The Girls' School reopened for classes 3.1, 3.2, 3.3, 3.4, 2.1, 2.2, 2.3 (304 girls). Shelters against Air Raid Bomb Explosions were provided but as the full number, 10, were not complete, classes 2.4, 1.1, 1.2, 1.3 were not to attend school until further notice. Each shelter has accommodation for 50 people. Five shelters along the North Boundary, two between the Girls' and Boys' Cycle Sheds, two behind the domestic Science block and one on the Field were ready for use; temporary arrangements were made accordingly and the girls had 'Air-raid shelter Practice'.

The War Years 1939–1945

Once the building of the air-raid shelters had been completed all year groups were able to return to school: the boys on 20 November and the girls on 27 November 1939.

But the war did not go well for the children of the UK during 1940 and 1941. There was the obvious disruption to normal life, with fathers and older brothers leaving home to serve in the armed forces, with no suggestion whatsoever of when or if they would ever come back. Evacuation from areas which were thought most likely to be attacked had taken place in August 1939 but the expected air attacks did not happen and some youngsters returned home.

On the other hand, pupils were immediately introduced to the very real threat of being bombed, the Air Raid Warning System being explained to them: 'raiders approaching' signalled by a siren being sounded, a machine producing a loud on-and-off wailing sound, never to be forgotten once it was realised what might or did follow. Orderly, even regimental, passage to and from the air-raid shelters was frequently and regularly practised, a first entry into these dark oppressive places, only recently erected and smelling of the still-drying cement and with cement dust in the air, must surely have been a very unwelcome experience, if not a frightening one.

The 'all clear', a continuous wail, inevitably brought a temporary relief.

In May 1940 British forces in France were retreating and by June the evacuation from Dunkirk was underway. Enemy forces were then no more distant than the width of the English Channel, and, at their closest, only twenty-two miles away across the Straits of Dover.

Considering the development of air travel between the wars, anywhere in the British Isles had become accessible to bombers from mainland Europe, and this included Darlington.

The threat of invasion was very real. On 9 April 1940 the children would have learnt of Germany invading Denmark and France; on 10 May, Holland, Belgium and Luxembourg were invaded and with effect from 11 June, there was a further threat when Italy declared war on England and France.

As though emphasising the danger in the north-east, Middlesbrough was the first industrial centre to be bombed, in May 1940, just after the surrender of the French to the Nazi invaders and at the time when the Luftwaffe was regrouping and making trial sorties across the North Sea. The expectation was for worse to come: aerial bombardment followed by invasion, the enemy's, by this time familiar, lightning strikes from the air and rapid invasion on land, known as the blitzkrieg. There was, perhaps, the hope that the natural moat of the North Sea and English Channel would deter the latter, but the Battle of Britain in the air, which commenced in August 1940, made it quite clear that there was no escape from the former.

During the afternoon of 7 September, 375 bombers and fighter escorts attacked Woolwich Arsenal, Beckton gasworks, the London docks and West Ham Power Station. They had left by 6 p.m. but returned the following night. There were deaths and injuries from explosions, falling buildings, and from flying debris, sharp fingers of glass, fragments of brick and stone.

Some 50,000 tons of high-explosive bombs fell on London during the period from September 1940 to July 1941.

A *Northern Echo* report of Friday 7 April 1942 refers to the bombing of a north-east town, not identified by name, presumably for security reasons, as doing so could provide useful information to the enemy. It says 'bombs were dropped in a crowded part of the town' and says that twelve houses were destroyed and others seriously damaged, people being left homeless. Five mothers and babies had been killed and other people treated in hospital or at first-aid posts. Rescue and demolition squads had worked throughout the night attempting to rescue those trapped.

There were also reports of incidents illustrating the amazing element of chance which so often seems to arise in times of devastation. In one house a family of six had been killed, while next door, separated only by a thin wall, a family of seven escaped with only minor injuries. Two men were said to have been blown out of their beds by the explosions yet were fit enough to join in the rescue operations.

Luckily Darlington did not suffer the devastation of some other places but that was not to be known until after the war, and the anticipation of what might come did nothing to ease people's anxiety. After all, the workshops of Darlington were responsible for maintaining a supply of railway equipment, among other things, surely making it an attractive target for an enemy intent upon destroying the United Kingdom's ability to defend itself.

Even so, the only record in the schools' log books of a potentially destructive incident was the fire discovered in a waste-paper basket between 8.30 and 8.45 p.m. on 17 January 1940 in Room 19, Domestic Science Room I. This seems to have been a mystery and one can only assume that, as there was no report of a hole in the roof or foul smells of an incendiary bomb, nor any sign of enemy agents in the place, it must have been caused by the careless discarding by the firewatcher of a lighted match or cigarette end.

It was reported on 15 January 1941: 'Miss Maughan left school at 11.5 a.m. to attend a meeting at the Education Office about "Fire Watching in School".' It is important to emphasise to those ignorant of World War II that this subject was nothing to do with gazing into the warming flames of an open coal fire in the middle of a severely cold spell of weather, no matter how much the lady probably wished it was! It was the far more serious matter concerning the dropping by enemy aircraft of fire bombs, or incendiary devices, capable of igniting conflagrations capable of destroying whole rows of houses, workshops and, of course, schools.

Consequently, as from 31 March 1941 'Fire Watching Parties' for day and night patrol of the school began duty. School staff volunteered their time to operate this scheme but it was reported that there were insufficient people available to cover every day and night of the week. This was no rave up! The duty consisted of the serious business of watching for falling bombs, finding where they landed and then extinguishing them.

An observation in the log of the boys' school for 31 January 1941 states that the timetable was suspended for an hour and forty minutes in the morning for a lecture on 'Incendiary Bombs, Stirrup Pumps, and

Redhill Containers' and there was 'a demonstration of how to extinguish an incendiary bomb using a Redhill Container, sand, shovel and rake'. An officer of the Air Raid Precautions authority was in charge.

Further advice was given in October 1942 in the girls' school on action to be taken in case of an air raid: 'Everyone in the ground floor rooms to lie down flat and take cover afforded in the room, all classes upstairs to proceed to ground floor under balcony in hall and in the entrance hall.'

On 9 April 1942 the *Northern Echo* published a warning to children: they were told not to touch items such as bottles, thermos flasks, metal balls or tubes found lying in fields or by the roadside as they may not be what they seem. There was concern that the enemy had dropped anti-personnel bombs disguised as such items. There was the additional warning telling them to stay away from the fire service water storage tanks, which had been set up to supply water in cases of fire.

The first reference to any actual air raid taking place is the entry in the girl's school log of 29 January 1940, when the pupils and staff took cover in the air-raid shelters between 9.27 a.m. and 10.30 a.m.

A further event is recorded on 22 February 1940 in the following manner: 'A Public Air Raid siren was heard at 12.58 p.m., the children and staff took cover in the Air Raid Shelters until 1.08 p.m. when the "All clear" was given.'

Normal school activities were continued whenever possible but not without disruption in the form of frequent visits to the air-raid shelters and practising the wearing of gas masks. During the week of 5 May 1940 air-raid shelter practice was taken each day, so that classes were in different rooms for each practice; on 24 May 1940, a practice was taken with gas rattles and 'raiders passed' signals. It was during this month that Miss E. A. Richardson and Miss Owen had to attend the 'Report Centre' for instruction in how to fit the 'Coutex' to respirators; and Miss Fenby reports with her usual concise efficiency, on 28 May: '"Coutex" fitted to every respirator in the school. Except for Domestic Science, specialisation was cancelled 9.30–12.30 so that the work was completed.'

Apart from regular air-raid shelter practices and respirator inspections, these seem to be the only events of war entering the records until July 1940 when it was reported: 'Thursday 27.6.40 and Monday 1.7.40 a "rest" period was taken at the beginning of the afternoon session, the first lesson at 1.55 p.m., as during the night previous to these days Public Air Raid Alarms were sounded after midnight.' The situation seems to have been one of expectation; a kind of 'raiders might be coming this way but did not quite make it'.

On 12 July there is reference to Local Authority Circular 40/44 and subsequent actions taken by the school: 'When the raiders passed signal is sounded after 12 midnight the school session on that morning will begin at 10 instead of 9 o'clock.' This explains the late start of school between September and December 1940, and again in the early months of 1941, signifying that air raids were taking place somewhere in the area during the night, and further observations point to there being daytime raids as well.

On 20 June it was reported that there had been an air raid the previous night which had lasted about five hours, from 11 p.m. to 4 a.m., and that only 71 per cent of the boys attended school next morning. By July 1940, due to the occurrence of night-time air raids, school regularly started at 10.00 a.m., an arrangement which continued into September. By November school was starting at 9.00 a.m. but in March 1941 it was again opening at 10.00 a.m. and still doing so in October. An instruction was issued in June 1942 that if the 'alert' came after midnight school should start at 9.15 a.m.

This is the period of the Blitz and further advice and additional precautions were considered necessary. In mid July 1940 Miss Fenby wrote: 'During the week practices have been taken in every class in different rooms in accordance with the order that "children should in no circumstances leave the school building in the event of bombs dropping in the neighbourhood, without warning. In such circumstances, the children should take up the safest positions available in the building itself, away from windows, and if necessary lying on the floor. The children therefore will take up 'crouch position' under the desks, then arms over their ears and hands clasped behind their heads, which will be inclined to one side and the jaw slack."'

Interruptions to the normal working day occurred with such frequency that it must be wondered how the children concentrated on any kind of school work during these times. Even when there were no air raids, practices were regular and frequent: exits made from the hall to the air-raid shelters, exits from different classrooms to the air-raid shelters, exits in the morning, and at lunchtime.

One cannot help wondering what sort of excitement was caused by this constant chasing about and whether learning of school work became a mere respite from the more physically active rushing about the building, diving under desks or suffering the tummy rumbles at the sound of Moaning Minnie (the air-raid warning siren, for those too young to know the expression).

There are further excitements! Entries in the girls' school log for 20 and 27 June 1941 say: 'Gas Masks worn by all girls for 5 minutes', and again on the 4 July: 'Respirators worn by children in school'. My own experience of the wretched contraptions, strapped tight around the face and with a misty window for seeing out, during rare trials, caused me to conclude I would either die of gas poisoning or suffocation!

The Eastbourne Schools were not evacuated, those in London were, and perhaps that is the reason for my opinion: for a period of some months, I was not evacuated, did not go to school, and had no forced spells of confinement behind the black rubber-smelling pig-like snouts.

At Eastbourne there were regular monthly inspections, when faulty masks were reported and presumably rectified. It is recorded that in March 1941 ARP staff visited the school for the fitting and overhauling of gas masks. While the Eastbourne pupils had their respirators fitted in school, we had to report to the Civil Defence Hut individually, and, apart from this visit made with a friend of the same age and without any parental escort, I do not remember anybody inspecting our stifling contraptions. We only seemed to carry them, in their cardboard boxes, upgraded bags or cylindrical tin cans, for a short time, and this must have been due to the lack of schooling in London – children being sent to parts of the country judged to be unlikely targets for attack from air raiders.

There was one of many respirator drills (the wearing of gas masks) and inspections at the girls' school on 28 January 1941, when it was reported: 'Without respirator 10, Defective 66, Wrong Ownership 4, In good condition 259.'

In spite of having experienced the sound of a torpedo whistling overhead and seen the yawning gap where houses had stood and the tattered strips of clothing, shattered glass and piles of broken bricks strewn across the road after the tremendous ear-shattering roar of the explosion; heard anti-aircraft guns pounding the sky with exploding shells; seen the site of a wrecked house still containing an unexploded bomb; smelt the mortar dust in the air; had parts of one's own school destroyed by a land mine dropped by parachute; seen another destroyed by a rocket falling from the sky and watched flying bombs pass overhead, on reading this so many years after the event I cannot help but see the funnier side of it all.

Wartime staffing

In the Emergency Powers Act of May 1940 the government took absolute control over all aspects of people's lives, giving the Minister of Labour authority to order anybody to do whatever was seen as necessary to win the war. This was essential in the struggle for survival and the safeguarding of the long-term freedom for the people, who would otherwise have become the subjects in a fascist state – and this was, after all, when the invasion forces of Hitler's blitzkrieg were massing on the French Channel shores.

The first people to be called to serve in the armed forces were members of the Territorial Army, and in August 1939 army and air force reservists were also called up and the navy mobilised. The early involvement of women is illustrated by the formation of the Women's Auxiliary Air force (WAAF) in July 1939.

People could be directed to work in munitions factories, their conditions of work, including wages, being determined by the state: for example, workers in aircraft factories were ordered to work a ten-hour day for seven days a week.

As well as the conscription of young men to serve in the armed forces, older men and women were directed to work in industries supporting the war effort and women replaced men in the jobs they had vacated.

Parliament had already, in April 1939, introduced the Military Training Bill making conscription compulsory for men between twenty and thirty-six. A national register of youths under twenty-one was also proposed with a view to giving them six months' military training followed by their placement in the Territorial Army or Special Reserve. The Bill received the Royal Assent in May and the first conscripts were enlisted on 3 June. By January 1940 two million 19- to 27-year-old men had been called up.

In March 1941 another law was enacted making it obligatory for women aged 20 and 21 to register in order to provide labour for the war industries and auxiliary services.

In December further regulations were brought out to 'call up' single women between the ages of 20 and 30 to cover clerical work vacated by the call-up of men to military service, to work alongside men in anti-aircraft gun crews, and to act as police officers and firefighters. For men, the call-up age was lowered to 18 ½ and the upper limit raised to 50 years of age. Both married and single women below the age of 40 had to register, and both boys and girls between 16 and 18 years of age had to register for appropriate pre-military training.

The *Northern Echo* for Saturday 7 March 1942 reports that the first women aged between 20 and 21 years were conscripted for service in the Auxiliary Territorial Service (ATS). They had attended for medicals a fortnight previously and were to report within the week to their designated depots. They were given a railway travel voucher and a postal order of value 4 shillings.

A little later, women of conscription age could choose to serve in the WAAF, the WRNS (Women's Royal Navy Service) or industry, in which case they would be sent to work in one of the Royal Ordnance factories established for the manufacturing of armaments. One such factory near Darlington was at Aycliffe. Those with special, appropriate previous training would be sent to work in agriculture or hospitals.

A further order, in December 1943, required one in ten men aged between 18 and 25 to work in the coalmines. They were chosen from conscripts by ballot and became known as Bevin Boys, taking the name from the then Minister of Labour, Ernest Bevin.

As late as May 1945, there was yet another government order making part-time work for women aged 18 to 45 compulsory, that is, those with no domestic responsibilities. Part-time hours were defined as thirty hours per week or fewer. Although a voluntary system had brought some 600,000 to work, it was argued that thousands more were needed to fill the gaps left by men being conscripted into the forces. However, the orders were not long lasting, apparently being of between three weeks and six months!

The significance of much of this, as far as girls were concerned, is the social change giving significance to females in the workplace. For instance, in education before the war, once a young woman teacher married, she would no longer be employed.

In relation to the registration of the younger age group, there is a telling quotation attributed to Winston Churchill: 'We must be careful particularly, that our boys do not run loose.' How significant this is when we look at the behaviour of some of the younger population today.

While the staff of the boys' school was disrupted by the direction of men to service in HM forces and war work, the core of the girls' teaching force remained remarkably stable with the exception of permanent domestic science teachers being involved in the arrangements for the promotion of wartime cooking among the adult population. Members of a team of local authority temporary teachers worked off and on in the school at this time.

There follows a number of entries made in the school log books which illustrate a little of the reality of the situation at Eastbourne:

'Mr R. Newton was interviewed in Middlesbrough on the afternoon of 19 February 1940 with reference to his joining the RAF, he had his medical on the 10 May and by June had joined the Service.'

'Mr T. A. Tweddle, aged about 35 years, was out of school at his National Service Interview on 4 March 1940 but by 26 July had become the head teacher at Gladstone Street School. Presumably he was not called up.'

'Mr J. R. Farrage, metalwork teacher aged 49, attended an ENSA Conference in York on 9 May 1940, ENSA being the Entertainments National Service Association, and on 13 June 1941 left Eastbourne to be a shop manager in the Royal Ordnance Factory at Aycliffe for the duration of the war.'

'Mr T. Tranter, aged 45, attended for a medical in connection with the registration of his age group for service in HM forces on 30 June 1941, and was called up on 1 August. He resumed his teaching career at Eastbourne on 1 November 1945 and on 19 July 1946 became Youth Warden at Gladstone Street Boys' school.'

'Mr G. Steele, aged 32, had his medical on 1 July 1941, his interview on the 17th and was conscripted on 1 August.'

'Mr J. Peacock had his interview relating to his joining the RAF on the 1 July 1942.'

There is a telling entry in the girls' school log for September 1940: 'Mrs J. Thompson returned to duty, absent one working day – acting as Train Escort to Overseas Evacuation Children, at the request of the Authority.' There is a report in the *Northern Echo* of 17 March 1942 of a 14-year-old Darlington boy, formerly living in Eastbourne Road but then in Canada, who had raised money for the war effort. He had been one of the evacuees sent abroad in 1940.

The school dental inspection was cancelled in February 1940 because the dentist had been instructed to report for duty in HM forces.

A note dated 17 September 1940 relates to Mr L. Walton finishing his duties as caretaker in the afternoon as he had been called up for armament work. A previous log-book entry for January that year indicates that the school domestic science flat was occupied by Mr and Mrs Walton, caretaker from Sherborne Camp, Saltburn, requiring alterations to be made to the domestic science teaching timetable. Apparently Mr and Mrs Walton's stay was short, the flat being back in use by 22 January 1940.

There is evidence of women coming in to take the place of male staff. When the boys' school opened in 1939 the staff consisted of the head plus thirteen other teachers, all male; at the same time, the girls' school was staffed entirely by unmarried women; but in September 1940 three women were appointed to the boys' staff: Miss J. M. Shinfield, then aged 46, Miss P. Vivian, aged 21, and Miss G. Todd, aged 33. Sadly Miss Shinfield died only three and a half years later, the other two leaving the school in 1943 and 1945 respectively.

Four more single women joined the staff of the boys' school in September 1941. They were Miss C. Connolly BA, an English specialist aged 25 who had trained at Liverpool University and who quickly transferred to the Darlington Boys' Grammar School; Miss E. M. Hamil, aged 21, who left at the beginning of November 1945; Miss K. L. Adamson, also aged 21 and newly qualified, who was transferred to North Road Secondary Girls' School in September 1943 but later returned to Eastbourne; and Miss M. Askew, aged 22 years, who is recorded as leaving on 31 July 1944.

Another team of young women joined the boys' school in October 1943 and they were Miss V. Horner, aged 22, who left on 30 April 1945; Miss M. E. Nicholson, aged 22, who transferred to The Day Technical School on 2 December 1945; Miss J. Bone, aged 25, who left on 21 September 1944; and Miss P. Bell, aged 21, who left on 20 July 1945.

Mr J. J. Goynes, aged 23, who had trained at Bede College between 1935 and 1937 and commenced duty at Eastbourne in August 1937, left on 27 July 1940 when it was recorded that his engagement was terminated by Town Clerk's Notice of Council Minute. Mr Goynes was registered as a conscientious objector and had attended a tribunal in

Newcastle on 26 January 1940. There is no further information given in the log book but it is generally known that conscientious objectors registered their claim to be exempt from military service. Some were able to satisfy their consciences by serving as medical orderlies on active service, placing themselves in the same theatres of war as their arms-bearing colleagues.

The notes below give rather different, but equally informative, reasons for staff being absent from their teaching duties.

'Sadly, on 23 June 1941, Miss W. Storer was absent from duty due to the news of the loss of her brother at sea, reminding us that ships, both those of the Royal Navy and Merchant Navy, were in constant danger of enemy attack.'

'On 20 July 1942 Miss M. L. Dixon was absent from duty having been granted leave of absence without pay due to "special circumstances" which were "to visit a friend on embarkation leave".' [Embarkation leave was leave from one's service unit before being sent to war zones overseas, with knowledge that the serviceman might not come back, or if he did, when this would be and in what state of fitness and health he would be in.]

Mrs W. A. Steele BA was granted leave of absence without pay for five working days in 1942 and again in 1943 due to her husband being on leave from HM forces; and from 13 to 19 September 1943 Mrs M. Brown, a domestic science teacher, had a similar spell of leave.

Under happier circumstances, Mrs Steele BA left the service of the authority on 31 August 1945 to return to Southampton, prior to her husband being demobilised from HM forces. There was also the head teacher's comment: 'No supply teacher available – timetable adjusted'; with the further note: 'Timetable adjusted because of staff shortages'. In the case of Mrs E. Mayo being granted leave of absence for the same reason a temporary teacher was appointed to cover her teaching duties.

Among others, Miss K. A. McLeish BA reported for temporary teaching duty on 5 November 1943, but eventually became a permanent member of staff in the girls' school, and the head of the English department on the comprehensive school staff, before retiring after some forty years' service in the Eastbourne Schools.

There are notes on staffing difficulties in early 1944 when, for instance, there were apparently three fewer permanent staff than there should have been in January – two staff were absent sick, and one was lost from the domestic science staff, requiring timetable alterations to be made in order to cover the classes.

A further rearrangement was made in February 1944 when there was 'Curtailment of half-classes for needlework and science in the 2nd year', the combining of classes in music, while classes 2.1L and 2.2L were not able to begin their domestic science course. This meant that these two classes had to be catered for over five days instead of four (by non-domestic science teachers), where there was already a shortage, and had to have extra needlework, English, mathematics, games, and first aid.

At the boys' school there were staffing problems in October 1944 when the teaching of art was discontinued until a new art teacher could be appointed. It was also recorded that a simple course in biology was to be introduced for A and B streams in the first and second years and a modified general science course for the A and B streams in the third year.

Courses for teachers

The *Northern Echo* for Thursday 16 July 1942 reported that Mr Chuter Ede, Parliamentary Secretary to the Board of Education, and Member of Parliament for South Shields, had visited Darlington to see some of the nursery classes, school kitchens and play centres, before speaking that evening at the inaugural meeting of a short course for junior school teachers.

He praised the Darlington Education Authority for arranging the course, for their school meals service in which some 30 per cent of the children participated, and on their provision of wartime nursery classes and play centres. He referred to the controversy that had been raging for some twenty years over the structure of junior education and praised those authorities which had already incorporated specific junior departments into their systems.

The head teacher of the Eastbourne girls' department, Miss Fenby, recorded the visit in the following words: 'Mr Chuter Ede, DL, JP, MP, CA Parliamentary Secretary to the Board of Education, accompanied by the Chairman of Darlington Education Committee (Coun R. Luck), Chairman of the Health Committee (Ald Best JP), Medical Officer of Health, Dr Dawson, Chief Education Officer, Mr W. F. Houghton MA and Mr J. P. Scothorne HMI, visited the school pm. prior to Mr Ede speaking at the inaugural meeting of the Short Course for Junior Teachers at the Darlington Training College.'

She also reported that Miss E. A. Richardson BA represented the Eastbourne staff at the course, attending the training college for all sessions; and that Miss N. Soper also attended at the request of the Chief Education Officer and HMIs to help with the group activity 'Study of Environment – Natural History'. The headmistress and other members of staff also attended individual lectures, the timetable being adjusted to meet the requirements.

A domestic science conference and lunch were held at the school on Saturday 25 July 1942, and a further course, this time for infant school teachers, took place in the following October.

Even during wartime, Darlington, and Eastbourne in particular, seems to retain a position at the forefront of educational development, the Eastbourne Schools still being only 5 years old and the newest buildings dating from late 1938 and early 1939.

School organisation

In relatively peaceful Darlington, the Eastbourne Schools continued with their task of educating the young. There was a routine, a curriculum and discipline, even if such matters were disturbed by the demands of a country at war.

In spite of the disruption, much of school progressed with at least some semblance of normality. The Eastbourne Schools hardly ever closed, many routine aspects of life continuing as before the war, with an intake of 11-year-olds from the primary schools twice each year, leavers going out to work when they reached the school-leaving age of 14, and others transferring to the high, grammar or technical schools.

The sizes of the schools

The schools were not large, the average size of the girls' department being about 447, with a maximum of 491 and minimum of 420; while the boys' average was 423, maximum 467 and minimum 382. From the information available, on the other hand, the average teaching group was larger than today at about 40-plus, and the pupils placed in groups according to their abilities. If the slowest learners were placed in smaller groups, it is obvious that the more able were taught in even larger groups and, as previously stated, there were half-classes in domestic science and science.

An examination of the data, in particular that for the girls' school, also give some indication of the changes in size of the schools during the year, as pupils left to attend the selective secondary schools or to take up employment.

In February 1943, we are told that thirty-three 14-year-olds had left to enter the world of employment, leaving a total roll of 491 arranged into eleven full classes, that is forms or groups which would be taught together for certain basic subjects but as half-classes for practical subjects such as domestic science and science, giving an average of nearly forty-five in each form.

Transfers to the boys' grammar, girls' high, and technical schools are discussed elsewhere (see School examinations, Chapter 1).

By February 1944 the girl's school roll had fallen to 431 but was still organised into eleven classes, giving an average class size of about thirty-nine. By September 1945 there is evidence of the formation of a class which would take a School Certificate course, requiring the group to remain in the senior school until they were sixteen in order to take the examination.

Unfortunately, there is less information given in the boys' school log compared with that of the girls' school but there is the additional reference to evacuees being in the building, making half-time schooling necessary.

There is a little more information about the inclusion of junior pupils in the schools: in September 1941 there are fifty children of junior age on the roll of the boys' department, who apparently returned to Dodmire Junior School in November 1941.

The intake of pupils from primary schools

The figures for the number of pupils entering the Eastbourne girls' and boys' departments from the contributory primary schools during the war years appear to show an anomaly, as junior pupils seemed to be transferring to the senior schools before they reached the prescribed age.

On 3 June 1940, twenty-seven girls and boys from Dodmire were transferred to the senior boys' school, accompanied by their teacher, Mr Taylor, returning to Dodmire on 4 November 1941.

In June 1940 Miss Fenby writes: 'A mixed class being transferred from Dodmire Junior School, to the Eastbourne Boys' school, arrangements were made for the 25 girls in the class to share cloakroom, playground, hall accommodation, Assembly and an air-raid shelter in this school.' The entry explains the later transfer of 11-plus children to the grammar and high schools from the Eastbourne Schools and reminds us of the strict segregation of boys and girls at the time, a division which was to become a marked characteristic of the schools. In February 1941 another group of junior pupils, thirteen boys and seventeen girls, was taken into Eastbourne boys' school from Dodmire.

Routine

The basic distribution and lengths of terms, holidays and daily sessions followed the pre-war pattern but suffered change from time to time due to the threat from air raids and other wartime events. For example the normal hours for the boys' school were 9.00 a.m. to 12.10 p.m. and 1.40 p.m. to 4.00 p.m., but, apparently, following changes early in 1940 they were resumed from 26 February. On 25 November 1940 the school opened at 9.30 due, it was said, to the 'Continuance of Summer Time' and it was reported that lessons would consequently last for thirty minutes.

The logic of the latter situation is puzzling: during the war years there was a scheme designated 'daylight saving'. As man does not determine the length of daylight hours, a function of the Earth's movement along its orbit round the sun during which the duration of daytime changes from winter to summer in the latitude of the British Isles, any changes to the clocks is merely a change of distribution of these hours according to man's conception of time. The daylight-saving, double summer time, scheme consisted of retaining the one-hour-forward (in advance of) Greenwich Mean Time for the summer months in place during the following winter and then advancing the clocks a further hour the next summer: all nothing more than a manipulation of daylight hours in order to use them to what was thought to be the best advantage.

After a period during which the girls' school was opening at 10.00 a.m., frequently the time of air-raid warnings, in November 1940 this changed to 9.30 a.m. and was expected to remain so until the end of January 1941.

Daily routine started with registration, assembly and religious instruction lasting from 9 a.m. to 10.00 a.m., followed by half-hour lessons from 10 a.m. to 10.30a.m.; 10.30 a.m. to 11.00 a.m., 11.10 a.m. to 11.40 a.m.; and 11.40 a.m. 12.10 p.m. Details were not given for the afternoon sessions.

On 24 November 1941 Miss Fenby reported: 'In accordance with circular 41/57 the School opened at 9.30 a.m. and until January 30 1942 the school sessions will be 9.30 a.m. to 12.10 p.m. and 1.40 p.m. to 4 p.m.'

On 17 February 1941, for a trial period, times for the opening of the boys' school were 9.15 a.m. to 12.15 p.m. and 1.30p.m. to 4.00 p.m. On 3 March the hours changed to 9.15 a.m. to 12.15 p.m. and 1.45 p.m. to 4.15 p.m. and these times were still being used in February 1942. In August 1945 new times for the sessions were from 9.00 a.m. to 12.30 p.m. and from 2.00 p.m. to 4 p.m.

The continuation of the school day up to 4 p.m., and sometimes later, is in contrast to today's end of normal teaching sessions at or even before 3.30 p.m.

After the mid-term holiday, when the girls' school reopened on 4 November 1941, the head teacher refers to the introduction of a simple house system, which is the first mention of what was to become a significant aspect of school life.

Movement about the school

An instruction issued as a reminder of expected standards in September 1943 states the rules for the movement of classes between lessons, on leaving class at recreation times and at the end of morning and afternoon sessions: pupils should move in twos as a class, keeping to the right both in the corridor and on staircases, from room to room or to cloakrooms, and in the charge of the teacher of the concluding lesson or the class teacher at the beginning of a session.

Entry to the premises was via The Fairway from Yarm Road and through the main gate, assembling in the central yard. On the blowing of a whistle by the duty teacher pupils would stand still (freeze would be a more accurate description) and, on a second blast of the whistle, line up in class order to be marched single file into the building, escorted by the class teacher.

Pupil behaviour and discipline

The social climate applied to the supervision of the young has changed: an autocratic discipline has been replaced by more democratic guidance – for better or for worse. During the war years there was concern that the disruption to family life would result in a rise in disruptive and delinquent behaviour among the young.

As an example: the Chief Constable of Middlesbrough commented on the situation when talking to the West Hartlepool Rotarians in 1942 (as reported in the *Northern Echo* on 1 April) saying that the prime cause of juvenile delinquency was lack of parental control and that 'namby-pamby treatment was as bad as sheer neglect'. He referred to the development of entertainments which took parents from their homes night after night, leaving children to their own devices. He even suggested that 'schools do not pay enough attention to discipline and Christian teaching'.

Yet reports on life at Eastbourne do not support the notion that either the boys' or girls' schools were places of indiscipline but they were certainly more strictly controlled than today's schools.

Considering for a moment 16-year-olds, who in the early 1940s would have been in employment, if not following courses at the grammar and high schools, there is a telling note in the *Northern Echo* of Tuesday 28 April 1942. Some 720 16-year-old girls had had to register the previous Saturday and it was clearly expected that they should be members of such approved organisations as the Girl Guides. The report concluded: 'Those who do not belong to an accepted organisation will be called for interview by representatives of the local authority.' It was understood that young people would have to play their part in wartime activities and prepare for eventual enlistment into the forces or essential work, but the tone of the summons must come as rather a shock to young people in our please-yourself society today.

Punishments

It is interesting to see that the cane was used as a punishment for misbehaviour, inattention, talking in class and general disobedience, something that may be seen as rather harsh when judged against today's standards. Bearing in mind the reported disrespect shown to teachers today, it can be seen that such behaviour among the boys at Eastbourne in the late 1930s and early 40s would have resulted in a caning. It is also clear that disobedience was recognised, not tolerated, and punished.

The record of punishments (officially recorded corporal punishment) given here only applies to the boys' school.

The highest figures are those for truancy, a total of some thirty seven cases over a period of some five and-two-thirds school years, or an average of something like five cases per year. This is in an average annual school population of 418, giving a recorded truancy rate about 1%. As it is unknown whether or not there were other cases of truancy not dealt with via the recorded punishments system, this may not be very significant. We do know, however, that three cases, two 13-year-olds and one 12-year-old, were absences of boys potato lifting, an established annual custom among some, bringing into the family home some much-needed extra cash.

The incidents arising from lessons indicate an element of rule breaking and/or dislike of lessons. Truancy could therefore be the result of either a dislike of school, boyish disobedience, or a need to do something seen as more important by the family.

The incidents of bullying included the sticking of pins into other boys, and the cases of vandalism were one of an 11-year-old scratching a desk top and another cutting a bench with a knife.

The stealing, at this time, was largely scrumping, or the stealing of apples from the gardens of properties bordering the school grounds.

It is interesting to see that the cane was used as a punishment for misbehaviour, inattention, talking in class and general disobedience, something which may be seen as rather harsh when judged against today's standards. Bearing in mind the reported disrespect shown to teachers today, it can be seen that such behaviour among the boys at Eastbourne in the late 1930s and early 40s would have resulted in a caning. It is also clear that disobedience was recognised, not tolerated, and punished.

Corporal punishment was not used in the girls' school and it seems from the comments made by ex-pupils when questioned later in life that discipline was strict and maintained by an autocratic head teacher, at a time when it was acceptable for teachers to exert this style of control in schools and classes.

One ex-pupil, Shirley Donner, in notes kept in the Darlington Public Library, commented: 'We knew the rules, held her [the headmistress, Miss Fenby] in awe and kept out of sight of her when possible! Let me make it quite clear though, we [Donner and her sister] cried when we left [Eastbourne] for Newcastle in 1945.'

Miss Fenby patrolled the school regularly, entering classrooms and inspecting exercise books, seeking ink blots and spelling errors. It was clear that behaviour outside school was also expected to be courteous and of a good standard, the head demanding that the girls queued in an orderly manner while waiting for the trolley bus and gave up their seats to adults. Any incident outside school which was reported to the head would usually be dealt with in a severe manner.

The teaching of responsibility

The prefect system
There is evidence that both the boy's and girl's departments operated a prefect system. The girls' school log entry of 4 November 1941 refers to the election of the head girl and prefects.

An element of local government
On 9 November 1943 ten prefects representing the girls' school joined with a party of ten boys from the boys' department and, accompanied by Mr Welford, attended a meeting of the town council at 2.30 p.m. in the council chamber, when the election of mayor took place, the mayor elect being the councillor representing the Eastbourne ward.

The girls' school committee
It is clear that Miss Fenby's objective was to educate the Eastbourne girls in both the learning of knowledge and behaviour; the establishment of a prefect system and school committee illustrating some of her ideals. The school committee, in particular, sounds very progressive, as such committees, or councils as they are often called today, are suggested as a proper means of involving pupils in their education, giving them a say in the making of the school rules and so on. But there is a significant difference between then and now: that is the very different attitude of adults to children and the very different expectations.

In Miss Fenby's era, the rules were clearly laid down, understood and adhered to before the pupils were placed in any position of responsibility, no matter how minor that responsibility may have been. Miss Fenby knew the required standards, the girls knew those standards, the starting point was clear: what would be tolerated and not tolerated was also quite clear.

The School Committee
Nora Fenby writing in the girls' school log book, July1943

The School Committee – comprising two representatives from each class, two from the Prefects, the Chairman (the Head Girl) and a Staff Representative – was inaugurated in this School after Whitsuntide. In the short time it has been functioning it has been most successful – every girl in every class in the school being contacted and made to feel her responsibility. Every girl is familiar with the constitution and feels she has a responsibility. In a school of this type it is felt that such an arrangement is preferable to the house system where it is difficult for some of the retarded children to understand the significance or feel that everyone has a part to play. It is a most promising committee and should do much to prepare the girls to take a full and active part in the Youth Organisations which, obviously, will be developed more and more and will be important to the girl on leaving a school of this type. Already it has become evident that youth needs this preparation.

School Committee officers for the current term were elected and the inaugural meeting held on 10th September 1943.

Here are some entries in the school log book illustrating some of the activities of the School Committee:

22 December 1943: 'At the request of the School Committee, Class 3.1 gave a physical training demonstration to all first-year pupils. There was also "entertainment" arranged by the Committee.'

19 December 1944: 'The Committee organised an exhibition of work completed by girls during their leisure time. Categories included literature, writing, needlework, domestic science, crafts and models. Adjustments were made to the school timetable to permit all pupils and staff to visit the exhibition in groups and it was expected that group discussions and criticisms of the work would follow.'

School holidays

Just as the school closed for the Whitsun holiday on 10 May 1940 Germany invaded Holland, Belgium and Luxembourg and consequently an emergency order from the Board of Education cancelled all holidays and school reopened on 14 May, instead of the 21st. The news was broadcast by the BBC but Miss Dover, domestic science teacher, did not hear it, returning to work a day late!

On 10 November 1941 the boys' school closed for pupils aged 12 and over 'to enable them to assist local farmers in potato lifting'. The school reopened on the 17th and Mr Welford reported that the average attendance for the school during the period had been 229 with a total roll of 382.

Holidays at Home Schools Week

During the war travel was restricted and in July 1942 the taking of holidays at home was promoted in schools through the 'Holidays at Home Schools Week'.

Previously, at Easter, people had been warned that they should not take the opportunity to travel, a notice appearing in the *Northern Echo* on 19 March 1942:

> Warning
>
> This Easter people must not travel for pleasure or on business that is not vitally important, because the lines are urgently required for goods.
>
> If the public disregard this warning many will find themselves stranded.
>
> Lord Leathers

The 'lines' are of course the railways, the means by which most people would travel if permitted to do so: the mass car-owning culture had not yet arrived.

On 28 July 1942 a group of girls and members of staff visited South Park during the morning in connection with a Holidays at Home Schools Week rehearsal and on 30 July girls and members of staff visited South Park during the morning and Darlington Technical College in the afternoon for further rehearsals.

On 20 July 1943 the timetable was suspended for an hour during the afternoon for sports in connection with Holidays at Home. Heats took place in preparation for the Wednesday evening meeting.

At this time, in accordance with the Board of Education's circular 1596, and at the request of the education authority, arrangements were completed for the school to remain open during the summer vacation for those girls who wished to attend, some forty indicating that they wished to take part. All members of staff volunteered for supervision duty and a rota was drawn up. It was intended that the school would be open each school day in August except for the 3rd and 31st. But by 14 August the experiment of opening the schools during the holiday proved to be a failure, with less than 6 per cent of pupils attending, and the schools were consequently closed from this date.

A note about the weather

After hearing so much about the bad spell of winter weather during late November and December 2010, the reports of difficulties with travelling and the apparent necessity to close schools, some observations on life at Eastbourne during the cold weather experienced in the 1940s are of interest.

It had been reported that the Thames froze over in January 1940 for the first time since 1888 and on the 27th of the month the worst storm of the century struck the country.

On 7 January 1941, when the Eastbourne Schools reopened at 9.30 a.m. after the Christmas vacation, it was said that the weather was severe; there had been a thaw after heavy snowfall and burst pipes had caused flooding in the kitchen of the flat.

On the 20th of the month Miss Thursfield, a domestic science teacher, was absent due to excessive snowfall and lack of transport. Pupil attendance in the girl's school fell to 50.9 per cent in the morning and 44.4 per cent in the afternoon. At the boys' school, following a heavy snowstorm, the numbers present were 235 in the morning and 223 in the afternoon when the total attendance for each session should have been 475.

With the continuation of the severe weather on 21 March attendance at the girls' school was 42.8 per cent in the morning and 42.4 per cent in the afternoon, while the boys managed an attendance of 229 in the morning and 216 in the afternoon.

Another bitter winter followed in 1942 when on 20 January there had been a heavy snowstorm and intense cold prevailed. On 23 January it was reported that after a week of severe snow and frost, a thaw set in and in several places in the school there were floods, the worst being in the library, where water soaked through the ceiling. On the 26th there were floods in the domestic science flat with water coming through the roof and ceiling in the bathroom and bedroom.

On 3 February a very heavy fall of snow and severe frost caused a low attendance. Transport was disorganised and no school milk was delivered.

The *Northern Echo* reported in early March 1942 that villages in Wensleydale and Coverdale were cut off by snow following the worst snowstorm for twenty-six years. The collection of milk from the farms was disrupted and sheep lost in drifts.

In March 1943 there was a different problem resulting from exceptionally strong winds, reaching gale force, such that outdoor games and play times had to be cancelled.

Once again, in January 1945, there were adverse weather conditions with heavy snowfalls, hard frosts, blizzards, and intense cold. It was said that everything possible was done for the welfare of the pupils but circumstances were not easy, in particular due to the difficulties associated with the obtaining of fuel supplies. The country was still recovering from shortages caused by the war and one of these was the shortage of fuel – the school was cold. At 9.30 a.m. recorded temperatures were between 37 and 45 degrees Fahrenheit. There was no coke for the boilers although some arrived next day. The head teacher of the girls' school observed that due to the severity of the weather, inadequate clothing worn by the children and illness, attendance was low, at about 67 per cent. But the school did not close. On 30 January, due to the intense cold, with deep snow drifts caused by heavy storms and blizzards during the night, frost and ice, the attendance was only 57.1 per cent in the morning and 58.2 per cent in the afternoon.

Cleanliness, health and fitness

Although recent scares (in 2007–8), such as the spread of MRSA in our hospitals, have caused us to focus our minds on the question of personal cleanliness, we can claim to be a cleaner nation than in the 1930s – at least in many respects. Occupations are cleaner, the smoky grime of belching chimneys largely eliminated and houses fitted out with modern sanitary and washing facilities. In the 1930s it was more difficult to keep clean and easier to get dirty: many men worked in heavy industry and women cleaned the home by hand. It is with this scenario in mind that the need for following note, issued by the School Medical Officer, Mr G. A. Dawson, in September 1936, can be understood:

DARLINGTON EDUCATION COMMITTEE

AUTHORITY TO EXAMINE SCHOOL CHILDREN
UNDER
SECTION 87 OF THE EDUCATION ACT 1921

I HEREBY AUTHORISE the HEAD TEACHER (or, in his absence, the ACTING HEAD TEACHER), of the EASTBOURNE SENIOR MIXED COUNCIL SCHOOL to conduct in the School an examination of the person and clothing of any child attending there who is suspected of being verminous or filthy, except that, for such examination of girls, MISS N. FENBY and MRS I. THOMPSON only are authorised as above.

Signed: G. A. Dawson

School Medical Officer

9th September 1936.

Hair inspections were made regularly, special visits sometimes made in relation to the health of a select minority of girls, and in July 1943 the head teacher called in the clinic nurse to complete a cleanliness inspection of the whole school. There was obviously some concern about the health and cleanliness of some of the pupils.

At the time of writing (2010), the government again showed concern over the state of the nation's health, particularly the fact that a large proportion of our children have been described as obese: a concern involving what they eat rather than with their cleanliness, but health problems are nothing new!

A drive to promote physical fitness

As early as 1935 the Central Council for Recreative Physical Training (CCRPT) had been set up to promote the pursuance of physical fitness through keep-fit classes, a campaign which gained great support with thousands of young men and women wanting to take part and creating a great demand for gymnasia. Modern schools, of which the Eastbourne Schools were an example, were provided with gymnasia, hard-surfaced play or recreation areas and playing fields, while earlier buildings were largely three- to four-storey structures behind high walls and gates.

In 1937 there was a further drive to make the population healthier and fitter, extending the provision of gymnasia, playing fields, swimming baths and camp sites; and creating a national college of physical training.

On 10 March 1939 the school closed 'on the occasion of the National Fitness display held in the Baths Hall. A class of boys in the charge of Mr Moss and a girl's class in the charge of Miss Storer took part in the display.'

During the early years of the war the local authority's physical education adviser, Miss M. Potts, frequently visited Eastbourne School, and in February 1940 arranged for teachers' physical education classes to be held in the school gymnasium. In April she returned to discuss a programme of physical education lectures and later again with Miss E. W. Scott, a member of the CCRPT staff, to discuss arrangements for a preliminary course for women and junior leaders in physical education.

On 16 September 1940 Miss Scott took a physical education class for all girls eligible to leave at the end of January 1941. Classes began at 7.30 in the evening.

Colleges of education were soon training specialists in the subject and Eastbourne saw students from Darlington Training College coming to the school to practise this element of their courses.

On 22 April 1940 Mr G. Richards, an organiser from the CCRPT, gave a talk to all third-year boys at 4 p.m. on 'Physical fitness after leaving school'. The significance here is again the importance of fitness among the boys and the notion of staying on after school hours to gain knowledge of it.

On Wednesday 24 April, Thursday 25 April, Wednesday 1 May and Thursday 2 May courses for junior and senior leaders were held in the boys' school hall.

The CCRPT also promoted the physical fitness campaign by showing films in schools. In March 1941 the girls were shown films on physical education and, in May, on tennis, swimming and physical training.

It can be seen how the school curriculum and its allied extra-curricular activities reflected this search for physical fitness. Very early in the development of the Eastbourne Schools physical education, games, camping and excursions into the countryside were encouraged.

Health

There are health scares and campaigns today: immunisation for the elderly against influenza and numerous injections given to children, with the suggestion that more are necessary.

With the food shortages of wartime conditions, there was no fear of there being an obesity problem but there is evidence from the girls' school log of other more obviously life-threatening diseases.

At the start of the 1939 September term Miss W. Storer was absent from duty suffering from diphtheria, a very infectious disease in which a membrane forms in the air passages of the throat, threatening death by suffocation and poisoning the body system: clearly a very serious medical problem in places such as schools where people are in close proximity to each other.

On 19 December 1940, Miss Fenby left school at 1.45 p.m. to report to the education office that one girl had been removed to the Isolation Hospital on the evening of Monday 16 November and another girl in the same class had been taken at 1 p.m. on 12 December. (It is easy to imagine an anxious Miss Fenby almost running out of the school, to catch the trolley bus perhaps, in her hurry to report this event as it is clear from her log entry of 9 October 1941 that only then was a telephone, number 4357, installed in the head teacher's room.)

Infectious diseases

Darlington County Borough Education Committee Regulations for 1938 explain this apparently rapid exit of the head teacher.

Note 32 Infectious Diseases

1. Head Teachers shall forward immediately to the Chief Education Officer notifications by parents or guardians

of infectious diseases occurring or suspected in persons residing with them.

The term infectious diseases includes: -

Smallpox, Diphtheria, Croup, Erysipelas, Scarlet Fever, Tuberculosis, Infantile Paralysis, Measles, German measles, Whooping cough, Chickenpox, Scabies, Ringworm and Influenza.

2. Head Teachers shall exclude children from school in accordance with the Schedule of infectious diseases.

The seriousness of the matter is illustrated by the visit to the school on the same day made by the School Medical Officer, Dr Brown, who examined the throats of girls in classes 3.1 and 1.1, returning to re-examine them on the following day.

He came to the school in January 1941 to complete the routine medical examinations of pupils but first, yet again, re-examined the throats of the same girls (for symptoms of diphtheria) and returned the following day to carry out a further examination.

In March 1941 Dr Dawson, the Schools Medical Officer for Health, visited the school with reference to the cases of reported diphtheria and arranged for a programme of immunisation. This was followed by Dr Brown again visiting the school, to begin the immunisation of 207 girls. A second injection was given a month later.

Tragically, on 7 April 1941, Mabel Martin (of Geneva Road) an Eastbourne girl, died in the municipal hospital after being a patient there for seven weeks suffering from diphtheria, and on 29 September 1942 it was reported that Patricia Gent of Eastbourne Road and Class 1.1, had died after suffering from the same disease.

Earlier, in February of the same year, the school was informed that a pupil (Theresa Martin of Brankin Drive) had died of pneumonia, and in July 1945 there was the death of pupil Isabel Pigg of class 1.1L after an operation, emphasising the fact that ill health was, at a time preceding the discovery and use of antibiotics in treatment, a significant problem.

The familiar regular dental inspections and routine and leavers' medical examinations were already taking place, and the examination of girls' throats continued. Health education was advanced; for instance, in January 1942, at the request of HMI, certain classes in the school listened to *Health Talks*, broadcast by the BBC each morning between 11 and 11.15 a.m., for a period of fourteen days.

There was also concern over the nation's diet, this being a period of food shortages and rationing. In March 1942 the Assistant Schools' Medical Officer for Health began a nutrition survey involving fifty girls who were taking school dinners and fifty girls who were not, with a follow-up a year later. A similar survey was made of all first-year girls in 1943.

School milk

In the drive to ensure the better health of children free milk was issued and schools organised a system of distribution to pupils in their classrooms. Health and Safety officers today would probably be horrified at the effect of spillages, which left classroom tables forever smelling of sour milk.

In February 1944 there was a shortage of school milk for pupils at Eastbourne, Miss Fenby reporting that only 150 one-third-pint bottles were received and a resulting arrangement whereby an average of eleven bottles were allocated to each class per day and under 'careful supervision' every girl who wanted milk allowed to receive it in rotation.

Rationing

During the years 1939–45 the British Isles were isolated, mainland Europe was in enemy hands and the surrounding seas and oceans dominated by the destructive fleet of Hitler's submarines, the U-boats. These densely settled but small islands rely on the import of a great deal of food in order to provide a nourishing and attractive diet for its people. Consequently, there was a severe shortage of necessary foods during the war years and the government response was rationing.

Butter, sugar, bacon and ham were rationed in January 1940, householders being required to register with a local shop in order to obtain their supplies, and meat rationing commenced in March 1940. In March 1942 the Board of Trade announced the rationing of coal, gas and electricity.

There was much discussion about bread, a necessary debate because large quantities of wheat had been imported from the vast grain-producing areas such as the Canadian prairies and a national loaf, made from wheatmeal, introduced.

Clothes rationing

Clothes rationing started in June 1941 and it was estimated that the average family spent £20 per head before the shortages and only £7.10s subsequently over a similar period. Shops were required to display the number of coupons needed as well as the price for each item. For example, for a raincoat sixteen coupons had to be given up, for a man's suit, twenty-six, boots, seven, and gloves, two. The making of such items as double-breasted suits was prohibited. A special extra allowance was provided for 'extra large' children, and entries in the school log books reflect this arrangement:

> 'All girls weighed and measured to meet requirements of Circular 41/56B re Extra Coupons for Clothing – 38 applicants.'

> 'Board of Trade Vouchers OC4 for extra coupons were distributed to eligible girls'.

On Saturday 11 April 1942 the *Northern Echo* reported: 'A Cut in Women's Clothing'. A Board of Trade Order was issued which increased the austere nature of clothing, making garments shorter and tighter. A fashion was imposed! There would be no trimmings on coats and they would be restricted on dresses; no artificial pockets, no back pleats and a limited number at the front, and no wide sleeves. It was decreed that skirts would be no longer than seventeen inches from the ground and not flared.

Reflecting on the influence of such conditions as relative poverty and rationing on children's dress, it is seen that there was far less opportunity for youngsters to demand fashionable clothes.

Ration books

Ration books were printed containing the coupons, and there are interesting log-book entries which state that certain classes in both the boys' and girls' schools were given the task of writing appropriate particulars on the covers of ration books before they were issued. Children were expected to play a part in wartime activities and this was clearly seen as an area in which they could carry out a necessary clerical task in an appropriately short time. As the youngsters were all under 14 years of age one might be amazed at their perceived competence and reliability.

The headmistress reported that specialisation, that is the normal timetable, was suspended, the addressing of ration books being seen to be more important than taking classes in arithmetic, English literature and so on, while needlework, library lessons, physical training, games, domestic science, singing and gardening were to continue wherever possible.

Here are some examples of entries in the girls' school log books relating to the writing of details on new ration books:

16 June 1941: 'Complying with instructions received, the necessary arrangements were made for a group of senior girls, with members of staff in charge, to write out the new ration books, during the coming two weeks, from today. During the two weeks, the timetable to be adjusted, specialisation cancelled except for needlework, library, P.T., games, domestic science and singing, gardening to be carried on whenever possible.' By the 25th of the month 12,000 ration books had been completed.

3 June 1942: 'In accordance with instructions received from the Chief Education Officer, 15,000 ration books were received for completion, suitable arrangements were made for senior girls to undertake this work immediately – necessary adjustments made to the Timetable.' [Completion took about one week.]

Again in May 1943 classes 3.1 and 2.1 involved in this work. Here are some entries in the boys' school log book:

16.6.41: Timetable suspended 9.30 a.m. onwards for classes 3.1 3.2 2.1, no specialisation for the rest of the school. The three classes named engaged in writing ration books. [Continued 17–23 June.]

8–12.6.42: Timetable suspended – Writing up Ration books. 15,000 Ration Books Completed – normal timetable resumed.

11.6.45: Room 25 placed at the disposal of the Food Office for the distribution of Ration Books.

23.6.45: The distribution of Ration Books from room 25 ended.

23.6.47: Room 25 occupied by the Food Office Staff for the purpose of issuing ration books.

Food and other shortages

Shortages of food, clothing and, in fact, just about everything, brought restrictions and what we may now consider at least odd and at most unbelievable solutions. Bath water was to be no deeper than five inches; people were expected to take fewer baths and to share baths. (Did they mean, share the bath water? After all, this did already have to take place in some of the poorest homes.) The soap ration was one tablet per month.

It was reported that beetroot juice was used as lipstick, soot for eye make-up, gravy browning to tan legs and eye liner to paint dummy stocking seams up the back of ladies' legs.

More restrictions appeared in 1942. The milk ration was reduced to two and a half pints per week and 'no person shall put sugar on the exterior of a cake after the same has been baked' (Ministry of Food Regulation). Cakes purchased in the shops were to contain no more than 20 per cent oil or fat, and no more than 30 per cent sugar.

Notes on a necessary obsession with food

Food shortages required the economic use of available supplies, resulting in various initiatives to help people obtain the best results from what they had, to use formerly unused items and to 'Dig for Victory', for example, digging up the lawn to grow vegetables.

The government established British Restaurants to supply meals as extra food for the population and that in Darlington was opened in the Corn Exchange in early to mid 1940. It catered for 240 people at a sitting and twenty workers were employed full-time to run it.

Wartime cookery for mothers

In March 1940 two HMIs visited the school to give a talk on 'Wartime cookery for mothers'.

On 27 September 1940 one member of the domestic science staff visited Borough Road for a briefing relating to the equipment needed for the wartime cookery demonstrations. Arrangements were made, on 15 October, for the opening meeting of the 'Borough Road food demonstrations'. These seemed to take place in a 'junior school room'.

23 October: Miss M. B. Reed, domestic science, and six senior girls visited Borough Road Junior School to prepare for and take part in the inaugural meeting of the food demonstrations to be held there.

Emergency feeding centres

The displacement of people from their homes resulting from bomb damage or evacuation to areas of presumed safety required arrangements to be made for accommodating and feeding them. Schools were convenient, available premises.

Consequently, log book entries such as that of 27 January 1941 inform us that Lady Havelock-Allan visited the school during the afternoon in order to arrange for the storage of clothing for the emergency feeding centre; and that Mrs Glover, the joint officer in charge of the centre, held a meeting in the school at 4 p.m. of members the Women's Voluntary Service (WVS) helpers and school staff.

On 15 May an Emergency Feeding Centre representative visited the school during the afternoon to make arrangements for cooking rehearsals; and on the 16th the Chairman, Vice Chairman and a representative from the Public Assistance Committee visited the school in the morning to inspect arrangements for establishing the centre.

In March necessary stores were delivered; Mrs Davison, the supervisor of Feeding Centres for School Children, visited the school in April, and in May she was making arrangements for cooking rehearsals.

In October Doctors Metcalfe and Beddows, from the Ministry of Health, Dr Dawson, Medical Officer, and Mr Shaw, the Public Assistance Officer, visited the school in relation to making available first aid, accommodation for aged people and the Emergency Feeding Centre.

Other indications of the attention given to the question of feeding the nation:

14.5.41: Headmistress left school at 11.20 a.m. to attend a meeting with the Chief Education Officer at 11.45 a.m.; re Scheme for Fruit Preserving.

28.5.41: The Head Teacher, Miss Reed and Miss Thursfield attended a meeting with HMIs, held in Reid Street Senior Girls' School, to discuss 'Food Campaigns in Schools'.

19.6.41: In the afternoon the first of a series of Food Demonstrations was given by Miss M. Thursfield. Twenty-five visitors were present. The subject 'The Use of Wheatmeal Flour'.

1.7.41: Demonstration on War Time cookery given by Miss M. D. Reed D Sc 'Breakfast and Dinner'.

8.7.41: War Time Cookery demonstration given p.m. by Miss Reed D Sc 'High Teas and Suppers'. And:

The ARP Controller for Darlington, the Chief Public Assistance Officer and Officials visited the School p.m. to inspect Emergency Feeding Centre arrangements.

The introduction of school meals

The emergency feeding centres developed into school canteens and the school meals service was born. Under war conditions there was a mass enrolment of mothers into the national work force, a new development from a situation in which the mother's role had been to maintain the home, washing and ironing clothes, shopping for necessities and providing meals for the family, particularly for working men and children coming home at midday.

Working mothers

In September 1940 an HMI visited the girls' school in order to ascertain details of mothers out at work, the type of work in which they were engaged and what provision was made for girls' dinners. At the end of January 1941 Dr Brown and the clinic nurse examined certain girls with reference to their being given free meals – it does not say free school dinners. It is clear that there was serious concern that children may not be receiving adequate food, a concern relating to those from the poorest families and also to those from more comfortable families where war conditions had brought about the breakdown of the traditional provision of the midday dinner.

State intervention

The perceived need for the state to intervene in the feeding of children has again (in 2007–8), for better or worse, become a significant aspect of government policy – there is an apparent obesity problem, but during the war this was certainly not the case.

The problem on 10 July 1941 was the fear of undernourishment, when the Organiser for School Feeding, an official from the Borough

Surveyor's department, visited the school in the morning to arrange for the installation of equipment for the cooking of meals for schoolchildren.

The head teacher left school at 3.50 p.m. on 30 September 1941 to attend a meeting of the Education Committee Subcommittee re School Feeding. It is clear that, by this date, the Education Committee had a School Canteens Subcommittee, a Schools Canteen Organiser had been appointed and planning was underway to provide meals in schools at midday.

By 22 October, when the schools canteen organiser visited the school in the afternoon, Mrs E. Knott, the newly appointed cook for the school canteen, reported for duty. On the following day two school canteen helpers reported for duty. The serving of midday dinners commenced on 10 November 1941, the circumstances recorded in the following girls' school log book entry:

> 10.11.41: The School Canteen was open for the first time; and the midday meal served at 12.25 p.m. The cooking arrangements were carried out for the Eastbourne Boys' and Girls' departments in room 16 in this school [the girls' building], under the direction of the Cook, Mrs Knott, who had three kitchen helpers. Until the complete equipment is available, temporary arrangements have been made for the boys to dine in their own hall, and the girls to use Domestic Science Rooms 17, 18 and 19. Each day three members of the School Staff undertake supervision, one for each room. A dining room helper is on duty for service. A two course dinner is served each day at the rate of 4d per child.

The service seems to have been popular among families and the numbers taking part increased. On 5 December the opportunity to stay for school dinner was extended to all girls who wished to do so, the number attending the canteen being about 200 as against 110 previously. The total number of girls on roll was 418, giving an approximate 50 per cent take-up.

A growth in the demand for meals

In the boys' school on 8 December, sixty-four more pupils were permitted to take school dinner, the total then being 179 when the number on roll was about 380, about 47 per cent take-up.

There was a change of location for serving the meals in the girls' school in January 1942 when, having received all of the necessary equipment, arrangements were made for school dinners to be served in the hall.

A comment made on 10 February 1942 provides another detail about how things were done – arrangements were made for dining tables to be put up and taken down by boys from the senior boys' department.

At this date there were three school canteens in operation at Lowson Street, Dodmire and Eastbourne, serving a maximum of some 1,800 meals per day and costing the corporation 6½d. each, although there was a subsidy from the Board of Education which covered some of the difference between this cost and the fourpence charged to the children. Four more canteens were expected to be open by Easter, proving meals for about half of the school population.

It was not very long before the question of dining-room supervision raised its ugly head.

On 27 November, the head teacher reported 'special duty all week'. This seems to mean that she exercised supervision of the dining arrangements, concluding that the organisation as far as the girls were concerned was very satisfactory but, as the service was so slow, the girls had little time for leisure and recreation.

At this time the head teacher was making representations to the LEA with the intention of trying to have more dining-room helpers appointed and in answer to this request the organiser visited the school and a third was quickly provided. Even so, the head's estimate was that there should be six! By the start of the second half-year in 1943 the number had risen to four but without cover if one or more of these was absent, a frequent occurrence. In addition there was a problem with retaining the dinner helpers – the result of problems arising from their need to discipline large groups of children, perhaps.

Board of Education recipes

In March 1942 the schools canteen organiser visited the school to observe the success or otherwise of the Board of Education recipes which were being tried out in the canteen; and Miss G. H. Bolam, newly appointed domestic science organiser and supervisor of school canteens, visited the school to see the canteen kitchen and dining-room arrangements

A few problems

In the early morning on 19 October 1942 there was a gas explosion in the school canteen kitchen Room 16 when the kitchen assistant attempted to light one of the Eagle ranges. The assistant suffered shock and was given first aid, and although her injuries were not detailed, she was taken home by taxi and the doctor called.

It is interesting to read that during the 1942 November holiday only ten girls attended the canteen for the midday meal.

The canteen organiser and CEO made one of their many visits to the school in mid February 1943 when there was concern about the arrangements for storing equipment and extra accommodation for washing up.

On 2 February 1943 an increase in numbers taking the midday meal to 285 was reported with resulting congestion in the hall. It was decided to serve sixty in the domestic science room. The shortage of equipment and helpers also caused difficulties and a few days later there were 292 staying for dinner.

In June 1943 there was a problem with the increasing numbers wishing to stay for school dinner, in particular toilet accommodation, accommodating some 60–70 per cent of the number of pupils on roll and the positioning of hot cupboards.

By the end of 1943 ideas were being considered for the building of a new canteen kitchen and sculleries, separate from the other existing school buildings: the CEO, domestic science organiser and a representative from the Borough Surveyor's department visited on 13 September to view possible sites. It is clear that the temporary arrangement for providing school meals in an emergency situation was already taking on the characteristics of a permanent service.

Problems associated with accommodating the number of diners continued: two first-year girls' classes were given their dinner in a domestic science room, while all of the older girls dined in the hall.

On 3 March 1944 the charge for midday dinner increased to 5d. per day.

The possibility of building separate canteen units took a step forward when on 7 December 1944, the School Canteens Subcommittee – Chairman (Councillor Luck) and Alderman Best together with the CEO (Mr Houghton), HMIs Mr J. P. Scorthorne and Miss E. M. Nicholls, an official from the Borough Surveyor's office and Mr Welford, headmaster of the boys' school – met at 2.45 to discuss the canteen arrangements and the possibility of building entirely separate units, each comprising dining room, kitchen and scullery, for each department.

As a final note on the subject of school meals in wartime, on 6 June 1945 Miss Fenby noted that owing to the potato shortage only one half of a potato and a half a slice of bread were served with the midday meal.

Darlington a reception area for evacuees

As well as the school being assessed as a feeding centre, on 15 January 1942, a Ministry of Health representative and Emergency Feeding Centre officials visited the school in the morning to inspect the building as a potential 'Rest Centre'.

Later, in 1944, the south-east of England found itself in the path of flying bombs and rockets, the forerunners of today's missiles, and on 12 July there was a meeting at the Education Office when information was received from the Ministry of Health that Darlington was to become a reception area for 800 evacuees from the London area and that Eastbourne School was to be a rest centre.

Officers from Public Assistance and rest centre personnel visited the school to make provisional arrangements on 13 July and on Monday 17 July the Education Officer ordered the closure of the school at 4 p.m. until further notice when the building was prepared as an emergency feeding centre to be manned by volunteers from the school staff. Plans were put in place to receive 600 evacuees from the London area, but 691 actually arrived in Darlington on 28 July, when 581 were admitted to the Eastbourne Centre, the party consisting of mothers with children under 5, mothers with children over 5, and expectant mothers.

August 4 should have been the start of the summer holidays when 518 evacuees were expected to be accommodated in the boys' and girls' schools. They had arrived from London on Friday evening, 28 July, and many were still in residence awaiting placement in billets.

The rest centre closed after fourteen days but further preparations were made on 16 August for it to reopen as a second batch of 800 evacuees was expected.

When the school reopened on 5 September the boys attended for the morning only as more evacuees were expected and the senior girls only attended in the boys' department during the afternoon between 1.45 and 4.14.

The rest centre was again closed, equipment removed and school furniture restored on 6 September, and normal full-time schooling resumed the next day, but there was a further interruption to schooling on 7 December 1944.

On 12 December at 4 p.m. the school opened as a rest centre for evacuees returning home to the south coast towns and who had been billeted in outlying districts, for example at Skelton, Middlesbrough, and Richmond. Arrangements were made for their sleeping in the hall and feeding in the domestic science rooms. The cooking was undertaken by the canteen staff. This is an extract from the girls' school log for 7 December 1944:

> By arrangement with the Chief Education Officer, the Public Assistance Officer (Mr Shaw), with members of his staff and Mrs Glover WVS, visited this school in the morning to make arrangements with Mr Welford, Headmaster of the Boys' Department (who was also present) and myself for a rest centre to be opened for one day, Tuesday 12 December–Wednesday 13 December 1944 as a collecting centre for 'returning evacuees' from the outlying districts of Darlington. The Ministry of Health's information is that there will be 99 mothers and children and twenty-three unaccompanied children arriving here Tuesday, for one night and they will leave Darlington station 10 am. on Wednesday 13th.

The war effort

Food shortages and the need to raise money for the making of war weapons and the obtaining of materials for their manufacture gave rise to national campaigns to involve the people in the war effort.

In 1939, with food shortages expected, the campaign for producing more at home was introduced: pasture was ploughed for crop production, derelict land cultivated and everyone was urged to 'Dig for Victory'. Roadside verges were planted with potatoes, parkland farmed, and individuals dug up their lawns for growing peas, beans and cabbages. Hens and rabbits were kept for eggs and meat.

There is a telling entry in the girls' school log for 13 June 1941: 'As from this week groups of girls will undertake school gardening. Members of the staff will be in charge and supervise.'

Alternatively, Miss Fenby seemed quite enthusiastic, in October 1944, when a memo from the CEO agreed to gardening in the girls' school being discontinued and the plots handed over to the boys' department!

Salvage

Those today who enthusiastically promote the recycling of waste products could learn a thing or two from the salvage campaigns of wartime Britain, when park and garden railings were cut from their foundations, aluminium cooking utensils were collected (it was claimed, for making aeroplanes), paper for pulping and re-making (often producing writing surfaces only slightly removed from blotting paper), and potato peelings for pig food. The efforts, of course, were not then born from the well-meant general saving of resources but from the essential reuse of what was available while importing goods from abroad was extremely costly in terms of the loss by destruction of both lives and shipping by enemy action. The Eastbourne School records illustrate some of the effort put into these salvage campaigns.

On 3 January 1942 there is the brief log book entry: 'Salvage collected by the Girls during the "January special effort" one ton 5 hundredweight.' The content of the salvage was not given.

However, it was St Augustine's boys who won the schools' monthly contest for the *Northern Despatch* trophy by collecting 52 tons 8 cwt of waste paper in March 1942.

In July 1943 a member from the Ministry of Supply visited the school to introduce the Book Salvage Drive which was to last for two weeks starting on Monday 19th. Special arrangements were made in the school to support the campaign.

In the summer of 1944 it was recorded that the school had collected 6,592 books.

War savings

During the war 'good money' could be earned in the munitions factories, a strange state of affairs when there were severe shortages of food, clothing, furnishings and so on, and therefore little available on which to spend those wages. Bearing this in mind and understanding that fighting a war costs the country a great deal of money, regular campaigns were organised to encourage the raising of funds to purchase weapons. Savings stamps (costing two shillings and sixpence) and National Savings Certificates (valued at fifteen shillings) were introduced whereby people could put their money into a government savings scheme, the money to be used for the war effort and then be available for repayment in peacetime some years later.

In April 1941 the Assistant Commissioner for War Savings showed films and gave a short talk, encouraging support during War Savings Campaign Week. On 10 October 1941 forty girls and two members of staff left school at 10.25 a.m. to visit the tanks in the Market Place at 11 a.m. This visit was in connection with the Army Tank Column being in Darlington, supporting the war savings movement. Savings schemes were associated with raising money for specific causes such as that in 1940 which was designated War Weapons Week.

Warship Week

The campaign for 1942 was titled Warship Week and Darlington set itself the target of raising enough money to replace the destroyer *Matabele* which had been lost in action some months previously. It started on 24 March when there was a parade on High Row, Rear Admiral W. G. C. Maxwell CMG RN taking the salute, and a naval exhibition was held in the new telephone exchange in Barnard Street. Local newspapers reported that £185,000 was raised on this first day.

At Eastbourne school, during the afternoon, a bring-and-buy sale organised by the pupils and staff was held, parents invited and the opportunity taken of showing them round the school.

Different days in the week were allocated to different groups in order for them to take an active part in the ceremony of raising the indicator on High Row to show the total amount collected. For instance, on Wednesday 25 March there was Ladies' Day, when Lady Havelock-Allan, centre leader for the WVS, announced a total of £328,000 and on Thursday 26th, described as Workers' Day, Mr Powell, a blacksmith at the North Road LNER workshops, raised the indicator to show the total of £380,000.

On Friday 27 the Eastbourne head girl, Nancy Elliot, represented the school at the Children's Day ceremony on High Row to witness Frank Robson, head boy at the grammar school, raise the indicator. In the afternoon at Eastbourne a special assembly was held after the break when a programme comprising the work of different classes was presented, and contributions to Warship Week made.

On 15 May the same year notification was received that one girl in the school was successful in the slogan competition held during Warship Week.

In the boys' school it was reported that the total savings generated through the sale of Savings Certificates and deposits in the Trustee Savings Bank for the week ending 27 March 1942 was £377.6s.5d. In addition £50 was raised by a concert performance of the school choir and other means which was given to the government as a 'free gift'. The free gift to the government seems to be a response to a government initiated charity.

An extract from the girls' school log 30 March 1942:

> At 3.15 p.m. His worship The Mayor (Coun Jackson), The Chairman of the Education committee (Coun R. Luck), The Chief Education Officer (Mr W. F. Houghton) and the Chairman of the War Savings Committee (Mr Hawitt) visited the school. The Mayor was presented with a cheque for £61.4s.9d., the sum raised in this school during Warship Week, as a free gift to the Government. The Head Girl, Nancy Elliot presented the cheque.
>
> The total raised in war savings and bank deposits was £825. Since the War Savings Group was formed in this school in June 1940 £2,155.12s has been raised, during the first year £1,204.7.0d. The membership is 172.

Wings for Victory Week

On 1 June 1943 three groups of fifty girls each and members of staff visited the Drill Hall, Darlington, 10 a.m.–11.30 a.m. where there was a Royal Air Force exhibition in connection with Wings for Victory Week. During the afternoon, many parents and friends were entertained at an open day given by the school, a bring-and-buy sale was organised by the staff and girls, social entertainments were carried out and the opportunity again taken to show the visitors round the school.

On 2 June three groups of fifty boys attended the Wings for Victory exhibition held in the Drill Hall at 10.00 a.m., 10.30 a.m., and 11.00 a.m.

On 4 June a prefect, Averil Noble, represented the school at the Children's Day ceremony on the High Row, when the Wings for Victory schools' totals were announced and the indicator on the display moved by a pupil from an elementary school. The total amount raised by the girls' school during the Wings for Victory Week was £1,688.

On 7 October 1943 two senior prefects, Florence Dobinson and Kathleen Dawson, attended the meeting of the town council to witness the presentation of plaques commemorating the successful achievements in the town during Warship Week 1942 and Wings for Victory Week 1943.

Salute the Soldier Week

In May 1944 the head girl, Margaret Carrick, represented the school at the Indicator Ceremony – Schools Day for Salute the Soldier Week. The total amount raised by the school was £600.11s.0d. and a 'free gift' of £84.19s.11d.

The boys' reported on 8 May that their target had been £250 plus a £50 free gift but the total raised was £642.17s.11d. which included an £82 Free Gift which was given to the Mayor of Darlington's Prisoner of War fund – the nature of the Free Gift Charity becoming clearer.

Merchant Navy Comforts Service Fund Appeal

On 3 October 1944 at 3.30 p.m., during the week of the Merchant Navy Comforts Service Fund Appeal, His Worship the Mayor, Councillor Trees, Mr Kirkland Bridge, Director of the Merchant Navy Comforts Service fund, Major Hawitt and Mr Milner, local officials, spoke to the girls about the activities of the Service.

Wartime emergency activities

Examples of other charitable activities in which the girls were involved are demonstrated by their supply of garments to such organisations as the British Red Cross and the nursery school in Hundens Lane. In July 1943, 153 pairs of knitted socks were sent to the British Red Cross for distribution to prisoners of war and the Hundens Lane Nursery School were given 70 knitted garments, 140 overalls and 140 pairs of knickers. The nursery school in Borough Road was sent 120 towels and 108 soft toys. Laundry cloths were provided for three canteens.

All this work was completed extra to the following of the normal timetabled subjects.

The wartime curriculum

The relatively basic and uncomplicated timetable of subjects taken during the pre-war years continued during this period: there was a sound, straightforward basic academic programme with emphasis on literacy and numeracy, with history, geography, science and physical activities, broadened through a significant extra-curricular programme (see further explanation in the chapters referring to the post-war years).

Subjects were generally taught in forms, the streamed classes staying in their form rooms except for the subjects requiring specialist rooms, thus limiting movement about the building.

Pens, perhaps better referred to as writing instruments, would hardly be recognised by today's schoolchildren, consisting of a wooden pencil-like stem with a curved pointed nib. The nib had to be dipped into the ink well at the top of the desk: too much ink and an unwanted blot would splash onto the page. Ink monitors had the job of keeping the ink wells topped up, carrying a spouted can from one desk to another.

Religious education

Religious education continued to form a major part of the life of the schools: for instance in October 1940 arrangements were made for scripture to be of normal duration even when the morning session was shortened due to air raids taking place during the night, the registration period being from 10.00 a.m. till 10.05 a.m. and religious education from 10.05 a.m. till 10.25 a.m. There were three half-hour periods for other lessons and ten minutes' recreation or break time. In November times were: registration, school assembly and religious instruction from 9.30 a.m. till 10.0 a.m., lessons 10.0–10.30 a.m.; 10.30–11 a.m.; break time 11–11.10 a.m.; lessons 11.10–11.40 a.m., and 11.40–12.10 p.m.

For the National Day of Prayer on 3 September 1942 the girls assembled at 11.00 a.m., and took part in the religious service broadcast between 11.00 a.m. and 11.15 a.m., but there is no mention of this service in the boys' school log.

Carol services took place at the end of the Christmas term and, certainly in the girls' school there was a special Easter service with Easter music and the participation of the school choir.

Visits to the school by HMIs

Regular visits to the two schools by HMIs were recorded in the school log books, and as many of these visits were made to see the teaching of various subjects, entries give a useful indication of curriculum content. For instance, on 20 February 1940 an HMI visited the boys' school to see the teaching of metalwork under war conditions; another visited to see the teaching of art. In June a visit was made to the geography classes, and in July the visit was to see the teaching of science.

In October 1941 Mr E. F. Welch HMI and Mr F. Rayment HMI, visited the school in the morning with reference to horticulture and biology. Miss A. J. Martin's morning visit was in connection with work done in art, and related to the promotion of 'Education in Art' on behalf of the Leverhulme Trust who had awarded a grant.

The observation that on 10 September 1941 the principal of the Darlington Technical College visited the school during the morning with reference to commercial classes for girls suggests that such classes were at least being considered, if not already taking place.

As well as evidence from HMIs' visits, it is clear that history, geography, English and mathematics were a prime part of the syllabus in 1940 because training-college students attended the girls' school in order to work with classes taking these subjects.

Physical and cultural activities

In 2008, schools have been instructed to offer pupils and students five hours of physical activity and five hours of 'culture' each week, and there is something about this which shows a lack of understanding of the long-understood teachers' vocational desire to encourage the young people in their charge to take part in a vast field of activities, so that individuals are given the opportunity to develop their unique talents and interests.

A study of the development of the Eastbourne curriculum and programme of extra-curricular activities shows how this was done in a controlled, disciplined and supportive, but not stifling, environment. Today's initiatives suggest an atmosphere of autocratic intervention and compulsion which may well generate a hostile opposition to what started out as good intentions.

There can be little doubt that sport and physical activity were significant aspects of the curriculum during the 1930s and 40s. The earlier reference in the section on health and fitness makes this quite clear, with the involvement of the Central Council of Recreative Physical Training. Among the activities arranged were the annual sports days.

The briefest of notes for the boys' school on 24 July 1940 reads: 'Annual Sports held at 7 p.m.' The period from early July to the end of the summer term was a period of disturbance because of the regular warning of air raids, with school starting at 10 a.m. each day owing to the 'raiders passed' signal being given after midnight.

On 30 July 1941 the timetable was again suspended for the girls, this time from 3.45 p.m. when the school assembled in the quadrangle for inter-class sports.

The schools' cinemas (the halls, with their built-in projection rooms) were also used to promote physical activities, for example in March and May 1941 when films on physical education, tennis, swimming and physical training were shown to the school.

In 1942 the annual sporting activities in the girls' school were apparently delayed until September due to preparations for a part of the Holidays at Home Scheme being made in July. On the 10th of the month in the girls' school, 'heats for the Holiday at Home sports held p.m. all classes engaged'.

Again, during the afternoon of 17 September 1942, the timetable was suspended, and organised sports were held in the quadrangle, 'all girls in the school took part and were most enthusiastic'. And for 26 July 1943 Miss Fenby writes: 'Organised school sports in the quadrangle pm. – a most enjoyable and successful afternoon; every girl in the school took part, cup presented to the winning colour.'

One wonders whether they had any choice in the matter; there is an unstated expectation that you will take part, you will be enthusiastic and you will enjoy yourselves! But, of course, this was a different era: children did as they were told – and did, with some exceptions, enjoy such activity.

The holiday scheme did not prevent the holding of the sixth annual boys' school sports, on 8 July 1942 at 6.30 p.m.

Two references to physical training made in late 1943 are of interest because of the particular items mentioned. In November the headmistress inspected the physical training costumes of all the girls there, 'revealing an alarming shortage of rubber shoes, the small supply from the Authority being inadequate for the demand'.

The LEA supplied rubber shoes and the girls of the school committee saw physical training as a significant activity, echoing the opinions of the time. The proposal of the Authority, made in December 1943, to purchase land adjacent to the school as an extension to the playing fields is further evidence of the importance attached to health and fitness.

More recently, at the turn of the twenty-first century, political initiatives saw the opposite of this trend in the selling off of parts of school playing fields. The extensive Eastbourne site was consequently reduced.

In March 1945 there were 'Organised School Team Sports for whole school in the quadrangle'.

By the summer of 1945 both head teachers were referring to the annual sports, those at the girls' school being held on the playing field on 12 June at 6.30 p.m. when there was a 'Large attendance despite most unfavourable weather conditions; most enthusiastic and enjoyable sports programme'.

Other log book entries demonstrate the schools' attention given to physical activities. For instance there were end-of-term competitions such as the finals of the rounders tournament held on 2 May 1941, the netball tournament held on 5 April 1944 which was arranged for the whole school by the School Committee, and the finals of another rounders tournament held in July 1945.

Darlington Athletic Association annual sports

On 4 July 1945 the school closed at 12.12 p.m. for the afternoon so that teams could take part in the first meeting of the Darlington Schools Athletic Association annual sports since the outbreak of war. The events seem at least a little strange compared with what is expected in secondary schools today, the final results for the girls' school being:

Flat Race for girls over 13: Eastbourne 1st, 2nd, and 3rd
Flat Race for girls under 13: Eastbourne 2nd

Flat Race for the younger girls: Eastbourne 2nd
In both the High Jump and the Obstacle Relay Race:
Eastbourne 2nd
Obstacle Relay Race: 2nd
In the One Lap Relay 1st Coronation Trophy one lap
relay race the school gained 1st place.

Mr Welford records the closing of the school for the school sports at Feethams but gives no details.

Swimming

A programme of swimming lessons was intended to continue during the war: a reference on 9 May 1940 refers to 'Swimming classes at the Public Baths began for girls from this school. Classes 1.1, 1.2, 1.3 and about 20 older girls who have never been to such classes, owing to change of schools, will attend each Thursday morning. The timetable has been adjusted accordingly. Misses Hunnam and Linford are in charge of the classes.' However, at the end of May all swimming classes were cancelled until further notice and there is no reference to classes taking place during 1942.

On 25 May 1943 the boys' swimming classes commenced 9.15 a.m. The only details given were that they were in three groups. A little more information is given for the girls: their swimming classes began on 27 May and took place from 9.20 till 10.20 a.m. Again three classes are mentioned 'of approximately 60 each from first and second years. Mrs O. Wearmouth to attend as instructor'. Three classes of sixty each seems to be inappropriate. There was an intake of 101 in September 1942 and 88 in February 1943, giving a first year of 189 pupils, so it was possible to make up three groups of 60 each from the first year alone.

At the same time of the year in 1944 arrangements were made for girls to attend the baths for swimming instruction, referring to Circular 44/186 which clearly indicates that this was a LEA scheme:

> Girls from all 1st and 2nd year classes given the opportunity to attend – those able to accept, about 170 – three groups 9.20; 9.40; 10.00 a.m., the 1st and 2nd groups to meet at the Baths, only one staff to act as escort to each group, owing to depletion of

staffing; these arrangements submitted to the Chief Education
Officer for confirmation. Timetable adjusted accordingly.

If this arrangement applied in previous years, the notion of three
groups of about sixty girls attending at three different times makes
sense. They were then presumably divided into groups of twenty when
at the baths, one of three instructors or teachers taking each group. It
is not clear whether the teacher-escort took any part in the supervision
of pupils when they were in the water.

It appears, from the entry of 1 June 1943, that at least one member
of the school staff also worked in the town baths: 'Mr Haynes i/c
swimming for the Town children attending the Baths and therefore
absent from school duties Tue a.m., Thu p.m., Fri a.m. each week'.

The swimming lessons led to swimming qualifications. Towards
the end of the summer term in 1945, '45 girls and a member of staff
left school 3.30 p.m. to attend the swimming Baths for the tests for
Swimming Certificates', and a further thirty-one girls and staff left school
3 p.m. on 6 September to attend swimming baths to take similar tests.

Culture in the curriculum

On Wednesday 13 February 2008, some seventy years after the opening
of the Eastbourne Super School, the headline on page two of the
Daily Telegraph read: 'Pupils will get a daily "culture hour"'. The article
explained that teenagers, in an effort to 'unlock the creative talent of all
young people' would be taken to the opera; opera and ballet companies
would be invited into schools; pupils would be given the opportunity of
learning a musical instrument; and they would be taken to art galleries
and museums.

Reading and remembering from one's own career the various
experiences provided for the young people in Eastbourne School
during the three-quarter century of its existence, one wonders where
our leaders went to school. Did they not have art departments which
enthusiastically encouraged them to struggle with the making of clay
pots, dabble in the painting of landscapes and still life, design repeated
patterns for wallpaper, attempt to advertise the school production by
providing handmade posters and so on?

Did their schools not have music teachers who brought children to
sing in choirs, performing in concerts and taking part in competitions?

Did their LEAs, governing bodies and head teachers not arrange for them to see and listen to operatic presentations, ballet, and dramatic performances?

Over the generations, the children and young people who attended the Eastbourne Schools had the opportunity to experience all of these aspects of what is now to be called 'culture'; experiences provided during the school day, approximately between the hours of 9.00 a.m. and 4.00 p.m.

These activities continued both after school and during school holidays.

Music and drama

Log book entries clearly emphasise the significance attached to music and drama education in both the girls' and boys' schools.

During the last week of the 1940 summer term the timetable for the girls' school was suspended during the latter part of one afternoon to enable the children to perform musical and dramatic items: 'the school assembled in the Hall and each class contributed either singing or dramatic work, community singing was included'.

An entry in the boys' school log for 15 November 1940 reads: 'In connection with the Music Scheme of this school, Conniscliffe Road Methodist Choir and the Darlington String Sextette (leader Madame Gomez of Elton Parade) visited the school and gave a concert to pupils and parents.'

On 22 November 1940 a concert by the English singers was held in the girls' hall at 7.00 p.m. with artistes Miss Winifred Radford and Frederick Woodhouse. The accompanist was Grace Shearer.

Records show that in January 1941 and 1943 the boys' school held their annual inter-house competitive musical and drama festivals.

A drama afternoon was held for all first-year classes in the girls' school on 9 September 1942 when each class performed in front of the other three classes, the same play being presented by different classes in some instances and the whole programme being managed by the girls themselves. The head teacher recorded this event as 'a most successful and enjoyable experiment'.

During the afternoon of 7 December 1942 fifty girls and two staff attended a matinee in Eastbourne Senior Boys' School hall, given by The Market Theatre and arranged by the Darlington Education Authority. The boys' school log recorded that The Market Theatre presented a dramatic and variety show which was attended by 500 children from the senior schools in the borough.

In December 1942 it is recorded that the third annual girls' school concert was held in the evening when there was an audience of 500. There were presentations of singing, dancing and drama, the drama being representative of school work. The programme was repeated for 500 children the following day.

In May 1943, as an opening for Wings for Victory Week, the girls' school timetable was adjusted during the afternoon and a musical programme arranged consisting of contributions by the pupils. Auditions had been held and the girls were responsible for the organisation. The head teacher made a point of emphasising the educational value of the exercise and a part of this was the expectation that the girls would take responsibility for the production.

On the afternoon before the half-term holiday in February 1944, 170 girls and 4 staff attended the Baths Hall to hear a special programme of orchestral music, played by the London Women's String Orchestra, in connection with a CEMA matinee performance arranged by the Education Committee for children of the town. There were also 140 pupils and 4 staff from the boys' school who attended.

Again, in March 1944, 160 girls and 130 boys attended the Baths Hall for a concert by the London Philharmonic Orchestra, also arranged by the Darlington Education Committee. Pupils were afterwards expected to write their impressions of the concert, as requested by the Authority.

In October the following year, during the autumn holiday, 130 girls and 123 boys attended a special performance for schools by the Halle Orchestra. Once again this was a musical experience organised by the Education Authority and demonstrates its commitment to the broadening of the young people's musical experience.

School visits and field studies

Field excursions, visits, school journeys and the boys' school annual camp were eventually to become major aspects of the schools' educational programmes but due to the wartime disturbance of 1940–41, with precautions taken against air raids and staff leaving to serve in HM forces and so on, such activities were not then a priority and it is perhaps surprising to discover the girls' school in particular being involved in out-of-school activities as early as September 1941.

Nature walks

Although these excursions were for only a very few girls they demonstrate a wish and willingness on the part of some staff to at least initiate this significant aspect of a school's curriculum. Other one- or part-day walks from school show that this was more than a one-off event, with the geography and science staff developing a practical field-study element in their subject teaching.

Nature walks are reported to have taken place in October 1942 to Salters Lane (a journey on foot, presumably, of ¾ mile) between 1.50 to 3.20 p.m., involving Classes 1.1. and 1.2; to Middleton One Row with second-year classes; but in January 1943 several of the walks were cancelled because of heavy rain. Whether this was the case at the girls' school or not, there was evidence later in other schools of some staff seeing the taking of children out of school as a soft option but a thought about the time of year, term or holiday time and the need to supervise pupils out of the confines of the classroom should deny this idea. In particular, residential courses require 24-hour-per-day supervision, and time-consuming pre-journey planning and follow-up afterwards.

In June 1943 at 3.45 p.m. a party of twenty-five girls from the top class, and two members of staff, Misses N. Soper and O. Hunnam, left school on an educational excursion to Langdon Beck Youth Hostel. The visit – from Wednesday 2 June to Saturday 5 June (including the Ascension Day school holiday on the 4th) was 'for science, geographical and social purposes – the programme being similar to those of September 1941 and 1942'.

There was also an active Junior Youth Centre Field Club, illustrated by the report of the visit of 17 May 1944 when junior members went 'With Misses Soper and Hannum to Langdon Beck Youth Hostel from Wed May 17th to Saturday May 20th. The party left school 3.40 pm. to catch the train to Middleton-in-Teesdale. As much preparation as possible, including geography, science and domestic science, was completed in school prior to the journey. The 18th was the Ascension Day closure.'

Girls' school field-study visits

It is only in the girls' school where field-study visits continued during the war years, unless such visits did take place in the boys' department but were not recorded. The latter seems unlikely as other visits were recorded by Mr Welford.

Miss Fenby's record of excursions from the girls' school is informative, starting with the expedition made by a relatively small group of senior girls to Langdon Beck Youth Hostel for a weekend stay in September 1941. The physical activity involved, as well as the educational programme involving botanical and geographical studies, is particularly notable, as is the use of the train to get into the Dales.

An entry in the girls' school log for 26 September 1941states:

> 3.50 p.m. 20 senior scholars and 2 members of staff left school, proceeding to Bank Top Station, Darlington to go by the 4.12 p.m. train to Middleton-in-Teesdale, continuing the journey from there to Langdon Beck Youth hostel which was to be their headquarters for their weekend educational visit to Upper Teesdale.
>
> The following educational excursions were made: -
>
> Saturday September 27th Climb Cronkley Fell (1793 feet); study of Alpine plants and sources of streams, following cairns back to Cronkley Bridge along Yorkshire side of Tees. Early evening – visit caves formed by action of water on limestone.
>
> Sunday September 28th Follow Tees along Durham side to Cauldron Snout, return along top of Falcon Clints, and over Widdybank.
>
> Monday 29th September Follow the Tees on Yorkshire Bank from Cronkley Bridge to High Force on Durham side for study of High Force Woods. Educational aims:
>
> Study of torrent stage of the river Tees from Cauldron Snout to Middleton-in-Teesdale. Characteristics of plants adapted to dry surroundings. Alpine Flora of upper Teesdale. Birds of the Moors. (Films shown previous to visit.)
>
> The visit ended Monday evening the party returning home by train.

A similar excursion, but this time apparently using camping-style residence, took place during the Whitsuntide holiday in May 1942.

Earls Orchard

The Darlington Education Authority leased the house known as Earls Orchard, situated on the outskirts of Richmond, in 1944 and prepared to open it as a youth hostel as soon as possible. It was expected that accommodation would be for groups of between thirty and forty members of Darlington youth organisations at weekends and during holidays. In addition it was anticipated that senior school pupils would be able to use the centre for short periods during term time and a scheme was eventually developed whereby each school was allocated particular blocks of days, Monday to Friday, for their visits.

Misses Soper and Hunnam were quick to use the facility, albeit almost a year after the idea was advanced, when on 9 May 1945 they took twenty-seven third-year girls to the hostel, leaving Darlington at 4.00 p.m. and returning home on Saturday 12th.

The boys' school was not far behind, Mr Hunt taking the older half of class 2.1 (second year, top stream), in total eighteen boys, on a residential course at the hostel 4–9 July 1945. Mr Welford, Mr M. J. Peacock, Miss E. M. Hind, Miss M. E. Nicholson, Mr J. Towers and Mr F. Haynes visited the party during their stay, suggesting plenty of interest was being shown by the school and its staff. The younger half of class 2.1, 23 boys, were taken there from 11th to the 16th of the month.

In the October of 1945 there was a meeting at the Education Office relating to Earls Orchard and we can surely assume that the initial success of the venture was discussed because parties continued to visit the centre throughout the secondary modern and comprehensive school years.

A course in child welfare

A different element of the education of girls was introduced in 1944 following instructions received from the Education Authority on 7 February for the school to arrange for a course in child welfare for the third-year girls. The course, lasting one hour per week, was taken by the health visitors.

In July third-year classes visited Hundens Lane Nursery School in connection with the child welfare course

Sex education

In February 1945 the Education Authority adopted a policy on sex education, approving for use in schools a syllabus drawn up by a representative body of teachers. Mrs Fenby's log entry explains that the whole staff were willing and anxious to co-operate in the implementation of the new scheme. She reported that sex instruction was already included in the biology scheme for the school, and certain aspects of the new initiative would be covered in physical training, and domestic science; and the moral aspect would be 'given full attention'. The school leavers, as had been the custom, would have the 'leaving talk' with the headmistress. It was not anticipated that there would be any difficulty concerning the attitude of the parents towards the programme.

On 1 March 1945 a log entry states: 'All 3rd year classes attended the film "Sex in Life" (a Central Health Council Film); with discussion and explanation following, previous to a second viewing.'

Films

The two school halls were equipped with projection rooms for the showing of films, a relatively new aid in education in the 1930s but by the 1940s a very popular and well-used means of entertainment en masse in cinemas.

The schools used their own projectors to show films promoted by various educational and instructional bodies, but also made use of a mobile cinema for promoting, for example, War Savings when on 9 November 1942 the log says: 'Mobile cinema displayed films etc on "War Savings" to the whole school a.m.' Otherwise, the selection of film showings given below gives some idea of the more usual use of the medium.

14.5.40: Film display in the girls' Hall 9.40 to 10.20; Geographical films 3.1, 2.1U and 1.1U shown films from 'Maize', 'Newts' and 'Market Town'. Discussion and written appreciation followed at the request of HMI.

30.5.40: Film display by the ministry of Information: 'Mulberry Harbour'.

9.2.44: Film on China duration about 1 hour shown to all year groups in turn.

Schools also used the town cinemas, for example on 31 October 1945 'A School party comprising of six classes, 3.1, 3.2, 2.1, 2.2, 1.1 and 1.2 [i.e. first and second streams in each of years 1, 2, and 3] in charge of Mr Welford, Mr Haynes, Mr Hunt, Miss E. M. Hammil, Mr E. M. Hind, Mrs M. E. Nicholson attended the Odeon cinema at 9.00 a.m. to see the film "Henry V". A total of 214 attended.'

Examinations

Internal school examinations

In the 1930s and 40s the only external school public examinations were those taken by pupils in the secondary schools and for the most part were those associated with the General Certificate of Education (GCE). Risking repetition in order to emphasise the situation, Eastbourne was at this time a senior school from which children left to enter employment when they became fourteen, the only examinations which concerned them being the internal class tests taken twice yearly in January and July. For example, on 15 January 1941 the boys' school held its half-yearly examinations.

Special Place and Secondary School entrance examinations

As outlined in the development of pre-war education given in Chapter 1, the Special Places system was introduced in 1932, and its perceived importance is regularly illustrated by the annual entries in the Eastbourne Mixed School log book 1936–1939.

By 14 March 1940 it is clear from the entry in the boys' school log that the examination had become the Special Place and Secondary School Entrance Examination, the Special Place part being for those of the 13-plus age group. The examination was held between 10 and 11 a.m. and there had apparently been a practice test on the previous day. The normal school timetable was suspended and Mr Scott, Mr Towers and Mr Tranter were out acting as invigilators, the examination seemingly taking place in the primary schools. The girls' school log tells a slightly different story: 'Misses Maughan, Richardson and Bellis were invigilating at other schools, while Misses Rush, Langley and Henderson "carried out duties at this school where there were 80 pupils".'

The intelligence test

An entry for 1 May 1940 states that 'a second intelligence test for the Special Place and Secondary School Entrance Examination was held in the Girls' Hall and Mr Scott acted as invigilator at St Augustine's Roman Catholic School'.

Preliminary scholarship test

In March 1941 there is an entry in the girls' school log saying 'Preliminary Scholarship Test held at 10–10.25 a.m.', but the entry for the boys' school says this was the 'Special Place Examination'. The significance of the term 'scholarship', as previously noted, is that the parents of children selected for secondary education were charged a fee according to their ability to pay and consequently the selection examination was seen as the means of earning subsidised entry into the grammar schools – a scholarship examination or simply 'the scholarship'.

Log book entries relating to internal examinations

Some indication of the nature of and importance attached to these internal examinations is seen in the following log book entries:

3 January 1942: 'School closed at 4 p.m. when the term and half-year ended; class examinations being completed, results filed and individual reports given to the pupils. In spite of the difficulties of the times – bi-annual examinations and individual reports have not been curtailed in any way, except to be as economical as possible in the use of paper.'

29 January 1943: 'For the Girls 'School closed at 4 p.m. when the term and half-year ended; class examinations being completed, results and individual reports given to the pupils; details on grade cards completed. All details of individual pupils maintained in spite of war conditions.'

6 July 1943, girls' school: 'Time Table adjusted during the day – examination in English and Arithmetic.' The nature of this entry does not indicate that it was a routine half-yearly exam, although the time of year suggests that it must have been.

31 January 1944: 'Class exams were completed, individual reports given to pupils, and individual grade cards completed.'

As a part of the internal examinations a composition exam was held on 4 July 1944, and once again, on 17 July, Miss Fenby noted that all examination results and reports had been completed.

It is clear that the end of term and half-year at this time did not coincide with the Christmas holiday.

Again, in July 1944, there is a report of the recording of examination results and reports being completed. The entry for 4 July 1944 suggests that a part of the bi-annual examination was the writing of a composition.

Here is some evidence relating to those who took part:

11.3.42: Secondary Schools Entrance Examination held a.m. 72 girls were eligible but 10 were absent.

Misses Rush, Appleby and Turnbull invigilated at Eastbourne, Mrs Thompson and Misses Bellis and Linford in other schools.

Based upon the results of the examination, five girls were offered Special Places in secondary schools in June 1942: Audrey Bird, Aileen Bulmer, Joan Dalkin, Joyce Rosemary Hutchinson and Edith Rhoda Johnston.

3.3.43: Entrance Examination to Secondary Schools held am. There were 87 girl entrants but five were absent.

12.5.43: Entrance to Secondary Schools Examination (Part II) held 10.05 till 11.00 am. 32 girls in this school took the examination. The results were received on 29th June 1943 when a total of 69 girls were successful, 17 attending from the Eastbourne school: Ann Sheila Ashmore, Kathleen Nora Bell, Eva Clarke, Sylvia Connolly, Marjorie Dickinson, Eileen Gowland, Rhoda Hall, Greta Harrison, Audrey Holmes, Doreen Jameson, Constance Mary Lax, June Mabbott, Elizabeth Rutherford, Norma Shafto, Zoe Brown Thomson, Edwina Anna Wastell and Sheila Wrightson.

There is no equivalent entry in the boys' school log.

There is an entry, referring to the girls' school, for 7 July 1943 stating that seventeen pupils attended for interview at the high school in the afternoon, presumably those who were successful in the examination.

The examination for 1944 took place on 1 March when seventy-eight pupils entered but five were absent.

On 4 April 1944 the second intelligence test of the Entrance to Secondary Schools Examination was held in the morning from 10 to 11 am, when twenty-three out of the twenty-four girls eligible were present. The significance of this entry lies in following note where it is shown that nine girls eventually transferred to the technical school, four to the high school at 13-plus and thirteen to the high school at 11-plus. The question arises here: what were girls of the 11-plus age group doing in Eastbourne Senior Girls' School? It seems that these girls were 11-plus pupils from a Dodmire class accommodated in the Senior Girls' School.

Miss Fenby recorded the second part of the examination, which took place on 30 May 1945, when seventy-eight girls were eligible, although five were absent, and says that it continued during the morning and afternoon of 1 June. On 12 July twelve girls accepted offers to transfer to the Darlington High School: Marjorie Allen, Joan Burrows Elcoat, Margaret Winifred Goodwill, Norma Haggie, Patricia May Howe, Dorothy Hutchinson, Joan Mary Leng, Agnes Adams Milroy, Eileen Rodrup, Georgina Margaret Sandford, Mary Eileen Seymour and Rita Stephenson.

The nature of the examination as demonstrated in log book entries

23.5.41: Secondary School Entrance Examination, second Intelligence Test was held 10.00–11.00 a.m. in the school hall. Twenty-two girls (one absent) from this school and thirty-four pupils from Eastbourne Senior Boys' school took the test, Miss Rush from St Augustine's and Miss E. Johnson from St John's School acted as invigilators.

10.3.42: Secondary Schools Entrance Examination Preliminary Test held a.m.

2.6.42: Eleven girls reported at the Technical College for a further test – Entrance to Secondary Schools Examination.

In 1945, the examination took place on two days in March:-

7th the Intelligence Test between 10.5 and 11.00 a.m.

8th the Arithmetic Test between 10.05 and 10.55; and the English Test between 2.12–and 3.05 pm.

For the boys' school for 6 March 1945, the headmaster reports:

'Secondary School Entrance Examination in the morning.'

7.3.45: Part 1 in the Hall.

8.3.45: Morning Arithmetic, Afternoon English.

The Day Technical School and the Day Technical School examination

Day Technical School opened in September 1943, plans having been previously made for there to be an entrance examination for 13-plus pupils hoping to attend the new school, and there was a panel meeting relating to the examination on 2 April, chaired by the CEO. Subsequently the Day Technical School Examination was introduced.

On 18 May 1943 thirty-three girls aged 13-plus took the Day Technical School Examination and the results were published in mid July. The headmistress of the girls' school recorded the results as follows:

'Commercial course – 20 places for boys and girls; this is a new school opening in September 1943. Successful candidates from this school: Doreen Dodd 3.1, Kathleen Forbes 3.1, Averil Noble 3.1, Brenda Lambert 3.1, Jean Harrison 3.1, Pamela Stabler 3.1, Eva Goldsborough 2.1.'

In March 1944 the girls' school entered thirty-seven pupils for the examination and nine transferred to the school in the following September. There is an additional note relating to the examination on 9 March 1944: 'Technical Day School entrance exam. Mechanical Aptitude Test. 3 girls attended the Darlington Technical College.' The reference is to a technical school, with courses designed with a clear view of qualification for employment in the workplace and with less apparent purely academic or intellectual exercises.

On 24 May 1944 the CEO held a meeting to discuss the Board of Education Circular regarding transfer of children at 13-plus to secondary schools. The possibility of transfer at 13-plus was supposed to cater for those children who were said to be 'late developers', that is those showing an academic learning ability at 13 which had not been evident at 11-plus.

A meeting was held in the girls' school on 8 June in order to present parents with information re Special Places for late entrants to secondary schools, and on the 16th late entrants to secondary schools in the 14-year-old age group were interviewed and an 'at home to parents' held in the evening. On the 19th correspondence was distributed to prospective fee-paying pupils at the high school, evidence that there were parents of children attending Eastbourne who were ambitious for their children to go to the high school and were willing to pay for this type of education. The following girls were listed and it would be interesting to learn of their experiences within the system: Marjorie Beckwith, Mavis Close, Freda Deacon, Joyce Hancock, Myra Marshall, Joyce Millar, and Joyce Ridley.

High school interviews

Eastbourne girls on the Special Places in Secondary Schools list attended the high school for interview on 21 June and on the 22nd prospective fee-payers to the high school attended for interview. Selection apparently included not only the examination but also a face-to-face interview.

Selection for secondary education would become controversial and be used by campaigners for the development of comprehensive schools, who claimed it was stressful to children and had serious long-term effects on their future prospects, labelling the unsuccessful as failures.

Late entrants

There were thirty-nine applicants to take the late entrants' examination held at the high school on 30 June 1944 between 10.15 a.m. and 2 p.m.; three were absent.

On 7 July a total of seventy-four girls were granted special places in the secondary schools, of which six were Eastbourne girls. This means about 15 per cent were therefore successful, but were the majority, the other 85 per cent, really seen as failures? That is, failures forever, when they had merely taken a test for entry into one type of course when there were others available to them where they could gain different success?

The girls' school reported that the technical and secondary school late-entrance examination was held on the morning and afternoon of 26 April 1945 and seventy-eight pupils were eligible to enter, although three were absent. Part II of the examination was held on the morning of 30 May and seventy-three out of the seventy-eight pupils were present.

On 12 July 1945 eleven girls attended for interview at the technical school and eleven transferred to that school at the start of the autumn term, appearing to show a pass rate of about 15 per cent.

A meeting for parents

A parents' meeting was held at the girls' school in February 1945 relating to the examination, involving both the 11-plus and 13-plus age groups, which 325 girls were eligible to enter; 100 parents attended.

External examinations: examinations as qualifications

There is evidence of the staff of the Eastbourne secondary schools being involved in the external examination system: for instance, on 15 February 1942 Mr P. Longstaff of the boys' school staff attended a committee meeting of the Northern Examination Council in Newcastle and in May 1943 he attended a meeting of the Junior Commercial Advisory Committee in Newcastle, but the involvement of Eastbourne *pupils* does not appear before 1945. Not until March 1945 is a meeting held concerning reorganisation and the mention of a class taking a School Leaving Certificate. On 6 July that year a meeting (of a subcommittee of the Education Committee), attended by Miss Fenby, was held at the Education Office to discuss the arrangements for a selection of girls of 13-plus to make up a School Leaving Certificate form. On 10 July the headmistress interviewed fifteen parents and fifteen girls who had been offered a place in the School Leaving Certificate form in the Eastbourne girls' school. A further interview session took place on 18 July when six girls and their parents were invited but only three attended. At the start of the new autumn term a number of girls joined a selection of Eastbourne girls to make up a fourth-year class. The girls from other schools entering the school's fourth form came from the High School (2), North Road (1), Reid Street (3) and, Cockerton (1). Eastbourne girls' school included, for the first time, a class which would study an appropriate syllabus leading to external examinations, the School Leaving Certificate of the University of Durham.

School leavers' preparation for work

The move towards the taking of external examinations by some selected pupils raises the subject of staying in school for an extra year or two for a few pupils, but the majority were still destined to enter the adult world of employment at 14 years of age. So what guidance, if any, did they have provided for them by the school?

In 1942 the head teacher of the girls' school apparently interviewed youngsters about to leave school and attempted to guide them into appropriate employment; in fact she says, at the end of the 1943 half-year: 'All leavers interviewed and as many as possible guided re: suitable employment. Many parents interviewed too, for advice re: girls' welfare.' The school was not lacking a caring, pastoral staff.

On 27 September 1944 there was a meeting between senior department head teachers and representatives of the Ministry of Labour when it was decided:-

1. Talks would be given to leavers by Ministry of Labour representatives;
2. Visits to works and business organisations would be arranged for them;
3. Leavers' interviews would take place in school during school hours; and
4. Head teachers would have the opportunity to attend in an advisory capacity.

The first recorded interviews took place on 11 December 1944 when fifteen girls attended but only three parents. On the following day thirteen girls were interviewed and five parents attended. This may be an indication of the need for both parents to be working.

The first recorded visit by leavers to workplaces took place on 29 January 1945 when twenty-two school leavers visited the Lily Laundry at 2.15 p.m. The log entry says that the visit was arranged by the Ministry of Labour in connection with vocational guidance.

On 27 and 28 March 1945 twenty boys attended Rise Carr Rolling Mills at 2.30 p.m. in the charge of Mr Peacock; and on 18 June a party of thirty leavers from the boys' third year, in the charge of Messrs J. Peacock and G. Brockway, visited Darlington Forge in the afternoon. There was a similar visit to Rise Carr Rolling Mills on 25 June.

School parent meetings

It has already been noted that meetings of parents were held to explain matters of current interest and in the girls' school, meetings referred to as 'At home' were regular events. On 14 September 1942 there was an 'At Home to Parents of Newcomers' when about fifty visited during the afternoon. There was a new intake of 101 pupils at this time.

There was another 'At Home' in July 1942 when the school was open to parents during the afternoon from 2 p.m. Over 100 parents visited the school, where they were shown round by their own girls and introduced to and talked to the staff. The event was described as 'a most successful afternoon'. A similar meeting was held in February 1943 when there were sixty visitors from an intake of eighty-eight girls.

In September 1943 seventy parents and friends visited when the intake of new girls was ninety-seven, and in February 1944 fifty parents and friends attended from an intake of seventy-two, the head reporting at the time that the visitors showed particular interest in the building and the work of the school. The building was still a leading example of a well-equipped and modern school for pupils over the age of 11.

In February 1945 about forty parents attended from an intake of ninety-three, and in September about seventy-five attended from a total admission of eighty-one. Clearly, the number of parents taking the opportunity to come into the school varied, but it is evident that parents of the winter intake of February 1945 may well have been deterred by the weather.

The attendance rate varies between a low of about one visitor for every two pupils and a high of almost one visitor for each girl. This may reflect variations in parental interest from year to year, or may be dependent upon other factors, such as the weather (already noted), the wartime absence from home of fathers and employment requirements on the part of mothers.

Celebration of national events

During the pre-war and wartime years schools celebrated certain annual and one-off national events, promoting a national identity, a sense of belonging and a pride in the nation.

One occasion was Empire Day: on 24 May 1943 being 'recognised in the usual way and the school assembled 11.0–11.30 a.m. for the Empire Broadcast'. Again, in 1944 the 'Empire Day message read to all girls who also listened to the special broadcast'.

Armistice Day, the occasion for the remembrance of those who had given their lives during the 1914–18 war and particularly pertinent during the Second World War years, was observed on 11 November 1942 with a Remembrance Service during school assembly at 9.30 a.m., and by the sale of poppies which raised £7.7s.0d. In 1943 there was again a special assembly when the 'official message' was read and the sale of poppies raised £7.16s.0d.

A thought on the question of litigation

The concept of suing the school, although not new, was little heard of before the days of Health and Safety and children's rights, therefore the log entry for 27 October 1944 is unusual: 'Mr Crowe of Eastbourne Road reported that an injury to his daughter resulting from a faulty landing made in the gym on the 4th of the month may be more serious than at first expected, calling for the involvement of a solicitor. The father was reported as making serious accusations against the school.'

Accidents do and will happen as on 18 October 1943 when, in domestic science room 17, Doreen Clarke, 3.1 turned on the gas, left the oven door closed, and afterwards applied a light. The result can be imagined and it was reported that she received singed hair and burns on the neck and hand. First aid was applied and the pupil taken to the clinic.

The end of the 1939–45 war

Both the boys' and girls' schools recorded the end of the war in Europe with summaries of the celebrations of VE Day.

7.5.45 girls' school log entry: School closed at 4.15 pm. During the evening, the BBC announced the Government's instruction, that as the Prime Minister would broadcast to the Nation on Tuesday May 8th 1945 at 3 pm. 'the cessation of hostilities in Europe took place at 2.41 a.m. on May 8th 1945', that day would be regarded as V E (Victory in Europe) Day and both it and the day following, May 9th, would be regarded as national holidays.

8.5.45 boys' school log entry: The school did not assemble by reason of this being V E Day i.e. Victory in Europe. The surrender of German Armed forces unconditionally being announced at 3 pm. by the Prime Minister Mr Winston Churchill.

Wednesday 9.5.45: School Closed – a National Holiday.

Thursday 10.5.45: School Closed. Ascension Day holiday.

Friday 11.5.45: School reopened at 9.15. A Service of Thanksgiving was held in the Hall at 9-30 am.

VE Day celebrations

Boys' school log:

2 July 1945: School Holiday.

3 July 1945: Victory Celebrations Films, Assembly, Sports. No tea could be provided owing to catering difficulties and the Ministry of food Regulations.

4 July 1945: p.m Town sports at Feethams.

Girls' school log:

2.7.45 School closed all day for local VE Day Holiday.

3.7.45: School reopened 9.15 a.m. VE Day Celebrations took place as requested – circular 45/42.

In the morning the opening assembly was made appropriate to the occasion; the headmistress recalling to mind the long ordeal through which the Country has passed and the exertions and sacrifices which have made possible the Victory now being celebrated. The opportunity was taken of explaining the possibilities of the future and the responsibilities of the Youth of today – the meaning of "Service" for them and the address was concluded with the reading of "A Legend of Service" – Henry Van Dyke and the singing of the National Anthem.

Time was allowed for decoration of the school, at 11.00 a.m. the school assembled for a film programme. The afternoon was spent on the Sports field where there was a large variety of individual and team sports, about half the girls in the school winning prizes in the form of National War Savings Stamps fixed on suitable cards. These were presented at the closing assembly at 4 p.m.

Although all arrangements for tea and ices had been made, these were cancelled as instructed in circular 45/43.

A note: education future planning

In spite of the necessary concentration on wartime matters, the latter years of the conflict did not prevent plans being made for the future. The log entry of 22 May 1944, referring to the Rebuilding Britain Exhibition, is an example: 'Two parties of 20 each: 20 3.1, 10 3.2. and 10 3.3. with staff visited the Rebuilding of Britain Exhibition in the Public Library.'

The entry for November 1944, referring to reports being submitted to the Education Committee by the head teachers of the town's senior and high schools on the reconstruction of education, and to a meeting of head teachers and the subcommittee of the Education Committee being held to discuss the proposals, is a clear indication that the reform of education for pupils over the age of 11 was ongoing at this time.

1944 Education Act: classification of pupils for secondary schools

In December 1944 there was a meeting of all head teachers with the CEO who explained the proposals of the Education Committee for the classification of pupils for secondary schools.

In January 1945 there existed a teachers' panel concerned with the examinations for entry into the high school and technical school at 13 years of age.

The 1944 Education Act

A new education system

As the end to the devastating worldwide war approached, the government was able to turn its attention to the immense task of reconstruction. The disruption to society's traditions, as well as the destruction of much of its physical basis, provided the opportunity for change. In education, change was to manifest itself in the Education Act 1944, known as the Butler Act, where the primary objective was to establish for the first time a free secondary education system for everyone. The concepts of primary and secondary education were established and it was clearly stated that there would be separate primary and secondary schools with a division at the age of 11. Only in the case of the provision for the physically and mentally disadvantaged was it envisaged that all-age schools would exist. Much of this was already in place in Darlington by the end of the war.

The philosophy of the Act was based upon the simple notion that all schools should have an equal share of available resources. Premises would be equally good; the teachers equally qualified and equally paid. The maximum class size would be the same for all children; the provision of books and equipment the same for all types of school. Even the length of the school holidays would be the same. And, perhaps, it was this notion which led to the misconception that if the environment was made the same for everyone, all would flourish equally. The Eastbourne Schools already had the most modern premises for the time, although lengths of holidays, class sizes and teachers' salaries were clearly three of the differences seen between the senior schools and the grammar schools.

The outcome of the Act, a matter which the Ministry of Education pamphlet number nine, *The New Secondary Education* published in 1947, largely the work of the socialist education minister Ellen Wilkinson, clearly addressed, is reflected in the development of the Eastbourne Schools in the post-war years. The intentions of the government promoted an education for all in which the individual child is placed first and a great variety of provision envisaged to suit different individuals but not different income groups, and where success was seen to be obtained through the arousing of the individual child's own interest. There was even the statement that 'No child must be forced into an academic education which bores it to rebellion' because that education is thought to be more socially desirable: an interesting concept because there was certainly one child who qualified to enter the high school but soon chose to be transferred into the Eastbourne girls' department.

The pamphlet opens: 'Everyone knows that no two children are alike', and continues: 'schools must be different too, or the Education Act of 1944 will not achieve success'. There can be no doubt that those who were motivated to bring about this great reform also appreciated the need to provide different styles of education for different people. Variety was seen to be necessary, in the curriculum and in teaching methods, to cater for children with different aptitudes, being at different stages in their development and having different levels of achievement. There was an acceptance that such individual differences require different schools, and an assumption that it is right to expect some children to remain in school to a later age than others. But there was also the expectation that the different schools would carry equal prestige, and this illusive ideal has dogged the education system ever since.

It was argued that a majority of children learn best 'by dealing with concrete things and following courses rooted in their own day-to-day experience', and do best 'in a school which provides a good all-round education' a school 'which will give them a chance to sample a variety of subjects and skills'.

The school for this majority was to be the 'modern school' and its curriculum such as to allow the pupils to sample a range of subjects and skills, and to pursue those which 'attract them most'. These became the secondary modern schools.

Another group of children, it was claimed, were able to decide at an early age which career they wanted to follow, or displayed particular aptitudes: for example in science or mathematics or music and the arts. The underlying concept, that different people have different aptitudes, is still vigorously pursued in career selection today, in spite of the development of a common curriculum and leaving certificate. Such youngsters, it was surmised, would need specialised courses, and that these would be provided in secondary technical schools. Darlington opened its technical school in 1943.

Thirdly, another minority were identified in terms of their having abilities and aptitudes which thrive on 'books and ideas', and which appreciate an 'abstract approach' to learning. These children would attend the grammar schools, being expected to follow an academic course leading to external examinations at sixteen and being likely to follow a similar but more advanced course into the sixth form, and eventually progress to university.

In spite of this three-school philosophy, there was an expectation that there would be similarities between the schools. All three would be involved in both book and activity learning: 'the proportions in which these two ways of learning are to be combined should be determined by the capabilities and needs of the individual pupil.' The existence of native ability, although a vague concept based upon intellectual ability and imprecisely defined special aptitudes, was accepted. Emphasis was placed on the idea that the child should work at those things in which it can be expected to achieve success and not be presented with subject matter which it cannot appreciate and which will only cause it frustration. It was also stressed that attention must be given to the whole child: to intellectual, social, emotional and physical development and spiritual growth. The inclusion of the spiritual aspect of education is noteworthy due to the subsequent developments in the perception of religious matters, including, eventually, the influx of people of faiths other than that based on the Christian teachings.

The provision of school libraries and timetabled library periods, during which every child would be taught how to use books for both entertainment and the finding of information, were proposed. The Eastbourne Schools each had its library but how many schools today still provide library periods? How well has this initiative succeeded when a significant proportion of the population sees little use for books and there are frequent complaints of illiteracy among the workforce? It is all very well to point to the upsurge of computer-aided learning, but the operator must first be proficient in basic reading and comprehension before being equipped to obtain the greatest benefits from modern technology.

Already in 1944 the significance of presenting material through media other than books was recognised. Schools were to be provided with cine projectors, film strip and micro-projectors, gramophones (the predecessors of the record, tape and disc players we have seen in more recent years) and radios, and these were brought into Eastbourne. It was even foreseen that television could one day be used to great advantage. But now of course, in spite of the existence of the Open University, schools broadcasts and educational programmes, a large part of the finance and technology applied to audio-visual presentation is invested in popular entertainment.

At the time of the Butler reforms, politicians were concerned with what they understood as education for good. They included the statutory requirement that each day should start with an act of collective worship, and the notion was promoted that each child should be encouraged to develop as a member of the community, learning citizenship, the workings of local and national government, the system of rates and taxes and the judiciary. But not politics, which some people today think can be taught objectively and without indoctrination, an objective dependent upon the neutrality of the teacher and his or her willingness or ability to present different views in an unbiased fashion.

It is the curriculum that defines the pupils' work programme and in the light of more recent initiatives it is worth considering the views advanced on the matter in 1944. It was stated quite clearly that the head teacher had responsibility for the curriculum: the Ministry of Education did not lay down subject matter or the time allocation given to each part. The only requirement was the compulsory provision of religious instruction and the daily act of collective worship. The curriculum was in the hands of the professionals: they were acknowledged as the experts, trained in their discipline and consequently the best people to do the job. They were trusted with this responsibility. How things have changed!

Education was seen to be a partnership between the Ministry of Education, LEAs, school governors and teachers. It is interesting to note that parents, members of local industry and commerce, and representatives of the community at large were not included.

With regard to the appointment of staff, the head teachers of all schools were given 'the same measure of responsibility in the appointment and retention of their assistant staff as is commonly enjoyed by grammar school heads'. The intention seems to have been that the head teacher should have the responsibility for appointing, supervising and disciplining assistant teachers. There was a professional attitude to management which has since been replaced by a broader spread of responsibility throughout a governing body.

What has become known as the hidden curriculum was expected to play a large part in the social, emotional, physical and spiritual education of children. It was understood that not only the timetabled activities but 'the general life of the school' and staff attitudes would work towards this broad education. A moral tone should be established in the school to ensure that 'every pupil is in constant contact with people … who are fired with generous ideas and set an example of creative and unselfish living'. Teachers, they said, can encourage pupils 'to treat others with courtesy and consideration, to be sensitive to the feelings of others and to respect their point of view'. The way in which teachers behaved towards each other, as well as towards their pupils, was given importance. Once again the Eastbourne Schools recognised and developed these ideas – but within the social climate of the day.

The significance of school clubs was recognised when, in particular, it was argued that they help those with learning difficulties. Many teachers have observed the improved pupil–teacher relationships which develop during club and school-journey activities being carried over into the normal classroom. There develops a greater mutual respect which brings increased pupil motivation and a lessening of the strains arising from confrontational discipline.

Little was said about the harsher discipline that was common in most schools at the time but comments were made on teaching styles. There had been too much emphasis on written work at the expense of other activities. The child's curiosity about things was to be the main stimulus to learning and the teacher's job was to arouse this natural curiosity and relate schoolwork to real aspects of life. Children were seen as showing great enthusiasm and skill in the pursuance of a chosen hobby and this motivating force should be harnessed. It was thought that this eagerness could be applied to homework, where the youngsters were expected to become keen to collect and tabulate data, draw diagrams and make things. It is a fascinating fact today that such a notion is not only rejected by some pupils and parents but also by some responsible educators.

Science should play its part in directing this curiosity through the application of scientific methodology. (Eastbourne Schools were equipped with science rooms.) There should be discovery through the consulting of sources, interpretation of information and the establishing of principles. Field work in history and geography (again already brought into the schools' teaching) should be used to further develop this principle of discovery and in mathematics the practical approach, through doing and measuring, was to be advanced. All of this was a part of the general advice for the development of the modern school but with value for pupils in the other schools as well. It becomes clear, as the pamphlet is studied, that the foundations, albeit often superficially defined, to much subsequent thinking were laid down in the immediate post-war years. Referring to the subject disciplines, it was said that 'hard and fast lines between subjects' were 'generally inappropriate', and this concept remains an area of contention today. Even subjects at university level now have different contents under the same titles, and similar contents under different titles! The introduction of new subjects and the redefining of the content of the more traditional disciplines have made this no less of a problem at school level. But some form of packaging of information is essential if learning is to progress efficiently. Perhaps modules, where smaller amounts of learning material are placed together, are a more useful way of handling subject content. A single module can apply to more than one subject: for example, the graphical representation of data, which is generally taught in mathematics, is probably taught again in science lessons and again in the geography class. It would be more efficient to teach the unit once and then to apply its techniques to the analysis of data in other areas.

The famous, or for some infamous, project method of teaching was promoted. The approach identifies a particular area of study and then draws upon several disciplines for its content. Its failure is illustrated by the geography teacher who had been involved in a project on the Trans-Siberian Railway only to discover that his pupils afterwards remembered such details as the number and type of wheels on the engines but nothing of the railway route or its commerce! Perhaps the failure lies in the whole being used in an attempt to teach the parts, when it would be more logical to teach the appropriate parts first and subsequently use them to investigate a greater whole.

The teacher in all of this was seen to be a supervisor and counsellor rather than as an instructor and this is yet another aspect of education theory, with its roots in the post-war years, which still gives rise to considerable controversy. For instance, there is a move to introduce teaching styles in which individual learning programmes are negotiated between teacher and student, rather than imposed by authority.

With regard to the composition of teaching groups it was said: 'It is obviously sensible to group the abler children together so that the teaching may be especially suited to their needs, and the pace of their work need not be slowed down to give a chance to the less able children, who in any case, require a different approach and a simpler presentation of their subject matter.' This seems to be sensible stuff. Clearly, it was intended that children who found learning school subjects easy should be placed in one group, those with moderate learning ability in another group and the slowest in a third group. Unfortunately, such groups, referred to as streams, soon became boldly labelled top, middle and bottom, emphasising success and failure rather than mere differences in learning and teaching strategies, and leading to the system being criticised for its divisiveness, denigration and perceived social injustice. Both of the Eastbourne Schools and certainly one of their intake primary schools became rigidly streamed in their organisation. Even in 1947, the reformers wrote of the social disadvantages of streaming: 'It is arguable that abler children benefit from rubbing shoulders with their less able comrades, and less able children are stimulated by the presence of the brighter ones.' A debatable point!

With regard to common leaving examinations, it was reported that 'it is impracticable to combine a system of external examinations, which presupposes a measure of uniformity, with the fundamental conception of modern school education, which insists on variety'.

Alternatively, emphasis was placed on the keeping of individual records, where it was intended that the child's development and progress would be plotted throughout its school career, tests and teacher assessments being used to diagnose difficulties. The Darlington Education Authority had instigated such a system by this date. Evidence relating to the young person's character was also to be included, then, on leaving school, a complete picture of the young person would be available for vocational guidance, fitting the candidate to a job or further education or training. Again an element of post-war thinking demonstrates the origin of yet another more recent innovation: records of achievement.

Back in the refreshing idealism of the forties, an idealism in which all children would be surrounded by good books, pictures, decorations and good-quality buildings, and all teachers raised in status to those working in the grammar schools, with equal pay, holidays, class sizes and expectations, the future looked good. The tripartite system of secondary education was in place and the roots of many of the theories and practices which were to dominate the sixties were put down.

In spite of the damage to and loss of school buildings during the war sufficient repairs and new building were accomplished to provide both grammar and secondary modern premises. The relatively new senior schools built during the 1920s and 30s provided well-constructed, pleasantly laid-out accommodation, but the older Board Schools, located in the inner urban areas, were hardly conducive to the fostering of the new education. There also developed a type of building (consisting of such features as flat roofs, extensive glass areas in external walls and thin internal partition walls) which was susceptible to easy damage by both the weather and the occupants, leading quickly to shabbiness in appearance. But such physical handicaps did not detract from the efforts of education authorities to develop secondary education for all.

Grammar schools took more children from less-well-off homes, relying on selection by ability rather than wealth, and secondary modern schools developed courses in keeping with the new philosophy.

The Darlington Education Subcommittee met at the Town Hall at 2.30 p.m. on 19 September 1944 to discuss post-war secondary education. Miss Fenby reported that she attended a meeting of all head teachers at 3.00 p.m. on 13 December 1944 in the Kendrew Street School library to meet the CEO who explained the suggestions of the Education Committee, referring to the classification of pupils for secondary schools under the Education Act 1944, due to come into operation on 1 April 1945.

The girls' school held a parents' evening on 16 February 1945 relating to the Education Act when the Entrance to Secondary Schools Examinations for the 11–12 and 13–14 age groups were explained. A letter from the CEO was discussed and questions answered. Miss Fenby stated that 325 girls were eligible to take the examinations and that over 100 parents had attended, which she declared to be very successful.

The boys' school held their parents' meeting on the topic of 'Schools Reconstruction', which was addressed by M. W. F. Houghton, CEO, on 19 February.

Mr Welford attended a meeting with the CEO at 2.20 p.m. on 13 March 1945.

The Fenby–Welford Years
By Way of Introduction

The post-war years

It will be difficult if not impossible for those who did not experience the conditions of war to realise that in the late 1940s, apart from the cessation of hostilities, living conditions were in many respects not unlike the war years due to shortages of both necessities and luxuries. In 1946 food rationing continued – the wheat content in bread falling to the 1942 level, the butter, margarine and cooking fat ration actually being cut from 8 to 7 ounces per week – and it was decreed that rice was not to be imported.

Shortages of fuel added to physical discomfort, a matter which the present generation of pampered central-heating dwellers needs to experience in order to fully comprehend the harshness of the situation. For instance, on 13 February 1947 the government issued the instruction that no electricity was to be used between 8.30 and 11.30 a.m. and between 1.30 and 3.30 p.m. due to the shortage of coal, the predominant source of energy used for its generation at the time.

Although some men who had been conscripted to serve in life-and-death situations across the world returned home, many did not, and those returning often displayed the physical and mental scars associated with the experiences thrust upon them in the devastating inhuman conflicts of battle and prison camps. People at home, even if they had escaped the effects of bombing raids, flying bombs and rocket attacks, had to face the problems associated with the reintegration of military personnel returning to civilian life.

115

At Eastbourne Mr T, Tranter returned to duty on 2 November 1945 after his release from HM forces; Mr J. R. Farrage on 3 December 1945 after his release from war service with the Royal Ordnance Factory at Aycliffe; and Mr W. A. Brown commenced duty on 6 May 1946 after his demobilisation from the army.

The weather

The weather did not help. It was at this time that Miss Fenby wrote about the extreme cold and severe weather conditions with persistent snow and freezing temperatures, during which the school carried on as usual! Snowfall, extreme cold and frosts were recorded for January 1946, and in the following September there was a period of heavy, incessant rain. Swimming classes were cancelled and there was no heat in the building. By mid September, when the heavy rain had continued for several days, making conditions in school cold and damp, a request was made in writing to the Education Office for permission to turn the heat on!

By mid December conditions had become severe, all roads and paths being dangerous because of ice and made worse by dense fog. During the week of 7 February 1947 extreme weather prevailed, with intense cold, snow, wind and freezing conditions. In the following week there were heavy falls of snow and blizzards; on 20 February, when the school reopened at 9.00 a.m. after the mid-term holiday, weather conditions were still severe, with more snow, and on 24 February following more blizzards and snowfall on the previous Saturday and a subsequent slight thaw, parts of the corridors were flooded. Even after this lengthy period of severe winter weather the heaviest snowfall was experienced on the 26th of the month, lying deeply on the ground when it was also windy. Equipment and food for the midday meal had to be brought through the school to the hall, and there was no transport from Catterick, causing the absence of a domestic science teacher. On the following day the Co-operative Dairy could not deliver the milk.

The log book entry for 13 March 1947 illustrates that the conditions continued when the weather was described as the worst of the winter with yet more heavy snow the previous evening continuing during the day. Pupil attendance was very low at 69.1 per cent.

By May excessive heat was being given as the reason for suspending the timetable for ten minutes at 3.15 in the afternoon!

Although the 1947 winter weather was exceptional, further log entries point to intermittent spells of unexpected exceptional events. At the end of January 1950 Mr Welford commented on the heavy snowfall influencing attendance. A sudden and severe storm on 17 September 1953 caused one of the swimming sessions to be cancelled. Severe weather again disrupted the swimming sessions on 18 January 1955. On 20 January snow, ice and fog caused the swimming sessions at the public baths to be cancelled in the afternoon and on 21 March 1955 the severe weather returned with snow, gales and intense cold. One of the boilers failed!

During the first week of January 1956 there were heavy snowfalls and extreme cold, causing swimming lessons to be cancelled; the severe weather continued through February. Again, on 24 February 1958, there were extreme winter conditions with deep snowdrifts, continuous snow and temperatures below freezing. Yet it was said that pupil attendance was remarkably good even though a teacher living in Cockfield was absent as there was no transport into Darlington. On 26 February inclement weather continued; swimming was cancelled.

During this period there were two outbreaks of influenza, events remarkable enough to be recorded in the school records.

Influenza epidemic November 1954
There was a serious outbreak of influenza in November 1954, as illustrated by the log entry for the girls' school of the 26th of the month which refers to the daily attendance figures.

> Attendance at the girls' school during the influenza epidemic of autumn 1954:
>
> Monday 81%
>
> Tuesday 77%
>
> Wednesday 71%
>
> Thursday 67%
>
> Friday 59%

During the same week Mr Welford, head of the boys' school, was himself a victim and reported a low 68.3 per cent attendance for Monday 26 November and an average attendance for the whole week of 75 per cent. By 13 December, however, the annual boys' school pantomime went ahead as usual.

Miss Fenby reported continued health problems at the beginning of December: due to the influenza epidemic continuing and extreme weather conditions, rain accompanying strong gales, attendance had been between 56 and 57 per cent. The following week swimming classes were cancelled due to the prevalence of severe colds and coughs among the children. The internal school examination programme was disrupted, fourth-year pupils receiving their reports and testimonials as usual but no formal reports being prepared for first, second, and third years.

Influenza outbreak 1957

Attendance at the girls' school during the influenza epidemic of September–October 1957:

16 September 82%

17 September 76% 140 absent

18 September 67% 192 absent

19 September 56% 253 absent

20 September 49% 295 absent

26 September 37%

27 September 35%

Week of 4 October 64–70%

Attendance at the boys' school during the influenza epidemic of September–October 1957:

16 September 76%

17 September 72%

18 September 63%

19 September 58%

20 September 50%

23 September 44%

24 September 44%

25 September 44%

26 September 42%

27 September 42% am & 38% pm

30 September 68%

1 October 68%

2 October 71%

3 October 72%

The girls' school visit to London on 23 September went ahead with the expected group of twenty-five reduced to seventeen. Swimming sessions were cancelled and several staff were absent for between five and seven days at a time, after which attendance returned to normal.

There are similar weather reports for mid February 1962, when there was intense cold with gale force winds and at the end of the month blizzards, snow, ice and gales.

Extreme weather conditions were reported for January 1963 when the cold was described as intense with severe frost, heavy snowfalls, and ice: transport was disrupted, and on 1 February there was a further heavy fall of snow followed by a week of severe weather.

Efforts to save resources, another concept foreign to the present wasteful generation, little considered before the introduction of campaigns to recycle materials, continued after the end of the war. In June 1948, following instructions received from the CEO, arrangements were made for a representative of the Ministry of Supply to speak in school assembly on the subject of the Book and Paper Drive. The war had been over for about three years and yet the idea of collecting salvage continued.

Influenza – staff absence
Staff absence during the Influenza epidemic of September–October 1957: The girls' school: Miss Hall, 1 day; Miss Bullyment, 7 days; Miss Grieve, 1 day; Miss Wood, 2 ½ days; Miss Dover, 7 days.

The boys' school: Miss Moran, 3 days; Mr Barlow, 5 days; Mr E. L. Robson, 7 days; Mr Welford, 2 days;

Mr Jacobi, 1 day; Miss Wilkinson, 1 day; Miss Pedley, 2 days; Mr Unwin, 9 days; Miss Dodd, 1 day; Mr Sheppard, 1 day.

Health and fitness

Today, 2008, taking note of government health warnings, obesity comes into focus: too many children are too fat! There is nothing about being too fat in the records of the post-war years, rather, there is concern about illnesses which are little heard of today. Diphtheria had been a problem in 1939, and a case of scarlet fever caused concern in December 1946.

In March 1946 there was still concern about the possibility of children becoming ill with diphtheria as Schick Tests were made available to any Easter leavers who wished to have them: tests to determine a patient's susceptibility to diphtheria were invented by the American Dr Schick in the early 1900s. A diluted diphtheria toxin is injected into the arm to produce a reaction. If there are not enough antibodies present the skin becomes red and swollen and the patient needs to be immunised. Schick Tests took place in June 1946 and in the following September fifty pupils were immunised.

On 18 December 1946 the Medical Officer for Health sent a nurse into the girls' school to examine pupils following the notification the previous week of one case of scarlet fever. Appropriate letters were sent to all the parents of girls in the same class as the patient. Again, in March 1974, a nurse visited the school concerning pupils who had been in contact with cases of infectious diseases, and on 10 June the head teacher requested that the nurse inspect pupils in class U2.1 following a further report of a case of scarlet fever and reported all precautionary measures taken. On the 19th of the same month the nurse came in to school again to see class L3.2, as one girl had had contact with a victim of scarlet fever, returning a week later to complete a follow-up investigation.

In mid September 1946 the head teacher reported that, during a particularly cold and damp spell of weather, illness among the pupils was significantly higher than normal and that their clothing in many cases was inadequate, giving some evidence of the relative poverty on the part of some families.

The head requested permission to put the heating on, school rooms being cold and damp, and poorly ventilated because of the need to keep the windows closed. A picture of masses of children in steamy smelly, probably sodden, clothing is easily envisaged.

A log book entry made at the start of the 1949 autumn term states that the school nurse was called in due to the 'appalling state' of two of the girls, being evidence of possible poverty and/or neglect. The nurse afterwards conducted a cleanliness inspection of the whole school, but this was a matter of routine.

In September 1955 there was a report of an investigation into the head's action regarding the 'state of cleanliness' of a pupil: the child's mother was eventually called into the school by the educational psychologist.

There was also concern relating to the infectious disease tuberculosis, commonly referred to as TB, which, in 2008, is described as difficult to catch. The poorly nourished and those weakened by alcoholism are thought to be particularly vulnerable and, due to poverty and the effects of the recent war, some youngsters in the Eastbourne Schools would certainly have been likely subjects. Strangely perhaps, most people who are infected do not become ill! Screening programmes were introduced to detect the symptoms of the infection and in October 1946 arrangements were made for girls to be X-rayed, the most common form of the disease being pulmonary TB when an inflammation develops in a lung.

In November 1948, 71 girls from the fourth year attended for mass radiography tests at the municipal hospital and in May 1950, 153 senior girls attended Feetham's Health Centre. There is a boys' school log entry for 23 May 1950 stating 118 boys went for X-rays at the health department. Mass X-radiography became a part of a regular screening programme.

On 4 February 1954 Miss Fenby attended a meeting at the education office with reference to BCG vaccinations. BCG is the abbreviation for the bacillus of Calmette and Guerin, used in the vaccination process to produce immunity to TB, and on 5 May 1954 there is the first report of Eastbourne girls being treated when eighty-two pupils attended the health centre for the vaccination. Some eighty-nine letters had been sent to parents requesting their permission for the treatment and there were seven refusals. On 12 May two groups of some forty pupils each paid a second visit to the health clinic for preliminary tests. On 1 July eleven girls attended the health clinic for additional checks.

There is a log book entry for 27 September 1946 referring to the Fever Hospital, the Borough Hospital for infectious diseases labelled on the Ordnance Survey map for 1923 and located to the west of the school site: a reference reinforcing the dangers perceived and action necessary to deal with diseases which at the time were not easy to treat and could result in death. The log entry itself is associated with dog bites! Apparently, during the dinner hour, two girls were bitten on the legs by a dog from the Fever Hospital. The matron of the hospital was informed immediately, as on a previous occasion when a girl was bitten by the same dog; first aid was given and both girls taken by the head teacher in a car to the clinic where they were given treatment. There is the additional point of interest: in 1946, the headmistress had a car!

All school leavers were given a medical examination during their last year; there were regular dental checks of the whole school; hearing tests and tests of eyesight took place; and the nurse was a regular visitor making health checks, particularly of the hair. Nitty Nora was a well-known expression but, of course, never used in the hearing of the nurse. In addition, children with particular learning or behaviour problems were also seen by the educational psychologist. For instance, on 1 March 1950 Mr Saunders, educational psychologist, visited the school to test six boys and continued the following day.

With such ongoing inspections and the observations of teachers a child in need or at risk would surely be identified: in fact examples of the head teachers' intervention have already been noted. The physical education staff, in particular, would observe the youngsters in different clothing and out of the classroom setting. It is amazing, in 2008, why, with social services established and abundant instructions from government, children in need are still apparently not getting the support essential to promote their welfare.

Initiatives of the war and post-war years, such as the issue of free school milk and the setting up of the school meals service, indicate the government's well-intentioned actions to support the poor. It was at the start of the 1946 autumn term that the Darlington Education Office issued instructions to schools concerning the distribution of free milk to those pupils wishing to have it. This was the time of the birth of the Welfare State. But with these developments came a question: how responsible should teachers be for the physical, mental and social well-being of their pupils? How involved should they be in such matters? The main task of the teacher should be to teach and not to be overwhelmed with matters of child welfare. It is for teachers to recognise health and social problems and to pass their observations to other specialists.

The growth of the school meals service

The introduction of the school meals service during the war years has at least partly given rise to the question of how involved teachers should be in welfare matters. Their initial involvement in the supervision of the meals during a time of national emergency has developed into a requirement; teacher trade unions have seen this as an imposition, and some consideration has been given to their concern by the appointment of non-teacher midday assistants.

Barely six months after the war ended the numbers of girls staying for school dinners increased: by early February there were 350 girls staying for school dinner, partly, perhaps, due to the severe weather. By August/September the LEA determined the working hours of dining-room helpers to be 2½ hours daily – it is not clear what this figure actually means.

In February 1947 there were 367 girls wanting to stay for school dinner. The weather was again very cold. In February the following year, on instructions from the CEO, school meals were limited to a total of 400 and to do this, priority was given to pupils living in Haughton Road and beyond, in Geneva Road beyond number 150, in Lingfield Lane and beyond the railway and Falmer Road; and to those with working mothers. All others had to go home at midday unless they could show special circumstances and arrangements were then made, where possible, for them to stay one or two days per week on a rota basis.

In September 1947 the position had eased a little, the school roll being 432, of which about 375 required a school dinner, which was then being served in the hall and two domestic science rooms. It was at this time the head raised her concerns with the CEO relating to the school canteen and the inadequate accommodation due to increased numbers, staffing and equipment.

The days of the working mother had been introduced during the war but were becoming more prevalent with the desire on the part of families to increase their income and raise their standard of living.

A further difficulty is demonstrated by the head teacher's request, made in September 1948, that arrangements should be made to avoid using the girls to put up and take down dining tables. It is clear that the school meals service was using provisional accommodation: it was not until 1950 that a purpose-built dining room was made available.

As a break from the more serious aspects of life, the observation in the girls' school log for 20 March 1947 is included for the sake of curiosity: 'Miss Bolam, Domestic Science Organiser, visited the School Canteen at dinner time to supervise Orange Juice Jelly.'

The new canteen

Between the outbreak of war and 25 February 1942 there were no events which brought the elected members into the school; then a whole delegation of dignitaries descended on both the boys' and girls' departments to see the school meals service. The size and make-up of the party is surprising, the emphasis clearly orientated towards feeding the youngsters and nothing to do with school in the traditional sense.

Boys' school log 25 February 1942: 'Visit of the Mayor and Mayoress of Darlington, Councillor and Mrs Jackson; the Chairman of the Education Committee, Councillor R. Luck. The Chief Education Officer Mr W. F. Houghton MA, Miss M. E. Nichols HMI and Members of the Darlington Town Council and Education Committee visited the school 12.50 pm to inspect the school canteen. After seeing the boys having dinner they dined with the girls in the Senior Girls Department.'

Girls' school log 25 February 1942: 'After a tour of inspection of school canteens and nursery classes in the borough, His worship the Mayor, the Mayoress, the Chairman of the education committee (Councillor R. Luck) and Mrs Luck, Members of the education committee and their wives, His Majesty's Inspector (Miss E. M. Nicholls), the Chief Education Officer (Mr W. F. Houghton MA), the Medical Officer of Health (Dr Dawson), the Schools Canteen Organiser (Mrs W. Davison) visited this school at 1 pm; and inspected the school canteen. The visitors remained to lunch which was served, as usual, in the school hall, for the children who pay fourpence each. Menu: Meat Pie and vegetables (carrots and potatoes). Steamed Sultana Pudding and Custard.'

Liaison between the Education Committee and the head teacher Mr Welford resumed in September 1944 at a subcommittee meeting when post-war education was the subject for discussion. There is no reference to Miss Fenby attending this meeting although she did attend subcommittee meetings relating to the preparations being made for the introduction of a school record for all pupils.

The Canteen Committee met at the school during the afternoon of 8 December 1944, the group consisting of Chairman Councillor R.

Luck, the CEO Mr W. F. Houghton, Alderman Best, Mr J. Scothorne HMI, and Miss M. E. Nicholls HMI. Miss Fenby and Mr Welford were present and discussion took place concerning the possibility of building entirely separate school meals premises, comprising of dining room, kitchen and scullery for each of the boys' and girls' schools.

There was a visit by the school meals organiser in June 1950 with reference to arrangements for the opening of the new canteen.

The new purpose-built kitchen–dining room at the girls' school opened on 10 July 1950 with accommodation for 200 and meals were served in two sittings. When school opened after the Whitsuntide holiday of 1950 Mr Welford reported that the boys' new kitchen–dining room was open for use. Both the boys' and girls' units were still in use during the first fifteen or so years of the comprehensive school but during a visit in July 2008 the unit at the girls' end of the premises was no longer used by the school, being excluded from the school grounds, and that at the boys' end, although still part of the school, had been put to other uses.

In April 1951 the price of the school meal was raised to 7d. per day.

Road safety

Present-day scholars could be forgiven for thinking that the road-safety precautions – seen in terms of speed limits, speed-restricting humps and road narrowing outside schools, cycle safety checks and cycling proficiency classes – as a modern introduction to education. They would be quite wrong.

Only two tragic accidents are recorded in the log for the girl's school between 1945 and 1959: one on 28 May 1948 when it was stated that Janet Kitchener, aged 13 nearly 14, of 87 Stooperdale Avenue, died in hospital as a result of an accident on the way to school in the morning. The head teacher, one other member of staff and 17 girls from 5.1 attended the funeral on 1 June. The other was on 3 July 1950 when Anne Beatrice Reid of 106 Eastbourne Road, aged 13, was fatally injured on Friday 30 June 1950 at 5 p.m. when she was knocked down by a motor wagon at the junction of North Eastern Terrace and Parkgate.

Neither of these accidents occurred close to the school, the entrance in any case being at the end of The Fairway. It is at the exit from the Fairway to Yarm Road where the greatest hazard would be expected but precautionary measures put into place there would not have prevented the above tragedies. The safety of secondary school pupils needs to be promoted through education but even then it cannot be guaranteed that an individual will not, on the spur of the moment, make the mistake of taking some purely accidental, although sometimes thoughtless, fatal step. The action of the mind is a creature of the moment.

The premises

Once the war was over the new school was in reality no longer new, being 9 years old, and, neglected during the time of conflict, was beginning to experience some problems. Perhaps the most obvious was due its growth in pupil numbers.

Overcrowding

As early as September 1947 there is evidence that the school buildings occupied by the girls were becoming crowded, if not overcrowded, as increased numbers on roll made it necessary to use the medical room as a classroom and for registration classes to be accommodated in all specialist rooms. The total number on the school roll in September 1947 was 549 when the new intake from primary schools was 100. In addition twelve extra pupils transferred at 13+ from Reid Street, North Road and Nevilles Cross to make up a School Certificate group of twenty-eight girls.

At the start of the second half-year, in February 1948, because the specialist rooms were being used for teaching non-practical subjects it was not possible to provide a full domestic science programme, and some science lessons had to be taken in an ordinary classroom.

An HMI, Miss E. Johnson, visited the school on 12 February to enquire about the number of pupils on roll and to look at the problem of overcrowding. Admissions from primary schools were taking place twice each year, and there were also School Certificate classes in the senior school, that is, with girls over the school-leaving age, explaining why the total on roll had risen to 665.

Miss Fenby's observations on the inspector's visit are interesting: when Miss Johnson left she had nothing to discuss, presumably realising that everything possible was being done to continue the teaching of the curriculum under difficult circumstances.

In September 1948 classes were very large in the first two years, being up to fifty in some cases, and the roll of 671 was some 150 more than the official accommodation figure. It was said that it was not practical to make smaller classes (presumably due to the accommodation problem) although the large groups were divided for teaching whenever possible.

By January 1949 the number of pupils had fallen to 618 with the loss of some 53 girls at the end of the Christmas term who had reached the leaving age of 15, a further 48 leaving at the end of the spring term. As no further observations are recorded on the subject, the school presumably continued to work under these less than ideal conditions until the numbers of pupils declined.

The boys' school had a total of 446 pupils in September 1947 and did not suffer the problems associated with overcrowding.

In October 1950 the girls' hall was largely out of use due to repairs being made to the oak panelling and the floor being resurfaced. At the end of the month work started on the cleaning and renovation of the oak panelling in the boys' school hall

Additions, modifications, fittings and equipment

The following examples provide a partial picture of how the Eastbourne building and its site were maintained and changed during the late 1940s and 1950s.

On 8 January 1946 the CEO and members of his staff visited the school to consider the provision of an electric plug in the staff room to enable the tea urn to be boiled, and to investigate the possible rewiring of the hall clock to connect it with the electric clock in the quadrangle. These appear to be rather trivial matters which could surely have been dealt with by one professional.

In June 1946 decorators were working in the girls' school hall and school meals and school assemblies could not take place there for three days, this being evidence of the school hall still being used for serving midday meals.

In September 1947 blackboard frames, each holding three blackboards, were erected in rooms 23 and 24 – they were probably those still in position in the comprehensive many years later. Blackboards were the teachers' chief visual aid for many years, only fairly recently replaced by the electronic white board.

The forty new chairs and forty new single desks delivered to the boys' school in September 1947 is another reminder of how things were. Desks faced the front, arranged in regimented rows.

At the time of the inspection in December 1950 the accommodation at the girls' school was: eleven classrooms, one specialist room for each of art, science and needlework, and four domestic science rooms, plus the flat; there was also a library, a medical inspection room, a gymnasium and the hall.

Concern was expressed that all of the building did not come up to modern standards.

Housecraft room 16 had been used for the school meals canteen kitchen and had just been returned to use for teaching purposes.

The gymnasium was said to be dark with poor artificial lighting and inadequate heating. Access to the changing room, directly from the playground or through a small door at the rear of the hall stage, was said to be poor, the changing room small and dark.

The library, situated on the upper floor near the hall balcony was, due to the increased size of the school, being used as a normal classroom. This, it was claimed, hindered the use of the room for reference purposes, although lending facilities were well developed and used. The girls were encouraged to borrow books and understand the ticket system, to encourage their reading and use of the public library when they left school.

In January 1951 domestic science room 16 (formerly housecraft room 16) was ready for use after being refitted with unit kitchens. There were then four domestic science rooms and the flat.

Recommendations made by the school inspectors visiting the boys' school in March 1951 reiterated the significance of the ubiquitous blackboard, suggesting more were needed; but also give some indication of the importance of the workshops, advancing the need for a lathe in the metalwork shop.

In September 1951 there were plans to construct a covered way (in the girls' school) to the gymnasium and for a new coalhouse – the school was heated by coal-burning boilers.

In February 1953 discussions were taking place concerning the making of changes to the centre quadrangle and to the proscenium arch to the stage; and in March 1954 there were proposals for changes to be made to the staff cloakroom, which were eventually completed during summer vacation of 1955.

In 1953 bollards were erected at the south-west corner of the building, presumably as a protection against traffic using the area, and the authority's decorators began painting the exterior of the building.

During the Easter holiday 1956 extensive alterations were made to the girls' gymnasium and changing rooms, the work continuing during the following term. After the summer holiday the changes made to facilities in the gymnasium, the new entrances and exits to and from the stage, and modifications to the area between it and the gymnasium were ready for use: the normal programme of physical education was once again able to take place.

On 24 February 1956 the electric light at the front of the school was placed in a central position to light up the school drive.

On 7 June 1956 members of the Borough Architect's Department and the Northern Electricity Board visited the school in relation to the fixing of bells for the inter-communications system, apparently in response to the third request made by the head. Originally, the signalling of times for sessions, the changeover and end of lessons was achieved by a member of staff or appointed pupil monitor going around the school ringing a hand bell.

In July 1956 groups of girls attended the North Eastern Electricity showrooms in Skinnergate for a talk and demonstration on the use and care of modern electrical equipment.

Twenty dual desks and ten chairs were delivered in September 1956.

In 1959 the lighting of the building was changed from suspended bulbs and shades to fluorescent tubes.

The school was equipped with a network for the receiving of radio programmes in each classroom and in 1959 obsolete speakers were replaced.

The Isolation Hospital

The Isolation Hospital was the smallpox hospital shown on the Ordnance Survey map of 1923 and sited in the area known to later Eastbourne generations as the walled field, the surrounding wall being the only evidence left standing. On 22 September 1949 an inspection of the site was carried out by the CEO and Borough Surveyor with a view to using the building or grounds for school purposes and in March 1951 it is recorded that the CEO and headmaster visited the Isolation Hospital which had recently been acquired by the Education Committee.

The front of the school

As well as the building having an imposing frontage every effort was applied to making the approach attractive. The main entrance to the school grounds had always been via the Fairway, between brick pillars which once held gates, meaning that both boys and girls walked up the main drive, but at different times. There was a strict division of the two populations, with the boys and girls arriving when possible at different times, passing through the central arch, girls to the left and boys to the right of the imaginary central line.

On 5 March 1949 the Group Managers, the Chairman, Alderman Luck, Councillor Buckborough and the CEO visited the school in the afternoon in relation to the removal of the grass plot in the centre front of both schools.

On 19 June 1950 the Gas Department repaired the surface of the quadrangle in front of the cycle sheds, the interest here being the involvement of the Gas Department when the gas supplied to the town was coal gas and tar a by-product of that industry. On 15 June 1956 the schools organiser (Mr Duggan) visited the girls' school to investigate the perceived need for an extension to the cycle accommodation. Plenty of youngsters cycled to school, if it was too far to walk or if the trolley bus routes were inconvenient.

The Coronation ceremony and the planting of trees on the drive

Generations of ex-pupils will be familiar with the burst of spring colour seen along the drive leading to the central arch provided by rows of trees on each side – until they grew old, died, or were cut down to make room for the security fence which became necessary in the later 1990s. Some will even remember how they came to be there.

In December 1953 the headmistress of the girls' school reported that in commemoration of the Coronation of Her Majesty the Queen an avenue of cherry trees was planted in front of the school from the west corner along the drive to the main gates, indicating that the left-hand line followed the path around the front of the building. The ceremony was attended by the Chairman of the School Governors, Councillor Buckborough; the Chairman of the Local Education Committee, Alderman Bell; the headmistress, Miss N. Fenby; the Staff First Assistant, Miss J. Owen; the Old Girls' Association, Vice chairman, Miss S. Donner; and for the boys' school, the headmaster Mr G. Welford, in addition to the captain of each school house; and the whole school, old girls, and other members of the school governing body. Some money to pay for the trees was raised by the Old Girls' Association.

No reference was made to the 1953 planting of trees by the boys department but on 2 March 1957 Mr Welford did report a similar ceremony for the planting of trees along the right-hand side of the school drive, when trees were planted by Mr J. Peacock, and pupils Brian Stabler, Frank Morton, Michael J. Carr, Cyril E. Lenagan (spelling not clear), Thomas K. Inglis, Eric Wilson, John M. Sutherst, C. R. Robinson, Arnold L. Wilson and Keith Flint, who had all been chosen by ballot.

The headmistress reported on 15 March that a concrete kerb had been placed round the grass verge from the main gates to the west corner, more trees planted, and semi-circular beds set out and planted by the Parks Department, all of which she said greatly improved the approach to the school. Thus the pleasantly enhanced and much-admired drive up to the impressive building frontage came in to being.

Another matter relating to the appearance of the grounds was the visit to the school by the Deputy CEO with reference to the work to be done on the drainage and layout of the lawn in the domestic science area.

Playing fields

In the 1950s the fashion, if that is what it should be called, was for the further provision of playing fields, the converse of what was to happen in the 1980s, when Darlington was a part of County Durham and when a large area of the Eastbourne grounds was lost to housing development.

In October 1950 it was the state of the existing playing fields that was giving rise to concern and no 'stick games' were played during the whole term. But by the summer of 1950 plans were being made for the extension of the playing fields, when visiting inspectors also commented on their poor condition. Much to the delight of the girls, no doubt, the inspectors also said the boys' had too big a share of the existing provision!

On 5 June 1951 the new extensions to the playing fields were seeded with grass, but in July concern was shown about their state as they were choked with thistles. Nevertheless, in the summer of 1952 the grounds were ready for the annual sports.

Again, in July 1955, there was a meeting in the school of the Deputy Education Officer, the physical training organiser, Mr Welford, and

Miss Fenby to consider the further development and tidying of the school playing fields. In June 1956 there was discussion of plans for the layout of the playing fields and in April 1957 there was a meeting chaired by the CEO to discuss priorities in playing-field improvements. By May 1959 a meeting took place referring to the completion of the first of three stages in the development of the playing fields, development going on through 1960.

A reference to the curling pond

The curling pond was situated behind the boys' school in what was to become the shale area, a name derived from the material used for the eventual filling and surfacing of the site for use as tennis courts. The pond was a valuable resource for the science department's practical work in biology but a hazard when unsupervised. There were several warnings given to the girls, such as that recorded for 17 September 1943, concerning the dangers associated with playing around the site, and they were instructed that the area was out of bounds during the dinner hour.

Supervision of the large school site has always been a problem. In early 1943 there were intruders, out of school hours, who interfered with beehives which were kept on the school field and police supervision was requested.

School garden

In May 1952 a school garden was proposed. In July the Parks Superintendent and Surveyor visited the school in relation to the garden and pond. In March 1954 the Deputy Education Officer visited the school in relation to the 'conditioning area for school garden'.

Security of premises

The advantages of having a low extensive building with numerous entrances, some at the rear, expansive grounds with official access from both Hunden's Lane and The Fairway, and much of the rear not being built up, were countered by the problems associated with keeping the site secure, problems which, with the development of a more liberal approach to discipline, were to take on a major significance.

The first difficulty was recorded on 14 February 1947 when there had been an overnight burglary, intruders entering the school via a door from the quadrangle into the corridor. The head teacher's room and staff room were entered and about ten shillings taken. There was extensive damage done to door locks, cupboards, and drawers, mostly in the head teacher's room.

A recurring problem was illustrated by the report in September 1948 of thieves removing lead sheeting from the cloakroom roof.

At the end of March 1949 the school was entered via the circular window in the caretaker's store next to room 12 but the intruder was unable to force open the door lock to gain entry to the rest of the school.

During the night of 12 April 1949 intruders broke into the headmistress's room via the window, where a pane of glass was removed and the frame damaged. Some seven locks were damaged during the forcing open of cupboard doors and desk drawers and two shillings taken.

The vulnerability of the buildings at the extreme west of the premises was demonstrated by the break-in to the school canteen during the weekend of 16–17 February 1952 when damage was done and goods taken. A similar event took place on the night of 2 June 1954.

The school corridors were bounded by large areas of glass windows, each divided into small panes and opening onto the playground areas at the rear of the premises and out of sight of the residential area to the south. During the Easter weekend of 1956 an entrance door from the north quadrangle was forced open and five rooms entered with the apparently unnecessary breaking of windows.

During one weekend in June 1961 unknown youths came into the school grounds and damaged meteorological equipment. The standard equipment on the school site would have been a Stevenson's Screen, to hold thermometers, and a rain gauge set into the ground.

The twenty-first anniversary and the lectern

Miss Fenby recorded on 22 July 1957 the Service of Thanksgiving to commemorate the twenty-first anniversary of the foundation of the school, another example, with the planting of the avenue of trees along the drive, of the generation of a spirit of care for and pride in the school.

The service, held in the girls' school hall starting at 11 a.m., was conducted by the Reverend Brown, vicar of St John's Church; the Reverend Wilkins, the minister at the East Road Methodist Church;

and Councillor the Reverend M. Beaton, minister of Geneva Road Baptist Church. Mr Welford, the headmaster of the boys' school; the Mayor and Mayoress, Councillor and Mrs Turner; Chairman of the Education Committee Alderman Bell; Alderman Luck; other members of the Education Committee; the Chairman of the School Governors, Alderman Buckborough all attended the service along with school governors, administrative staff, parents, friends, ex-staff, Old Girls, all the pupils at the girls' school plus twenty pupils and staff from the boys' school.

The address was given by Councillor the Reverend Beaton and the headmistress and head girl read passages from the Bible.

It is quite clear that the occasion was a very significant event in the life of the school and that it was very strongly based in the traditions of the Christian Church.

The lectern bearing the school badge, dedicated during the service, together with an accompanying chair and three garden seats, were gifts presented by the staff and pupils to commemorate the occasion. The lectern and chair were intended for use at the daily act of worship and continued to be used in the comprehensive school, eventually finding a home in the St Aidan's Church of England Academy.

In September 1958 the Old Girls' Association presented the school with a display cabinet for school trophies.

The Fenby–Welford Years
The Making of Successful Schools

Although the roots of the two schools had been put down before and during the war, it was to be the subsequent lengthy and relatively stable period which was to see the development of what was to come to be seen as the Eastbourne School.

During its early years the school was at the forefront of the education system and went on to develop into two extremely well-thought-of departments, one for boys, the other for girls, maintaining a strongly held belief that boys and girls were best educated separately.

The relative strength and interaction of government, LEAs, governors, head teachers and teaching staff are the ingredients which controlled the functioning of state schools, and although the characteristics and proportions of these inputs have changed during the lifetime of the Eastbourne Secondary Schools it was during the Fenby–Welford years that the government had laid down the fairly straightforward framework of the tripartite system which was administered by a small intimate LEA, where people knew each other, met face to face and talked regularly, and where the governors for the most part were the LEA. The teachers worked within clearly understood bounds, as equal-status and equally remunerated assistants (there were originally no special allowances or responsibility posts), except for the informal recognition of experience due to length of service. For instance, there were reserved seats in the staff room for the long-serving staff, an informal but well-understood tradition.

The Darlington Education Authority was small and its area compact, a situation in which the Education Committee, its officers and teaching staff could be in close and frequent contact. There is evidence that the Authority did indeed keep tight reins on its staff, the schools subject to instructions from above. Instructions to head teachers were regularly received from the CEO, the senior professional of the LEA, rather than the government, although it is clear the he and the Education Committee were themselves subject to government directives. It is the nature and proportion of each that are significant, the government laying down a framework in which the LEA could operate.

Examples of instructions received from the CEO regularly appear in the school log books. Miss Fenby reported on 6 November 1946: 'Official Copy of timetable of present term submitted to the CEO received duly approved and signed.' So it appears that, although the head produced a timetable for the school, it had to be formally approved by the LEA.

An officer regularly came to the school to inspect the attendance registers: there are frequent log entries along the lines of 'Registers checked and found correct', dated and signed.

There are occasions such as that in September 1947 when permission was granted by the CEO to suspend swimming classes due to school visits.

The head teachers

It was within this system that the head teachers, with their individual leadership styles, developed the unique ethos of each of their schools. They remained in office for some twenty years and became well-known, respected characters, a part of the establishment, which people still remember today.

Miss Nora Fenby served as head teacher of the Eastbourne Girls' School from August 1939 until her retirement in April 1963, a period of twenty-three years and two terms; Mr George Welford served as head of the mixed school and boys' school from August 1936 until his retirement in December 1959, a period of twenty-two years and one term. The post-war period, some fourteen to eighteen years, was a long time during which the foundations laid before and during the war were consolidated and strengthened, a time of little major change. Following the introduction of the 1944 Education Act the Eastbourne Schools remained secondary modern schools until comprehensive reorganisation in September 1968.

This long period of continuity under the direction of the same head teachers and with an established understanding of what was required and how things were done, is a major factor in the success and recognised public perception of the schools during these years. Those who attended as pupils still, in 2008, speak highly of their experiences of the system as it was – it worked very well.

Miss Fenby was aged 41 when she became head teacher of the Eastbourne Girls' School on 28 August 1939. She had trained at Goldsmiths College, University of London between 1918 and 1920, being awarded a First Class Certificate as a trained teacher, and had been on the staff of the mixed school since it opened in 1936.

From discussions with former pupils and staff, the personality of Miss Fenby emerges as that of a formidable lady and not one to be ignored or taken lightly. There can be little doubt that the first head teacher of the Eastbourne Girls' School was an autocrat, but her actions suggest she was driven by a strong desire to give the pupils in her care a sound foundation for their future lives within what she understood to be the clearly defined boundaries to behaviour and her responsibilities as a professional educator.

One story told by a former pupil sheds some light on the character of the lady. This child had returned to England with her parents after being abroad and was suffering from a disrupted education. As there were most free places in the bottom stream, where classes tended to be closer to thirty-five than thirty in size, the young girl was placed in that form. She said she quite quickly graduated to the third stream but stood no hope of going any further because the upper classes were too big. At the time of the Late Entrants to the Grammar and Technical Schools Examination the youngster wrote a letter to the Authority and claims she was given the go ahead to sit the examination, although the school said only those from the top two streams were eligible to enter. She passed the examination. The response from Miss Fenby was first to question what the girl's mother knew of all this and, as the truth was she knew very little, immediately called the parent into school and demanded to know what she thought her child was doing, going against the procedures laid down by the school. It seems the parent said very little and left school thoroughly berated.

The child was told in no uncertain manner that third-stream girls could not and did not pass this examination: the emphasis being firmly placed on the 'did not', whether anyone else thought they could or not.

The ex-pupil also related the occasion of her hair being too long. Glared at by staring eyes, pointed at with a stabbing finger, and bawled at in terms of, 'You, girl,' she was expelled from the class and made to stand outside the head's room. There she stood, dreading the moment the door would open and she would be commanded to enter – remaining there awaiting the head's pleasure. On final entry and after a further humiliating dressing down, she was forced to turn around, and a piece of string was yanked under her hair to tie it up. Further humiliation came from being forced to move around the school with hair so obviously attended to by the 'dragon'.

Another ex-pupil reported that there was no corporal punishment, no detentions, nor exclusions, but there was Miss Fenby! 'We knew the rules, held her in awe, and kept out of her sight when possible!' The latter was not easy because the headmistress regularly walked around the school and into classrooms, looking for blotted exercise books, wrong spelling, and anything else that was not strictly in place according to Fenby law.

The teachers were treated similarly; for instance, lesson plans for the following week had to be submitted in writing to the headmistress every Friday, being thoroughly examined, commented on and almost marked out of ten in red ink.

There is another story. A new refrigerator was required in the domestic science department and a request, duly signed by Miss Fenby, sent to the area office. So far so good, but it was known that such equipment had recently been supplied to the school and there arose the serious debate about who should be sent to tell her she could not have another one. In due course, Miss Fenby was supplied with the apparatus she demanded!

Under Miss Fenby's leadership there developed a strong staff hierarchy where senior teachers held considerable status and newcomers felt distinctly disadvantaged and repressed. The number of young, newly qualified staff who did not stay long in the school may have been the victims of this social climate, while those who weathered the storm of early problems rose above the repression to become stronger for their experience.

The teachers in the boys' school appeared to be treated more as members of a friendly club, newcomers being helped with their integration into the team. Their involvement in the annual camps, the Ascension Day treks and pantomime productions reveals this club-like spirit.

Both head teachers became leading and influential figures in the community: for instance in 1962 Councillor Spense, re-elected chairman, welcomed Councillor G. W. Welford to a meeting of the governing body, making it quite clear that the head of the boys' school was an elected councillor and on the governing body of the girls' school. By this date, of course, Miss Fenby and Mr Welford had been colleagues working in the Eastbourne Schools for a quarter of a century. Mr Welford served on many committees relating to education in Darlington, becoming a Justice of the Peace in 1945 and Chairman of the Juvenile Bench in 1950.

On 10 November 1947 Miss Fenby was installed as Mayoress of Darlington for the Municipal Year 1947–48 and in the summer of 1960 Miss Fenby attended the Royal Garden Party at Buckingham Palace.

School governors

School governors do not appear during the pre-war and war years, although school managers were evident from time to time but references made to them in the school log books are rare. On the other hand, in Darlington, elected members were directly involved in the schools, as illustrated by those people attending the first Eastbourne School prize-giving held at 3 p.m. on 3 November 1937. The Mayor, Councillor R. Luck, presented the prizes and was supported on the platform by Lady Starmer, Mrs Whalley, Alderman J. Hinks, Councillor M. Gallagher, Mr C. H. Leach MA OBE (Ex-Alderman and Chairman of the Education Committee), and Miss Waters. The headmaster Mr G. Welford presided over the meeting.

The Chairman of the Education Committee visited the school during the afternoon of 12 November 1937 with the CEO Mr H. Whalley BSc, Mr E. J. Edwards HMI, Archdeacon Owen, and the Reverend Nye.

On 9 December Councillor Luck was again in the school with Councillors R. Dodd and J. Clayton and the CEO to consider protection for the gymnasium windows, box blinds for the hall, and the position of clothes posts near the domestic science block. This close involvement is surprising when assessed against later arrangements but is in part explained by the nature of the prestigious, modern newly opened school and small compact LEA.

The newness of and incomplete premises were reasons for the visit by the Chairman, Councillor Luck, Vice Chairman, Councillor Bell JP, and Mr Whalley, CEO, on 17 May 1938 when they considered repairs and new extensions. Further visits were made later in the year and during 1939.

Mr Welford was directly involved with the planning of the new extensions in early 1939, attending the subcommittee meeting of the Education Authority.

On 13 November 1946 guests at the annual school concert were the CEO and members of the Education Committee. There is no mention of governors.

All school business seems to be conducted directly with the CEO and Education Committee or its subcommittees at this time.

Involvement of governors in the life of the school
After the end of the war there is a revival of the involvement of members of the Education Committee in school functions. For instance, on 5 November 1946 a subcommittee of the Education Committee, Chairman Alderman R. Luck, Alderman Hudson, and Miss Stanton, together with the CEO, Mr Houghton, and Mr Scarr visited the school to discuss pupils' attendance, staffing and the stage curtains; they also inspected the field club and the needlework exhibits for the Local Government Exhibition, all of which sounds like school governors' business.

On 2 September 1947 Miss Fenby refers to 'Education Committee Managers for this school' listing Alderman Bell as Vice Chairman of the Education Committee, Miss Stanton, Alderman Hicks, and Alderman Hudson. They attended the school and discussed the proposed plan for the layout of the grounds for both the girls' and boys' departments, and modern electric and gas appliances for the domestic science rooms and flat.

The established tradition of members of the Education Committee regularly attending school functions continued for many years and when school governors, largely LEA councillors, came into existence in late 1950, their close involvement continued.

The governors were appointed to a group of schools, Eastbourne governors being referred to as Group 2, serving both the boys' and girls' schools. The meeting held on 16 July 1952 was held in the boys' school and as the business was concerned only with that department the headmistress did not attend. This was the first meeting attended by the new CEO, Mr David Peter MA MEd. Governors present on this occasion were the Chairman, Councillor H. Buckborough, Councillor B. E. Pigg, Councillor G. E .Wilson, Councillor R. Barker, Councillor K. Loraine, Councillor Mrs Lyonette, Mrs G. A. Osborne, Miss E. Hutchinson and Mr A. E. Burley. A survey of alterations and repairs was made and various repairs put in order of priority.

The meeting of the Appointments Committee held on 17 September 1954 demonstrates a responsibility of the governors, and possibly a problem with the procedures, when an application for the post of art specialist was considered but no appointment made because the candidate had accepted a post elsewhere.

The annual Speech Day ceremony for the girls' school was held on 13 October 1954 when the Chairman of the governors, Councillor Buckborough, presided, other governors being present.

On 15 October the boys' school held its first public Speech Day in the hall at 7 p.m. when T. H. Summerson Esq. JP presented the prizes. The Chairman of the governors, Councillor H. Buckborough, presided, supported by other members of the governing body and Mr D. Peter MA MEd, CEO, and prefect Peter Liddle proposed the vote of thanks.

At the annual girls' school swimming gala in July 1955 one of the awards was made by the Mayoress, Mrs Neasham, who was also a member of the school's governors. The Chairman of the Governors, Alderman Buckborough, presided at the girls' Speech Day in 1955 and Mrs J. Neasham, presented the awards, addressed the school and donated a cup for a speech competition to be awarded annually. Other governors also attended. The first speech competition for the Neasham Cup was held on 1 December 1955.

Civic dignitaries at school functions

By the time of the governors' meeting on 22 June 1956, Councillor Alderman Buckborough, re-elected Chairman, was the Mayor of Darlington, and Councillor Loraine was re-elected Vice Chairman. Other governors present were the Rev. M. Beaton, A. Lunn, Mrs Grant and Mr A. E. Burley. On the occasion of the girls' school annual concert, the Mayor and other governors attended. In July 1959 Councillor Buckborough was once again elected Chairman of Governors, when Councillor Laughton replaced ex-Councillor Spense, and Councillor Stokoe replaced the late Councillor Farrage. There is the additional observation that 'all other governors continued', suggesting little change in the make-up of the governing body.

There is overwhelming evidence of long-standing, respected elected members of the local authority being regularly, frequently and closely associated with the school for many years during the headships of Miss Fenby and Mr Welford: there was a core of interested, involved and influential people who were well known to each other associated with the overseeing and running of the schools.

The teachers

The Eastbourne Schools were perceived as successful, having developed from their inauguration in 1936, through the war years and into the 1950s and early 60s. One aspect of this success, some will claim, is the long service of some teachers in the schools, not least that of the head teachers Miss Fenby and Mr Welford, which provided a stability, an absence of change; and this idea calls for further examination.

Initially, in 1945, there was still disturbance resulting from men being taken from their school duties to serve in both the armed forces and essential industry; and from women replacing men, and from married women being employed as teachers for the first time. It took time for these disturbances to settle down. Temporary women staff were being replaced in the boys' school as the men returned to their jobs, and there was a general shuffling of teachers from one school to another. In addition, government legislation immediately required children to remain in school until they were fifteen, having previously left when they reached 14 years of age, thus requiring more teachers to staff each secondary school. To make up for the shortfall, colleges were established for the emergency training of teachers, and men and women qualifying in this way were classified as emergency trained.

The significance of the number of long-serving teachers working in the girls' school between 1945 and 1963

During the period Miss Fenby was the head teacher of the girls' school there were four other women teachers who served with her. The most senior was Miss J. Owen, who had graduated from Bangor University and became the school's first assistant mistress during the year 1945–46, the first assistant being the equivalent of the head's deputy. She retired just one term later than Miss Fenby, having served for twenty-four years. Both Miss Richardson and Miss Dover served throughout Miss Fenby's years, both retiring from the school some years later after serving twenty-nine years each. Miss Thompson joined the school in 1939 but left before Miss Fenby in 1950.

The total number of teachers working in the school during each of the years 1947 to 1950 varies between head teacher plus 26 and head teacher plus 17, giving an average staff size for the period of head teacher plus 22. During the first five or so years of the secondary modern school, when Miss Thompson is included, there were five out of about twenty-three members of staff who formed a lasting senior team; that is, some one fifth of a relatively small group of teachers. They formed a strong stable core working under the firm leadership of Miss Fenby during a period when teachers in general were respected and commanded authority.

During the period 1944–1963, the time during which Miss Fenby was head teacher of the secondary modern school, four more teachers had joined the staff and continued to serve throughout these nineteen years, making a long-serving team of head plus 7 teachers: and in addition, three more teachers joined the team in 1945.

For the secondary modern school years 1945 to 1963 there is therefore a long-serving team of head plus 10 teachers in a total staff of between seventeen and twenty-six. During the years 1951–1962 the average total number of staff was head plus 21, which means that about half the teachers did not change.

Furthermore, there were at least six other teachers who served for about half the period 1945–1963, providing a continuity which, with the head's policy enforced from above, produced a long-lasting ethos.

Another relevant factor is that the teachers were all relatively young unmarried ladies and, although having lives outside school, they did not have the responsibilities attached to marriage and the bringing up of their own children. They had energy and freedom to devote to the school in so far as teaching responsibilities could be given and this many did with loyal enthusiasm.

Conversely, there was an element of change: from time to time there was an influx of young newly qualified teachers who did not remain on the staff for very long. For instance, during the years 1945–1950 there were almost twenty teachers who worked in the school for something like two or less years, some leaving after one year and others after one or two terms.

Ten teachers left after a short period in order to take up a post elsewhere, suggesting that for various reasons Eastbourne was not their priority choice in the first place. Further examination shows that five moved to other schools in the Darlington Authority and were perhaps contracted to the Authority and not the school, and were transferred. Ten took posts with other authorities, emphasising that the changes were from personal choice.

The next largest number to leave the school was those marrying and moving away, probably to the area where the husbands worked. Three gave the general reason for leaving as domestic circumstances; three cited health reasons and three left the profession.

At the start of the new school year in 1957 five new teachers were appointed to the school having just qualified and having no experience; four completed about one year each and the other remained on the staff for only two years. In addition, two married ladies were employed on a temporary basis for one month each, teaching domestic science. The latter situation in particular points to difficulties with finding experienced teachers to fill vacancies.

In 1959 six newly qualified inexperienced teachers were appointed to the school: three served one year, two served for two years, and one resigned after three years and one term.

Entries in the log book point to the continued special position of the domestic science teachers on the staff, and problems with staffing that department: the total number of teachers on the staff is always given as x plus the number for domestic science.

There is an observation as early as March 1946 that there were only two domestic science teachers instead of three, and consequently the timetable adjusted: all third-year classes being given one day per week; twenty-four girls from two second-year classes having one day per week; but the other two second-year classes having one day per fortnight. An interesting comment following on from these arrangements was that there was a special timetable for the class remaining in school, emphasising the domestic science department's physical position outside the rest of the building, in what is clearly regarded as a separate unit. This *going to a special place* would have given the girls the feeling that the subject had extra significance.

Teacher shortages in the girls' school

Again, after the Easter holidays in 1946, there was only one instead of three domestic science staff, causing the normal programme to be continued in the third and fourth years but in the second year, girls had to be given extra needlework, hygiene, games, maths and English instead. In January 1947 no replacements could be found for staff who left in November and December, leaving the school short of a domestic science teacher. There were no replacements for Miss Armitage and Miss Snowdon, except Mrs D. Carmichael, who came as a temporary replacement and who ceased duty on 24 July 1947. In February there was a domestic science teacher and one other short at the start of the new half-year, when the head teacher interviewed the CEO!

Domestic science was not the only subject to be disrupted by a shortage of teachers: in February 1946, third-year biology was also suspended due to staffing difficulties.

Post-war raising of the school-leaving age

It must be re-emphasised that the school-leaving age was raised immediately the war ended and more children were obliged to stay at school. More pupils required more teachers at a time when the country was emerging from the disruption caused by the war, and, in spite of the Emergency Training Scheme, there were too few to satisfy the demand. Miss Fenby also complained about the strain placed on staffing by the introduction of a School Leaving Certificate class having repercussions on the staffing of the rest of the school. This was in 1947 when the number of pupils on roll was 463 with, for example, one first-year class having forty-eight pupils and another forty-seven, when there was no possibility of having half-classes for any subject. It was stated that many of the teachers had only two periods free from teaching for marking pupils' work and the preparation of lessons. Even with more such 'free' periods most marking and preparation was certainly completed outside pupil-contact hours.

Length of service of teachers working in the boys' school 1939–1963

Just as there was a core of long-serving teachers in the girls' school so there was in the boys' department: three, the head teacher, Mr Peacock and Mr Tranter, serving through the whole period 1936 to 1963.

In addition, Mr Farrage, metalwork teacher and a strong influence in the musical work of the school, was on the staff in 1936 but retired in 1950. Mr Foxon was appointed in 1946, became chief assistant master in 1952, serving a total of nine years, but returned as head teacher on the retirement of Mr Welford, serving a further eight years.

Mr Thornhill, appointed in 1948, taught mathematics for more than 28 years, becoming head of department. Mr Sherwood, appointed in the same year, was head of English, becoming deputy head in 1960, leaving after fourteen years to become a head teacher in Bedford.

Mr Foord was appointed metalwork teacher in 1951, became head of the craft department in 1967, and retired in 1974 after twenty-three years. Mr Sheppard joined the school in 1953 eventually taking over responsibility for music and retiring from the comprehensive school.

In addition, a further ten teachers served for between five and seven years during the period 1945 to 1963, taking over key positions as some older members of the staff moved on, largely having achieved promotion. Of this group three were described as emergency trained, in other words, completing their training in the colleges set up after the war to provide teachers during times of shortage and the raising of the school-leaving age. They served in the school for between five and six years each. Mr Brown, Mr Shipley, Mr Rand, Mr Pierce, Mr Robson and Mr Bullock only left the school on achieving promotion to other schools, clearly all competent and experienced members of staff.

In a school where the average total teaching staff for the period 1947–1962 was approximately head teacher plus 19 full-time permanent (and some unknown temporary and part-time) staff it is clear that there was a sizeable stable core of experienced teachers to promote an established ethos.

During the period 1944–59, apart from part-time and temporary staff, there were only some seventeen teachers who stayed in their post for between one term and two years.

In the early days of the Eastbourne Schools the staff consisted of head teacher and assistant teachers: in other words there were no differences in status, other than in terms of length of service, between assistant teachers, and it may be argued that the introduction of posts of responsibility, with salary enhancements attached, produced a previously non-existent rivalry between members of the teaching team.

Assistant teachers

The assistant teachers' team consisted of those qualified in the traditional teacher-training establishments, colleges catering specifically for those intending to enter the profession; the university education departments, turning out graduates; and the emergency-trained teachers from the emergency training colleges set up in response to the post-war demand for extra teachers, catering for those not returning from war service and the extra places required due to the raising of the school-leaving age.

Emergency-trained teachers

Various entries in the schools' log books indicate that emergency-trained teachers served in both the girls' and boys' schools. In October 1946 for example, Mr William Evans, emergency trained teacher, commenced duty and taught 'backward' children for five years. Similarly Mr E. Smith was appointed in April 1947 and taught in the school for eight years before moving to Newton Aycliffe Secondary Modern School. Mr K. Sherwood joined the school in august 1948 having followed a two-year course of training for teachers, probably as a part of the same scheme, and after serving for almost fifteen years as the head of the English department and deputy head, moved to become head teacher at the Jubilee School in Bedford.

At the girls' school Miss O. M. Nicholls was recorded as coming from Leavesden Green Emergency Training College, serving for nearly three years before marrying and moving abroad. Miss C. B. Veitch came from Drake Hall Emergency Training College and taught in the school for almost four years, after which she transferred to North Road Girls' school. Miss E. Coxon trained at the Warton Emergency Training College in Preston, and taught for seven years before moving to Windsor in Berkshire. Another was Miss B. Auckland from Wymondon Emergency Training College, who taught in the school for about six years before moving to Canada.

It is clear that the number of emergency training colleges was considerable and many continued to become recognised as established teacher-training colleges qualifying the ever-growing number of teachers required by an expanding system of secondary education.

It is also clear that students from the new colleges attended the Eastbourne Schools for their period of school practice: for instance on 24 March 1947 four emergency training college students attended in order to obtain schemes of work in connection with their school practice. In the following October a student from Peterborough Emergency Training College attended school in the morning to obtain details of the school practice due to commence on 10 November.

The newly qualified teachers were subject to visits by government inspectors: for instance, on 6 March 1950 Miss Johnson, HMI, visited the boys' school specifically to see the emergency trained teachers.

Graduate teachers

Courses for those intending to become graduate teachers usually lasted for four years and were conducted by the universities: for the first three years students generally concentrated on learning their subject disciplines and in the subsequent post-graduate year entered university education departments to follow courses in education theory, teaching methods and teaching practice.

Responsibility posts

Miss Fenby recorded that Miss J. O. Owen served as first assistant mistress for the periods 1946–47 and 1947–48; Mrs S. Thompson was responsible for special duties during 1946–47 and Miss E Gatenby for 1947–48, but their particular duties were not given.

A note for 4 July 1947 says that certain posts of special responsibility were granted – but there is no mention of who did the granting!

In March 1948, when Miss Owen was first assistant, posts of special responsibility were held by Miss E. W. Dover for domestic science and Miss E. A. Richardson for needlework.

At the boys' school in 1946 Mr William Robinson Richardson was chief assistant master and had been on the staff since the school opened in 1936. In January 1947, following the death of Mr Richardson, Mr John J. Clarke became chief assistant master but moved on to become head teacher at the Corporation Road Primary School, with Mr William Alan Brown, on the staff of the school, being appointed first assistant master with effect from 13 October. Mr Brown gained promotion to a headship in the West Riding and was replaced by Mr H. Foxon in April 1952. Mr Foxon had been on the staff since 1946, became head teacher at Albert Road Boys Secondary Modern School in 1955, returning to Eastbourne as head in January 1960.

The continuity, produced through the appointment of chief assistants from the staff, is a further factor in the maintaining of an established ethos in the school over a lengthy period.

In April 1949 first assistant was Miss Owen B.A. and there were two other responsibility posts held by Miss O. Hunnam B.Sc. and Miss C. McLeish BA.

In April 1950 holders of posts of responsibility were given as Miss J. Thompson and Miss E. Gatenby.

There is clear evidence from the boys' school, from a meeting of the school governors held at 2 p.m. on 16 July 1952, that a whole range of responsibility posts came into existence, apparently backdated to 1 April of that year.

Mr E. L. Robson became head of the physical education department (special responsibility payment £75), Mr G. Steele became head of science (allowance £75), Mr J. Peacock head of woodwork (allowance £50) and Mr J. Main head of art (allowance £50). Mr K Sherwood was appointed head of the english department in September.

Thus the hierarchical system of staff responsibility posts came into being.

The oversight of teaching standards

In a profession with the professionals themselves being trusted to manage and monitor standards, there have long been officers overseeing the work of teachers: at local authority level, school organisers or inspectors; and, at government level, teams of inspectors.

School Organisers

As well as having the professional appointments of chief and deputy officers to oversee the Education Service there were also school organisers, advisers, or local inspectors who were in schools regularly questioning teachers and monitoring the teaching.

According to the Eastbourne School log book records for the Fenby–Welford, years Darlington employed a schools organiser, a school meals organiser, an organiser for physical education and an organiser for domestic science. The latter was referred to, on one occasion, as an adviser, and there were visits to the school by a music adviser, the differences between 'organiser' and 'adviser' being unclear. Certainly, the organiser for schools seems to have had general oversight for all matters relating to primary and secondary schools. Miss Fenby recorded on 5 May 1952 that Mr J. Duggan was re-designated Organiser of Schools, as well as being associated with adult education.

It is also clear that there was an LEA Organiser for Youth Clubs, Miss Storer holding this position in January 1954, attending the school with the Deputy Education Officer Mr D. Green and the Youth Warden Mr E. R. C. Smith with reference to the youth centre canteen.

On 21 May 1952 Mr Duggan (then described as the LEA Organiser for Secondary and Primary Schools) visited the girls' school to consider the proposals for a school garden and on 24 June his visit was concerned with organisation and staffing. He visited the teachers and attended lessons. During his next visit on 30 September he again attended lessons and made enquiries about the aims and objectives of the education of pupils in the fourth year, the enquiry being continued on 6 October.

His Majesty's Inspectors of Schools (HMIs)

HMIs were the government's officers who frequently visited schools, inspecting staff, checking on equipment, viewing the teaching of subjects and generally looking at the life of the school.

During 1937 and 1938 particular interest was shown in the provision for domestic science and handicraft. This is in part due to the showpiece nature of the new school, illustrated by one HMI bringing his father on a visit!

One visit was made to inspect student teachers taking part in their biology teaching practice and two inspectors called with reference to those children now referred to as having learning difficulties.

The frequency of the visits of HMI Mr Walek recorded in the log entries points to his particular responsibility for the oversight of the Eastbourne Schools and others within the local geographical region.

The HMI Miss E. Johnson was a regular visitor by 1949, concerned with the general business of the schools: staffing, teaching and teacher appraisal, accommodation and grounds; but also attending special school functions such as the girls' school concert, their residential course at the LEA's youth hostel at Richmond and the Inter-house Music and Speech Festival at the boys' school. She is described as the District Inspector for Primary and Secondary Schools in Darlington as from 1 September 1947.

HMIs with special subject responsibility are also evident; Miss Dane for domestic science; Mr Dove and Mr Grimsdale for handicraft. There is the HMI with a non-teaching responsibility for the now established School Meals Service, Miss Erskine, illustrating the beginning of the move from an emphasis in schools on child learning to a greater concentration on child welfare.

From time to time, teams of HMIs went into schools for a period of a week or more, with individual inspectors making visits during previous weeks. At the end of 1950 the girls' school was subjected to a thorough inspection by a whole range of HMIs responsible for various subject disciplines and a full written report published. The boys' school general inspection took place in February 1951 and these were the only long and thorough inspections recorded as having taken place at Eastbourne during the Fenby–Welford years.

From the girls' school log 5 December 1950:

His Majesty's Inspectors of the Ministry of Education began the general inspection of the school.

The main panel of inspectors were –

Miss E Johnson – Miss Eacott – Miss Withers – Miss Daice [spelling not clear]

There was a one day inspection of the School Meals Service completed by Miss Erskine.

The inspection lasted from 5th to 8th December with a conference of the inspectors with the head mistress on the last morning.

Miss Johnson, accompanied by Miss Withers and Mr Ashurst, attended the Governors' Meeting held at 2.15 pm on 8th December and gave their report on the inspection.

A written report was received by the Education Authority on 14th April 1951.

There were visits of HMIs in the month prior to the general inspection 1950:

8.11.50: Miss E. Johnson all day attended the showing of the Fact and Faith Films – God of Creation and Dust or Destiny, shown to the Senior School.

21.11.50: Mr J. W. Horton all day Inspecting Music in the School.

22.11.1950: Miss Ghaleb pm continuing on 23.11.50 am Inspecting Physical Education.

27.11.50: Mr Hill all day Inspecting Art in the School.

With respect to the general inspection of the boys' school, there is almost an impression given that everything is low key and of no great significance. But the full report provided some interesting observations.

There is a strong impression that the physical and sporting aspects of the school are paramount, the inspectors stating that the physical education is a credit to the school. A special commendation was given for the voluntary work given by the head teacher, master in charge of PE and the many other staff in the organising and running of the annual outdoor activities, in particular the school camp.

The behaviour of the boys and their standards of work were seen to be very good; social training, turnout and courtesy being praised.

The building was still seen as well planned and attractive, with twelve classrooms, two workshops (each set out to take forty pupils!), art and science rooms, a gymnasium and library. The kitchen and dining buildings had at this time only been open for one year. The playing fields, shared with the girls' department, were said to be too small and in poor condition, drainage always having been a problem in the area. It was at this time the Authority was extending the grounds. There were grass areas in the quadrangle which were apparently more mud than grass, no doubt well run over and trampled on by the boys. There were, however, no gardening plots available for cultivation by pupils at this date, and their desirability was suggested.

The request for a lathe in the workshops arose from the fact that the original had been taken away for use elsewhere during the war.

The curriculum subjects were the same as those in the girl's school, except, of course for the provision of workshops for boys, with good reason, as the 15-year-old leavers were expected, very largely, to go into heavy industry, joinery and motor maintenance in garages.

A significant point is made where the inspectors comment on the number of teachers taking classes in several academic subjects: English, mathematics, geography and history. For example, fifteen teachers out of a total of twenty-four took classes in English. Specialists in charge of subjects set the syllabuses and gave support to assistant staff. The teaching of elements of English, as seen on the report forms, was emphasised, and in addition, reading for pleasure and the enjoyment of poetry. Form teachers took their own classes (that is, the registration groups) for mathematics. Standards of teaching were said to be high on the part of all teachers.

History included current affairs but was timetabled separately, being taken by the form teacher in half of the classes, the other half being taken by a part-time teacher. There was the additional observation that pupils listened to radio programmes through the school's Rediffusion system.

Concerning teaching methods, it was clear that class teaching, using such techniques as asking leading questions and requiring hands to be raised in the giving of answers, was used. Personal note taking was encouraged. A criticism was that there was too much direction from the teachers and not enough individual work, a fashionable trend leading to pupils working in groups on various projects. It was also said that common approaches were often used for all classes irrespective of the pupils' ability.

The general inspection of the boys' school was in February 1951. The following were the pre-inspection visits by HMIs:

9.1.51: Miss E. Johnson re: Inspection due in February.

10.1.51: Miss Johnson all day re: Inspection.

12.2.51: W. G. D. Inspected Art.

15.2.51: Mr L. F. Grimsdale inspected Woodwork, Metalwork, and Practical Drawing.

The General Inspection
27 February 1951 to 2 March 1951
The Panel of Inspectors
Miss E Johnson – Mr H. L. Willoughby – Mr T. B. LeCren
Mr A. H. Howlett – Mr K. L. Ashhurst
Miss Erskine inspected the kitchen the School Meals arrangements on 1 March 1951

2 March 1951 The Panel of Inspectors had a conference with the head master between 9.45 and 12.45.

In the afternoon HMIs Miss E. Johnson and Mr H. L. Willoughby reported to the Governors at their routine meeting.

An entry in the log book records that the inspectors expressed the need for a lathe in the metal workshop, more blackboard and display facilities and some storage arrangements for pupils' personal kit for physical education.

Teaching methods

Under the group title of handicrafts, woodwork, metalwork and technical drawing were taught. The workshops, however, were not fully used due to the shortage of teachers, there being only two specialists when four were required. It is noticeable that the great significance given to domestic science in the girls' school was not evident in the provision of workshop experience for the boys, raising the question of whether or not this was intentional. The school was very much physical and male orientated, giving the expectation that there would be an emphasis placed on practical activities, but there is strong evidence of attention being paid to academic study: an interesting point.

There is a similar question relating to the teaching of art. Although crafts, including lino cuts and clay modelling, were included, evidence suggests the further development of practical work could be achieved, particularly in the more senior years.

Music was a significant part of the curriculum but at this point in time some enthusiasm seems to have been lost due to the departure of the teacher in charge and the vacancy only being filled by a temporary appointment. Once again there was comment on the scheme of work not taking into account the different abilities of the boys. In spite of this, a school choir made up of boys selected from the junior classes was doing well. There was also a voluntary recorder-playing group and plans for the development of a group to play brass instruments were underway.

Positive comments were also made on the annual pantomime, house speech competitions and annual concerts.

The size and organisation of the schools

It is during the period of post-war years through to the start of the 1960s that the Eastbourne Schools developed their characters and established their reputation as successful places of learning. In some respects an established ethos and routine remained unchanged, but a more careful consideration of events demonstrates that significant changes were taking place. The intake of young people from the primary schools was one example, particularly in the mid 1950s when new primary schools were opened. Pressure on the schools, due to the growing numbers of youngsters wanting to attend, created problems. The school-leaving age, which was raised with the introduction of the 1944 Education Act to fifteen but allowed leavers to depart at Christmas and Easter as well as at the end of the school year, made changes necessary to the organisation of senior school classes throughout their final year, with the associated disruption associated with such changes in routine. The oldest could apparently leave early and go into the perceived more adult world of employment, while younger reluctant learners were bound to remain in school.

The unchanging aspects of the schools were the daily routine and the routine annual events, including the regular competitions organised through a competitive house system. There was also the interest generated through the celebration of national events, all of these occurrences adding to the creation of a positive ethos.

The intake of pupils from the primary schools

Between 1945 and 1947 pupils entering the schools came from primary schools in areas of the town which had not changed significantly since they were established in the developing industrial environment of the late nineteenth and early twentieth centuries: Dodmire, Haughton, St John's, Gurney Pease, Beaumont Street and Borough Road.

The 1950s peak for the girls' school intake could, without too much thought, be a reflection of the post-war baby boom; but with fathers returning home from 1945 into 1946, the bulge should reach the secondary schools in 1956–57, not five or so years earlier.

There is a steady rise in the numbers entering the girls' school between 1946 and 1950, while the change in the boys' school is more sudden, in 1949. In both schools during this period there is a significant growth in the intake from the main contributory primary school, Dodmire, suggesting an increase in the number of pupils attending that school.

Similar increases in numbers are seen in the figures for the other contributing schools although each always sends fewer children to the secondary schools each year than Dodmire. No comment on these increases is made by either of the head teachers, possibly supporting the notion of an understanding of the general growth in population.

There was, however, a significant growth in the total numbers of boys and girls coming to the schools: the girls' school intake growing from 82 in 1946 to 174 in 1950 with a fall back to 134 in 1951; the boys' school showing a continuous rise from 78 to 164.

The increase in numbers entering the schools continued throughout the post-war Fenby–Welford years although the upward trend was not uniform, there being a number of peaks and troughs in the otherwise steady rise.

The peaks of 1953 and 1955 in the boys' numbers are not seen in the figures for the girls' school, where fewer pupils entered the school between 1951 and 1953 followed by a steady rise peaking in 1959. The boys' numbers remained fairly uniform between 1955 and 1960 while the girls' were lower following the 1959 maximum. The low of 1961 is seen in the intakes of both schools.

Any sizeable variation in the intake requires changes to be made in the distribution of children into classes and in the number of classes in the year group. For instance, in September 1950 the girls' school has five classes in the first but only four in the second year. In 1959 there were six classes in each of the first and second years, four in the third year and three in year four.

In both departments 1952 is a year when the intake figures fall, a reduction from the previous year of eighteen, about 13.5%, for the girls, and five, about 3%, for the boys. In 1951 the 134 girls were placed in four classes, that is between 33 and 34 per group. In 1952, 116 girls were placed in three classes of about 38, indicating the organisational difficulties created by the change in intake numbers and the increase in size of the teaching groups, which actually increase when the intake is smaller.

The first pupils arrived in both departments from the Firth Moor School in 1956.

Haughton Primary School sent its last pupils to Eastbourne in 1957 (18 boys) and 1958 (1 girl).

Daily routine

Daily routine continued more or less unaltered throughout the Fenby–Welford years with pupils approaching from the Fairway but with boys and girls arriving at different times. Even so, there was the rule that the girls kept to the right of the entrance drive and boys to the left (seen from the building), passing through the central arch and maintaining these positions in the central quadrangle. Staff talked of the invisible line down the centre of the playground across which pupils dare not stray. On the top corridor, above the arch there were doors which were kept locked, emphasising the isolation from each other of the two schools. The rules for entry to the premises – in silence, on the sound of a whistle – as established during the foundation years continued to apply. In the boy's school, failure to conform resulted in any culprit being punished with a stroke of the cane.

The marking of the registers followed, the recording of attendances and late arrivals being obligatory, with any spare time given to quick tests in spelling and mental arithmetic.

Similarly, the established pattern for movement into the school halls for morning assembly continued. The boys marched in twos, approaching their given rows along the central aisle and smartly turning to face the left or right hand wall before moving into line and then, on the command 'face front', turning to face the stage. They remained standing, no chairs being provided. The headmaster entered when all classes were assembled. If a boy should pass out, it was presumed due to his not having had breakfast, he was carried outside and sat on a chair provided for the purpose – suggesting that this was not an uncommon occurrence.

When all the girls were in position in their hall there followed an element of the dramatic, a theatrical entry creating an atmosphere of awe with the emphasis on authority: led by the head girl carrying an open bible, Miss Fenby processed down the central aisle to mount the stage. It was not her way to stay there: during the service she would descend to the floor of the hall and move along the rows of girls to listen for those not singing.

The organisation of the classes

The pupils entering both the boys' and girls' schools continued to be placed in registration classes or forms, strictly grouped according to their ability, and in charge of a form teacher: a classification known as streaming in which, formally or otherwise, classes were recognised as top, bottom or in between, with status being attached to the hierarchy. The streams were the teaching groups, subdivided for practical subjects. If a pupil improved he or she could be promoted and, conversely, demoted where test results demonstrated a decline in standards.

Leaving dates and transfer of pupils

Until the end of 1948 the transfer of children from primary schools to secondary schools took place twice yearly, at the end of August or beginning of September, depending upon the date of the start of term, and in early February; after that the once-a-year transfer system was adopted, that is at the end of August or start of September.

Pupils left at the end of the term in which they became fifteen (unless remaining voluntarily in school for further education), leading to the necessary reorganisation of the classes in the senior part of the school.

The last year in which 14-year-olds could leave was 1947 and Miss Fenby reported: 'In Accordance with the 1944 Education Act the Spring Term ended on 31 March 1947 when girls who had reached the age of 14 years up to and including 1 April 1947 were eligible to leave. These totalled 19 and came from classes UIV (2 girls), LIV (2) U3.1 (9), and U 3.2 (6).'

Other pupils leaving in significant numbers were those transferring to the girls' high and technical schools at 13-plus: these losses possibly making necessary the rearrangement of classes after the summer holidays.

Details of the organisation of the girls' school were written in the school log book by Miss Fenby each half-year (until 1948) or annually and this provides a useful insight into the running of the school. The system for allocating pupils to teaching groups continued to be one of rigid streaming according to academic ability and the log book entry for September 1949 illustrates how this allocation was completed:

'Entrance Tests completed for all 11 + transfers – from results an exceptional amount of transferring and reorganisation necessary – new registers made out for all first years and attendances transferred.'

And in 1950, 4 and 9 September: 'Entrance Tests for Primary Transfers. Temporary Registers for First Years for one week'; the practice being continued throughout the period of Miss Fenby's headship.

On 5 May 1947 Miss Fenby writes: 'The timetable is to be tested and adopted for the Summer term' and gives reasons for this as allowing for the introduction of a remedial reading class, the inclusion of swimming arrangements for the whole of the first and second years, and to rearrange the teaching of domestic science using two staff instead of three. The upper and lower fourth-year groups continued without alteration but classes L3.1, L3.2, U2.1, U2.2, L2.1 and L2.2 were changed to have only one day in alternate weeks. U denotes the upper group and L the lower in the fourth year.

The point made here is that the school timetable had to be changed, tested to see if it worked and only then put into use at the beginning of the third term of the academic year. There are frequent references to the modification of the timetable and to its suspension. The term suspension of the timetable referred to a day or part of a day being used for some other activity than that on the usual timetable: the showing of a film, perhaps, or a performance by a visiting drama or music group.

The timetable was apparently changed each term and tested during the first week, and then approved, before becoming routine. Working to the timetable was referred to as 'specialisation' so when the timetable was not followed, for example during examinations, visits and so on, specialisation was said to be suspended.

Due to the increased number of pupils on roll it was decided to experiment with a ten-day timetable in February 1948, allowing for the better use of specialist rooms and longer sessions for the craft subjects.

The sizes of classes in relation to the number of teachers on the staff
Staffing for February 1948, the start of the second half-year, is given as nineteen, plus four domestic science staff. It is not clear if the head teacher was counted as one of the nineteen but, clearly, the domestic science teachers were seen as something special in addition to the rest of the staff. The roll at this time was 665; therefore, taking nineteen, plus head teacher, plus four domestic science staff, total twenty-four,

as the full staff, the pupil–teacher ratio is approximately 28:1. But the domestic science teachers would take half-classes and the head teacher would not take a regular teaching timetable. Teachers also had time free from pupil contact in order to complete marking and preparation so the 28:1 does not mean that the size of the classes taught was as small as this figure suggests.

At the start of the 1948 autumn term there were 671 girls on roll when the official accommodation was for 520 pupils. By the autumn of 1948 the staff consisted of fifteen permanent, four temporary supply and four domestic science teachers, a total of twenty-three. Giving the figure for the domestic science teachers separate from the rest, about 17% of the total work force, once again demonstrates the importance placed upon the subject in the girls' school.

The classes were arranged as follows: there was one group 5.2, described as the School Certificate Group; six groups in the senior school, U4.1, U4.2, L4.1s, 4.1j, L4.2s and L4.2j; two groups in the third year described as 'transition', 3.1 and 3.2; ten groups in the junior school, five in each year 1 and 2, with classes streamed from 1 to 5.

An additional note indicates that first- and second-year classes were very large, with fifty pupils in some groups, resulting from the large number on roll. The lack of available rooms for registration made it impossible to make up more classes although the large groups could be divided for the teaching of many of the subjects.

A special effort was also made to ensure that all girls completed a full year in the last year of compulsory education by arranging promotions from the transition groups at Christmas or Easter and making the senior course last for one and a half years. There was also effort made to ensure 'long settled periods without change of either room or teacher'. This is another significant factor: a change of teacher causes a break in continuity of teaching subject matter and style, causing at least some disruption to the pupils' learning. The more classes move about the building, the more chances there are for misbehaviour and, in any case, movement is time consuming; teaching time is lost.

By May 1949, after some 48 Easter leavers had departed and one member of staff being recorded as having resigned her post, the total on roll was 583. The headmistress then put into operation what she referred to as 'extensive adjustments and alterations' to the organisation of classes: those in the fourth year were decreased by two; numbers were adjusted in the second-year classes and in year one the previous seven classes were made into six.

The house system

The first entry in the Eastbourne Schools log books which refers to a house system was written by George Welford on 3 February 1938 when he wrote: 'Time Table suspended at 3.20 pm and a House Rally held in the Hall when the new boys were allocated to their respective Houses and the House System explained'. There is no mention of the girls being involved and the entry suggests that boys already in the school had been allocated to their houses at some previous date. The first recorded inter-house event took place on 12 March, the timetable being suspended at 3.10 p.m. for the House Competitive Cross Country Run, but it is not clear whether both boys and girls took part and it is very likely that they did not. On 7 July 1938 both girls and boys were involved when the timetable for the boys and girls in the second and third years was suspended for the Inter-House Musical Contest and Festival. By 26 January 1939 the boys and girls are once again seen to be treated separately when: 'The Boys held their Annual Inter-House Musical Festival'. However, on 26 July 1939, the last event before the disruption caused by World War II was described as the 'Sports and House Competitive Events' and could have been for all the pupils.

When, in August 1939 the separate boys' and girls' schools opened, similarities and differences between their two house systems emerged.

The most obvious of the similarities were the concepts of competition and co-operation: competition being encouraged between the houses while co-operation was required by members within their house teams.

There was also an attempt, best illustrated by the records of the girls' school, to encourage competition across a broad field of activities in order to cater for the variety of pupil talent and ability, both intellectual and physical.

The house system in the boys' school

The boys' school had four houses, each having its own shield displayed on the panelling at each side of the stage in the boys' hall, two on each side, still in place in 2009: they were Vane, Stanley, Pease and Havelock.

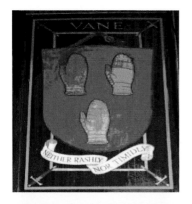

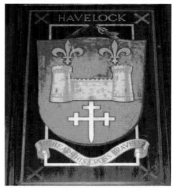

The log entry recording of the official opening of the school on 26 September 1936 demonstrates that the names used were those of families significant in Darlington, stating that The President of the Board of Education (The Right Hon. Oliver S. G. Stanley MC MP), kindly gave permission for the school house system to include one house to be known as Stanley House.

Although the school at the time had by necessity both boys and girls on roll, it is apparent that the initial house system was that which continued into the boys' school in 1939.

The house system in the girls' school

The lectern was presented to the school by the staff and pupils on the occasion of its celebrating the twenty-first anniversary of its foundation, held on 22 July 1957.

The six houses were given the names of abbeys situated in the north-east of England: Byland, Easby. Eggleston, Fountains, Rievaulx and Whitby, and the pupils in each class or form were divided and placed into houses. Members of staff were generally attached to one house and remained with that house. Exceptionally, the domestic science staff did not. The badge incorporates the symbols which represent each of the abbeys in the house system.

The Girls' school badge as carved on the lectern

The log book entry for 30 January 1948, 'End of half-year Special Assembly for House Competition Results and cups awarded; this being the first half-year since the adoption of the House system in this School', indicates that the house system commenced at the girls' school in 1947.

House activities in the girls' school

There was one major day-long outing held each year which encompassed the house system: the annual visit to the abbeys. Another annual inter-house event which was very positively encouraged was the domestic science competition and exhibition.

In addition there were the annual inter-house athletics meetings and swimming galas which led on to the equivalent inter-schools competitions held during the summer term. But there were also other inter-house competitions; in fact, almost any subject was considered suitable for inclusion in these events.

The girls' school domestic science exhibition took place during either the spring or summer term each year.

The perceived importance of domestic science in the girls' school continued from the foundation years, through the 1939–45 war and throughout Miss Fenby's years as headmistress, the annual Domestic Science House Competition and Exhibition helping to emphasise the significance of the subject

It is quite clear from log book entries that extra enthusiasm was generated for the subject by making it one element in the house competition. For example at 2.25 p.m. on 24 March 1954 there was an exhibition of cookery by finalists in the domestic science competition.

The girls prepared dishes in class and these were marked by the domestic science department teachers. The teachers were put under pressure to extract the highest possible standards of work from the pupils, encouraging them to display their work in an attractive manner. A special display was arranged for the best dishes produced by each house and other subject teachers, pupils and sometimes parents were invited to view the products. Miss Manfield, a long-serving teacher in the domestic science department, believed that, in spite of the pressure to do well, these occasions were enjoyable and sometimes amusing: she commented, some of the staff comments 'made me smile and keep my mouth shut!'

Other aspects of the girls' work were sometimes combined with the display of cookery and the whole school were taken to view the work of those girls achieving the highest standards, parents and friends being invited into the school during an afternoon session. Miss Fenby reported that on 18 July 1951, 'the school was open to visitors between 2 and 4 pm. Exhibitions of Needlework, Craft, Art and Domestic Science were arranged together with other school activities. Some 250 parents attended.'

The culmination of all the hard work and enthusiasm generated by the house system came at the end of the autumn and summer terms when the girls' school held its half-year and end-of-year house ceremonies, when the annual results of the inter-house competitions were announced and awards, cups, and trophies presented.

House activities in the boys' school

The writer of history relies on available evidence and it must be repeated here that, when relying on the reports in the log books of the Eastbourne Secondary Modern Schools, Miss Fenby always reports far more and in far more detail than Mr Welford. When it appears that the girls' school house activities are so much more inclusive than those of the boys' school this may be the actual situation or merely reflect the difference in reporting.

The boys' house competition events appear to be concentrated on physical activities: the Annual Cross Country, Annual School Athletics Competition and the Annual Swimming Gala. It is only in the years between 1946 and 1950 that there is any reference to different events, when an Annual Inter-House Music Festival is recorded.

From the log book entries shown below the Competitive Musical and Drama Festival was held each year between 1946 and 1950, and as that of 19 May 1949 is described as the thirteenth event this must have been an annual occurrence since the opening of the school in the year 1936–37.

> 17.4.46: Inter-house Musical Festival 2 p.m.–4-30 p.m.
>
> 23.7.47: In the afternoon, the Tenth Annual Inter-house Music and speech Festival held commencing at 2p.m.
>
> 13.5.48: Inter-house Musical Festival 2.00 p.m.–4.30 p.m.
>
> 19.5.49: 13th Annual Inter-house Music and Speech Festival was held in the Hall commencing at 2 p.m. in the afternoon.
>
> 10.5.50: Inter-house Music and Speech Festival held.

It is clear that the school year was punctuated by regularly held events, forming the basis of an established routine, a stability; and stability, minimum change, is significant in the running of the schools.

End-of-term activities

The final days of each term were invariably marked by both regular activities, occurring every year at about the same time, and special events arranged as circumstances dictated. For example, the end of the autumn term, the period approaching Christmas, was celebrated in the girls' school according to the traditions of the Christian Church. The regularity and similarity of the log entries relating to the carol service is certainly evidence of a strong tradition. There is no evidence in the log books of this being the case in the boys' school, where the major end-of-term event was the production of the annual pantomime.

The girls' school also held a concert, or drama or speech competition, at the end of the autumn term, the two schools demonstrating a different style in their presentations. The girls' department appeared to pay more attention to the Christmas traditions and to a more overt effort to educate the girls in music, speech and drama. The boys' wrapped up their music, speech and drama work in an apparently more light-hearted project, the pantomime.

The spring term

The following are regular activities recorded as taking place largely at the end of the spring term at the girls' school during the period 1947–1962. There may have been others which were overlooked. It is possible that some regular activities at both schools were thought to be such a matter of normal routine that they were not worth mentioning.

Opening after the Christmas and New Year holiday the approximate duration of the spring term was from the first or second week in January until late March or mid April, when the school closed at noon. There was a mid-term holiday at the end of February.

The needlework department produced costumes for productions and the domestic science department laundered the garments. Light refreshments were provided for governors and other visitors, again with pressure to produce the highest possible standards. School uniform had to be worn by pupils on duty and it also had to be perfectly displayed.

On a lighter note: at one event and at a crucial moment, the tea urn was plugged into a faulty socket and, somehow, when switched on, plunged the stage into complete darkness. It is an understatement to say that the domestic science department were not the most popular people present on that evening.

The regular activities taking place in the spring term at the girls' school fall into three groups: annual concert, domestic science exhibition, and house competitions.

The annual school concert, another of the regular events which focussed the school on a particular aspect of education, brought together the efforts of a wide spectrum of teachers and pupils and helped to develop the school ethos. At these annual events it could be said: this is the school we all belong to and are happy to do so. This is particularly noticeable in the work of the girls' school but less so in the boys' department.

28 .3.50: First Years held their Annual Drama Performance 2–3 pm in the School Hall.

15.3.51: Rehearsal for Easter music.

2.4.52: At 7 pm Annual Concert: Music, Drama, Mime and Dance. A successful evening – some 120 girls took part, and an audience of approximately 400 attended.

The regular activities recorded as taking place largely at the end of the spring term at the boys' school during the period 1947–1962 fall into two groups: outdoor physical activities and music and drama.

The recorded entries for music and drama suggest there was less enthusiasm for this style of activity during the spring term and show a decline in the number of such events taking place during the latter part of the period.

Outdoor physical activities:

10.4.46: Inter-House Annual Cross Country Run 3 pm.

23.3.49: Inter-House Annual Cross Country Run 3 pm.

13.4.49: Annual Staff v School 1st XI Football match at 3 pm.

5.4.50:   Annual Staff v School 1st XI Football match at 3 pm.

18.3.53: Inter-House Annual Cross Country Run 3 pm.

19.3.53: A tea Party followed by films arranged for all pupils who took part in the Annual Pantomime last December starting at 4.30 pm.

2.4.53:   Inter-House Annual Cross Country Run.

28.3.61: The Annual Cross Country Run over the Lingfield Lane course.

29.3.61: The school watched a match between the School 1st XI Football and the staff.

17.4.62: Cross Country run cancelled due to wet weather.

Not exactly physical but interesting:

5.4.50:   Cast of the Pantomime entertained to tea by the school.

19.3.53: A Tea Party followed by films arranged for all pupils who took part in the Annual Pantomime last December starting at 4.30 pm.

Other spring term events

Darlington Non-competitive Music Festival, later described as the Competitive Music Festival, also took place annually and continues to do so today.

17.4.46: Inter-House Music Festival 2 till 4.30 pm.

15.3.48: School Choir gave a concert at the North Road Wesleyan Church in the evening.

2, 3 and 4.4.52: Four One Act Plays presented in the evening.

4th year – The King's Highway

2nd & 3rd years – Scuttleboom's Treasure

2nd year – The Crimson Coconut

1st year – The Pie and the Tart

30.3 and 1.4.53: Schools Drama and Choral Concert held in the Hall each evening.

The introduction of pupils to music was established in Darlington's education system before the 1939–45 war and continued to play a significant part in the curriculum during the Fenby–Welford Years.

The summer term

The opening of the schools after the Easter holiday took place during the period of the second week in April and the first in May; the mid-term holiday was the week of Whitsuntide; and in addition Ascension Day was also a holiday.

There were also closures for municipal and parliamentary elections, and a half-day closure for the afternoon of the Darlington Secondary and Grammar School Sports.

Regular summer term events in both schools were: the annual inter-house sports competition; The Darlington Schools' Athletic Association Inter-School Sports; the annual inter-house swimming gala; and the Darlington Schools Inter-School Swimming Gala.

Regular events which became almost legendary were: the girls' school visit to the abbeys; the boys' school excursion day; and the boys' school camp.

The annual house sports

The annual school athletic sports were a part of the inter-house competition in both schools and generally took place in May or June.

The weather was not always perfect: in 1947 the meeting at the girls' school had been postponed after twenty minutes due to heavy rain and was eventually held on 26 June at 6.30 p.m. The boys' meeting had been held at 6.30 p.m. the previous evening.

The girls' school in particular reported that the spectators included governors, HMIs, friends and parents.

By 1950 the sports were being held in the afternoon. The grounds were not ideal. As early as 1947 the headmistress asked for favourable consideration to be given to the levelling and draining of the playing fields, and the total area was considered inadequate for both schools. By 1952 the Authority had acquired extra space on adjoining land.

Here are a selection of log book entries:

18.5.49: Boys' School 13th Annual Inter-House Athletic Sports held on the School playing fields commencing 6 pm.

30.5.51: Girls' School: Owing to inclement weather, the Annual School Sports arranged for this afternoon were postponed but the special Folk Dancing Display was held in the Quadrangle. Many parents and friends, including Miss E. Johnson HMI, were present. As a contribution to the Festival of Britain programme, the Folk Dancing included, English, Scottish, Irish and Welsh.

21.5.52: Boys' School Inter-House Sports held in the afternoon commencing at 2 pm.

28.5.52: Girls' School Annual School sports held in the afternoon from 2.15 in the new extension playing field. Attended by School governors, parents and friends.

29.5.57: Boys' school: The Annual Inter-house Sports were held 2 pm–4.15 pm.

5.6.62: Girls' School Annual sports held in the afternoon attended by many parents and friends. The Chairman of the School Governors, Councillor C. Spence presented the cup to the winning House.

The Darlington Schools' Athletic Association Inter-School Sports for secondary schools were at first held on the Feethams's Field, then at the Rolling Mills Sports Stadium and eventually at the Longfield site. The schools closed for the afternoon.

As illustrated by the log book entry for June 1956, trophies were awarded to schools winning the various events and, significantly, prestige was added to the competition by the organisation of an occasion when a good turn-out of civic dignitaries presented the awards: 'The Deputy Mayor and Mayoress of Darlington, Councillor Mrs G. Tremewan Supported by the Chairman of the Education committee Alderman H. P. Bell JP attended the School 9.30 a.m. and presented the Inter-Schools sports trophies won by the School.'

Some further log book entries:

30.6.49: The Girls' School closed at 12.15 pm Inter-School sports for Grammar and Secondary Modern Schools (Schools Athletic Association) Feethams Field 2 pm.

5.7.51: The Boys' School closed in the afternoon for the Inter-Schools Sports.

5.7.51: Inter-School sports held at Feethams at 2 pm School closed for the afternoon.

Eastbourne Girls won the coronation Cup for the highest number of points and the Eclipse Trophy for the senior relay.

22.6.54: School closed in the afternoon for Inter-Secondary Schools' Sports at Feethams Cricket Ground.

14.6.55: Inter-Schools sports at the Rolling Mills Stadium.

29.6.55: Girls' school Four pupils in the county sports.

Norma Greenwell 2nd in the discus, Moira Bowes 1st in the long jump 16 ft 8 inches. Moira went to the Nationals in Manchester (13–14.7.55) where she became the Schools National Junior Champion with a jump of 16' 9 ½". The

County Durham Team won the Championship Shield for the first time.

20.6.62: The Boys' School closed for the afternoon session for the Inter-School Sports at Longfield Road Stadium. We were second to the Grammar School. We won the three lap race.

The Darlington Education Authority encouraged all children to learn how to swim, establishing a programme of swimming lessons for the schools at the Town Baths which were located in Gladstone Street. As a part of this programme individual schools held their own swimming galas each year and took part in the inter-schools galas.

Here are a selection of log book entries regarding the annual house swimming gala

20.7.49: Girls' School Swimming Gala. The school held its first Annual Swimming Gala in the Second class Baths at 9 am (owing to very restricted accommodation it was with regret that parents and friends could not be invited – neither could all the pupils from the school be accommodated). Pupils who did attend were all 4th years, all swimmers, and 'Never Absent Never Late Group' 220 pupils in all, together with nine members of staff. The competitions were held under official regulations and outside judges from Darlington Swimming Club gave their services.

12.7.50: Girls' School Swimming Gala in Gladstone Street Baths at 2 pm. The Whole School attended together with visitors, parents of competitors, The Mayor and Mayoress (Councillor and Mrs Dougill), The Chairman of the Baths Committee (Alderman Chandler), Mrs Chandler and Members of the Education committee. The function was an outstanding success from every point of view.

21.6.51: Boys' School Inter-House Swimming Gala held in the Gladstone Street Baths in the afternoon.

24.5.55: Boys' School Inter-House Swimming Gala held in the Public Baths, in the afternoon 2 pm–4.15 pm.

13.5.60: Boys' School the Annual School Swimming Gala held at the Gladstone Street Bath. Owing to torrential rain only competitors were there at the start, but the rest of the school came down as transport available.

1.6.61: Boys' School The whole school attended the Gladstone Street Baths during the afternoon session for the Annual School Swimming Gala.

There was also a Darlington Schools Inter-School Swimming Gala Although Mr Welford may have applauded the boys' swimming in a similar way, he did not enter any details in the school log book.

In 1961 Mr Foxon did record: 'Town Swimming Gala. Runners-up to Grammar School, one point behind. Won Senior Relay Shield and individual Diving Championship Cup.'

The Darlington Schools Inter-School Swimming Gala
A selection of log book entries

17.7.50: Inter-School Swimming Gala at 6.45 pm. Girls Championship Trophy awarded to Eastbourne.

4.7.52: Inter-Schools swimming Gala. Girls Championship Cup won by Eastbourne Girls. The Cup for Diving was won by Denise Dixon, who was also first in the 1 length back stroke and 1 length breast stroke.

The boys' school annual Ascension Day holiday excursion

The boys' annual Ascension Day excursion was one of the major events of the boys' school year, the significance of which can only be appreciated by reading the entries made in the school log year after year about the journeys, by Mr Welford. Firstly there is the head teacher's enthusiasm for holding the event every year; secondly there is the willingness of staff to give up a day's holiday to take part; and, thirdly there is the high level of pupil attendance.

Some of the excursions take on the character of expeditions, albeit only day long, there being no overnight camping involved. To climb Helvellyn is no afternoon stroll – it is after all a mountain that is being climbed: its paths have steep gradients; straying from the paths, the unwary are suddenly faced with precipitous drops; the surface to be crossed is rough and rocky; and there is always Striding Edge to negotiate. This must have been a challenge.

On several occasions the large party was divided into two groups which were each taken to a different side of a piece of boggy Pennine upland: Dufton in the west and Langdon to the east. They then made their way above the great glacial trough below High Cup Nick, or by Cauldron Snout waterfall to meet up and cross each other's paths somewhere in the middle. Crossing the peat-covered upland, with its unsuspected rivulets of peat-stained water rambling here and there, the boys could easily stumble and fall in.

Eastbourne boys went this way – to the Lake District

Helvellyn and Red Tarn

26.5.49: Thursday. School on holiday. 125 boys, 18 masters and 7 guests went on expedition to climb Helvellyn. Four motor coaches were engaged and the mountain was successfully climbed. The day was highly successful and the weather perfect.

The Lake District 10.5.56: School closed. An Annual School Excursion to the Lake District took place. 308 pupils in charge of 17 staff and 3 York students. In addition 3 Staff and 27 members of the School Angling club went to Langdon Beck in Teesdale on a fishing expedition.

Striding Edge and Red Tarn

11.5.61

School closed. 115 boys & 10 adults visited Ullswater, down the Lake by steamer. Home via Kirkstone Pass. 160 boys & 14 adults visited Corbridge, Housesteads, returned via Allendale and Weardale.

Eastbourne boys also went this way – in the North Pennines

6.5.48: Three bus loads travelled from Darlington to Langdon Beck in Teesdale; three bus loads travelled to Grafton in the Eden Valley. The Langdon Beck party crossed the Pennines via Cauldron Snout, Birkdale, High Cup Nick to Dufton and the Dufton party travelled to Langdale Beck in the reverse direction. 187 pupils and 7 staff took part. The day was highly successful and the weather perfect.

18.5.50: Annual School outing to Bilsdale, Helmsley, Bylands Abbey, Kilburn etc returning via Thirsk and Northallerton. Six motor coach loads and party numbered 223 pupils and 20 staff and their wives.

3.5.51: 246 boys and 16 staff and 8 school friends crossed the Pennines. Half the party travelled from the west: Dufton, High Cup Nick, Birkdale, Cauldron Snout and Langdon Beck; the other half in the reverse direction.

View from above Cauldron Snout

22.5.52: Thursday. Annual school Excursion to Middleton-in-Teesdale, Holwick, High Force over the Fells to Falcon Clints, Cauldron Snout, Birkdale, Widdybank Fell and Langdon Beck.

High Force in Teesdale

27.5.54: 328 boys in charge of 18 staff formed two parties: one going into Swaledale, the other into Wensleydale. The divide between the two dales was crossed by each party. Ten motor coaches were hired for the occasion.

Swaledale

26.5.55: Pennine crossing 332 pupils and 23 adults joined the journey. Half the party started from Dufton in Westmorland, the other half started from Langdon Beck in Teesdale, County Durham.

The view from High Cup Nick

High Cup Nick

Ascension Day Excursions made by the boys in other years, demonstrating inevitable repetitions and variations

14.5.53: 273 pupils in charge of 14 members of staff and five friends travelled in 8 motor coaches into Cleveland – visiting Rievaulx Abbey, Helmsley, Ampleforth, Byland Abbey, Coxwold and Kilburn.

30.5.57: School closed. The Annual Ascension Day Excursion was held and 371 boys in 9 motor coaches and staff travelled to Holwick by motor and then walked via Juniper wood, High Force, Blea Beck, Cronkley Fell, Cronkley Crags, Falcon Clints, Cauldron Snout, Widdy Bank Fell, Cow Green to Langdon Beck where the whole party had tea returning for home at 6.15 p.m.. The weather was delightful.

15.5.58: Thursday. The Annual Ascension day Excursion was held and 354 boys in 9 motor coaches and in charge of 20 staff travelled via Teesdale, Barnard Castle and Weardale, St John's Chapel and over the divide to Langdon Beck in Teesdale again to Cow Green, Widdy Bank Fell and Cauldron Snout. Tea at the Langdon Beck Hotel after which returning to Darlington. Weather delightful.

7.5.59: Ascension Day. Schools Annual Exursion took place and 364 boys in 10 motor coaches and in charge of 20 staff travelled to Upper Teesdale. The coaches were left at Langdon Beck and the party walked to the Tees, joining near Cronkley Crags and proceeded up stream via Falcon Clints to Cauldron Snout, Birkdale, Widdy Bank Fell to Cow Green where we rejoined the motor coaches. After tea at the Langdon Beck Hotel we returned home – the outing was very successful.

George Welford retired at the end of 1959.

26.5.60

The School was closed for Ascension Day. 278 boys and 18 staff took part in an outing to Wharfedale.

The girls' school annual Ascension Day holiday excursion

Ascension Day was not the major outing day at the girls' school although small groups did take the opportunity of making visits on this holiday. For example, in 1952 a party of girls and staff visited Durham and this was repeated on several other occasions. By 1961 those girls working for the Duke of Edinburgh's Award, nearly fifty each year, completed the Expedition Section, visiting Marrick Priory and walking to Reeth.

Eastbourne Girls visited these places:

10.5.56 Ascension Day Closure: A party of 2nd year pupils visited Finchale Priory and Durham Cathedral.

30.5.57: One party visited Durham Cathedral and Museum, another Raby Castle and Auckland Castle.

15.5.58 Ascension Day Closure: School journeys to the Tees, Piercebridge and Gainford; and a party of 58 visited Raby Castle and Staindrop Church, Escombe church, the River Wear and Bishop Auckland.

On 26 April 1948 the first journey to the abbeys took place. The girls' houses took the names of abbeys in the area: Fountains, Rievaulx, Bylands, Whitby, Easby and Egglestone. Rievaulx and Byland Houses combined, visiting both abbeys, Bowes Museum and the Meeting of the Waters. The other two pairs of houses visited their abbeys and Ripon Cathedral.

These annual outings became a major event in the school year, taking place in the summer term, and were organised by the senior staff. The girls were expected to wear the school uniform on these visits and an educational content vigorously followed. When abbey staff were not available to act as guides the teachers were expected to be prepared to do this.

The minority of girls who did not go on the outings, perhaps due to their being subject to travel sickness or unwilling to pay the nominal charge, were expected to attend school for the normal hours.

Visits were rotated in such a way that each girl would have the opportunity to visit each of the abbeys during her spell of education in the school.

Reports of the girls' school visits to the abbeys

In 1948 the groups left school at 9.30 a.m. using thirteen private buses and returned at 7 p.m. Financial assistance of one shilling per girl was given by the Education Authority, the girls contributed four shillings each and the School Fund was used to cover additional expenditure. The weather was superb, with sunshine all day.

The 1949 journey took place on 18 July when 303 girls and 16 staff left school at 9.30 a.m. in 11 buses.

There were about 580 pupils on roll at this time, and as this was not a holiday, the remainder of the girls were in school in the charge of five staff.

On 23 June 1950 twelve busloads left at 9.30 a.m. returning at 7 p.m. The total number of girls taking part was 348 out of total roll of 564, and these were divided into four groups, 97 girls going to Whitby, 83 to Fountains, 83 to Easby and Eggleston, and 95 to Byland and Rievaulx. Fifteen staff accompanied the parties. There were also nine girls and their leader from Austria who went on the journey. Four staff with 164 girls remained in school with those who did not take part.

The importance attached to these excursions is illustrated by the annual entries made by Miss Fenby in the log, for example: 'The journey to the abbeys was, perhaps, the most successful yet held; the weather was ideal – and due to preparatory preparation – the girls derived full benefit in every way.'

15.6.51: Fourteen buses left school at 9.30 a.m. returning at 7 p.m.

The total number of girls attending was 428, accompanied by 20 members of staff, 56 going to Whitby, 82 to Fountains, 161 to Egglestone and 129 to Byland and Rievaulx. 125 pupils less absentees (8 on vacation and 28 other absences) remained in school with two members of staff.

With ideal weather conditions and thorough preparation for the journeys, the whole project was most successful. Included in the appropriate journeys were visits to Bowes Museum (especially the Festival of Britain Special Exhibition Rooms), Kilburn, Newburgh Priory and Ripon Cathedral.

27.6.52: 12 buses left school at 9.30 am and returned at 7 p.m.

331 girls took part, 96 going to Whitby, 97 to Fountains, 65 to Easby and Egglestone, 73 to Byland and Rievaulx, accompanied by 17 staff.

The weather was ideal, the preparation thorough and the whole project most enjoyable and successful. Included in the programme were visits to Bowes Museum, Ripon cathedral, Kilburn (Wood Craft mouse exhibition), Coxwold and St Mary's Church Whitby.

Note: following the weekend break, the internal school examinations took place

26.6.54: The Annual Visit to the Abbeys took place on 26th June 1954 when 349 girls took part supervised by 15 staff and the headmistress.

There were about 441 pupils on the roll and those not going on the trip were supervised by three staff.

The annual excursions to the abbeys took place every year during Miss Fenby's headship between 1948 and 1962.

The given number of pupils on roll is the figure for the previous September, consequently by the time the excursions took place in the summer term some girls will have reached the school-leaving age and left for employment.

The head teacher is sometimes one of the staff on the journey but at other times she remained in school as one of those teachers supervising girls who did not take part in the visits.

June 1955: 12 buses left school at 9.30. 373 pupils and 16 staff took part. Fountains Hall included this year. Summer weather prevailed and a larger number of pupils than ever enjoyed this pleasing project.

Visit to the Abbeys 1962: 499 plus 24 staff

Two staff and 15 pupils remained in school – 26 pupils were absent!

The weather was again described as "ideal" and the excursion as 'happy and enjoyable'.

Girls' School Annual Excursion to the Abbeys				
Year	No on Roll	No of Girls taking part	No of Staff taking part	No of guests taking part
1948	549	400 plus	22	
1949	671	303	16	
1950	653	348	15	
1951	648	428	20	
1952	595	331	17	
1953	512	347	17	
1954	517	349	16	
1955	520	373	16	
1956	525	388	16	
1957	522	397	18	
1958	578	422	18	2 students
1959	591	458	19	
1960	658	522	22	
1961	676	559	28	
1962	647	499	24	2 students

A few more observations on the visits to the abbeys

On 29 April 1948 a 'School Effort' is recorded. Contributions were collected for a jumble sale and these were auctioned from 6.30 p.m. onwards. The whole staff, prefects, house captains, vice captains and sports captains, were on duty. The purpose was to raise money to support the house outings, keeping the amount to be paid by the children to four shillings, which, the headmistress said, made it possible for all children to take part.

This was a splendid bonding of the school, giving a united purpose to all. Yet, some did not take part and there is no evidence showing who these people were or why they did not join in.

The Mouse furniture.
The log entry for 1952 includes a reference to the visit to 'Kilburn (Wood Craft mouse exhibition)' and it was in 1957 that the lectern, produced at the woodcraft centre, was presented to the school.

The boys' school annual camp

Another major event in the life of the boys' school was the annual camp, initiated by Mr Welford when the school opened. There are no camps recorded as taking place during the war years but they were resumed in 1949 and continued into the early 1960s when they were no longer held each year, being held for last time in 1964 at Newton Mulgrave. The significance of the event in the life of the school, the number of boys taking part, the staff involved and the organisation required are demonstrated in the frequency and fullness of the head teacher's log entries, which are noted here.

In the summer immediately preceding the outbreak of war the third annual camp was held at Eastgate in Weardale. There were fifty-four boys (including four old boys) and ten masters in the party. There is a report of the camp being held at Eastgate again in 1951 but there is puzzling note suggesting that Mr Welford explored the possibility of going into Wensleydale instead. One wonders if he meant to write 'Weardale'.

> 25.4.51: Mr G. W. Welford and Mr J. Waddleton visited Wensleydale re: Annual Camp – supply of tents, proposed site – left school at 11 a.m.
>
> 27.7.51: Friday. A party of 24 boys in charge of Messrs W. A. Brown, J. Waddleton, J. Peacock, and G. W. Lorraine left School at 10.45 a.m. to travel by the 11.25 a.m. train to Eastgate for the Annual Summer Camp – the remainder travelled to

Eastgate on the 6.45 p.m. train. Mr G. Welford, Miss Knott, Miss Beadle, Mr J. J.Clarke (visiting master).

Another site near Reeth was used in 1949:

22.7.49: An advance party of the School Camp in charge of M. W. A. Brown, Mr J. Waddleton, Mr E. Smith, Mr J. K. Farrage and Mr G. Brockway left at 10.00 a.m. by motorbus for Reeth. 30 boys were in the party.

Friday 4.15 p.m. School closed for the Midsummer Holidays. A party of 137 pupils in charge of the headmaster and 16 Assistant masters left school at 5 p.m. for a week's camp at Reeth, Yorks. Three guest masters (Mr J. J.Clarke, Mr J. Redpath and Mr D. Lockhart) and four guest boy campers also attended. The Camp was held 22 July to 29 July 1949 and the charge per head was One Pound Ten Shillings.

Another favourite site for the camp was at Castleton, North Yorskshire:

24.7.50: Twenty-one boys from year 1 in charge of Mr Foxon and Mr Richardson commenced a week-long residential course at Earls Orchard Youth hostel Richmond. This was arranged to recompense the boys who had volunteered to attend the annual school camp at Castleton and who were not accepted because numbers attending had to be restricted to Years 2, 3 and 4.

28.7.50: Friday. The advance party for the Annual School Camp at Castleton, North Yorkshire, consisted of Messrs W. A. Brown, J. Waddleton, J. Peacock, and E. Smith and 20 boys. They left for Castleton by the 6.58 a.m. train. The main body of 45 boys and Messrs G. W. Welford, J. J.Clarke, K. Sherwood, I. Harris, T. B. Shipley, S. J. Thornhill, S. Main, accompanied by Mrs G. Welford, Miss Knott, Miss Beadle left by the 5.29.

25.7.52: Friday. 9.15 pm 38 pupils in charge of Messrs J. Peacock, E. L. Robson, K. Sherwood and W. D. Peirce left as the advance party for the Annual School camp at Castleton, North Yorkshire. The following members of the Staff attended the camp later. The Headmaster, Mr S. Main, Mr W. G. Loraine, Mr S. J. Thornhill and two guest masters Mr J. J.Clarke and Mr J. Harris.

The School closed for the summer holidays 3.34 p.m.

There is something about this which gives the whole thing an element of an old boys' reunion or club – an atmosphere of all good mates together which characterised the school staff.

In 1953 the camp was at Dunsdale, near Guisborough, north of the Cleveland Hills.

> 24.7.53: Friday. Advance Party for the Annual School Camp 38 boys in charge of Messrs E. Smith, J. Peacock, E. L. Robson, K.M. Sherwood left school at 9.30 a.m. for Dunsdale near Guisborough and a second party of 33 boys in charge of M. J. D. Rand left school at 1.45 p.m. for Dunsdale. The camp week extended from 24 July–31 July

In 1954 and 55 the school held bring-and-buy sales to raise money for camping equipment.

Camps held in the Whitby area:

> 23.7.54: An advance party of 32 boys in charge of Messrs J. Peacock, W. D. Peirce, E. Smith, and E. L. Robson left at 9 a.m. for Whitby for the Annual School Camp. A second party of 35 boys in charge of Messrs J. D. Rand and C. E. Robson left at 2.00 p.m. The final party of 13 boys in charge of Messrs G. W. Welford., F. Foxon, B. Richardson, B. F. Sheppard, S. J. Thornhill, Mrs G. Welford, Miss Knott, Miss S. Henderson and three old boys also accompanied the party. Full camp complement was 103 persons. Mr J. J. Clarke was present as guest staff helper.

> 27.7.56: Annual camp held at Whitby 27 July–3 August 1956. Advance Party of 24 boys left in charge of Messrs J. Peacock, J. R. Foord. E. Smith, E. L. Robson, W. D. Peirce and J. T. Pauton. 8.30 p.m. [should this be a.m.?] A second party of 24 boys left

at 5 p.m. in charge of Messrs S. J. Thornhill, F. A. Jacobi, J. R. Bates, W. Hetherington and G. W. Welford.

25.7.58: Friday 4.15 p.m. School closed for the Midsummer Vacation. Annual Camp held at Moorgate Leas Farm Whitby 25th July–1st August. The Advance Party consisted of Messrs A. F. Foord, J. Peacock, W. T. Unwin and W. D. Peirce followed by 40 boys in charge of Mr B. F. Sheppard and later 40 boys in charge of Mr R. Whiteside, both parties travelling by motor bus (limited). The total party consisted of 80 boys, (lady cooks) Miss Knott, Miss Porrit, (Matron) Mrs Welford, Miss Judith Welford, Messrs G. W. Welford, W. Hetherington, K. M. Sherwood, J. Peacock, W. D. Pierce, J. T. Pautin, B. F. Sheppard, J. C. French, W. Andrew, H. C. Bullock, N. Matthews, R. Whiteside, T. Tranter.

At Newton Mulgrave, near Hinderwell, Staithes and Runswick Bay:

22.7.55: Friday. An advance party of 28 boys in charge of Mr J. D. Rand, Mr H. C. Bullock, Mr E. Smith and Mr A. R. Foord left at 9 a.m. for Newton Mulgrave near Runswick Bay for the Annual School Camp. A second party of 33 boys in charge of Mr E. L. Robson, Mr C. E. Robson, left at 2 p.m. A further party of 16 boys left in charge of Messrs G. W. Welford, and S. J. Thornhill at 6 p.m.

26.7.57: Annual School Camp held at Newton Mulgrave near Runswick Bay 26th July–2nd August.

An Advance Party in charge of Messrs J. Peacock, J. R. Foord, W. D. Peirce, and B. Sheppard (24 boys) left at 8.02 a.m.; in the afternoon 48 boys in charge of Messrs T. Tranter, and R. Whiteside left at 3.20 p.m. Both parties travelled by train. The total attending the camp included 72 boys Miss Knott, Miss Porrit (Lady Cooks).

24.7.59: Annual Camp held at Newton Mulgrave nr Hinderwell 24th July to 32st July.

The advanced party consisted of Messrs A. R. Foord, J. Peacock, and W. D. Pierce followed by 39 boys in charge of Messrs R. J. Whiteside and B. Stephenson 8.30 a.m. and later at 2 p.m. 38 boys in charge of Messrs J. O. Robson and P. Lyonette –

both parties travelling by motor coach (limited). The total party consisted of 77 boys, (Lady Cooks) Miss Knott, Miss Porritt, (Matron) Mrs Welford, Miss Judith Welford, Messrs G. W. Welford, K. M. Sherwood, W. D. Peirce, R. J. Whiteside, B. Stephenson, J. O. Robson, P. Lyonette, B. F. Sheppard, supported by Mr R. Peacock (student) and Messrs J. J. Clarke, J. T. Pauton guest masters.

22.7.60: The Annual School camp was again held at Newton Mulgrave from 22nd to 29th July. The advance party consisted of Messrs J. Peacock, A. R. Foord, H. C. Bullock. The party of 47 boys left at 9.30 in charge of Mr D. G. Whiteside. The whole camping party consisted of 47 boys, Messrs H. F. Foxon, K. Sherwood, J. Peacock, H. C. Bullock, D. G. Whiteside, G. W. Welford, R. Peacock (student), Mrs Welford, Miss J Welford and two lady cooks Mrs Porritt and Mrs Holdsworth.

Mr George Welford retired at the end of 1959, a camp taking place as usual. There is the record of the camp held in 1960, when Mr Foxon was headmaster, but there is no record of a camp taking place in 1961. There was another in 1962 and the last is recorded for 1964.

27.7.62: A party of 48 boys left for the Annual School camp at Newton Mulgrave. The boys were accompanied by the Headmaster, Mr K. Sherwood, Mr J. Peacock, Mr D. G. Whiteside, Mr B. Stephenson, and Mr T. W. Murphy from the staff. Also in camp were Mr and Mrs Welford, Miss Judith Welford, Mr R. Peacock and two lady cooks.

31.8.64: A party of 46 boys accompanied by the Headmaster, Mr J. D. Lovell, Mr J .Peacock, Mr D. G. Whiteside, Mr J. C. Carling and Mr J. K. Robson left for a week's camp at Newton Mulgrave.

The annual Speech Day

The ethos of a school is determined by a number of factors and among these is the attention given to ceremonial occasions. In the Eastbourne Schools particular attention was given to the ceremony of the annual Speech Day or prize-giving, as illustrated by the extracts from the school log books below.

The first point to note is the attendance and part played by local officials and dignitaries. At 2 p.m. on 21 March 1953, the annual Speech Day, the Chairman of Governors, Councillor Buckborough, presided and Miss W. B. C. Jewsbury, head teacher at the Darlington Girls' High School, presented the prizes and addressed the school. Staff and pupils attended, as did other governors, the CEO and LEA administration staff, pupils' parents and friends.

In 1954 the Chairman of Governors, Councillor Buckborough, again presided (he had been chairman for a decade). The ceremony was attended by old scholars, school governors, the Chairman of the Education Committee, the Chief Education Officer, administration staff, Lady Starmer, parents and friends. The inclusion of 'old scholars' illustrates a continuing active interest in the school on the part of at least some previous pupils.

The boys' school's first public Speech Day was held in the school at 7 p.m. on 15 October 1954. T. H. Summerson Esq. JP presented the prizes. The Chairman of Governors, Councillor Buckborough, presided supported by other members of the governing body and CEO Mr D. Peter MA, MEd. Prefect Peter Liddle proposed the vote of thanks to Mr Summerson.

In October 1955 the prize-giving/Speech Day at the girls' school was held at 2.15 p.m. The Chairman of Governors, Alderman Buckborough, presided and the Mayoress, and school governor, Mrs J. Neasham, addressed the school and presented the prizes. Mrs Neasham also presented the school with a cup for an annual speech competition. The event was attended by all pupils and staff, old scholars, school governors, the CEO, Mr Peter, the LEA's administrative staff, parents and friends.

In October 1956 the ceremony was again held at 2.30 p.m. in the girls' school. His worship the Mayor, Chairman of the School Governors, Alderman Buckborough, presided and was accompanied by the Mayoress. Lady Starmer OBE JP presented the awards and addressed the school The event was attended by all pupils and staff, old scholars, governors, the CEO, an HMI, the LEA's administrative staff, parents and friends.

On each occasion the meeting followed a formal pattern, with a chairman in charge, other dignitaries on the platform, a guest speaker, and someone to give a vote of thanks. In particular, it was the girls' school which adhered most closely to this formality, Miss Fenby, perhaps, being more supportive of ceremony than Mr Welford.

Other guest speakers were Professor Brian Stanley, Director of the Institute of Education, Durham University; Councillor Mrs M. Lyonette; and Miss Ella P. Jorden MBE, Branch Director of the British Red Cross (Northumberland Branch). In October 1960, the year of the Duke of Edinburgh's visit, Mrs P. Gordon Spencer of London, Secretary of the Girls Scheme for the Duke of Edinburgh's Award, presented the prizes and was guest speaker.

With the occasion being held in the afternoon at the girls' school and all pupils and staff expected to be present, it is quite clear that Miss Fenby intended the occasion to be of great significance in the education of the girls.

The celebration of special events during the period 1946–62

The celebration of special and national events also played a significant part in the education of the children, promoting a national identity. In 1946, just after the end of the war and immediately before the Whitsuntide holiday, the closing assembly included an appropriate ceremony for Victory Day, cards bearing His Majesty the King's message being given to every child.

Each year Remembrance Day was celebrated with Miss Fenby carefully recording the money raised by the sale of poppies, for instance £11.4s.8d. in 1948. On 26 April 1948 the schools closed for a half-day holiday on the occasion of the royal silver wedding. On 15 November 1948, at the suggestion of His Worship the Mayor of Darlington (Councillor S. Fenby) that the occasion of the birth of a prince to Her Royal Highness Princess Elizabeth, Duchess of Edinburgh, should be celebrated in schools, the schools closed for the afternoon.

In October 1949 time was taken during school assembly for the headmistress to give a talk on the United Nations Organisation and the National Savings movement. On 18 June 1951 celebrations as a part of the Festival of Britain included the final of a netball tournament held in the South Park at 7 p.m. when Eastbourne beat Reid Street 18 to 13.

The death of His Majesty King George VI was announced in the morning of 6 February 1952 and an appropriate special assembly held at 3.45 p.m. On the 8th arrangements were made for the pupils to listen to the broadcast of the Proclamation of Queen Elizabeth II at 11 a.m., and on the 15th, the day of the funeral of the late King, a special assembly was held to observe two minutes' silence.

In the afternoon of 10 October 1952, fifty-two girls and three staff attended the Baths Hall for the Civic Ceremony of Welcoming the Lord Bishop of Durham.

A national event of particular note took place on 2 June 1953, the Coronation of Her Majesty Queen Elizabeth II, and the schools closed at noon on 21 May to reopen on 5 June, this being the Whitsun holiday with extra days for the celebration of the occasion. The schools' particular celebrations took place on 5 June when one head teacher reported that the LEA allowed the provision of tea at 1s.9d. per head and prizes at 6d. per head, together with a coronation beaker. During the afternoon a coronation fayre was held, when tea was served at 3.45 p.m., and there was a fancy dress parade at 5 p.m.

The event was attended by an HMI, Miss Johnson, Councillor Mrs Lyonette (Governor), Lady Starmer J.P., Miss Storer, Youth Organiser, and Mr Green, Deputy Education Officer, together with parents and friends. Miss Fenby noted the school was most tastefully decorated and the function was enjoyed by everyone. In reply to a message of loyal greetings, a telegram was received from Her Majesty the Queen. On 10 June staff and pupils attended the Odeon cinema for the film *A Queen is crowned*.

School closed in the morning of 11 May 1955 on the occasion of the official opening of the new high school building in Hummersknott by HRH the Duke of Edinburgh.

The twenty-first anniversary of the founding of the school

In the true tradition of the girls' school, on 18 July 1957 an open day was held as a part of the celebrations marking the twenty-first anniversary of the foundation of the school. A large number of parents and friends attended, as did the CEO and the governors. On the 22nd of the month between 10 a.m. and 12 noon a service of thanksgiving was held in the school hall, conducted by the Reverend Brown, Vicar of St John's Church; Reverend Wilkins, Minister East Road Methodist Church; and Councillor Reverend M. Beaton, Minister of Geneva Road Baptist Church, also a member of the Education Committee and school governor.

All pupils attended plus twenty boys from the boys' school with two staff, Mr Welford from the boys' school, the Mayor and Mayoress, Chairman of the Education Committee, Members of the Education Committee, other governors, administrative staff, parents, friends and 'old girls'. The lectern bearing the school badge was dedicated during the service and Councillor Rev. Beaton gave the address. Scripture readings were given by the headmistress and head girl.

The lectern, with the accompanying chair for use in the daily worship, and three garden seats were gifts by the staff and pupils to commemorate the occasion.

A local civic occasion was celebrated on 1 April 1958 when thirty-six pupils and two staff attended the ceremony of the Presentation of the Freedom of the Borough to Lady Starmer OBE JP and Alderman Bell MBE JP, Chairman of the Education Committee, at the Baths Hall 7 p.m.

A further royal wedding, that of HRH Princess Margaret, was celebrated on 6 May 1960 by the closing of the schools.

School discipline

There is a well-founded belief that the behaviour and discipline of children and young people has changed drastically since the days when Miss Fenby and Mr Welford were the head teachers at the Eastbourne Schools, but, when seeking evidence of the way things were, subjective memory frequently overrides objective evidence. There is not a great deal of relevant material in the log books; there is in existence the punishment book from the boys' school which lists offending pupils, their misbehaviour and the number of strokes of the cane administered; and there is the spoken evidence given by those teachers and ex-pupils who are not shy of sharing their views.

The general opinion is that in the girls' school the children were taught self-discipline within an ordered environment where boundaries to behaviour were defined, clearly understood and generally accepted by society. The children knew the school rules, walked as expected in the building, respected their teachers and crept mouse-like by the head teacher's room. Old pupils and staff alike have repeated that the children knew they had to behave themselves.

As a part of the process of teaching responsibility senior pupils were appointed as prefects and their duties included keeping the cloakrooms, toilets and corridors clear at break and lunchtimes, an aspect of education favourably commented upon by HMIs. They were also expected to organise games during the lunch break, collect and deliver the class registers, ring the bell, and rarely, for the privileged, to exercise the head's dog.

Miss Manfield recalls the difficulties experienced during fire drills, when her departmental staff had to remain in the kitchens to check on food and any cooking in progress. She recalled two occasions when things were rather more unexpected than well ordered, when large fire engines appeared on the premises following an unexpected sounding of the alarm (set off by misbehaving pupils), creating much excitement, and clearly demonstrating the fact that even in this well-regulated school there were those quite capable of challenging authority.

The report of 29 November 1948, that the police made an enquiry relating to an 11-year-old pupil missing from home since 2.30 p.m. on Sunday 28th, is evidence that not all pupils were without their problems. The child was back in school the following day but all was not well: the child was later involved in an episode in which money had been taken.

A few boys and girls were under the supervision of the probation service, a situation arising from a child's delinquent, that is unlawful, behaviour and an appearance before magistrates in the Juvenile Court. For example, it is recorded that probation officers visited the school to see a number of girls on 9 December 1948, and similar visits were made in subsequent years. There were obviously children in both schools who had been brought before the Juvenile Court for various reasons.

Hearsay evidence suggested that Mr Welford, a magistrate serving in the Juvenile Court, threatened Eastbourne boys that, should they appear before him, they would be given twice the punishment of other offenders: an idle threat perhaps, but nevertheless a part of the mystique surrounding the keeping of order among hordes of lively, self-assertive young people.

There was the situation when a harassed young teacher entered the staff room following a particularly difficult time with a rowdy class, saying: 'I've just threatened the third year that if their behaviour does not improve there will be dire consequences. What are dire consequences?'

Much of the control of children is achieved by gaining their respect, but there are always those whose respect cannot be won. Miss Fenby had the reputation of maintaining order through the establishment of unbreakable rules and the force of her personality, a regime, it can be argued, that would not work today because the social climate has changed, encouraging the challenging of authority and permitting disruption to flourish.

Another aspect of maintaining order involves the recognition of the causes of rule breaking and the subsequent application of punishment or treatment. Some deviations from usual behaviour were recognised as maladjustment in the post-war years and educational psychologists, based in Child Guidance Clinics, were employed to seek causes for and give help in cases of educational failure and behaviour problems. For instance, in March 1950 the educational psychologist Mr Saunders was in the boys' school testing six pupils – most probably with reference to their educational ability rather than their behaviour.

A social worker was also attached to the Child Guidance Clinic, visiting pupils in school, as illustrated by the log book entry: 'Child Guidance Clinic Social Worker visited school' in the afternoon of 19 November 1954 'for reports on two girls'.

The responsibility for the welfare of pupils as well as their discipline was recognised in the secondary modern schools. there is an interesting report in the girls' school log for 29 September 1955: 'The Authority's welfare officer visited the school in the morning to investigate the action taken by the headmistress and the clinic nurse on Tuesday afternoon at the close of the school session 4.10 p.m. with regard to a pupil's condition, which was said to be extremely unsatisfactory, as far as cleanliness was concerned.' The School Welfare Officer had responsibility for school attendance and school–home liaison.

The headmistress met the parent of the pupil in school on 1 February 1956 at the request of the educational psychologist, clearly illustrating the involvement of the school with other welfare agencies in cases where the problem was social rather than disciplinary.

They were the 'Good Old Days', the description used by a teacher who taught in the boys' school for about eight years and subsequently in the mixed comprehensive school – and he was most emphatically referring to the former.

It was in the boys' school that corporal punishment was used throughout the period 1939–63. In some ways the school was less restrictive than the girls' department, the pupils less fearful but equally respectful of the head, and the staff relationships less hierarchical. Disobedience and unacceptable behaviour were certainly not tolerated, being instantly punished by strokes of the cane to produce what was perhaps seen as a more masculine ethos.

Entries of corporal punishments were made as required in the Punishment Book, which remained in the school, although disused, in 2009.

Children were being given corporal punishment for misbehaving in the classroom but the record does not provide us with the circumstances in which the misbehaviour took place. They could also be caned for talking or not paying attention in class and, perhaps even more astonishing seen through today's eyes, they could be physically punished for turning out poor classwork.

The misbehaviour recorded was either in some way exceptionally bad or repeated after many warnings and the application of lesser punishments.

Punishment for talking (presumably during silent working sessions) or for not paying attention is of course justified but there is the nagging doubt that, in the case of the inattention, the behaviour can result from the setting of inappropriate work or some medical condition. The case rests on the judgement of the teacher and at the time the teacher's authority was not challenged.

Corporal punishment was given in cases of general disobedience – pupils had to do as they were told, or they would be punished. Of the twenty-seven 14-year-olds punished in this way there was a group of boys refusing to go to their prescribed lesson. The nineteen punished for breaking a school rule, it is explained, were out of bounds and found breaking into a hut on school premises: that is, they were on school premises but in an area which they were not allowed to enter, that being the rule. They were also committing an act of vandalism and possibly involved in intended theft, matters which could have been referred to the police.

Impudence or rudeness to staff was not tolerated but it is clear that such disrespectful behaviour was perceived as being more prevalent among the older children. The lower number in the oldest category is explained by the fact that these youngsters were not compelled to stay in school once they became 15 years of age. But the leaving age had risen and would rise further; older youngsters were being compelled to remain in school when they would sooner not be there and, among some of them, challenges to the teachers' authority became more common.

The use of bad language was similarly punished although recorded episodes are small in number.

Another area that seems to have attracted corporal punishment is in the case of telling lies. The wrongdoer's first line of defence is very often to deny any involvement in the suggested misbehaviour and can be a sound technique for getting out of a situation if the truth cannot be proven. In the Welford days, when a teacher said he knew a boy was lying (and it was very likely that he did know) that was sufficient proof of guilt. The child knew that and knew the impossibility of not owning up.

Much is made of bullying others, with strategies and policies being imposed upon schools to deal with it, but it is not a new problem. Physical and spoken aggression was quite simply dealt with by applying corporal punishment. Two boys scrapped and two boys were punished. One boy attacked another and the attacker was punished.

There is no doubt that, among a school population, there have always been those who become involved in malicious and delinquent acts. The wrongful setting off of fireworks is dangerous and every year (now) there are television campaigns to inform young people of these dangers: yet some still find it amusing to risk injuring themselves and others, often seriously.

Cases of damaging property included smashing milk bottles (which were all made of glass at the time), scribbling on walls (before the days of spray-paint) and the destruction of school books. Once again the frequency of such events is greater as the young people grow older.

Instances of theft are recorded and the cases clearly dealt with by the school. The question of the school knowing the culprit is guilty and the culprit accepting the judgement is significant: if it becomes necessary to prove the guilt by calling witnesses and the case goes to court where this is necessary, the known culprit can get off, his arrogance growing with the knowledge that he cannot be punished and reinforcing his antisocial and/or delinquent behaviour.

Some children in both the boys' and girls' schools were taken before the Juvenile Court, as shown by the visits of probation officers. A probation officer visited the school during an afternoon in September 1949 with reference to one school pupil and 'loss of money on school premises'.

> 2.5.57: Two probation officers visited the school in the afternoon and discussed several cases of delinquents on probation.
>
> Early 1958: Police and Probation Officer in school re: delinquency on part of a few pupils.
>
> 23.2.60: Probation Officer in school re: three pupils.

Boys' Log 3.2.54: Knife incident

Mr Welford reported that a pupil was sent to hospital at 1.23 p.m. following a wound caused by another pupil with a knife. CEO informed.

Another area of misbehaviour which has attracted a great deal of attention in recent years is truancy. It is not a new problem and once again was dealt with by applying corporal punishment. In general the problem is seen to increase with the age of the pupil culminating with the reluctant scholar approaching the school-leaving age.

The same discipline was applied to behaviour outside school, not only when the boys were going to and from school but also outside school hours. In this way the school demonstrated its concern that behaviour should not only be proper in school but outside as well.

Digressing from discipline in the boys' school, it is clear that Miss Fenby's influence extended beyond the school gates. During the 1950s trolley buses served both the school and the new Paton and Baldwin's factory in McMullen Road: when using the service girls were expected to queue in an orderly fashion and give up their seats to any older person. This is also a further example of the understanding that children should behave in a civilised manner and that inappropriate behaviour would be punished, the realistic enforcing of a respect for others.

Parents' involvement in the school

As it is not known whether one or two parents are recorded per child the measure is far from ideal, but the attendance is shown to be generally good: parents are displaying interest and support.

Entries in the boys' school log are less detailed but demonstrate that regular meetings for the parents of new children were also held in that school in July each year: for instance, 'The parents of pupils and the pupils due to join the school on 1st September 1952, were invited to attend the School at 7 pm and were addressed by the Headmaster on the Aims, Policy and Rules of the school – the Headmaster was supported by members of the Staff'.

In some cases a follow-up meeting to that of July was held in September, once the pupils were settled in the school, and meetings for the parents of children in other year groups held at other times. That held for second-year pupils in October 1958 attracted an attendance of 90 parents for some 180 children. In the following year there was a turnout of 90 parents for a year group of 194 pupils.

A different kind of meeting took place when parents and friends were invited to attend bring-and-buy sales like that held in September 1959 when Miss Fenby wrote: 'Over 600 attended and there was a happy social occasion.'

The development of the curriculum

Darlington County Borough Education Committee
Extract from the Regulations 1938
Curriculum and Timetable

The curriculum and the timetable of the school must be approved by the Committee. The Head Teacher is allowed discretionary powers as to the time to be devoted to a particular subject of instruction, subject to these regulations.

No alterations of the curriculum and/or timetable which will involve additional expenditure shall be made without the Committee's previous consent.

Instruction in secular subjects shall occupy at least two consecutive hours in the morning, and at least two consecutive hours in the afternoon of each school day. Secular instruction shall begin, at the latest, immediately after the time for the closing of the registers.

A copy of the Syllabus of Lessons on the Hygiene of Food and Drink issued by the Board of Education shall be in each Senior School, and provision for such instruction shall be included in the curriculum.

Practice in intelligence tests and other forms of special coaching for examinations shall not take place in the school.

Compared with what is seen today, the curriculum was initially (1945–1950) lacking in complexity: it was uncluttered, covering relatively few and well-defined subjects which were taken by everyone. Nevertheless the pupils received an extremely broad and rich education because of the wide range of activities which supplemented the academic studies. Those integrated into the house competition system have already been mentioned.

The twice yearly examinations consisting of the writing of a composition, and tests in English, English literature and arithmetic, suggest a concentration on the basic skills of language and calculation.

Subjects listed on the report forms also support this view: arithmetic, algebra, geometry, reading & drama, composition, English language and literature, music, geography, history, art, needlecraft, biology, domestic science, woodwork, metalwork and physical education.

An entry dated 2 September 1947 demonstrates that the basic subjects were taught in the junior part of the school by the same teacher: 'the core of the school will be 2.5 years [the junior two and a half years of the school] English and maths to be taken by the class teacher whenever possible.' The class teacher was also the form teacher, the teacher in charge of the class for the registration and school assembly period each day, having charge of the same group for a significant proportion of the week. Such a policy reduced movement of classes about the building, increased the close supervision of the pupils, and produced a calmer, more stable environment.

As early as the autumn term 1946 it is remarked: 'specialisation to be extended to Mathematics in the A & B streams throughout the school.' This is apparently a change from merely teaching arithmetic, repeats the fact that the pupils were placed in classes in strict order of their perceived ability, and that top streams were given a more extended curriculum than the lower groups.

Remedial reading class
There was recognition that the language and reading skills of some pupils were below the acceptable standard and, once again, it is the detail included in the girls' school log which indicates something of the nature and size of the problem.

In mid March 1947, Mr Armstrong, the educational psychologist from the Child Guidance Clinic, began a testing schedule of backward readers with the intention of identifying those who would benefit from remedial reading lessons.

After testing it was agreed that twenty-five girls should benefit from attending a remedial class and, in spite of there being difficulties with staffing the programme, it was considered that this class was of such importance that it was agreed it should commence for two periods per day. The remedial reading class was organised in May 1947, to be taken by Mrs Thompson. There were frequent follow-up visits by the educational psychologist but the success or otherwise of the work was not reported in any detail. The head teacher does later report that progress was being made when she regrets that she cannot staff the desirable two classes.

In September 1947 it was estimated that more than forty girls should be in the remedial class but staffing did not allow for the organisation of two groups. It was concluded that the priority should be to teach twenty-five girls from the new entrants with the inclusion of some older girls. From this evidence it can be seen that at least 25 girls out of the intake of about 100 from primary schools were poor readers, one quarter of the intake.

An entry in the boys' school log for 11 February 1947 refers to the educational psychologist visiting the school with reference to the 'Remedial Classes', showing that there were similar needs to those of the girls' department and that there was more than one class involved.

This is a problem that never seemed to be resolved. In spite of efforts made over many years some children still entered the secondary schools unable to read to an efficient standard.

On 9 November 1962 a course in the teaching of 'Backward and Retarded Children in the Secondary Modern School' and another in the 'Teaching of Reading' was held in the school during the evening. In conjunction with the above the school staged the National Book League exhibition of 'Books for Backward Readers'.

There were a small number of children with physical problems in the school, for instance one attended the Child Guidance Clinic classes for the partially deaf.

Housecraft or domestic science

Practical subjects continued to be a major part of the curriculum. Housecraft, later called domestic science, was strictly a girls' activity and, whenever staffing allowed, pupils were given one complete day for the subject; that is, one fifth of their school week.

A further indication of difference between the domestic science teachers department and other staff was that they did not, as a rule, have a form to supervise at registration and assembly times, being expected to have kitchen preparation duties, such as the setting out of demonstrations, to carry out. They did attend the school assemblies, standing at the back of the hall.

The accommodation, built into the separate, almost isolated, wing of the school, continued to emphasise the difference between this and other departments. The flat, the purpose-built bungalow standing in its own site, continued to be well used by girls on a rota basis. Consisting of a sitting room, hall, bathroom, outside toilet, bedroom and kitchen, it was at least of an equal standard to that of the 1930s housing adjacent to the school – at a time when some of the pupils came from homes in older properties. The girls took turns to care for it and senior girls prepared meals for invited staff, giving them not only experience of cooking and serving, but also the prestige of being able to provide for their elders.

Miss Manfield, who worked in the department for many years and was head of department in the comprehensive school, recalled that the pupils learnt how to run a home, make a fire (referring to the open coal-burning hearths – there was no central heating), bed making, preparation of food, tea trays and so on. The tea trays were sent to the head teacher's room twice daily and often extra ones prepared for visitors.

There were no automatic cookers (meaning they had to be lit by match or taper), but they were exchanged for new ones every three or four years. There were originally six in each room but, as examination work increased, the number was increased to eight.

Electric irons for pressing clothing replaced the originals which had been heated by gas. Washing was done by hand, using scrubbing boards, which were eventually replaced by washing machines, the boards being given to skiffle groups to be 'played' as musical instruments.

The rolling and cutting of pastry was done on wooden boards, which had to be thoroughly scrubbed after use.

The pupils had to bring their own ingredients, a tricky point because of the cost involved, and the possible errors arising when the cooks were mere learners. There was a supply of basic ingredients kept in school and replacements given if errors were made and the dish had to be repeated, and some help was given to those from low-income families. Yet in spite of the potential problems, parents tended to be most helpful and co-operative.

Ingredients were also provided when dishes were repeated for display as a part of the house competitions or for demonstration purposes.

Consequently, the staff had to keep meticulous accounts which were sent to the Education Office every month. Miss Manfield said: 'Woe betide us if we were a farthing out!' Stock books were maintained for everything in the department and all equipment was carefully checked. 'We hoped too many breakages did not occur or teaspoons go missing.'

The syllabus included the care and use of equipment, including sinks and waste bins; safety in the home; and choice of foods, their nutritional value and cooking methods. In the 1950s, this included the use of dried egg powder in place of fresh eggs. The girls were taught how to budget and be economic when shopping.

In needlework new pupils made their own aprons for cookery and their own cap which had to be embroidered with their monogram. At least one girl, Shirley Donner, did not take to this activity, failing to complete any of these items. There was some concern with the threat of not being able to attend sports day if the tasks were not completed but apparently it was all hands to the pumps at home and miraculously the left-handed, impractical child produced both within three days. Everything was known and understood, but nothing said, and sports day was enjoyed.

After passing the test of making a satisfactory apron and cap girls graduated to knitting, embroidery and the making of other garments for themselves.

The domestic science rooms were regularly modernised, the head teacher always on the lookout for new equipment. For instance, in July 1950 Miss Fenby and Miss Dover (then head of department) visited Ripon Secondary Modern School to see the unit kitchen system in the domestic science department. It was at this time that the new school meals canteen was opened and room 16, which had been used by the school meals service, was to be reconditioned as a domestic science room. Earlier, in December 1947, the application for material for loose covers for furniture in the flat brought the School Management Subcommittee – Alderman Luck, chairman, Alderman Hudson, Councillor Wilson and the CEO – into the school.

In 1949 it was recommended that the settee and two chairs in the flat be sold and new ones purchased due to the high cost of repairs.

Woodwork and metalwork

The practical subjects taken by the boys were taught by male teachers who were industry orientated with specific City and Guilds qualifications in woodwork and metalwork and the classrooms formed a workshop environment, again being in a wing separated from the classrooms used for teaching the more academically orientated subjects.

Subjects reported on by the HMIs during their inspection of the girls' school in December 1950

Religious instruction

The subject, overseen by an arts graduate, was said to be very well taught with much effort having been given to the planning of the scheme of work which clearly interested the girls and influenced the complete life of the school.

English

Most of the work in English was taught by the form teachers and the inspectors found that the girls spoke easily and pleasantly about the books they had read. There was a suggestion that the emphasis placed on the neatness and correctness of the composition writing possibly detracted from the girls' willingness to be more adventurous with the content. Many of the essays were found to be uninteresting!

Speech and drama, strong aspects of school life, took up forty-five minutes of the week for most pupils. Speech was found to be good, even among the girls who had only recently entered the school. The school hall was used for drama, when the girls worked together in small groups.

At the time of the inspection history and geography were mainly taught within an integrated social studies scheme, which was described as being at an experimental stage. The more able girls were apparently taught the subjects as separate disciplines and the project raises the question of the desirability of integrating traditional subjects which have a clearly defined syllabus content. There is a danger in any integration scheme of losing this content within a less clearly defined series of projects. The motivation for integration is often an attempt to avoid time wastage by the teaching of the same topics twice or more in the different subject classes. There is also sense in the argument that skills, such as note taking in English lessons, should be used in other subject teaching: sometimes using, say, notes taken in science as subject matter in the teaching of English. This does not avoid duplication, as it is still necessary for the specialist subject teacher to discuss and or correct the facts relating to the special subject.

The inspectors noted that facts were accumulated without there being sufficient opportunity for the girls to pursue their own interests. The converse of this is, of course, that the girls would go off along their own lines of interest and thought and learn very little of the content of the traditional subjects. Surely, a sensible approach is for the teacher to provide facts and teach skills, and then encourage the pupils to use this knowledge to investigate suggested historical and geographical topics.

It is interesting to note that in September 1951 there was a change to teaching history and geography as separate subjects, social studies being dropped from the senior school timetable.

Mathematics

Mathematics teaching was overseen by the senior mistress, who taught the senior classes while the less experienced teachers were helped by the detailed schemes of work produced.

Senior school mathematics was taught via topics relating to the home, giving the subject a real and practical purpose, essential for young people who are by their nature losing interest in what they see as child-orientated teaching.

The neatness of the work, the careful attention given to the proper layout of exercises, and the extremely thorough marking of exercise books were remarked upon by the inspectors and from other evidence it is clear that these aspects of teaching and learning were emphasised and expected by the head teacher. In spite of the hints that more freedom of expression could be allowed in the girls' work, one cannot but feel the school was right. Learn the rules and when that is done apply them to a wider field of learning.

Science

The scheme of work in science covered simple aspects of physics and chemistry, plant and animal biology, and health education.

Art

A specialist art teacher taught most of the classes, supported by two others, and the scheme of work included the use of colour, patterns, lettering, figure drawing, object drawing and interior decoration. It seems that the tools of the trade were being carefully taught but the inspectors were not happy; they wanted to see more exploration, greater use of the lettering and imaginative painting – again going beyond the teaching of the basics.

Housecraft

During the late 1940s and early 1950s the purpose-built housecraft department was suffering from a lack of experienced teachers; it was reported that there had been fourteen different teachers appointed over a period of eleven years. There should have been four teachers for the subject but there were often only three and sometimes only one or two. Continuity had been provided by the senior member of staff who had been working in the school since it opened and continued in post until her retirement in 1970.

Needlework

The girls were encouraged to provide their own basic sewing equipment and were taught use them skilfully: again the teaching appears to be aimed at providing basic skills which will be of practical use. There were eleven sewing machines in the school and the girls were encouraged to use them from year one.

There was only one specialist needlework room and the inspectors commented on the undesirability of girls having to use other rooms where the furniture consisted of sloping-topped dual desks. The sewing machines were of the treadle type and distributed among the various rooms, quite unable to be moved about more than absolutely necessary.

Music

In 1950 music was taught by four teachers, none having a specialist music qualification, illustrating, as seen in other subject areas, a shortage of staff. The school-leaving age had been raised but the provision of necessary providers not achieved, even with the introduction of the emergency training colleges.

It was noted that there were two gramophones with electrical amplification and some good gramophone records!

Physical education

Four teachers shared the work of the physical education department; one, the youngest and newest, was a specialist in the teaching of gymnastics.

The growth of a senior school curriculum

The 1944 Education Act required that the school-leaving age be raised to the term during which the pupil reached 15 years of age, making necessary the provision of an extra year of school education. In Darlington discussions about the implications and requirements of this legislation took place in February 1947, and this came into effect in March 1947.

The girls' department was already experimenting with examination courses for the academically more able pupils, following the pattern of the grammar schools, and developing an orientation towards employment. This is evident in October 1947 when a visiting teacher was appointed to teach the shorthand section of the business knowledge section of the School Leaving Certificate. There were to be two sessions of three hours on each of Wednesday and Friday morning and two sessions of 1 hour 25 minutes on Wednesday and Friday afternoons. The significance of this course is its vocational orientation.

An optional element in the curriculum of the girls' school

In many ways, the girls' school appeared to have a progressive outlook towards education. For instance, at the beginning of September 1947 Miss Fenby introduced, as an experiment, an optional period for the last three-quarters of an hour on a Friday afternoon when pupils could choose from a number of activities: the choir, crafts, discussion, physical education, drama, and other unspecified activities. However, the practicalities of running the optional classes seem to have put constraints on what could be done in some of the subject areas.

Field work and out-of-school visits had been a part of the curriculum during the war years and were subsequently developed further. For instance, on Saturday 13 September 1947 a visit to Gainford Hall was organised by the girls' geography staff, and with the kind permission of Mr Harrison, for the purpose of making a farm study. In the following November one half of L2.1 (lower school second year, top stream) visited Peases Mill.

It is also clear that there was a junior field club at the girls' school, which is mentioned in the entry of 8 April 1949 when a party of pupils under the leadership of Miss Hunnam and Miss O. M. Nichols left school at 3 p.m. for Barnard Castle, where they stayed at the youth hostel until the Saturday evening. The importance of there being teachers willing and enthusiastic enough to organise such activities cannot be ignored.

In 1932 Mr James Campbell of London (brother of the Darlington councillor and one-time mayor G. R. Campbell) offered the leasehold of a house known as 'Cliffden', at Saltburn, to the local authority. The lease had thirty-four years to run and the ground rent was £25 per annum. It was estimated that repairs and redecoration would cost £400, the price of a small semi-detached house at that time. Nevertheless, the offer was accepted, subject to the approval of the Board of Education, and was clearly used for school visits. Miss Fenby's log entries, such as those for June 1946 when twelve girls from UIV (the upper fourth year) spent the weekend at the Cliffden Hostel, Saltburn, and for the Whitsun Holiday in 1952 when twenty-eight girls and five staff spent the week at Cliffden, Saltburn with Miss O. Hunnam in charge, are examples of the use of this facility. In 1949 twenty-nine girls from the second stream in the second year in the care of four staff spent the weekend at Cliffden.

The hostel at Grinton was another base for the girls:

> On Ascension Day 1949 24 girls from 2.4 [fourth stream in the second year] with two staff, Miss O. Hunnam and Miss J. Mudd, left school at 8.0 a.m. to take part in a two day residential course at Grinton Youth Hostel. A further group of 21 from the 4th and 5th years spent a weekend at the Hostel.

Also, in 1949, twenty-nine girls from 2.2. with four staff spent the weekend at the Cliffden Hostel, Saltburn. During the Whitsun holiday of 1948 two groups of girls from U2.1 (30) and L 3.1 (25) and six staff visited Saltburn, staying at Cliffden for three days.

Barnard Castle Youth Hostel

On 23 April 1948 a party of 20 girls from 5.1 [the top stream in the fifth year] and two staff left for a two day visit to Barnard Castle, staying at the Barnard Castle Youth Hostel.

The Nent Hall Holiday Fellowship Hostel

During the Whitsun Holiday of 1951 a party of 54 girls and six staff stayed at the Nent Hall Holiday Fellowship Hostel at Alston for one week visiting the Roman Wall, Houseteads Fort and Hexham, also having organised walks in the area.

Earls Orchard continued to be well used during the secondary modern school years: for instance on 11 June 1945:

Class 2.1 The younger half of the class, 23 boys taking a residential course at Earls Orchard Youth Hostel. Mr J. L. Hunt in charge. The visiting teachers for the week, they are in residence, will be the same as last week except that Mr Brockway will substitute for Mr Peacock on Tuesday. Party returned to school.

On 16th June 1947 a party of 22 pupils from 2.1 in charge of Mr W. A. Brown and Mr T. Shipley left for a week's residential course at Earls Orchard Hostel, Richmond.

The London excursion

Another of the regular school journeys organised by the girls' school was the London excursion, the first recorded as being made in September 1952 when, on Sunday 14th, Miss McLeish and Miss Hunnam departed from Darlington with a party of twenty girls on a five-day educational visit. The same teachers took a similar group away in 1954.

There was another journey to London in 1955, with twenty-one girls from the two top streams in the third year, once again accompanied by the organisers, Miss McLeish and Miss Hunnam, departing from Darlington on Sunday 5 May for a six-day visit. A similar visit was made in 1956 when twenty-two pupils took part.

In May 1959 the excursion to London left on Sunday 31st, when it is reported that girls from third-year classes took part. It is interesting to note that eleven of the pupils were from the top stream, six from the second and three from the third. It would be more interesting to learn the reasons for their taking part while others presumably did not do so.

The visit in May 1960 to London was once again taken by Miss McLeish, this time accompanied by Miss Giles, with twelve girls from top third-year stream and eight from the second stream.

The last recorded London trip was made in June 1961 when eleven girls from the top stream, seven from the second and two from the third took part in a week-long educational and social programme.

Local studies

Local studies, sometimes described as 'nature walks', were taking place before the 1939–45 war and various excursions continued to be organised by the girls' school during the war. School journeys into the countryside were a significant part of the curriculum and were further developed after the war when one such excursion among many took place on 12 October 1953 when class 1.2J with Miss Coxon and Mrs Thompson left school at 1.30 p.m. to walk from Piercebridge to Gainford, returning at 6 p.m. Class 1.1J completed the same excursion on Saturday 10 October.

The curling pond was still used for practical work in science in 1946 when a third-year group visited it for about three-quarters of an hour in October, but there are no references to it being used in subsequent years, although there is a note for June 1959 when 1.4S (the bottom stream in the first year of the senior school) carried out a science practical pond study between 9.15 and 10.45 a.m. It is not clear which pond is referred to!

In July 1961 there are visits being made by first-year classes to 'The Pond' in McMullen Road, as a part of their science course. In July 1962 senior classes visited The Pond.

In 1956 there is a report of classes visiting Lingfield Lane: 'The top stream in the second year of the lower school walked to the site in two groups as a part of their work in science, one during the morning and the other in the afternoon.' First and second streams in year one made their visits in science lesson time in May 1960.

In September 1955 Miss Coxon had taken the top two streams in the junior half of the second year on half-day science trips to Lingfield Lane and Wood. It was also Miss Coxon, a young teacher recently transferred from North Road Girls' School, who took a group of first-year girls to Piercebridge and Gainford on Saturday 23 September 1956.

Other local visits

June 1950: First year Nature Walks to Nunnery Lane and Tees Bank returning early evening.

October 1950: Classes 1.4 and 1.5 were taken to Bank Top Station for a local study. They were given a talk by the Station Master and were shown No.1 Engine.

Class 1.3 visited St Cuthbert's Church and the Market Cross as a part of their local studies during the afternoon of 17th October 1950.

18th October 1950: Half of 1.1S visited the Gas Works in the afternoon as a part of their Science course.

Juniors also visited the Waterworks in later 1950.

And 2.3S visited Salter's close housing Estate, Haughton, in connection with their project 'The Home'.

6th May 1953: 24 senior girls and two staff left school at 3.30 pm. for a school excursion to Gainford and walk through Selaby Woods.

During the school closure on election day 1955: 1.1S with Miss Hunnam and Miss Auckland to Thickley Wood and Skerning Lane.

1.3S with Miss Raynor to Richmond.

1.1J with Miss Coxon and Mrs Thompson to Piercebridge.

June 1959: Planned walks around the Tees for 1st year pupils for wild flower collection now completed. Trips taken after school during several evenings.

October 1959: 1.1J and 1.2J visited Nunnery Lane re Science – after 4 pm.

1.J and 1.4J visited Cemetery Lane re: Science – after 4 pm.

June 1960: 1.1J visited the Waterworks: different days half at a time 2 till 4 pm.

A few more out-of-school visits

On the 18th June 1946: 'Third Year pupils visited the 'Needlework and Embroidery Today' exhibition at the Public Library.'

During the Autumn Holiday in 1948 a party of 24 girls aged 14-15 and three staff visited York for the day.

In May 1952: '274 girls and 7 staff left school at 3.55 p.m. to attend a performance of Chipperfield's Circus.'

In May 1955: 'the Arts council and Needlework Development Scheme presented an Exhibition of embroidery in the Public Library. Two parties of thirty, each made up of four representatives from each class in the school, visited the exhibits in the afternoon.'

Use of films and the cinema

Films were shown to pupils using the projection facilities in the two schools but for special presentations they were taken out to the cinemas, for instance 96 senior pupils attended the Odeon cinema to see the film *Hamlet*.

In May 1949, 131 girls from fourth and fifth-year classes visited the Odeon cinema to see the film *Scott of the Antarctic*, arrangements having been made by the Education Authority. The girls paid 9d. each.

In October 1950 the timetable was suspended for the showing of the film *Centenary of the Public Library* and on 8 November Fact and Faith Films, *God of Creation* and *Dust or Destiny* were shown to the senior school by arrangement with the Rev. Clements, Rev. Francis, and Mrs Dresser. A visiting HMI also saw the films.

In the afternoon of 28 January 1953 a special programme of films was arranged for the senior school, including *Papageno* (the work undertaken for the school concert at the end of the spring term), *Carmen, Instruments of the Orchestra* and *Steps of the Ballet*.

In January 1954 at 5.10 p.m. 203 girls attended a performance of the film *Julius Caesar*.

Physical education

The following log entry is evidence of the national promotion of physical training, the support from schools continuing in the post-war years: Miss J. Mudd was granted one day's leave to attend, as one representative, the Recreative Physical Training Youth Rally, held at Wembley in June 1948. The wartime emphasis on physical training continued, it being a separate part of the schools' physical education programme. However, change would eventually come with the notion that such education should be more recreational and the games programme broadened to cater for the preferences of the children.

Swimming

The Darlington Education Authority's programme of swimming lessons for pupils was in operation before the 1939–45 war, as illustrated by Mr Welford's log entry for 1938: 3 May 'Swimming – (Boys) commenced 9–9.30 a.m' and 5th May 'Swimming – (Girls) commenced 9–9.30 a.m.' As there are no log book entries for the early years of the war, it appears as though, like many things, swimming lessons ceased, but by 1943 the programme was in operation again.

There is a hint of *there will be swimming, whether the pupils want it or not*: everyone must learn to swim. Miss Fenby wrote in May 1946: 'All 1st and 2nd year pupils visited the swimming baths weekly "in accordance with the Authority's instructions". The timetable had to be adjusted accordingly.'

In September 1946 the time taken for each class to attend the baths was reported to be two hours due to transport problems; for example, a first-year class left school at 9.00 a.m. and returned at 10.50, another left at 9.55 a.m. and returned at 11.55, causing disruption in school. In addition more and more girls were not attending swimming because of colds.

The school inspectors commented in 1950 that one and a half hours were being taken out of teaching time for a class to have a twenty-minute swimming lesson.

At the end of the course children took swimming tests. Certificates were awarded for one width, one length, five lengths, quarter-mile, half-mile, and 1 mile.

Awards made in January 1947 for the courses ending in the previous summer at the girls' school were:

One width 25 pupils, one length 43, five lengths 19, quarter-mile 3, half-mile 1 and one mile 2.

Another award which the pupils could strive for is reported in the log entries for 1954 and 1962. In 1954 Life Saving Certificates and bronze medals were presented to those girls who had qualified by Mrs J. Neasham, a school governor.

In 1962 the following girls qualified for Royal Life Saving Society Awards:

Intermediate: Vera Adamson, Barbara Akers, Barbara Barras, Judith Holmes, Carol Jackson, Sandra Spears, Sylvia Weatherill and Elizabeth Wright.

Bronze Medallion: Annette Wood, Sandra Chapel, Wendy Bland, Margaret Emmerson, Sandra Brassington, Joan Thompson, Carol Evans, Caroline Williams, Angela Stockdale, Pamela Hughes, Heather Thompson, Evelyn Darke, Denise Richardson, Elizabeth Kitching, Joan Walker.

Bronze Cross: Judith Abbott, Denise Dawes, Elizabeth Stephens and Patricia Wells.

As well as so much time being required for the normal swimming programme to function, occasionally the situation was made worse by other problems. On 26 June 1959: 'Swimming Classes – according to the summer timetable – first-year group arrived at the baths for the first session at 2 p.m. The Gladstone Street Bath was reserved for a Gala; The Kendrew Street Bath was packed beyond capacity (4 per cabin), a waiting queue of the general public – the pupils from this school had to return here and all other groups (168 pupils) cancelled for the afternoon. Temporary arrangements made in school.'

Again, on 2 September 1959: 'Swimming sessions commenced following the winter timetable, arrangements being made for classes to attend the baths as expected. Groups of 51 and 49 pupils left school at 2.40 p.m. and another 45 at 3 p.m. At approximately 3.10 p.m. a telephone call was received from the Education Office informing the school that the baths were overcrowded and one was closed for a Gala. Another group of 46 pupils was therefore kept in school while 145 pupils and 3 staff returned to school, walking and arriving at 3.55 p.m.'

One episode which demonstrates elements of danger, a little heroism and even, when looking back, some humour, took place during the afternoon of 6 July 1950 when a group of first-year girls were at the swimming baths: Marlene Wade was spotted in difficulty and was rescued by Veronica Hewitt who, in turn, collapsed in the water and was rescued by the instructor, Mrs Rowell.

The question remains: was the programme worthwhile in terms of efficiency? Certainly a few pupils achieved a great deal and it is a school's responsibility to encourage each according to his or her abilities. A large proportion achieved something but one is left wondering what effect the compulsory trip to the baths had on the less motivated and less physically able. There did appear to be an obsession that everyone should be able to swim and one wonders why: people live on dry land and can generally choose whether they go near water or not. And the taking up of almost two hours, more than one-third of a week's teaching time, for the satisfaction of producing a handful of expert swimmers and a majority who could perhaps enjoy some swimming in later life, does seem excessive, indeed, inefficient.

That those who have talent should be encouraged to develop that talent cannot be denied. Young people need to be challenged and guided into gaining success in as many worthwhile occupations as possible. Those who are successful should be applauded and it is at the sports meetings, among other activities, where some pupils can gain self-esteem, the majority supporting them as members of a team. It is through the membership of such groups that a sense of belonging, the recognition and value of the different contributions recognised, and co-operation fostered. The school swimming galas were one of the annual sporting events.

The first annual girls' school swimming gala was held at 9 a.m. on 20 July 1949 in the second-class baths. Miss Fenby comments: 'Owing to restricted accommodation it was with regret that parents and friends could not be invited – neither could all the pupils from the school be accommodated. Pupils who did attend were all 4th years, all swimmers, and "Never Absent and Never Late" Group – 220 pupils all together with nine members of staff. The competitions were held under official regulations with judges from Darlington Swimming Club.'

On 12 July 1950 the school gala, held at 2 p.m. at the Gladstone Street baths, was attended by the whole school, visitors, parents of competitors, the Mayor and Mayoress (Councillor and Mrs Dougill), the Chairman of the Baths Committee (Alderman Chandler), Mrs Chandler, and members of the Education Committee.

As well as the attendance by the members of the local authority, that of the whole school, parents and other visitors added to the significance of the event in the life of the school and helped to promote a community spirit. This pattern of involvement continued throughout the Fenby–Welford years, as in 1961 when the Mayor and Mayoress (Mrs Lorraine), Councillor Reverend Beaton and Mrs Beaton, Mr Cameron, the Organiser for Physical Education, and parents attended, with the whole school present as competitors or spectators.

School teams in turn gave the best swimmers a chance to measure their performances against those in other schools, have the honour of representing their school, and advance the achievements of the school in the eyes of the public. A major occasion when the teams could compete was the annual Inter-Schools Swimming Gala when for instance in July 1950 at 6.45 p.m. the girls' school won the Championship Trophy. Judging by her entries in the log book, Miss Fenby always applauded the successes of the school teams.

Music in the curriculum

The Darlington LEA had introduced music into the schools before the 1939–45 war and a pattern of activities including the inter-house and inter-schools annual festivals continued to be followed during the Fenby–Welford years. The annual school concert was also a strong element of education in the girls' school and regularly took place between 1945 and 1961, but it does appear that there was a change in policy in the boys' school when Mr Farrage, who was involved in both the workshops and the music department, retired in 1950.

The annual school concert

There is, however, evidence of school concerts and or music competitions taking place in both schools, leading to the entries into the Darlington Musical Festival. For instance, the annual girls' school concert which took place on 13 December 1946 involved 150 pupils. The timetable was adjusted in the morning on 12 December for a full dress rehearsal and the concert took place at 7 p.m. on the 13th. The programme included music, drama and dancing, illustrating the work of the school in these subjects. There was an audience of some 500 including the CEO and members of the Education Committee.

The concert was repeated for the whole school during one morning a little later in the week.

On 26 February 1948 when the school choir performed under the direction of Mrs I. Thompson with Mrs E. Watson playing the piano, the headmistress commented that the singing by both the choir and soloists was of a high standard. There was an audience of about 600 people including the Mayor, Councillor S. Fenby JP, the Mayoress Miss N. Fenby (headmistress), Miss E. Johnson HMI, the chairman (Alderman Luck) and members of the Education Committee, and the CEO (Mr Kilgour).

There can be no doubt that music played a large part in the curriculum as is well illustrated by events listed in the log books, and none of these productions would have been possible without the involvement of plenty of pupils and the majority of the teachers.

The boys' school were using similar talent and effort in the combined staff-pupil production of the annual pantomime. These productions were being performed in schools with no sixth-form students and where those who wished could still leave school when they became fifteen.

The first post-war log book entry which refers to the Darlington Non-Competitive Musical Festival was dated 23 November 1948 when the Eastbourne Schools closed for the day. The Darlington Teachers' Association was responsible for the organisation of the event, which took place in the Baths Hall: the boys' and girls' schools each entered two choirs, that from the girls' department comprising pupils from classes 2.1 and 3.1.

The schools' involvement in the Darlington Non-Competitive Music Festival initially continued after 1950; for example, on 1 November 1951 Mr A. Robinson, the music master, attended the Baths Hall in the afternoon for a rehearsal in connection with the festival. Mr Robinson had only held his post since September 1951 and so there was perhaps a change of policy at this time: a decision not to hold the annual school function. Mr Robinson left in the summer of 1954 and Mr B. Sheppard, who had been appointed in August 1953, became the music master, but there are no log entries that suggest there was an enthusiastic involvement in the music festival until 18 November 1959 when an entry reads: 'Wednesday. The School closed for the Darlington Schools Non-Competitive Music Festival in which the school took part.'

Music was certainly not neglected, boys being taken to the Baths Hall for various musical performances, as on the 22 February 1957 when 120 pupils and four staff attended a concert given by the Liverpool Philharmonic Orchestra.

The next festival after 1948 seems to have been held in October 1951 (no references were found for the years 1949 and 1950), when the girls entered three choirs. Auditions were held in the Baths Hall at 4 p.m. on 30 October, schools closed the following day for the festival and a concert took place on 1 November. Both the girls' and boys' schools had children who took part in the concert: a selection of girls from the choirs with three teachers and fifteen boys from 2.1 with Mr A. Robinson attended a rehearsal at the Baths Hall between 2 and 4 p.m.

Festivals were not held in the next two years but in 1954 Mr Bennett the Music Adviser visited the girls' school for an hour on 5 November in relation to a forthcoming festival and the girls had two entries (details were not given) on 17th of the month. No reference was made to the festival by the boys' school. It is possibly significant that Mr Robinson, the master in charge of music, left the school in August 1954.

At the end of the school year 1957–1958 Miss Fenby recorded, in her end-of-year summary of achievements, the results of the 'Darlington Competitive Music Festival' but the date of the event was not given and there is no record of a festival entry for the boys during this year.

Folk dancing Class 2 under twelve years old gained a Certificate of Merit

Class 3 12 to 15 years team 1 gained 82 marks; team 2 82 marks; team 3, 83;

and team 4, 81

Class 4 over 15 years of age gained a Certificate of Merit.

Choirs A and B earned Certificates of Merit

Hymn Singing Choirs A and B gained Certificates of Merit

The event was described as 'competitive', which it clearly was. The entry gives some indication of the festival programme and the involvement of the girls' school.

In 1959 the festival described as non-competitive was held in the Baths Hall on 18 November, when, once again, the schools were closed. The girls' choirs and recorder groups attended rehearsals on the 19th and 20th as preparation for concerts given in the evening. The boys' school record of the event concisely states: '18.11.59 Wednesday. The School closed for the Darlington Schools' Non-competitive Music Festival in which the school took part.' It was in January 1960 when Mr B. Sheppard was appointed to the post of Responsibility for the Teaching of Music, just after the retirement of the head teacher, Mr Welford.

In 1960 the Competitive Music Festival took place on 3 and 4 March and Mr Foxon, the new head teacher at the boys' school, wrote: '3.3.60 A Junior and a Senior Team took part' and '4.3.60 Teams of boys, and girls from Eastbourne Girls' School took part in the Country Dancing'. Miss Fenby did not record these events.

In 1961 the festival took place on 2 and 3 March, again described as competitive, and Miss Fenby did record: 'Choirs and Folk Dancing Teams entered from this school.' Mr Foxon wrote: '2.3.61 two school choirs participated in the Darlington Competitive Music Festival' and '3.3.61 Teams of boys, and girls from the Girls' Department took part in the Folk Dance'. Do the entries echo the fact that the girls' school was very much a girls' department, not to be mixed with the boys, and a move on the part of the new boys' school head towards the integration of boys and girls?

The LEA's wish to promote an appreciation of music is further illustrated by its organisation of orchestral concerts for children For example on 12 November 1946, fifty-five girls from the third year and U2.1 and three staff attended an afternoon performance given by the Lemare String Orchestra at the grammar school; on 24 November 1950 the Yorkshire Symphony Orchestra gave a performance at 2 p.m. attended by 279 girls with 8 staff and 80 boys; and on 22 February 1957 there was a performance for schools by the Liverpool Philharmonic at the Baths Hall when 112 girls with 6 staff and 120 boys with 4 staff attended.

Drama

The opportunity to experience drama productions and to take part in school-produced plays, and the boys' pantomime, was yet another aspect of the broad curriculum offered by the Eastbourne Schools. The girls' school regularly held drama concerts and the boys' annual pantomime was one of the cornerstones of the school year.

Two aspects to a drama concert given on 18 March 1948 in the girls' school are interesting. Firstly is the fact that the performance was given by the drama club with 'a wide range of girls'; and secondly there was an audience of some 500 including, as was the pattern at the time, members of the Education Committee and the CEO. Three plays were presented: *King Melow, William Tell* and *Twice is Too Much*. Secondly, those involved belonged to a club, presumably a voluntary activity taking part outside lesson time. Some of the plays seem to be the work of the teachers.

During the afternoon of 19 December 1951 the junior school assembled in the hall for a drama recital given by first-year girls and in July 1955, for the production of a play written by member of staff, Miss Auckland, performed by class 2.1J between 11 and 12.30.

In 1952 there is reference to the annual concert of music, drama, mime and dance, in which 120 girls took part and 400 people attended, taking place at 7 p.m. on 2 April and being repeated in the morning of the following day for the pupils in school.

Drama was clearly an aspect of the curriculum encouraged by the local authority, encouraging the Children's Theatre Company Ltd to give performances in the schools, as on 16 November 1948 when 240 girls and 9 staff attended a performance of *Androcles and the Lion* given by the company in the boys' school.

From Mr Welford's observations, performances were given during the mornings and afternoons of 15 and 16 November when pupils from other Authority schools attended as well as those from Eastbourne.

A similar programme took place on 17 and 18 October 1949 when the company gave performances of *Tobias and the Angel*. Eastbourne girls, a total of 222 from the second, third and fourth years, attended, and, no doubt, so did the boys, but no number was recorded.

The Education Authority arranged a week-long course of lectures in October 1951 given by Miss N. Lambourne, a staff tutor at the British Drama League and a specialist on stage settings and costumes. On the 10th of the month Miss Lambourne visited the Eastbourne Schools to give a talk and demonstration to the pupils and staff. Miss Fenby refers to eighty pupils attending but Mr Welford only states that the event took place: it is not therefore known whether the eighty pupils were boys and girls, or only girls.

Performances by the English Children's Travelling Theatre Company were given at the girls' school on 21 February 1957 when the audiences included pupils from the following schools: Larchfield RC Girls, Beechwood RC Boys, and Eastbourne Girls. Some 200 Eastbourne boys attended at 10 a.m. but no figures are given for the numbers coming from other schools. The programme consisted of two plays: a drama *Down to the Sea* by Stuart Brady and a comedy, *The Proposal.*

Details of numbers attending the Children's Theatre Performance given on 26 November 1959 are given: 'Eastbourne Boys 175 and Girls 175, St Augustine's Boys 70, St Augustine's Girls 30. A programme of two plays was presented: *The Tinsel Duchess* by Philip Johnson and *The Anniversary* by Anton Chekhov. An HMI attended.'

In November 1962 performances of dance, song, drama and mime were presented in the boys' school at 2.30 p.m. All fourth-year girls and 200 boys attended plus 67 pupils from St Augustine's Girls' School.

Examinations and the reporting of progress

The girls' school log records that on 23 June 1947 the half-yearly test in arithmetic took place in the morning and on 25 June 1947 the English test took place, again during the morning. The programme was apparently limited to these two subjects and illustrates a simple, straightforward situation. In January 1948 the tests are referred to as 'class examinations' but by the end of 1948 they included four subjects: during the morning session on 30 November there was the examination entitled 'Composition', on 1 December 'Arithmetic', on 2 December 'English', and on 6 December 'Literature'.

A similar pattern was followed in June and November/December 1949, the duration of the papers being given for the winter timetable: composition, one hour forty minutes; literature, one hour thirty minutes; arithmetic, two hours ten minutes; and English, also two hours ten minutes. It is emphatically stated that the composition examination was for 'the whole school', possibly suggesting that the other subjects were not – there is a hint that the duration of the papers was aimed at the senior classes. There is no doubt however that the examinations were becoming more sophisticated, taking longer and involving more subjects.

June 1950 Examinations for the whole school

29.6.50 Composition 10.40 till 12.30

3.7.50 English language a.m.

5.7.50 Arithmetic 10.45 till 12.30

6.7.50 Literature 10.45 till 12.30

June 1951 Examinations

25.6.51 Essay am and pm Literature

28.6.51 Mathematics 10.45–12.30

19.6.51 English Language 10.45–12.30

4.7.51 Year Group Arithmetic 9.15–10.15

November 1951

19.11.51 Mathematics Two hours

30.11.51 Composition 1 ½ hours

3.12.51 English 1 ½ hours

4.12.51 Literature 1 ½ hours

27–29 June 1955

Monday Mathematics 10.30 till 12.30

Essay 2 till 4 p.m.

Tuesday English Language 2 till 4

Wednesday Literature 10.30 till 12.30

In June 1951 the subject mathematics is introduced, the paper taking one and three-quarter hours, while 'Year Group Arithmetic' lasts for one hour. In November 1951 the mathematics paper lasted for two hours.

The established pattern for internal examinations continued to be given in the girls' school log up to 1962 and the essay or composition section was always included, clear evidence that, in that school, considerable importance was attached to this aspect of the curriculum.

There is an example in 1946 of the LEA's promotion of essay writing among school pupils. Following a visit to the Local Government Exhibition in November of that year the timetable was suspended as instructed by the CEO for the girls to enter an essay-writing competition, when first and second prizes were awarded for the best essays in the upper and lower school.

There was also the Annual Clara Lucas Essay writing competition established before the 1939–45 war.

Entrance tests

The girls' school carried out annual testing of new pupils in September each year. In September 1949 entrance tests were given to all of the new 11+ girls and the head reported: 'from the results an exceptional amount of transferring and reorganisation was necessary'. It would appear from this evidence that information on standards reached by children coming from the primary schools was unreliable, probably because of the varying standards from school to school. The project was repeated in September 1950, with the first-year classes being rearranged as a result, presumably to give the intended grouping by ability for the strict organisation of classes into streams, and continued throughout the time Miss Fenby was head teacher.

The Entrance to Secondary Schools Examination

Subsequent to the 1944 Education Act all secondary school education was free, the Eastbourne Schools being designated 'secondary modern schools' to exist side by side with the girls' high and boys' grammar schools. The category of fee-paying pupils therefore ceased to exist and the facility for parents to pay for their children to have a grammar school education was eliminated.

There is evidence to suggest that some pupils and or their parents did not wish to be involved in the 13-plus selection procedure. Where the figures are available there is a discrepancy between the number of girls eligible to take the examination and the number of actual candidates. This becomes more obvious from 1957 onwards. As early as 1948 it is recorded in the school log that two girls were absent, producing medical certificates, and two others were absent and gave no reason why. In February 1959 Miss Fenby noted 'from a total of 164 pupils eligible to take the examination, 104 opted to do so (parents' choice) 13 were absent', suggesting that, even when some parents wished their children to taken the examination, some absented themselves. Although the data for the boys' school is far less than that given in the girls' school log, an entry by Mr Foxon for 1960 seems to suggest the boys were absent because of their reluctance to take the examination.

The log book entries for the girls' school show that the school was involved in a selection system for pupils at the ages of 11-plus and 13-plus.

What appears to be a special sitting of the examination was held in January 1947 and may have been for children with some medical problem, but it is not clear whether the log entry refers to all five entrants or just the older child.

The log entry for 11 March 1947 shows examinations were held for the 11-plus age group on three consecutive days, while the entry for 13 March shows the 13-plus children were tested during the morning and afternoon of that day.

There were ninety-nine candidates for each examination but a few were absent. Another fifty-two girls, presumably not taking the main examination, were due to take the intelligence test but nineteen of these were absent and this may have been significant. The weather was described as the most severe of the winter but it was perhaps the least motivated group of girls who experienced the highest absence rate.

Entrance to Secondary Schools Examination log entries 1947

There was an Entrance to Secondary Schools Examination held in January 1947 – for children aged between 11 and 12 years, when five pupils were eligible (four aged between 11 and 12 years and one aged between 12 and 13 allowed on medical grounds). The children attended an appropriate centre in the primary schools when the tests took place during three morning sessions and one afternoon session.

11.3.47: The Entrance to Secondary Schools Examination, referred to as the 11+, was held in the morning of 11th March 1947.

Morning – Intelligence Test – Possible entrants 99, of which 5 were absent. Three teachers from North Road invigilated and three Eastbourne staff invigilated at North Road.

The examination continued on the following day in both the morning and afternoon.

13.3.47: Entrance to Secondary Schools – Late entrants

Referred to as the 13+

a.m. and p.m. Entrants 99, 7 absent

Girls in the same year group not taking the examination were given the same intelligence test. There should have been 52 girls present, 19 were absent.

In July 1947 there was a meeting of the General Purposes Sub Committee of the Education Committee to discuss Late Entrants – Transfers to Secondary Schools.

1947 Results: to the High School 5/20 and to the Technical School 12/32.

Those to go into the examination class at Eastbourne were to be given later.

The figures for the boys gaining entry to the grammar and technical schools again demonstrate a demand on the part of parents for the chance for their children to qualify. The figures demonstrate a greater demand and/or success (the data alone does not tell us which) in the case of the technical school and this is particularly the case in the latter years. It could be that the boys and their parents favoured entry into what they saw as a technical rather than purely academic establishment or it could be that the system was designed to cause more to qualify for the technical school than the grammar school.

The reluctance to take part could be used as an argument in favour of abolishing the procedure: the system being seen as placing undue pressure on the children; favouring those with ambitious parents; and emphasising the psychology of failure. Much was to be made of the so-called failure of children to qualify for grammar and technical school places at the tender age of 11 and 12 but surely the concept of failure was misused by adults, particularly the professional idealists. In a situation designed to ensure that a large majority do not reach a qualifying standard does it matter? Surely, what should matter is that there is a broad enough range of activities provided to give the majority a good chance of qualifying in something.

In 1958 there was clearly dissatisfaction shown concerning the existing 11-plus system of selection as the Education Committee approved a recommendation of the Teacher's Advisory Committee to modify the procedure. Previously two sets of tests were taken with a gap of about one month between them and each consisting of papers in three subjects. The change required the pupils to take one set of tests on a day that was not made public beforehand and this test would provide only 50 per cent of the marks used to prepare the order of merit lists. The other 50 per cent came from merit lists prepared by the teachers in the primary schools. In cases where the recommendations from the schools and the test results did not agree, information taken from record cards was to be considered as well.

It could be argued that the new system was less objective than the old, relying on teachers' judgements. In addition it could be said that the testing system, albeit made up of two different tests on two separate days, put children under unreasonable pressure and that selection (if there was to be any at all) should be made on the continuous assessment of pupils' work over a longer period.

The desire for change primarily came from those who were not in favour of any form of selection at 11 years of age, although it was accepted by the Authority that transfer from one type of school to another could take place at any time on the recommendation of the head teacher.

Whatever one's views may be, the selection procedure came to an end after the 1961 examination.

The difference in numbers of girls and boys transferring at the 13-plus stage to the grammar and technical schools during the period 1947–62 is certainly interesting. The significance of the difference is, however, by no means obvious from the data alone. It is often claimed that girls mature at an earlier age than boys, so, if this is the case, why do more girls than boys qualify for the grammar-type education at 13+? It should be the case that as the boys mature, they catch up with the girls and demonstrate a higher rate of qualification for the academic courses.

It could of course be the case that there are more places available at the high school than at the grammar school. Or it may be that girls in general are more academically inclined than boys – or that the examination is in some way less appealing to the boys' ambitions, or is orientated towards the girls' attitude to learning.

Whatever the case, the evidence surely suggests the need for more opportunities to be made available for young people to develop their various abilities and interests – more areas in which to qualify, not less.

Darlington Society of Arts – School of Arts Scholarship

Another examination which could be taken by the girls during the Fenby years was the Darlington Society of Arts – School of Arts Scholarship. Seven pupils took the examination in late June 1946 but it is not clear how many were successful. In March 1950 nine girls attended the Technical College School of Art in order to take the examination and in 1952 it is clear that the examination lasted from 9.45 a.m. till 12.30 p.m. The log entry for 1953 explains that the examination was in two parts: Part 1 on 3 March and Part 2 on 5 March.

In spite of a lack of information for many years it is clear that a small number of girls were entered for the School of Arts Scholarship and a few were successful.

The significance of the examination being available is that it provided another opportunity for pupils to achieve success in an area of particular interest to them and in which they had a special talent.

Barclays Bank Scholarship Examination

A 13-year-old, Janet Jackson, sat the Barclays Bank Scholarship Examination in January 1949.

There may well have been other such opportunities which were not recorded in the log book.

The development of the School Leavers' Examination

During the secondary modern years at Eastbourne the School Leavers' Examination system grew out of its initial stage, that seen in the grammar schools, towards a mammoth institution involving all 16-year-old young people. The developments at Eastbourne mirror the national trend.

In March 1945 a meeting took place between the CEO and the heads of the girls' and boys' schools to discuss the reorganisation and the possibility of establishing a course which would lead to a School Leaving Certificate. In June 1946 there was a meeting of the General Purposes Subcommittee of the Education Committee, held to discuss the transfer of girls at 13-plus to a School Leaving Certificate class at the Eastbourne Girls' School. In mid July 1946, in the afternoon, twenty-six parents of girls due to be admitted next term to the School Leaving Certificate course were interviewed. The class, and other groups, was inspected by an HMI in November 1946.

In January 1947 there was a meeting of the Maintenance Allowance Subcommittee of the Education Committee to consider maintenance allowances for School Certificate pupils. Clearly, the problem of cost was considered a significant factor in deterring some pupils from staying in school for the extra year necessary for the completion of the Certificate course.

There was also liaison with the high school staff to discuss School Certificate work, at least pointing to the different requirements and experience perceived as necessary for teachers involved.

Another significant factor in the development was the need to involve parents in what was then the unusual step of staying in school beyond the statutory school-leaving age when, for the second time, towards the end of July 1947, the parents of girls entering the School Certificate course in the following September were interviewed by the head teacher. Twenty-four of the girls' parents attended.

Matters did not entirely progress without doubts being raised about the suitability of having such a course in the modern school. In July 1947 one HMI spent a considerable time with the School Certificate group, reporting that they were a 'grand group of girls' and the staff were working with them at the correct level for their 'very limited ability'. There also seemed to be doubt expressed by the Eastbourne staff about the suitability of the girls for such a course because of what was perceived as their limited ability – limited being a relative term and applying to academic ability only.

On the 23rd meetings were held at 7.00 p.m. of parents of the School Certificate groups and of the twelve in U 4th all were represented; twenty out of twenty-one of L 4th parents attended. The following evening at 7.00 p.m. parents of girls offered entry into the School Certificate Group for the following September were interviewed. Twenty-eight places had been offered but one declined; they were Eastbourne 16, Reid Street 7 and North Road 4. Three girls were not represented by a parent.

In September 1947 sixteen girls from Eastbourne and twelve others transferred at 13-plus made up the School Certificate group. A decision of the Education Committee was that the group should continue at Eastbourne but one of the six subjects taught should be replaced by business knowledge, with the proviso that any girl found to be not suitable for the course after two years should take commercial training (including shorthand and typewriting) for one year instead.

The size of the group being offered the Certificate course increased: at the start of the second half-year in February 1948 Forms 5.1, 5.2, and 5.3 seem to be referred to as School Certificate groups. Two girls left 5.2 at the end of the first half-year.

In March 1948 ten girls from 5.3 began to attend the high school for mock examinations. Also in this month HMIs visited the school with reference to the School Certificate Business Knowledge course and to give consideration to having a commercial course in the school.

In 1948 ten girls from 5.3 attended the high school to take the School Certificate Examination. Their results, published in the summer, showed seven of the girls gained a certificate. The head teacher remarked 'exceeded expectations and the experiment, begun 3 years ago, proved most interesting'.

The only reference in the boys' school log relating to this examination, dated 12 March 1945, states: 'The headmaster attended the Grammar School at 3 pm. Re: School Certificate Course'. There is no reference to any such course being organised in the school.

> Number of Exam Papers taken by the ten girls (having failed to gain entry into the high school at 11+ or 13+): 69
>
> Number of papers awarded at the Credit standard: 28 – about 42%
>
> Number of papers awarded at the Pass standard: 29 – about 43%
>
> Number of papers failed: 12 – only just over 17%

A further observation made at the start of the autumn term related to class 5.2 (the second year of the School Leaving Certificate course): owing to business knowledge being dropped from the course, numbers were depleted, leaving only six girls in the group, who were transferred (for staffing reasons) to the High School. All girls who qualified in the previous term's 13-plus were admitted to the High School; therefore there were no girls from Eastbourne to start the first year of the School Leaving course, and no group to commence a course in the autumn. A full report of the experiment was submitted to the CEO.

At the end of the 1949 summer term eight girls from the School Certificate group transferred to the High School to complete their course, and miss Fenby noted: 'School Certificate Course closed'. Apparently, at the examination in 1949, four of these girls passed and two failed. There is no record of what happened to the other two. An indication may be found in an observation made by a former High School girl many years later: some of the girls transferring from the secondary modern schools for their last year were talented, for instance, playing the violin, but never seemed to adopt the ethos of the grammar school.

Northern Counties Council School Certificate
The next reference to a School Leaving Certificate for pupils at the Eastbourne Schools is dated 26 February 1957, the concept expecting pupils at the schools to be in need of such an examination lying dormant for about eight years. A meeting took place at the Darlington Technical College at 4 p.m. involving all of the heads of the secondary modern schools re: 'Examinations in Secondary Modern Schools'.

A question immediately comes to mind: if the earlier experiment in the girls' school came to an end because it was felt that the pupils did not have the required level of academic ability to succeed in the School Certificate Examination, would any new examination designed for the modern school pupil be easier? Did the intake of pupils between 1949 and 1958 display higher levels of ability? Was the new examination designed to be less academic in style?

The Northern Counties Council School Certificate was introduced in September 1958 and there was a good turnout for a meeting of third- and fourth-year pupils' parents at 7 p.m. on 16th of the month when the LEA policy was introduced. As the examinations took place in the fifth year it was necessary for candidates to remain in school beyond the school-leaving age which was then 15.

In October 1958 the head teacher of the girls' school became a representative on the Northern Counties School Certificate Standing Committee and attended regular meetings in Newcastle. The word 'Council' was eventually dropped from the title.

Valuable information relating to the subjects taken by the pupils – and, in the girls' school, the results achieved by the candidates – was recorded in the schools' log books. For example, in May it was recorded that the Northern Counties School Certificate Examination was scheduled to take place for the first time from 27 May1959 till 10 June 1959, in the girls' school, arrangements being made for subjects to be taken by twenty-two candidates, and in the boys' school for thirty, each taking papers in five subjects. The total number of pupils originally entering this year group was 154 and 193 respectively and this provides a very approximate indication of the proportion eventually taking the examination.

Eighteen girls were awarded a certificate, while the other four failed to qualify. Note the absence of any commercial subjects, such as shorthand and typewriting, introduced into the girls' school during the experimental period of the School Certificate Course.

The timetable for the examination period provides a list of subjects taken by the boys. There are some subjects common to both boys and girls but others are clearly intended to belong firmly in the realm of one or the other, the education of boys and girls still being seeing in terms of differing sexual roles. A comparison, shown in the table below, is worthy of perusal.

Boys' School first Northern Counties School Certificate Examination May 1959

Papers taken

27.5.59:	Technical Drawing	9.30 a.m.–12 noon.
28.5.59:	English Language Pt 1	9.30–10.30 Pt 2 11.00 a.m.–12 noon.
	Metalwork Pt 2 Practical	1.45 p.m.–4.15 p.m.
29.5.59:	Metalwork Pt 2 Practical	9.30 a.m.–12 noon
	Metalwork Practical Pt 2	1.45 p.m.–4.15 p.m.

(Candidates who opted for lathe work were divided into three groups and each performed the demands of the examination at separate times.)

1.6.59:	Mathematics	9.30 a.m.–11.30 a.m.
2.6.59:	Science	2 p.m.–4 p.m.
8.6.59:	Woodwork Pt 1	9.30 a.m.–11.00 a.m.
	Metalwork Pt 1	2.00 p.m.–3.30 p.m.
10.6.59	Woodwork Pt 2	2 p.m.–4.30 p.m.

A comparison of subjects taken by the pupils of the Eastbourne Schools at the first Northern Counties School Certificate Examination in 1959

Girls: English language – arithmetic – art – biology – English literature – housecraft

Boys: English language – mathematics – technical drawing – science – woodwork or metalwork.

The examinations started on 27 May and ended on 10 June; term finished at the end of July, meaning that, if the pupils were expected to remain in school until the end of the term, there were five or six weeks of schooling to be completed. A purposeful programme of learning should be required, but what will motivate those who believe their course has finished and are anxious to take up employment and earn money? The school-leaving dates at this time were still Christmas, Easter and summer: those examination candidates who had reached the leaving age by Christmas or Easter were therefore able to finish their schooling as soon as their examinations were concluded.

The recorded results for the girls' school show that the same subjects, with the exception of art, were taken at the 1960, 61 and 62 examinations: art being a minority subject and having no entries in 1960.

Practical examinations give an opportunity to pupils with poor language ability and/or skills to gain worthwhile qualifications and may be seen as a sensible strategy for use in this examination. However, theory papers were also taken by the candidates.

Practical examinations are costly in terms of examiners' and invigilators' time, placing an extra burden on the teaching workforce.

Northern Counties Exam 1960

Main examination

17–28 May: Candidates girls 19, boys 27

Practical Examinations

2 May: Housecraft preparation 2 till 4.15

10 May: Housecraft Examination morning and afternoon. 19 candidates. External examiner Mrs Harrison.

Practical examination: 4–5 dishes to be produced by girls of 14 to 15 years.

18 May: Metalwork Practical

1 June: Woodwork Practical

In 1961, when the main examinations took place from 2–18 May, the girls' school entered twenty-eight and the boys' thirty-two candidates. In addition to the subjects taken in previous years two boys also took the art examination and one took music.

A meeting of parents of third-year pupils was held at 7 p.m. on 17 July 1961 to discuss the Northern Counties Examination for 1962, and on the 18th of the month the CEO called a meeting of head teachers to discuss examinations in secondary modern schools, suggesting that the question of an examination for pupils not attending the grammar schools was still open to debate. On 9 November 1961 Dr Mills, a psychologist from the Child Guidance Clinic, visited the girls' school at 4 p.m. with regard to the proposed plans for the selection of candidates for the GCE course. In the girls' school at least there was apparently seen a need on the part of some pupils to sit the traditional and established examination. The views of the psychologist were not recorded.

At the examination in 1962 the girls' school entered thirty candidates and the boys' department thirty-nine. The girls took papers in English language, arithmetic, English literature, biology and housecraft. Geography was an additional subject taken and there was a minority group which took art.

The data below shows the timetable of examinations for the boys' school and illustrates the beginnings of a greater complexity. More subjects are being taken (but not necessarily by all candidates) and more papers are being set in individual subjects.

Northern Counties Examination papers taken by the boys in 1962

As recorded in the school log book

15th May: morning English Language, afternoon, Woodwork

16th May: Art Paper III

17th May: Mathematics and English Literature

18th May: General Science

21st May: Art Paper I and Practical Metalwork

25th May: Woodwork I

28th May: Music I and II

29th May: Metalwork Theory

30th May: Music III

Public examination system – staff out of school

With the development of the School Leaving Certificate came the involvement of teachers in the examination system, taking them out of school during teaching time and raising the question: should teachers be both teachers and examiners? The invigilation load was growing and more teachers were out of school taking part in subject panel meetings. The latter resulted from the involvement of classroom teachers in the setting, moderating and marking of examination papers, a policy which continued to be pursued in the development of the national Certificate of Secondary Education (CSE) examinations.

There was also a steady growth in the numbers of pupils taking the examinations with the boys having 57 candidates in years 1959–60 and the girls 51; and 71 and 58 respectively for the years 1961–62. Are more boys involved because their examinations seem to be more closely related to employment – male employment?

The most obvious adverse effect of teachers being out of school is that they are not teaching their timetabled classes and although it is true that someone else could take over during their absence this in itself is a problem. There is a loss of continuity of teaching.

Some of the teachers going out were reluctant to set work for the classes they left and, in any case, setting work is not the same as being with the pupils and interacting with them, guiding them, answering their questions, expanding on relevant aspects of knowledge and correcting their errors. In addition, extra work is placed on the shoulders of those who have to cover for their absent colleagues, leading to discontent.

During the Fenby–Welford years the concept of all school leavers taking an extensive course of examinations was in its infancy, the majority of senior school pupils not being involved. Equally, there were not many teachers absent on examination business.

The time during which teachers were out of school on examination business was negligible until early in 1958 when the involvement of staff in the Northern Counties School Certificate Examinations commenced.

The total number of days lost to teaching by staff being out of school during the years 1945–1962 was achieved from interpretations of log book entries, but the figures are estimates in half-days and the precise duration during which a teacher is out of school is not always clear; for example, a teacher leaving the premises at 11.15 a.m. to attend a meeting in Newcastle may or may not have returned by mid afternoon.

During the period from March 1958 to the end of 1959 in the girls' school the headmistress' absences count for about 2 ½ lost days, the head of English department 1 day, and the head of domestic science 1 day. The total loss of teaching appears to be of little consequence.

In the boys' school during the same period the head is only absent for one day, the deputy head 2 days, the head of woodwork 3 days, and one other teacher for an afternoon.

During 1960–62 in the girls' school the headmistresses' absences account for about 4 ½ of the lost days, the art teacher 1 day, the head of domestic science 2 days, the senior mathematics teacher 2 ½ days, and the head of English 3 ½.

In the boys' school during the same period the head is no longer involved, the head of woodwork is absent 3 days, the head of religious knowledge 2 ½ days, a mathematics teacher ½ day, the head of science 3 days, and the teacher in charge of music 1 day.

The head teacher's absences may be insignificant in terms of class teaching lost, the head usually only taking a small regular teaching timetable, possibly none at all, or filling for absent teachers; but he or she is the senior figure in the school and the one looked upon to set an example, take charge in cases of serious indiscipline and generally take action in cases of emergency. There can therefore develop a feeling among the assistant teachers that the head is 'always out of school' or 'never there when needed'.

The number of different teachers who take on examination duties increases during this period and their absence becomes more significant. In addition, it is the senior, most experienced teachers who are out of school, the temptation on the part of those left behind to accuse them of 'having a soft time', being out of contact with the pupils and their problems, and being in the more cosy environment of the committee. These are all factors in the changes influencing cohesion among staff so essential in the maintenance of a positive ethos.

The absence of staff on examination business is the second change during the period 1945–1962 in the erosion of staff cohesion, the other being the introduction of posts of special responsibility.

Standardised testing

During the testing of eligible pupils for entrance to grammar and technical schools, Miss Fenby recorded that other children also took the tests 'for record purposes'. On 16 February 1949 for example, she wrote: 'Late Entrants Examination to Grammar Schools and Technical School held am and pm (13-plus age group) 162 entries for transfer; 47 for record card purposes.' The log entry for 8 February 1950 makes it clear that those not taking the full examination took the intelligence test for record purposes, the scores being entered on the pupil's record card. It has already been noted that intelligence tests of the non-verbal type were introduced in order to identify able children who were handicapped by poor verbal skills, which were thought to be due to their social upbringing.

In 1948 a Mr Adams from the Aycliffe Approved School, as it was then, visited the school in connection with Professor Schonell's Testing. Schonell was an authority on standardised testing, as in the assessment of intelligence, and permission had been given by the Darlington Education Authority for an intelligence test to be given to the whole school. The testing took place between 9.45 and 11.00 a.m. on 22 September, when Schonell's Intelligence Test A was used. Intelligence Test B was given in January 1949. The purpose of such testing was to study the scores of large numbers of pupils in different age groups with a view to studying the distribution of the scores. When scores taken from very large populations of candidates are plotted on a graph they produce what is called the normal curve of distribution, that is, with most people in the middle range and a fall-off in numbers towards both the highest and lowest scores.

By comparing an individual's score with those in the normal distribution, his or her ability to answer the questions set in a particular test on one occasion can be shown to fall in the average, below average or above average categories for a year group as a whole. Clearly the categories could be refined to indicate various degrees of deviation from the norm: a candidate's actual score being matched to that score on the normal curve.

The purpose of giving the school both tests A and B was to look at the consistency of the candidates' scores on the two tests. A large difference between a large number of scores from many candidates would suggest that the two tests were not equivalent, and could not be assumed to give equal results. The two tests could not then be used to compare different groups tested on different occasions. The test constructors would also look for items in the tests which produce wildly different scores, suggesting that the instructions are not clear, or the question is badly worded or ambiguous. Such questions would be removed from the test.

Tests composed in this fashion are standardised assessment tests and may be used to compare individual scores with national standards in a whole range of subjects.

On 7 July 1950 the girls' school log says the 'Age Group Arithmetic Attainment Test' took place between 9.15 and 10.30; a standardised test being used to compare the girls' attainments with national norms. Such testing has its value, ensuring that standards being applied in any one school are not wildly out of agreement with the country as a whole.

Reporting progress

In 1945 regular meetings of teacher representatives were taking place at the Education Office for the planning of a new record card and local authority record cards were introduced for all pupils in September 1946. It seems that previously each school had its own method of recording pupils' progress, so this is evidence of the standardised recording of pupils' attainments for internal use by the professionals.

Parents were informed of their children's progress by the twice yearly issue of a school report which gave the marks obtained by the pupil on each subject taken in the twice yearly school examinations, the position of the child in its class when all subject marks were taken into account, the observations of each subject teacher, a comment on conduct and the number of times the child was absent and late.

In December 1954 the girls' log book tells: 'During this coming week [6.12.54] all half-yearly examinations will be held. Owing to the effect of Influenza Epidemic on attendance the examinations will be staggered. All fourth-year pupils will receive reports and testimonials as customary; no formal reports to 1st, 2nd and 3rd years but all results will be given.'

School leavers

The 1944 Education Act determined that the school-leaving age would be raised to 15 and from 1947 all pupils had to remain in school until the end of the term during which they became 15 years of age: consequently, during the Fenby–Welford Years up to 1962 pupils left at Christmas, Easter and Summer each school year. At this time there were still plenty of employment opportunities for young people and for those intending to leave when they became of age the Ministry of Labour introduced a programme of careers advice.

Each term representatives from the ministry came into school to give an introductory talk to the whole group of leavers and then in the following weeks each would be interviewed by an employment officer. Parents were invited to the interviews and, certainly in the case of the girls' school, the head teachers also sat in.

March 31 1947 was the last occasion that pupils reaching the age of 14 years up to and including 1 April could leave school at the end of that term: a total of nineteen girls took the opportunity.

In 1950 the task of interviewing and advising leavers became the responsibility of the Juvenile Employment Office, interviews for twenty-three girls taking place on 11 July when sixteen parents attended. On 13 July twenty-nine girls were interviewed and seventeen parents attended. Parental interest, demonstrated by their attendance, was generally good, although in the summer of 1949 the headmistress reported: 'Owing to many mothers being out working, it is regrettable to note the decline in numbers of parents attending the interviews.' It was apparently not expected that fathers would be able to attend at that date, very probably due to long working hours. The entries for the leavers' interviews given in the girls' school log provide some evidence of the parental support given to the children.

Talks by the Youth Employment Officer (YEO)

Introductory talks were given to the school leavers by the YEO and these were followed up by individual employment interviews.

> October 1950: Talk to Fourth Year boys on the Youth Employment Service given by Mr Pritchard.
>
> June 1950: Juvenile Employment Officer gave a talk to all girls due leave at the end of the term.

October 1951: School Leavers Talk given by YEO Mr Pritchard. 58 girls and four staff attended and an HMI came with the YEO.

October 1956: Juvenile Employment Officers (Mr Pritchard and Miss Watson) visited the school 3–4 pm. to talk to all pupils due to leave during the school year. 89 pupils were present.

Discussion followed the talks.

Visits to workplaces

Another aspect of careers advice and guidance for school leavers was the organisation of visits to places where the young people may be expected to work.

Most gained meaningful employment, adapted to the discipline of the workplace, were capable of being of value to their employers, earned money for themselves and their families, and gained a strong feeling of having entered the adult world, no doubt feeling more grown up than they actually were.

The programme of visits organised to various places of potential employment, demonstrates the nature of the employment prospects of the young people and reinforces the differences between the expectations of boys and girls. All school leavers received a medical examination in the term they were due to leave.

Examples of visits made by the girls:

3.4.46: Easter leavers (girls) visits to Peases Mill, Lilly Laundry.

Similar visits took place for Summer Leavers in July when 40 girls, in two groups, visited the Lilly Laundry and Peases Mill.

In October 1946 leavers also visited the General Post Office (GPO).

Visits for girls approaching the school-leaving age grew to include The *Northern Echo* works and offices, Messrs Alexander's factory, Messrs Paton and Baldwins' factory, the public library, Messrs Binns Store, Co-operative Dairy, General Post Office, Telephone Exchange, Memorial Hospital.

Senior girls continued visits throughout the 1950s although the number of places visited seems to become restricted in the latter years.

7.5.51: Two groups of 20 senior girls each visited Peases Mill in charge of Miss K. McLeish and Miss Raynor 2 till 3.30 pm.

31.3.60: A group of leavers visited The North Eastern Electricity Showrooms for a demonstration on modern equipment and another the Public Library.

6.11.61: Twenty senior pupils visited the Memorial Hospital – Miss McLeish in charge.

Twenty senior pupils visited Paton and Baldwins – Miss Brewster in charge.

12.3.62: Twenty senior pupils visited the Northern Echo Offices between 2 and 4 pm – Miss McLeish in charge.

Examples of visits made by the boys:

27.3.45: 20 boys attended Rise Carr Rolling Mills on a works visit, 230 p.m. in charge of Mr J. Peacock.

18.6.45: A party of 'leavers' from the Third Year in charge of Messrs J. Peacock and G. Brockway visited the Darlington Forge – 30 boys – 2.00 p.m.–4.15 p.m.

19.3.46: 18 Leavers visited Messrs Hawthorne and Stephenson Ltd 2.20 p.m. in charge of Mr Brockway.

21.3.46: 16 Leavers visited Messrs Summersons and sons Ltd at 2.30 p.m. in charge of Mr J. R. Farrage.

26.3.46: Leavers visited the Library for 2nd lecture in charge of Mr W. E. Taylor.

2.7.46: Leavers from 3.3 and 3.1 visited Whessoe Foundry in charge of Mr Farrage.

None recorded during the1946–58 period

12.6.58: Twenty-five boys visited the new College of Further Education.

12.2.60: During the afternoon session a party of leavers in charge of Mr Sparkes visited the Faverdale Wagon Works.

19.2.60: A party of leavers with Mr A. R. Foord visited the works of Stephenson and Hawthorn Ltd.

1.7.60: 4.1 visited the Power Station during the morning in charge of Mr H. C. Bullock.

14.10.60: In the afternoon session a party of leavers in charge of Mr J. Peacock visited the Faverdale works of British Railways.

The employment expectations of girls and boys
Some of the traditional industries of the town, heavy engineering, were the object of the visits made by the boys between 1945 and 1946, but there follows a gap in the programme during the 1950s. From a mere observation of log book entries it is not possible to determine the cause of this apparent break. Was it just a case of routine matters not being entered by the head teacher – although this seems to be unlikely? Was it perceived that the visits were not appropriate, possibly not reflecting changes taking place in the workplace opportunities? Or was it a matter of opportunities for visits being no longer available?

There is no obvious break through 1945–1962 in the programme of visits made by the girls and the direction in which they are guided is different from the boys, the girls being taken predominantly to such places as clothing manufacturers, shops, offices and the hospital. The latter demonstrates the guiding of girls towards the caring services. In the first instance it is clear that a major expectation of girls was that they would be the workers in the family home, as seen in the emphasis placed on the teaching of housecraft: cookery, washing and ironing, house care and needlecraft. In addition there is the programme of child care within the senior girls' curriculum, the expectation that they would be caring for their children. For instance, in 1948 class U 4 visited the Hundens Lane Nursery at 4 pm and Greenbank Maternity Hospital and clinic on another afternoon as a part of their course 'Care of young Children'.

During the 1950s the notion of girls being the mainstay of the home and family had grown to become a career ambition; nursing and commerce also being emphasised as providing career opportunities. Girls were being seen as people who would have a life in employment but, nevertheless, in those areas seen as mainly the preserve of women.

In February 1950 a meeting was held of the senior girls to introduce them to post-school courses: the Hospital Nursing Cadet Scheme and the Technical Commercial Course in Further Education.

In September 1953 a Mobile Nursing Exhibition visited the school in charge of a matron, Miss Makay, and all fourth-year girls attended a talk on the nursing profession and visited the exhibition in the van in small groups. The exhibition was brought to the school again in March 1955 when sixty fourth-year girls attended the talk and visited the exhibition. On 26 January 1955 a group of thirteen pupils from 2.2.S attended a film programme at the public library at 7.30 p.m. by kind permission of Mrs Lowther, librarian, as one film on nursing was thought to be of particular interest to those considering it as a career. In May 1959 there was a visit to the school by the King Edwards Hospital Fund for London Nursing Recruitment Service when a talk was given to all third-year girls and Miss Fenby reported 'a stimulating address'.

Another expectation of girls' employment was demonstrated during June 1951 by the showing of the film *Working in a Store*.

Conversely, in June 1951 all of the boys were taken in groups of 150 at a time to the Iron and Steel Exhibition associated with the Festival of Britain; and in June 1960 it was the headmaster of the boys' school who attended a meeting at Darlington College of Further Education in connection with a proposed follow-up course for boys leaving school and wishing to enter engineering.

Boys and the armed forces

Another expectation of the boys was that they would seek careers in the armed forces and consequently speakers from the army and RAF were invited into the school.

On 5 May 1951 Squadron Leader H. H. Henderson of the RAF addressed the whole of the fourth year on prospects for a career in the RAF. His talk was supplemented by films and on 28 May an army lecturer gave a talk to that year's leavers at 3.30 p.m. In 1953 there was a talk by a squadron leader on the RAF and careers to the Easter and summer leavers.

Paton and Baldwins

On 27 July 1951 alterations were made to the times of the school sessions as employees of Paton and Baldwins were expected to take up the accommodation on the trolley buses when the works closed for the summer holiday at 4 p.m. School closed at 3.30 p.m., when pupils would be able to use the buses provided.

In September 1966 Miss McLeish attended a teachers' Introduction to Industry course at Paton and Baldwins. This initiative was designed to give teachers, who tended to train in a college environment and then move into schools without ever experiencing the world of industry and commence, a better understanding of the employment their pupils were likely to take up on leaving.

The Armstrong–Foxon Years
Changing Times

Mr Welford, being the senior of the Fenby–Welford head teachers, retired in December 1959 while Miss Fenby continued until her retirement in April 1963. Both had established strong traditions within a fairly straightforward and uncomplicated education system lasting for almost a quarter of a century (Mr Welford 1936 to 1959 and Miss Fenby 1939 to 1963). Mr Foxon became head teacher of the boys' school in January 1960 but the complete change from the long period of constant leadership did not come to the girls' school until three or so more years had elapsed.

The following decade brought significant changes: the accepted traditions of the Christian Church began to fade, the firm autocratic leadership of the head teachers (particularly in the girls' school) became more democratic, teachers began to challenge the decisions of the school management (namely the head teacher), the curriculum expanded and the examination system became a dominant aspect of school life. The social climate relating to how children and young people should be treated became much more liberal, employment prospects for young people decreased, older youngsters remained in school (at first only those who volunteered but eventually all by direction of the state) and the changing attitudes to what should be taught and the methods employed brought confusion.

The school-leaving age had been related to the date the young person reached fifteen, but from the end of the 1963 autumn term legislation was introduced which no longer allowed pupils to leave school at Christmas.

At the time of the introduction of the Northern Counties Examination for school leavers the whole examination system began an immense growth, taking up much time and teacher energy during the summer term, which inevitably impacted on the organising of other traditional activities such as school journeys and sporting events.

The greatest upheaval and change in the schools came in 1968 when the education system changed from one of selection to that of the all-in comprehensive schools.

Changes taking place in Darlington

Apart from the internal changes to life in the schools, the 1960s were also a time of change in the geography of Darlington, developments taking place involving the clearance of old housing between the Eastbourne area and town centre and the construction of the ring road, in some respects cutting Eastbourne off from the heart of Darlington.

Town centre redevelopment

On Tuesday 17 September 1963 the *Northern Despatch* included a supplement outlining the report of the proposed redevelopment of the town centre. A further front page and inner spread appeared on 10 February 1964. The plans included pedestrian-only areas around the market place, part of Tubwell Row, the east end of Duke Street, Skinnergate and Post House Wynd. Main car parks were proposed for an area north of East Street, between Duke Street and Pewlet Street, and between Houndgate and Beaumont Street. A new town hall was to be built south-west of St Cuthbert's Church, between Feethams, Lead Yard and the River Skerne. A dual carriageway inner ring road was intended to remove traffic from the centre: it would also create a barrier between the suburbs and the heart of the town. However, pedestrian crossings were included in the plan, that connecting with Eastbourne, where there was already the River Skerne to cross, being via Tubwell Row and Parkgate, focussing on the established railway underpass.

Of more significance perhaps was that the 1930s exciting 'newness' of the Eastbourne area had declined, replaced by the emphatic changes taking place in the 1960s.

Some indication of the existing situation and state of affairs is illustrated by such reports as that of 2 November 1963, when the local authority Health Committee recommended the clearance of the Model Place, Dirk Place, Swan Street, Heal Street, Dales Yard and Hargreave Terrace area, south of Parkgate, describing at least some of the houses as being unfit for human habitation. Permission was granted for the demolition in the Russell Street area, in spite of objections and eventually with settlement payments being made to owners, of some well-maintained properties.

At the same time, in 1962, new developments were taking place in the Hummersknott and Mowden areas. In 1962 Caedmont Crescent, Barrett Road and part of Hummersknott Avenue had been completed. In 1964 a new road to link Hummersknott Avenue with Carmel Road was completed ready for the construction of eighty new houses. There were also new developments taking place at Branksome, Lascelles Park and Burnside Road (formerly the site of prefabricated post-war houses). The Lascelles Park development included the compulsory purchase of land in order to prepare for the provision of housing, open space and allotments; and the clearance of obsolete properties.

In July 1965 the council proposed to buy the twenty-five-acre Red Hall Estate, the site of the house or Red Hall built of limestone in 1830, the site also providing clay for the making of bricks.

In relation to the inner ring road, work was due to start on the construction of the first section, Victoria Place to Freeman's Place and Northgate, in September 1964. The first new building to be constructed on the ring road was the John Neasham Ltd. car dealership, completed in 1966. It was in the 1960s that the Darlington by-pass and motorway were constructed.

New schools and Darlington College of Further Education
At this time when the heart of the town was changing and new suburbs expanding, there was also the need to modernise the education system. New schools had been built in the 1950s and the programme of construction was continuing.

Changes in religious education and the application of the Christian ethic

The 1944 Education Act required every school day to start with an act of collective worship, and for religious instruction, in accordance with an agreed syllabus, to be a part of the curriculum. The first 'agreed syllabus' for Darlington Schools was established soon after the introduction of the 1944 Act. In the early 1960s changes in attitudes, and consequently requirements, had been recognised by the Authority and, while upholding the requirement that religious instruction was the only compulsory subject in the curriculum, a new syllabus was introduced.

It was the outcome of two years' work completed by a group consisting of six members of the Education Committee, five representatives each of the Church of England and Free Churches, and Darlington teachers' associations, and a representative of the Darlington College of Further Education.

Their task was not easy in a changing society. Much of taking part in the school assembly was regarded by most, without much thought, as a routine ritual and without much meaning. The key factor, belief or faith, was perhaps little considered. The teachers, who were expected to carry out the instructions of the Act, were becoming less accepting of ritual. But it was argued that education must recognise religious as well as social, cultural and physical needs. Teachers were expected to speak openly and frankly on their own beliefs and those of others, an admirable thought while most teachers subscribed to the beliefs of the Christian Church but quite clearly disruptive where teachers were displaying open hostility to these beliefs and refusing to take part in the traditional activities associated with them.

Debate included the intention to present facts but not to indoctrinate, enabling children to make up their own minds concerning matters of belief. The Bible was to be seen as a human record, including errors, and explanation was expected to show the place of God in history, that is the Christian God, not a general concept of god or gods.

Some of the group members saw that it was a duty and privilege to pass on the knowledge of the Christian faith and Bible, and to show an appreciation of Christian traditions. Others saw the new syllabus as weakening the place of Christianity in the United Kingdom.

The future, however, would be influenced by the prime aspects of religion, faith and belief, which are almost impossible to correlate with facts and for many to present objectively without displaying their own prejudices.

At the time of the Armstrong–Foxon headships the schools did still very largely follow the customs of the Christian faith. They celebrated the Christian Church festivals and held regular morning assemblies. During the post-war years there is clear evidence of support for the Christian faith in such events as the Bible Exhibition of June 1948 when forms 5.1, 5.2, Upper 4, Lower 4.1, and Lower 4.2 from the girls' school attended the exhibition in the public library, an event described as an excellent project in every way. In November 1949 films were shown to the whole school entitled *Fact and Faith, God of Creation* and *Voice of the Deep.* A further British and Foreign Bible Society exhibition, held in the Co-operative Hall, Priestgate in February 1954, was attended by classes 2.1S and 1.1S.

On 16 February 1961 the Women's World Day of Prayer was celebrated by the attendance of twenty-four fourth-year pupils at the service in St Cuthbert's Church. There were similar attendances in 1962 and 1963.

The traditional Harvest Festival was celebrated in both schools; for instance in September 1967, following the service in the girls' department, gifts were collected by members of the Women's Voluntary Service and two fourth-year girls accompanied them to distribute them to old people via the Meals on Wheels service.

The Harvest Festival service held in the afternoon of 11 October 1967 was linked with the Wells for India campaign.

The traditions of Christmas were celebrated in the schools although the boys' pantomime seemed to dominate their activities while the girls' end of term was more faith orientated. For example on 17 December 1963 at 3 p.m. a form concert was held, and on the 18th from 11.20 till 12.30 class 4.3 presented the 'Coventry Nativity Play' to the school, followed in the afternoon from 2.30 till 4.00 p.m. by form and choir carols. On 22 December 1966 at 9.30 there was a Christmas carol service, and again on 20 December 1967 the carol service was held, a nativity play presented and at 3.30 p.m. the final assembly included community carols and prayers. It is possible that similar services were held in the boys' department, as on 23 December 1964, during the morning session, a carol service with readings from the Bible was recorded as taking place.

The local authority continued to close the schools for a holiday on Ascension Day.

The building

By 1960 the modern building of 1936/39 was no longer new, being very old fashioned in style, showing signs of overcrowding and being in need of updating. As early as January 1961 Mr R. Heworth HMI visited the school and discussed with the headmaster the ministry's suggestion for a major extension of the school buildings.

In September 1962 the CEO and Borough Architect visited the boys' school to discuss the siting of two temporary classrooms.

At the start of the summer term in April 1963, when Miss Armstrong became head teacher, a new classroom was in the course of construction and the housecraft rooms were being fitted with new ironing points. By the start of the autumn term the new needlework room, at the front of the school, was ready for use but room 21, an art room, was still not complete and the porch accommodation was still not available. One first-year group was using the balcony (at the back of the hall) as a classroom.

It had been in February 1963 that Mr Foxon recorded that two HMIs, Mr R. Hewarth and Miss B. E. Hill, visited the school with plans for the new classrooms and at the start of the autumn term one, built over the south cloakroom of the boys' school, was ready for use. There were four new rooms constructed at this time over cloakrooms at the south-east, south-west, north-east and north-west corners of the main building; the two at the back of the building accessed via the stairway landings and those at the front via a step down through a small lobby from the corners of the upper-floor corridors.

There is evidence that the schools were regularly redecorated; for instance, at the girls' school, during the Christmas holiday 1963, the interior decoration of the canteen kitchen, dining hall and possibly the housecraft rooms, was taking place. In April 1964 the painting of the exterior of the building commenced and in March 1965 it was said that the painters were decorating the gymnasium, the rest of the school having been completed in 1964.

Following the announcement in September 1963 concerning the development of secondary education in Darlington, the future of the Eastbourne school buildings had to be considered with a view to their fitting into the new scheme.

There was a log entry for 24 February 1966 which recalls that the head teacher and science teachers attended a meeting in the girls' school to discuss plans for new science rooms, with Mr Ross, Deputy Education Officer. By 1967 major changes were underway.

On 13 April 1967 Mr Fletcher of the Borough Architect's Department and Mr Lomax, Clerk of Works, visited the school to discuss the remodelling with Miss Armstrong and Mr Foxon and in no time at all, later in April, contractors actually moved onto the site, and the Hundens Lane entrance was closed and the boundary of the site required for the construction of the new block secured.

On 23 May Mr Lomax visited the school to discuss with the headmaster and headmistress possible alterations to the premises which could be done between May and the summer vacation. In July the headmaster moved out of his office to allow alterations to the entrance hall to proceed.

The grounds

Shale area

In October 1960 the area which came to be known as the shale area was still being referred to as 'new' and throughout 1962 there were several inspections of the area made by the CEO, physical education adviser, and representatives of the Borough Surveyor's department.

Walled field

The grounds of the hospital once referred to as the Smallpox Hospital, were acquired by the local authority and in October 1964 the site had presumably been cleared as there was talk of 'levelling of the walled field', the surrounding wall being left standing. On 25 January 1965 members of the governing body and Education Committee visited the school to decide whether the wall surrounding the walled field should be repaired or rebuilt; and, in September the following year, Mr D. Peter (CEO), Mr Cameron (physical education adviser), Mr Jones (Parks Department superintendent) and Mr Gardener (a consultant) visited the school to inspect the work done on the walled field and the bitumastic wickets.

Security

In July 1966 a greenhouse, to be used for classes in gardening and rural science, was delivered: and as the extensive site was wide open it was, from time to time, subjected to damage by intruders.

The extensive grounds and open nature of the site has always left the Eastbourne School difficult to protect from intruders and there have always been those who have caused damage by their antisocial behaviour or desire to commit burglary. The diary of reported events indicates something of the nature and extent of the problem.

The teaching staff

In September 1960 there were about six new teachers who joined Eastbourne Boys' School, most coming straight from college (precise details of appointment not being known in each case). The head plus five others had served ten or more years in the school, four between 7 and 9, and two between 4 and 6, and another eight had only been at the school for between 1 and 3 years. Consequently some fifteen, almost half the teachers, were new.

By 1963 there were twelve teachers, nearly half the staff, who had been in post for only three or fewer years, although one of these is the deputy head and presumably an experienced teacher. Six had been in the school for more than ten years, two of them since before the war, and it can be expected that all, including the head teacher, were set in the traditions developed during the previous quarter-century. In this situation, where the staff is divided between a group of traditionalists and another of younger newcomers, it could be expected that change would be difficult to bring about.

In September 1965 those with ten or more years' service total six, while the middle (4 to 9 years) and fairly new (1 to 3 years) groups remain the same. There are, however, another four new appointments, including a new deputy head, the previous deputy only staying in the school for three years. The senior team, in terms of age, length of service in Eastbourne and experience, remained the same. The question arises: did tradition remain largely unchanged?

The 1967 figures show the group of four staff joining the school in 1960 having served for sufficient time for them to have become a part of the establishment: did they adopt the ways of the traditionalists, or did they begin to influence change? Within the group serving between 1 and 3 years is the deputy head, Mr Binns, who is in a senior and influential position, and Mr Shotton, who became the head of department for English in March 1966, being promoted to a headship elsewhere in 1970.

The staff of the girls' school in September 1963

Miss Armstrong became the head teacher at Eastbourne Girls' School in April 1963. In July that year came the retirement of Miss J. Owen BA Honours, the senior mistress/deputy head, who had commenced her service in the school in August 1939. She was replaced by Miss C. I. Hope.

Altogether nine teachers left at the end of the term plus one supply teacher, resulting in the appointment at the start of the 1963 school year of eight new teachers, four of them new to teaching.

The total number of girls on roll was 531 and the total number of teachers 22 (including one supply teacher, temporary until a permanent replacement could be appointed) plus the head teacher.

In April 1964 Miss Armstrong reported that forty pupils left at Easter to obtain employment and consequently the number of forms (classes) was reduced from sixteen to fifteen, when the fourth year became four groups instead of five. A shortage of three teachers was recorded.

The situation in 1965 is not so very different: the same six long-serving teachers are still in post, another has now served 7 years and six between 1 and 3 years. There are seven who have been at the school for less than 1 year and two of these are new to the school in September 1965.

There is, therefore, opportunity for a team of long-serving teachers to dominate the school and a large number, thirteen, to follow the established traditions. One of the newcomers is, however, the deputy head, who is an experienced teacher and, it can be expected, will be concerned with overseeing the introduction of new educational developments.

The pattern of a group of six long-serving teachers continued in 1967 with a small group of four now having been in the school long enough to have adapted to its ethos and brought their own ideals in so far as there has been the opportunity for them to do so. There is still a sizeable new group of which two have just joined the staff.

Teacher consultations and representation

In July 1933 the Darlington Education Committee refused to discuss with the representatives of the Darlington Teachers' Association, the local branch of the NUT, the matter of closer relationships between the teachers and the committee. The teachers were concerned about changes being made to education in the town and wished to place their views before the elected members.

A resolution passed by the committee informed the teachers that they felt no advantage would be obtained by meeting a deputation from the Teachers' Association as it was the responsibility of the committee to determine policy. They agreed, however, that there was time for the teachers to submit their views to the committee and that their views would be carefully considered.

Alderman Leach, the Chairman of the Education Committee at the time, was reported as saying that if the committee consulted teachers on matters of policy they would be putting themselves in a difficult position. He went on to say many decisions had recently been taken and no teacher had been adversely affected, none had their appointments terminated and none suffered loss of pay. It was his view that the Authority had dealt generously with the teachers during the changes, unlike some authorities, and that, really, was that.

It is clear that regular consultations with teachers' representatives did not take place, the Authority being seen today, perhaps, as rather benevolently autocratic.

In the 1960s the local branch of the NUT sought representation on the Education Committee and it is not surprising that the local authority saw difficulties arising, not least due to the fact that other bodies would seek similar representation and the existing system of co-opting people to committees would have to be completely reviewed. The Chairman of the Education Committee at the time, Alderman James Skinner (more usually known as Jim), was in favour of representation being considered, saying that Darlington was the only authority in the country which did not have a representative system of this kind in operation. His idea was that co-options should be limited to six and would be one or two teachers, and representatives of the Darlington churches.

The Teachers' Advisory Committee was in existence at this time and its composition being reviewed.

The position of the teachers in the schools was changing but still largely accepting of the head being the head: he or she made the decisions, listening to assistants if they so desired, and instructions were generally handed down with the expectation that they would be carried out without question. In the early days of the two schools, staff meetings to discuss school policy or arrangements were not recorded and possibly did not take place in any formal fashion. The schools were small by today's standards – the staff small in number and easily met and spoken with every day of the week. Nevertheless, in the case of the girls' school in particular, evidence suggests that only the most senior staff were recognised as having sufficient experience for their views to be considered.

This situation was to change. The social climate changed, the styles of head-teacher leadership changed and the idea that teachers' views should at least be invited and listened to gained acceptance. Reports of staff meetings taking place became more frequent.

At the boys' school there was a meeting held at 1.30 p.m. on 14 March 1960, the agenda being very briefly recorded as 'Registers and the House System'. Another in April 1961, again held at 1.20 p.m., considered the Ascension Day outing, future term events, the regrouping of the school and the introduction of a report book.

At this time the meetings appeared to be called when there was some specific matter to discuss; they took place in timetable time at 1.20 p.m., the pupils being on an extended break.

Agenda items – including such things as the discussion of dining-room supervision, whether or not to go ahead with the school pantomime, the house system (a more equable award of house marks between examinations and weekly competition, and sporting activities), reports, examinations, promotions etc. and the organisation of classes for the coming year – suggest areas of particular concern and the need to both inform and involve staff in the day-to-day running of the school. This was also the beginning of a more formal approach to staff consultations.

In relation to pupil behaviour, the question of discipline was raised for the first time at the staff meeting held on 17 September 1963, and again on 8 February 1965. Linked with the raising of school-meals supervision on several occasions, does this indicate the staff being less conscientious in the matter of general supervision of the school?

Another area of increasing significance apparent from staff-meeting agendas was that of school examinations, including the school-leaving examinations.

The first report of strike action by teachers was on 20 September 1961 when ten members of the National Association of School Masters were absent from duty. Eight classes were given the day off and no school dinners were served.

On 27 March 1963, a local representative of the NUT, Mr J. D. Lovell, was absent attending the House of Commons lobby by teachers, indicating a developing period of union action.

The size and organisation of the schools

The girls' school roll for September 1961 was 647. Miss Fenby reported: 'the pressure on accommodation continues, all special rooms, the balcony of the hall, the canteen, and Gym annex are needed.'

The Size of Eastbourne Secondary Modern Schools 1963–1968				
Start of Term	Girls' School Roll	Boys' School Roll	Girls School 1st Year	Boys School 1st Year
29.4.63				
2.9.63	539	608	4 classes	
7.1.64	539	608	3 classes of 40, 39 and 38 girls	
13.4.64	497	556		
31.8.64	?	566	3 classes	126
11.1.65	?	566		
3.5.65	?	?		
31.8.65	484	532	3 classes	?
25.4.66	465	?		
30.8.66	459	496	124 in 4 classes	111
10.1.67	?	?		
10.4.67	?	?		
4.9.67	?	?	4 classes	?
9.1.68	464	?		
By the end of the Autumn term 1963 a new Act had been introduced which no longer allowed pupils to leave at Christmas				

In 1960 concern was being shown about overcrowding in both the boys' and girls' schools, otherwise the internal organisation of the departments continued according to the traditions already developed. Both schools continued to place pupils in classes according to their ability, the system of streaming continuing, as illustrated in the staff deployment at the girls' school for September 1964. There were twenty-two teachers and fifteen registration groups, and consequently seven teachers did not have form-teacher responsibilities. They were Mrs Forrest (history), Mrs Forster (a supply teacher), Mrs Richley, and four housecraft teachers: Miss Dover, Miss Manfield, Mrs Butterfield and Mrs Clark.

In 1964 there was an 'O' level class due to take the examination in the summer of 1965; a fourth-year group intending to remain in school for a fifth year, presumably to take 'O' level; and another working for the Northern Counties Certificate in the following summer.

In the middle and lower school the first figure of the class title signifies the year and the second the stream. Therefore 3.1 is the top class in the third year, 3.2 the second from top, 3.3 the third and 3.4 the bottom group. The system was reintroduced by the new head teacher, Miss Armstrong.

Girls' school teacher deployment
September 1964

5 O level 1965 Miss McLeish

4.1 Mrs Watson – those pupils intending to stay for a 5th year

4.2 Miss Hope Northern Counties Certificate form 1965

4.3 Miss Giles a class with some Easter leavers

4.4 Miss Richardson a class with some Easter leavers

3.1 Miss W. Robinson, 3.2 Mrs Ellwood, 3.3 Mrs Fairless, 3.4 Miss Brewster

2.1 Mrs Brown, 2.2 Mrs Flowers, 2.3 Miss Nancarrow

1.1 Mrs Nicholson, 1.2 Mrs Clarke, 1.3 Mrs J. Robinson

The same detail, giving the names of the teachers in each case, was not given in the boys' school log. For 1964 the entry merely states that there was a first-year intake of 126 boys placed in four forms, and for the first time there was a fifth-year class of 14 boys.

Earlier, in January 1964, the head teacher of the girls' school reported staffing problems: no replacements were appointed for two full-time staff who left at Christmas and eighteen classes were reduced to sixteen. Consequently, there were two full-time staff short and only two part-time staff recruited. When forty girls left at Easter the classes were again reorganised into fifteen classes, one less in the fourth year than in the previous term. The head claimed that the school was then three teachers short and three part-timers had been appointed. A problem with part-time staff is that they would only be available when they chose to be, not necessarily when the school wanted them, therefore various part-time staff would be used to cover gaps in the timetable. A further problem is that part-time staff are not always committed to the school as a whole, only attending for their teaching hours.

At the end of the 1965 summer term the school lost six staff out of an estimated twenty-two, or about 27 per cent.

Girls' school teacher deployment
September 1965

Fifth year Miss McLeish

4.1 Mrs Watson, 4.2 Miss Brewster, 4.3 Miss Lumley, 4.4 Miss Richardson

3.1 Miss Giles, 3.2 Mrs Armstrong, 3.3 Mr Jones, 3.4 Mrs Wylie

2.1 Mrs Fairless, 2.2 Mr Hughes, 2.3 Miss Robinson

1.1 Mrs Clarke, 1.2 Miss Lonergan, 1.3 Mrs Forrest

Staff without class responsibilities:

Miss Hope and housecraft staff: Miss Dover, Miss Manfield, Mrs Butterfield, Miss Jackson

In 1965, when the number of pupils on roll was 459 in 15 forms, the deployment of staff in the girls' school was similar to that of the previous year, while the boys' school had 18 forms and a roll of 532.

The number of pupils in a form is given below for the girls in 1966, showing sizes of teaching groups, although half-classes were timetabled for practical subjects. (NC means Northern Counties; P means practical, but the meaning of PW and PG is not known.)

Girls' school teacher deployment
September 1966

Fifth year (16 girls) Miss McLeish

4 CSE (29) Mrs Watson, 4 NC (38) Miss Brewster

4 PG (24) Miss Giles, 4 PW (23) Miss Wylie

3.1 (38) Miss Fairless, 3.2 (35) Miss Wold, 3.3 (29) Mrs Spurr

2.1 (37) Miss Richardson, 2.2 (35) Miss Thornton, 2.3 (31) Mr Hughes

1.1 (38) Mrs Clarke, 1.2 (37) Mrs Forrest, 1.3 (26) Mrs Lonergan

1.4 (23) Mrs Armstrong.

Teachers without forms: Miss Hope and Mrs Brown

Housecraft staff –Miss Dover, Miss Jackson, Miss Manfield

Part-time staff – Mrs Paterson 5 mornings for housecraft, mothercraft and child care (a new course).

Apart from the 'O' level group, top streams in each year are the largest classes, allowing slightly smaller groups to be provided for slower-learning pupils. But even the smallest groups hardly allow for very much individual attention to be given to the girls.

The total number of girls in the school at this time was 459 and the number of teachers (excluding the head) the equivalent of 20.7, an average of about one teacher to every 22 pupils.

In a five-day week with a seven-period day there would have been 35 lessons per week to be given to each of the 15 classes, a total of 425 (at least, because practical subjects were taught in half-classes). The teachers, however, did not teach 35 periods each week, having time free from pupil contact for marking and preparation purposes. Taking the number of such periods per teacher as five, there were 20.7 teachers available for 20.7 x 30 teaching periods, a total of 621, so there are apparently 196 teaching periods spare, or 13 for each of the 15 teaching groups, allowing each of these groups to be taught in half-classes for about one day each week. This would not be possible if the number of classes was increased in order to reduce the number of pupils in each class.

The 'O' level group being only sixteen in number was expensive in terms of teacher time; the other examination groups, twenty-nine for the CSE class and thirty-eight for those taking the Northern Counties course, perhaps seem to be unfairly large. The problem was that only sixteen were either willing to stay in school above the leaving age or were judged to be capable of taking and succeeding in the examination of the harder GCE course.

Staff deployment in the boys' school
No annual deployment of staff was written in the log of the boys' school.

A note on part time staff
Although considered to possibly lack commitment to the school – i.e. to all school activities – and very likely to be mothers of school-age children and have parental and housekeeping duties taking priority in their lives, some part-time or supply staff were regularly employed on this basis and certainly did give their time to the school.

Girls' school teacher deployment
September 1967

Fifth Year Miss McLeish

4 CSE Mr R. Cummins, 4 NC Miss Dodd, 4.3 Miss Giles

4.4 Mrs Watson

3.1 Miss Clarke, 3.2 Mrs Spurr, 3.3 Mrs Fairless

2.1 Miss Richardson, 2.2 Mr J. Mather, 2.3 Miss Wylie

2.4 Mrs Armstrong

1.1 Mrs Brown, 1.2 Miss Lonergan, 1.3 Mrs Thompson

1.4 Mrs Forster

Teachers without forms: Miss Hope deputy head

Housecraft staff – Miss Dover, Miss Jackson, Miss Manfield

Three part-time staff

Mrs Forster was full-time supply

Traditions continuing and declining

The house systems in the two schools continued in their established form, a means of grouping youngsters for competitive activities in academic work, sport, music and drama. The competitive spirit generated was perceived as a motivating factor in bringing the pupils to be involved in the school, developing a group spirit, a feeling of belonging. The end-of-year ceremony in the girls' school is one clear indication of the importance attached to these competitive events.

For the boys' school it cannot be certain that all events were recorded in the log. It does, however, seem quite clear that the regular production of an annual Christmas pantomime ceased after 1965. Other fairly regular features of the end of this term seem to be the showing of a film to the whole school and a carol service.

At the girls' school, without any annual pantomime, the end of the autumn term continues to be orientated towards the traditional Christmas activities of the Christian Church: *every* year there is the mention of a carol service. The Christmas cake display was still an all-girls affair, although there is the introduction of a prefects' party and a fifth-year party to which boys were invited. The broadening of the event from 'prefects' to 'all of the fifth year' would possibly have been a manifestation of the social climate of the time when selection could be seen as elitist: if the prefects can have a party so should all the other fifth-year pupils. However, the fifth year at the time was still selective, self-selective certainly, but comprising only of those volunteering to remain in school. With the compulsory raising of the school-leaving age in future years the nature of the fifth year would change.

The end of the spring term in the boys' school was not marked by distinct events in the same way as those at Christmas: the only regular item appearing in the school log being the annual cross country run. Described elsewhere is the Darlington Schools Music Festival which was held at about this time each year. The one-off items reported give an insight into other things in which the school was involved.

The summer term is the particular period when sporting activities predominate with the inter-house swimming and athletics competitions; and the inter-schools gala and sports.

The pattern of Ascension Day outings and the girls' visits to the abbeys also continued until 1967. But after the retirement of the headmaster Mr George Welford, the enthusiasm for an annual boys' camp clearly declined: efforts were made in 1960, 62 and 64 when the number of boys taking part was just under fifty in each case, compared with a hundred or more attending some of the earlier camps.

By 1960 the school uniform for girls was a blue tunic with white blouse and in the summer, dresses in blue and white, green and white, or red and white. It is not known whether there was any significance in the colour choice.

The uniform for the boys was a green blazer and grey shorts, a sign of boys being seen as boys, rather than adolescents, until the age of 14 when long trousers were permitted.

Pupil behaviour and discipline

Remembering that the figures being compared refer to the awarding of corporal punishment recorded in the school's punishment book there appears to be very little change from 1945 to 1968 in the category of Misbehaviour in Class. It is among the more senior pupils where punishment was apparently seen as necessary, although the overall figures are low, almost insignificant statistically, with only fifteen applications recorded for the 14-year period 1945–59 and seventeen for the 9-year period 1959–68, in a school with a maximum roll of some 650 pupils.

There are two sides to the argument relating to the significance of these figures. Firstly it may be said that as they are so low the punishment is irrelevant and may as well not be used at all. Secondly, as the application of the punishment is a last resort, the misbehaviour therefore very serious, its use provides a meaningful sanction against serious offenders. The action demonstrates to all of the pupils that such behaviour will not be tolerated and acts as a deterrent to others.

The higher figures in the older age groups suggest a possible rebellion against the expectations of school-style discipline among some of the senior pupils.

The disappearance of corporal punishment for the category Poor Classwork may reflect a change in attitude on the part of the education establishment from one in which poor work must be regarded as the fault of the child to one in which there is a realisation that some youngsters have particular disabilities which, although they possibly give their best, it does not appear that they do so.

Similarly, punishment for lack of attention in class is apparently no longer applied in the latter years, although talking in class remains a punishable offence.

The subject of homework is introduced in the later of the two periods, another indication of changing attitudes to learning: the compulsory taking of work home becomes a part of the process.

General misbehaviour seems to increase in the latter period, once again being more noticeable in the senior classes. It is from the age of 13 upwards that the sanction is being applied.

There are some nineteen recorded incidents of breaking a school rule during the period 1945–59, all in the 14-plus age group. During the second period there are only three recorded incidents in this category, two in the junior school, and one senior.

When general disobedience is considered there is a surprising fall in the number of punishments awarded from the earlier to the later years. Do the young people become more conforming in their behaviour? Was there a weakness in the competence of some of the staff during the earlier period? Did teachers become more tolerant of aspects of behaviour which were previously unacceptable?

The same questions arise when considering the recorded incidents of impudence or rudeness to staff: in particular, is society becoming more tolerant of, even encouraging, a more challenging attitude from young people? It is generally accepted that children have been allowed greater freedom of expression, their expected behaviour being far less restricted.

Another indication of changing attitudes towards the discipline of children may be the recording of swearing and the use of bad language, albeit only three recorded incidents in the first case and none in the second. The tolerance of the use of rude or crude language and swearing has certainly increased, not least in the case of certain areas of the media. At a parents' social evening the conversation with the father of a pleasant, co-operative young girl pupil included the mention of this subject. He was told by the head teacher that the school was trying to discourage such language and there was an unexpected reply of 'Why?' He continued: 'Why? When they [the children] hear it [crude, bad language and swearing] all around them, especially on the television, all of the time?' Such is the changing attitude towards decent standards.

There is a marked difference between the recorded incidents of telling lies or deceit between the two periods, due to the occurrence in the 13-plus age group. It is first of all noteworthy that this behaviour was considered serious enough to merit corporal punishment; secondly the attitude continues through both periods; and thirdly it is in the senior school where most (even though few in total) incidents are recorded.

The significance of this area of behaviour and discipline is underestimated. During the Fenby–Welford years, if a teacher said, 'I know you are not telling the truth, the truth of the matter is ...' the child would come to agree. Later, a more persistent denial of the truth developed in which the element of 'prove it' became the norm.

There were a few occasions in the life of the school when boys were involved in sufficiently serious fights in classrooms for them to have been recorded in the punishment book. As with most other events the precise circumstances are not given: it can only be assumed that a teacher was not present at the outbreak of the disturbance but arrived on the scene after the initial arguments, pushing and shoving had developed into full-blown conflict.

There is more evidence of fighting elsewhere, in the corridors perhaps or, more likely, in the playground, where the event would have attracted a sizeable audience. The approach of a master known for his discipline would disperse the crowd but the situation may have required physical action on the part of the teachers to separate the contestants in the brawl.

As the age of pupils staying in school was raised, either voluntarily or by compulsion, so the physical development of the boys increased: boys became young men, giving rise to another change in circumstances. There was a report from another school of the head teacher recording that there was a fight in the playground, and as he was of rather a small stature, there was not much he could do about it!

In these events there was a kind of one-to-one attempt to sort out differences; in the case of bullying it is a matter of one stronger or bigger than another, or a group, threatening or attacking a weaker boy, and it appears as though this kind of aggression became more common in the pre-comprehensive school years.

There has always been a number of pupils who, given the opportunity, would choose to escape from school or attend rarely, if ever. The figures for Eastbourne Boys during the 1945–59 and 1959–68 periods suggest that the problem was largely occurring in the middle years. After all, the older classes were where pupils still had the option of leaving and seeking employment. The problem, however, is greater in the latter period than during the earlier years, raising the question: is school becoming less attractive or the opportunities for absence easier? As it is made compulsory to remain in school longer, does the need for some to rebel become stronger?

Misbehaviour going to and from school and outside school on other occasions continued to be punished by means of corporal punishment during both the Welford and latter periods: the school still took the responsibility for the behaviour of its pupils outside school hours – and was still able to do so. The figures suggest that this was mainly a matter confined to the 12-plus and 13-plus age groups.

Although there are reports of the setting of fires or arson, a very serious form of misbehaviour, they are extremely rare with only one case during the period 1945–59 and two between 1959 and 1968. As they were dealt with in school it can be assumed that they were not sufficiently serious to be taken to court. Together with the ages of the pupils, 12-plus and 14-plus, it *may* also be assumed that the events were mischievous rather than malicious, and in this matter there rests an important concept. When are episodes of misbehaviour of such a serious nature to make it essential for the courts, rather than the schools, to judge the cases and award punishments?

For example, in December 1963, when a fourth-year child was caught taking money in school, the incident was reported to the Education Office and the Child Guidance Clinic asked for help.

Approved school

There was a report in the *Northern Despatch* for Thursday 12 September 1963 of a 14-year-old schoolboy who had appeared before the Juvenile Court being sent to an approved school. There is no evidence of this boy being a pupil at Eastbourne School but the case serves as an example of what could happen to a seriously misbehaving child in 1963.

The approved school referred to was probably for junior boys of between 10 and 15 years of age. It would be a boarding school at which the pupils' freedom would be restricted, probably meaning that any leave or days out would have to be earned by the collecting of points for good behaviour and classwork. Visits by family and friends to see the youngsters in the school were allowed at prescribed times.

The boy in the report had been living with foster parents and had run away from the home several times. It was clearly not a stable environment in which to bring up a young teenager. There is no mention of his natural parents.

It was stated that the boy had previously appeared before the court and been remanded to a remand home, where his freedom would have been restricted, his needs cared for and his behaviour carefully observed with a view to drawing up as thorough a report as possible on his situation. An educational psychologist would have seen the child and tested his educational attainments.

At the current hearing it was said that the boy had broken into a house during one of his episodes of absconding from home and stolen various items to the value of £10. The magistrates decided that it would be in the boy's interest that he should be sent to an approved school.

Although the action was implied to be in the interests of the child, others would certainly have seen being sent away as a punishment for wrongdoing, and this is significant as a deterrent to others.

A further report in the same edition of the newspaper reported that a 15-year-old girl was remanded to a home for being 'in need of care and protection' after being missing from home on several occasions – and that the parents were evicted from their house. The significance here is that the girl would have been left to her own devices had she not been placed under supervision. Again, the message sent to others would be that, no matter what your family circumstances, you cannot be allowed to be free from supervision.

There is no evidence from the log books that Eastbourne pupils were sent to approved schools but there are examples of probation officers and the police visiting to discuss delinquent youngsters; for example on 1 July 1963 a woman inspector visited the school in relation to the case of girl pupil.

Teenage pregnancy
There is a record in April 1964 of a pupil's father calling in to the school to report that his daughter was pregnant. It was claimed that the father of the child was unknown. The consequent action was that the Welfare Officer was informed, the Schools Medical Officer became involved,

and the child was taken off the school roll. The impression given is that such an occurrence was unheard of and that the child involved should immediately be removed from the school. There was disapproval shown and this disapproval was clear to the other girls.

Assault

On 22 April of that year Miss Armstrong recorded assaults on a fourth-year pupil both during the dinner break and at the close of afternoon school by three fourth-year and three third-year girls. She investigated the incident and established the truth of statements made. A report was sent to the CEO with the request that the girls be suspended from school dinner.

This incident was reported in the *Evening Despatch* and *Northern Echo* on 1 May and 2 May respectively and it was alleged that untrue allegations and attempts to photograph the girls were made. This is another significant development: that of the media reporting acts of indiscipline in schools with the risk of a situation being worsened.

On 5 June 1964 Miss Armstrong, Mrs Walters and Miss Hope, with police officers, interviewed fourth-year girls in relation to theft of money from a purse. The empty purse was found later and one named child suspected of theft.

On 6 July 1965 it was recorded that an Eastbourne policeman collected a wallet found in a toilet tank by Mr Cole, the caretaker, which contained the name of the owner, a temporary driving licence and photograph.

There seems to have been an unsettled atmosphere about the place in 1964, with the assault and theft reported, and staff leaving the school. The behaviour of the pupils is, however, not necessarily related to the changes in staff – but it may have been. There was a change of head teacher in 1963 and a new deputy head appointed at the same time. Four other newly appointed teachers were inexperienced, coming straight from their college training.

The involvement of parents in the life of the school

The pattern of year-group meetings for parents and, in the girls' school in particular, the invitation for parents to attend such events as the Domestic Science Exhibition, swimming galas, sports days and the annual Speech Day established during the Fenby–Welford years, continued.

In addition, all leavers were interviewed by the Youth Employment Officers and, in the girls' school certainly, the head teacher or her representative attended the interviews, as did most of the parents of the young people.

One or two entries are of particular interest because they indicate subtle but significant changes taking place in the schools. The earlier entries suggest a *come and see what goes on in the schools*, as in the Domestic Science Exhibitions and open days, and for the new entrants, *this is what is on offer*. There is also an element of *come and celebrate what your children are involved in and enjoy the occasion*.

There is an entry which says that advice will be given on courses, presumably becoming available in the 1960s, and the meetings concerned with the introduction of the new Northern Counties Examination.

Latterly is an entry concerning the school journey abroad, a development of the time, adding to, if not replacing, the existing outings.

The core curriculum

During the years of grammar and secondary modern education, on the surface at least, the curriculum in both types of school had a similar basic core: English, mathematics, religious knowledge, science, history, geography, music, art and physical education being the subjects taught. It was in the presentation and syllabus content where differences appeared; and while the grammar schools were dominated by the requirements of a public examination system the other secondary schools were less so.

Matriculation

At first the grammar schools sought to bring their pupils up to the standards required for Matriculation, defined by university entrance. In order to qualify for a certificate pupils had to reach the pass standard in English, mathematics, a science, a foreign language and one other subject – it was usual for the school to encourage them to take more, attaching importance to art and music, for example. Physical education was just that, emphasising the need to keep healthy and fit, and to participate in recreational sporting activities.

Although the core curriculum remained the same in the Eastbourne Schools from the 1940s into the 1960s, with the significance of the practical subjects most pronounced, particularly in the girls' school, and with the emphasis on mathematics and English, change was taking place. Not least as a factor in change was the growth in the examining of all subjects, in turn influenced by the introduction of school-leaving examinations for more, and eventually all, young people.

Internal examinations

A look at the subjects examined in the bi-annual internal examinations, and taught by the teachers appointed to and serving on the staff during the 1960s, gives some indication of the content of the curriculum. English, in the girls' school at least, has three elements tested: the writing of a composition, the elements of the language, and literature.

Observations made in the log books suggest the continued significance awarded to spoken English, both in specific competitive events and in the drama presentations. The importance still being given to domestic science subjects is seen in the continuation of the domestic science exhibitions.

The introduction of special responsibility posts, creating positions of heads of department, giving responsibility for particular subjects and defining responsibilities in other areas, suggests an all-round growth in the curriculum with extra emphasis being given to subjects that were previously more peripheral to the basic English, mathematics and practical disciplines.

There was the often controversial introduction of the teaching of French. Criticisms that come to mind are: why attempt to teach a foreign language when so much needs to be done among many pupils to teach them their native tongue? Why teach French rather than say German or Spanish?

With the core of English, mathematics and practical subjects there is the broader curriculum which includes compulsory religious knowledge (discussed previously), history, geography, science, music, art and physical education. Each subject was clearly defined and the syllabus of each understood.

Known subject teachers at the boys' school 1960:

J. Peacock and K. A. Wilkinson – woodwork and metalwork

A. R. Foord and B. Stephenson – metalwork

E. C. R. Smith – warden mixed YC and part-time teacher

Mr Hunt and S. J. Thornhill – mathematics

J. Minikin – mathematics special needs

K. Sherwood – English and religious knowledge

J. H. Jackson – religious knowledge

W. Andrews and T. U. Robson – English

J. C. Carling and E. L. Robson – physical education

H. C. Bullock – science

Miss S. E. Dodd and B. F. Sheppard – music

Mrs W. Doran – temporary, subject unknown

C. W. Sparkes – technical drawing

P. Lyonette – subject unknown

D. G. Whiteside – history

T. W. Murphy – geography

C. .H Parkinson – art

Subject teachers appointed to the boys' school staff 1961–68:

September 1961:	A. N. Spense for PE and games
May 1962:	D. Bayliss as Head of Science Department
January 1963:	R. L. Shotton as Head of English Department
January 1964:	R. W. Charlton for technical drawing
August 1964:	F. L. Mercer for science
August 1966:	A. L. Walker for woodwork
January 1967:	D. S. Hogg to teach French
January 1968:	J. Cousins graded post for woodwork

Known subject teachers at the girls' school in 1960

Miss K. A. McLeish – English

Miss C. I. Hope – deputy head

Miss C. A. Peacock – subject unknown

Miss Nancarrow and Miss C. M. Giles – PE games

Mrs M. Hall – subject unknown

Miss Brewster – subject unknown

Miss Potts – history and English

Mrs D. D. Watson – subject unknown

Mrs M. G. Brown – music

Miss Richardson – subject unknown

Miss Hunter – mathematics

Miss Cousins – geography and needlework

Mrs Shirley – supply teacher

Mrs Elwood – science and general subjects

Miss E. M. Fairless – subject unknown

Miss P. Nicholson – religious knowledge

Miss P. Robinson – general subjects

Miss Dover, Miss P. Hogg, Miss D. Manfield and Miss Richley – housecraft

Remedial education

It was recognised that some children were behind in their achievements in English and mathematics. The rigid system of streaming ensured that such children were placed in the lowest streams – where they remained for all subjects. There was little if any provision for a child who might display particular talent in one or more areas but achieve little in basic English and mathematics to be taught in a group where other higher achievers in these areas would have greater demands placed upon them.

Low attainment in the basics defined the standard of the child unless the school possessed a particularly forward-looking staff.

Special Educational Needs children

The concept of Special Educational Needs had not been recognised but children thought to be in need of exceptionally special education could be assessed by the educational psychologist for attendance at Glebe School. This school was variously described as being for the mentally retarded or sub-normal children, while Salters Lane, the open-air school, was for those with health problems. (Log entry for 19.1.68: Mr Gordon, Educational Psychologist, called at the Girls'

School to test a recently admitted pupil for admission to the Glebe School for the sub-normal child.)

Children with low achievements in English and mathematics were generally regarded as needing remedial teaching to bring them up to standard.

A course in the Teaching of Backward and Retarded Children in the Secondary Modern School and another in the teaching of reading began on the evening of 9 November 1962. In conjunction with the above, the school staged the National Book League Exhibition of 'Books for Backward Readers'.

The fact that some did not have the personal make-up to conform to perceived normal standards probably detracted from research into the many possible causes of low achievement. Teachers therefore continued to apply traditional methods to put things right. In some cases, where particular personal circumstances had caused a child to miss out on the early stages of teaching, such remedial strategies could bring those children up to standard but a proportion still left school without having adequate skills in written language and calculation. There was a kind of belief that repetition and going back to the initial teaching strategies should eventually work if only the child could be sufficiently motivated to learn.

A new initiative – The Newsom Report

Half Our Future

Principal recommendations as they affect the running of schools.

It was reasoned that for children of average and below average ability to have an 'effective education':

1. The school-leaving age should be raised to sixteen for all pupils entering secondary schools in 1965.

2. Research should be taken into teaching techniques, in particular to help pupils thought to be handicapped by their environment and poor language skills.

3. Social problems should be addressed, the significance of frequent staff changes and the size of schools be considered,

and the design of buildings be appropriate for community use.

4. Fourth and fifth year pupils should be given a choice of courses related to 'occupational interests'.

   Attention should be paid to the arts and the 'personal and social development' of the pupils.

   The fine grading of pupils by ability should be avoided.

   Older pupils should be given status in the school via organisation and building design.

5. Fourteen to sixteen year olds should work to an extended school day to include extra-curricular activities.

In addition, recommendations were made relating to religious instruction (being made more appropriate to the needs of young people) and necessary sex education.

Newsom Groups

On 2 November 1966 Mr P. Phillip HMI arranged to visit the boys' school with colleagues to see the work being done with Newsom Pupils. Mr Minikin and Mr Jefferson were involved in this work.

The title Newsom Children or Groups is derived from the name of the chairman of the Central Advisory Council for Education (England) in 1961, John Newsom, when Lord Eccles, Government Minister for Education, asked the council to consider the education of 13- to 16-year-old pupils of average or less than average ability.

The council's report, 'Half Our Future', was published in 1963.

The introduction to the adult world of employment and leisure was emphasised:

- There should be an internal leaving certificate based on internal assessment and school records.
- Pupils for whom external examinations are inappropriate should not be placed under pressure to take them.
- The extension of the provision for practical subjects was seen to be essential.

There were also recommendations relating to the provision of buildings and the appropriate training of teachers.

Mothercraft and child care

Some of the suggestions made in the Newsom Report were already understood and incorporated in the curricula of the Eastbourne Schools but would become more obvious in the future internal organisation of the schools.

In September 1966 there is clear evidence of mothercraft and child care courses being available in the senior part of the girls' school when Mrs Paterson was appointed as a part-time teacher for five mornings each week to teach them. Class 4 PG, it was claimed, using the Newsom approach, were offered courses in child care, mothercraft, home nursing and personal grooming. There is even the suggestion that the courses were new – yet it is clear similar work was being done much earlier.

Choice of activities was introduced in physical education. Pupils could take either needlework or art and craft, and efforts were made to make teaching groups in these classes small.

Extra–curricular activities

The Newsom Report called for the extension of the school day for senior pupils so that attention could be given to activities outside the normal curriculum, yet such activities had been a part of the educational programme of both Eastbourne Schools ever since they opened. The significant difference between what was done and what was being recommended was an increase in formality. Instead of activities being offered and children being encouraged to take part, a system was to be structured to ensure all took part, while still retaining and element of choice.

There is a fundamental principle involved in all of this. From a system in which children could choose to leave school and seek employment, one in which they could choose to remain within the school system to join in extra-curricular activities or not, they were to be retained in the school environment whether they liked it or not. While many did continue their education after the age at which they were allowed to leave school and many did take part in extra-curricular activities, others did not. This group have been equated with being underprivileged and a system devised to *ensure* that this *perceived* inequality of opportunity be rectified. Such compulsion, direct or indirect, does not bring about the change the reformers desired – it breeds hostility, encouraging rebellion in the form of truancy and antisocial behaviour within the school.

Evidence of the opportunities for pupils to become involved in extra-curricular activities at the schools is obvious from the details given in previous chapters, and from the items below.

One aspect of the Newsom recommendations was that children should have the opportunity to experience residential courses: and in Darlington the Earls Orchard system of visits was already well established and continued during the 1960s.

Several school journeys, such as those in 1967 and 1968, were made by the girls' school as a part of their extra-curricular programme.

Two of the London visits made by the girls' school in the 1960s:

24.5.67: Thirty-five girls in charge of Miss Hope and Miss Brewster with Mrs Watson, Miss Giles, Miss Lonergan and one other

Set off to London en route for the School Journey to Denmark.

Duration of the trip one week, party returning on Sunday June 2nd

Described as 'a very good holiday'.

27.5.68: London Visit

25 girls (5 form five, 20 form 4 CSE) In charge of Mr Cummins with Miss Hope and Miss Jackson

On the 30th they visited the House of Commons and House of Lords hosted by Mr Fletcher the Darlington Member of Parliament.

There are regular references to the school choirs taking part in concerts. On 19 February 1964 the girls' school choir sang in the 'Festival of Light' (organised by National Children's Homes) at 7 p.m. at the Baths Hall. Mrs Brown and Miss Nicholson were in charge, and it was the girls' school in particular that held an annual concert.

The tradition was established during Miss Fenby's headship and was continued after her retirement. The programme's content included singing, dancing, drama and physical education displays.

The Darlington Competitive Music Festival continued to play a significant part in the encouragement of participation of both boys and girls in the making of music, the annual events including categories for various skills. The inclusion of competitions for participating groups gave opportunities for youngsters with different abilities to be involved.

A significant development in the 1960s was the introduction of the playing of brass instruments. On 21 March 1964 Mr C. Bennett, Darlington Music Adviser, visited the boys' school to discuss the provision of brass instruments and in April letters were prepared for circulation to pupils' parents concerning arrangements for teaching those interested in the playing of such instruments.. The first lessons commenced for five boys during the evening of 3 February 1965.

The annual school sports days continued to take place but there is evidence of a change. For instance, in 1963 Councillor and Mrs Lorraine, Miss Fenby, Mr Cameron and 'a small number of parents' attended but during the previous year Miss Fenby stated: 'Many parents and friends of the school were present including the Chairman of Governors (Councillor Spence) who presented the cup to the winning house.'

At the boys' school it appears that heats were organised, suggesting that many, if not all boys were expected to take part at some stage. For instance, the log entry for 25.5.60 reads: 'Preliminary Heats of School Sports; Timetable suspended after first period in the afternoon.'

At the final event in the boys' school, on 24 July 1968, close to the end of term and the closure of the boys' school, and after two postponements due to the weather, the inter-house sports were finally held and Stanley House were the champions.

The internal inter-house sports continued to feed the most able competitors into the school teams for the annual Inter-Schools Athletics meetings (Town Sports) when the schools were still being closed for the afternoon.

The boys' school annual cross country run continued to be held in the spring but it seems that the girls had not yet been introduced to the sport. In the 1960s boys were boys and took part in boys' sports, girls were girls and took part in girls' sports!

Boys' school football teams were regularly involved in matches.

A few of the boys' football match results:

19.3.60: School defeated Gladstone Street in the Bousfield Cup Final 3–1

1.5.61: School First XI met the Technical School in the Pike Pease Cup Final – result 2–2 draw after extra time.

22.4.64: After School the First XI visited Bishop Auckland and beat the Grammar School 4–2 to reach the Final of the County Cup.

13.5.63: School team reached the final of the Durham County Cup but lost to Washington Grammar School at Usworth.

1966: School First XI defeated St Mary's in the final of the Pike Pease cup

Inter–Town Netball Tournament:

Saturday 3rd April 1965: 9 till 12 noon

Attended by Mayor and Mayoress, members of the governing body.

Lunch was served for 120 in the school dining room for players, staff and guests.

The Mayor presented the trophy to the winning team from Sunderland.

Duke of Edinburgh's Award Scheme

On March 2 1960 Mr Foxon recorded his attendance at the inauguration of the Duke of Edinburgh's Award Scheme which took place at the Town Hall. On 16 March Miss Storer, the Darlington Youth Organiser, called at the boys' school to enquire about the progress being made with the introduction of the Scheme and a meeting to discuss it was held on 10 May at 4 p.m. at the Education Office.

A start seems to have been made with a group commencing the first aid class, a part of the programme, on 11 May at 7.15 p.m. and there was a meeting of leaders involved in the Scheme at Eastbourne at 4.30 p.m. on 25 June 1960.

On 17 May a helicopter of the Queen's Flight made a landing on the school field as a part of the preparations for the Duke of Edinburgh's visit in June.

Mr Foxon reported that on 24 June 1960:

> HRH the Duke of Edinburgh visited the School to see the
> work being done in the town by boys working at his Award
> Scheme. All boys from other schools assembled here and
> many activities were on display. He arrived by helicopter at
> 12.15 and after lunching with the Mayor, returned here at 2
> p.m. and remained until 3.20 p.m.

Although there is no record of girls being involved in the Scheme at
this stage, Miss Fenby wrote at length on the visit by the Duke:

> An informal visit when the Duke inspected the work being
> done for the Bronze Awards of His Scheme – as organised by
> the LEA's Youth Service and Voluntary clubs.
>
> The activities were shown on the playing fields and in the
> boys' school. The Duke arrived by helicopter and the pupils
> of the school assembled on the fields for the welcome and
> departure. Mrs Gordon Spencer, Secretary of the Girls' Award
> Scheme, visited the Girls' School.
>
> Miss Fenby was included in the presentation party at 12.15 p.m.

On 19 April 1961 Mr Maddison commenced the expedition training
with the second group of boys taking part in the Duke of Edinburgh's
Award Scheme and during the evening of 2 June 1961 eleven boys were
presented with Bronze Badge awards.

It is clear that the girls had been involved in the scheme before this
date because on 17 November 1961 there was a special ceremony held
at 3.40 p.m. when Mrs Gordon Spencer, the Assistant Director and
Secretary of the Girls' Scheme, visited the school to present Bronze
Awards to forty-six successful candidates.

Outward Bound courses

Another opportunity for pupils to take part in adventurous activities was
the Outward Bound courses. It was recorded on 7 October 1960 that
two boys, Dennis McNiff and David Muckle, attended the Education
Office for an interview for a place at an Outward Bound school and

that they were both selected to attend the course at the Ullswater Centre in the following March. David F. Brown and Colin Egglinton took part in courses at the same centre in February 1965 and January 1966 respectively.

The girls' school also sent pupils on Outward Bound courses: on 31 January Anne Boyd departed to the Outward Bound school at Towyn in North Wales as one of Darlington's two representatives for the period 30 January 1967 till 20 February 1967.

In January 1968 Sandra Robson of class 4 CSE went to the Outward Bound school at Towyn (again as one of two from Darlington).

Examinations and reporting progress

The bi-annual internal examinations programmes continued during the 1960s; for instance on February 24 between 2.15 and 3.45 the pupils took papers in English and on the 25th between 2.15 and 3.45 papers in maths.

In the boys' school it is also clear that the examinations took place in other academic subjects: history, geography and science; and there were practical tests in woodwork and metalwork.

The woodwork syllabus consisted of learning the main joints used, and producing a stool and an airer, with the most able going on to produce a wooden bowl.

Marks for each subject were totalled and the position of each pupil in the class given in rank order.

The system of examination and transfer to the grammar and high school at 13-plus ended in 1961.

1960: 142 boys took the exam. Ten boys who wished to take the exam were absent in the morning and eleven in the afternoon.

1961: 124 boys sat the examination (*note: held for the last time*) three boys absent.

31 boys successful – 28 to go to the Technical school and 3 to the Grammar school.

The schools continued to enter pupils for the Northern Counties School Certificate Examination and that pupils eligible to leave at Easter were remaining at school to take the examinations in the summer term.

The Ordinary Level General Certificate of Education (GCE)
Just as the Newsom groups were not catered for, the top of the ability range were also thought to be missing out on chances of taking GCE courses because there was no longer the opportunity to transfer to the grammar and high schools via the Late Entry Examination. Consequently 'O' level courses were introduced (or reintroduced). An indication of the subjects being taking by the pupils is given in the table for the 1965 'O' level examinations.

First 'O'level candidates at the boys' school, 1965:

Examination described as the 'O' level of the GCE

25.6.65: English language and geography

28.6.65: Mathematics and geography

29.6.65: Mathematics

1.7.65: English literature and physics

5.7.65: History

6.7.65: Practical physics

Results: One boy 6 passes; four boys 5 passes; five boys 4 passes; three boys 3 passes; one boy 2 passes

A total of 84 papers taken and 57 passed.

First 'O' level candidates at the girls' school, 1965:
A note says: 'Form 5 Proficiency in Arithmetic – Cambridge Exam Board'.

June 1965

24th 1.30 till 4.30 pm. Art 'O'level

25th GCofE English Language am. Geography pm.

28th am. 'O'level Geometry and pm. Geography

29th am. 'O' Arithmetic

30th June am GCofE 'O'level Algebra

1st July 'O'level Literature and 2 till 4.30 pm. 'O'level Art Paper I

2nd July GCof E Cookery Theory

6th July GCofE General science am.

8th July 'O'level Science am.

12th July Art 'O'level 9.30–till noon Paper 2

The Certificate of Secondary Education (CSE)

While retaining the 'O' level for the traditional groups of pupils staying at school until they were sixteen, generally attending grammar or technical schools, a second examination was thought to be desirable for the majority of young people. That examination was to be the CSE in which a grade 1 pass was to be equivalent to a GCE pass.

On 30 October 1963 a meeting was held at the Education Office to discuss the 'new Certificate of Secondary Education'. In the evening on 1 May 1964 a meeting was held for parents of third-year boys at which the facts about the new CSE examination were given. At least 100 parents attended, showing significant interest. A further meeting took place on 29 May.

At the girls' school Speech Day on 1 November 1963, Miss Steele, Principal of Darlington Teacher Training College, invited to present the prizes, also gave a talk to the parents and girls on the new Certificate of Secondary Education.

The first CSE examinations took place in the summer of 1966, commencing in April. Candidates would be given one of five grades: grade 1 was to correspond to an 'O' level pass (without admitting that there were different levels of 'O' level pass, and without stating which was expected to correspond with the CSE 1). In reality, as there was no subdivision of grade 1 CSE, it came to be equated with the lowest 'O' level pass. Grade 4 CSE was defined as the standard reached by an *average* pupil taking the examination, while grades 2 and 3 were rather vaguely described as standards between 1 and 4. Grade 5 was awarded in cases where it was judged, although below average, it was appropriate for the candidate to take the examination.

The actual value of *average* relied on the number and quality of those taking the examination.

No one was to fail, an attempt to deny the concept of failure in the misguided belief that a failure in an examination labelled one an irreparable total failure for life. A strange concept, for those who have failed once may struggle again and eventually achieve success. Furthermore, failure in one area is not failure in all and different people have strengths in different areas: failure in one should lead to the struggle for success elsewhere. Those who did in fact fail to produce an appropriate standard of work in the CSE, yet were somehow entered for the examination, were to be given the odd grade U for unclassified.

A further confusion was that courses could be taken in three modes – Mode I, Mode II and Mode III – and a problem was created by adapting examinations to meet the abilities of the pupils rather than objectively setting standards in learning and requiring pupils to reach those standards in order to gain a certificate.

As the subject syllabuses were so numerous and varied, an average standard, labelled grade 4, was difficult to objectively describe in terms of real criteria. Furthermore, the story which was put about in the early days of the examination, before the statutory leaving age became sixteen, is worth repeating. The scene was a school corridor where a teacher had stopped one of his pupils (we will call her Julie) to enquire whether she would be staying on to complete the CSE examination.

'What do I want to do that for?' she enquired.

'To obtain some school-leaving qualifications,' the teacher responded.

'What grades do you think I could get?' she asked.

'Well Julie, I think that you could manage grade 4 in most of your subjects.'

'What does grade 4 mean, sir?'

'It means that you are a good average girl,' the teacher replied with confidence.

But the girl began to laugh.

'Why do I have to take examinations and be given certificates to show that I am a good average girl? I know that already!' And she walked away laughing loudly at what she saw as an absurdity.

Because the level reached by any candidate taking the examination relied on the concept of an average standard, problems arose associated with validation made by comparison with the theoretical normal distribution curve. Most candidates could expect to get, and would get, irrespective of effort, an average grade – and this is not an acceptable system of qualification. Qualifications should not be the same for everybody. Different qualifications are required for different occupations. In addition, they should define what the candidate knows and can do: in other words, be usable as a qualification.

The demands of the growing examination system

Even a quick look at the extensive examination timetables of the school-leaving examinations for the 1960s cannot fail to demonstrate the demands on teachers and teaching time. The start in late April or early May meant that normal teaching ceased for much of the summer term: in turn meaning that course instruction in the last two years of secondary school education leading to the examinations at age 16 lasted only for one year and two terms.

An examination system requires invigilators to supervise the candidates in the examination halls and teachers had to take on this task, taking them away from classroom teaching. Furthermore, the system is complicated, disrupting the normal lesson timetable because different members of classes take different examinations at different times. A teacher may be unavailable to teach because he or she is invigilating and, when free from this duty, a large proportion of his or her class is absent taking papers in a different subject. It may be a good idea to visualise classes continuing for purposes of revision but either the teacher or some of the pupils are not available to take part. If remnants of classes are combined, some learners will not have their original teacher, a factor that may be seen as insignificant, but in reality can confuse the learners.

The conclusion has been for lessons to cease for the candidates when the examinations start and excluding pupils from the school from May onwards. As the results of examinations are not published until August the young people have been placed in a limbo-like situation for something like three months. The conscientious and able spend their time privately revising for their examinations, finding vacation employment to earn much-sought-after cash, and possibly taking a structured holiday. Many, however, do not revise; even temporary employment is scarce and young people are left with time on their hands – life seems to be one long, rather aimless session of perceived pleasure and this is not a good foundation for subsequent disciplined learning or for the routine of the workplace.

The CSE examination introduced a greater reliance on internal assessment by teachers, a high proportion of marks being awarded for projects completed, in theory, through the private study of the young people. This was another aspect of the new examination which created a huge, time-consuming burden on teachers: each individual project had to be assessed by them and their assessments moderated by other teachers external to the school.

Projects in academic subjects proved to be of doubtful value in determining what a young person could do or had learnt. In the practical subjects, the craftsmanship in the making of wooden or metal artefacts, the production of items of clothing or the cooking of culinary dishes, and the talent of the artist in the crafting of pots, design, painting and photography, can be measured – and the work known to be that of the candidate.

Many of the academic projects proved to be no more than a conglomeration of materials copied from elsewhere – and possibly the result of assistance by well-meaning parents, not entirely the work of the candidate.

A further impingement on teaching time was the decision to involve teachers in the construction of the syllabuses and the examination papers, that is, in deciding what shall be taught. A whole host of staff were suddenly required to be out of school attending subject panel meetings.

In addition, the notion that teachers should decide what to teach and what is to be examined is flawed. Too many individuals and groups suddenly produced their own ideas on what a subject discipline should contain. No longer was it possible to know from a nationally produced syllabus what was being taught. Consequently, any grade in any examination on any subject so compiled became meaningless – unless the user of the results was prepared to personally study a vast mass of individual work programmes – an unrealistic situation.

Leaving school, careers education and changing employment prospects

In some respects, careers advice and visits to workplaces continued during the early 1960s in much the same way as before but with signs of change. The boys continued to be taken to such places as Robert Stephenson and Hawthorne Ltd, Darlington Forge, the Power Station, the School Furnishing Company, Faverdale Works of British Railways, and the Waterworks. There were still introductory talks and visits made with a view to introducing boys to careers in the armed forces. For instance, on 30 March 1960 Squadron Leader Fanthorpe gave a talk to leavers about careers in the RAF; in February 1961, Captain Corrigan of the army team of lecturers gave a talk, illustrated with films, to the fourth year, and in 1964 Major Marshall from Catterick Camp visited the school to discuss a possible visit by pupils to the camp. On 12 March 1968 a party of boys with Mr Shotton in charge left school at 8.00 a.m. to visit the Army Apprentices School at Carlisle.

No reference was found to the involvement of girls in careers talks related to the military except for that of 21 February 1968, when there was a visit by a speaker from the Queen Alexandra's Royal Army Nursing Corps (QARANC) to talk to leavers and show films about careers in the army with special reference to the nursing service. This is indicative of, on the one hand, the expectation that girls should be interested in careers with the military but also of an adherence to tradition: it was appropriate for girls to be introduced to careers in nursing.

There was a hint of a growing encouragement of school leavers to continue into further education. There was liaison between the secondary schools and the College of Technology, with its new building in Cleveland Terrace (the Ceremony of Laying the Foundation Stone was held on 2 June 1961). For instance, in June 1960, a meeting was held at what was then referred to as Darlington College of Further Education in connection with a proposed follow-up course for boys leaving school and wishing to enter engineering. In July boys in 3.1 and 3.2 who took classes in metalwork visited the college to see the display of students' examination work. In September 1964 there was a conference held at the college with the theme Education and Industrial Opportunity.

In 1967 the head teacher of the boys' school recorded a number of pupils attending the college in order to sit entrance examinations for pre-apprenticeship courses: on 18 May four boys took tests for a building course and on the 19th three for catering and two for painting and decorating.

In February 1961 the headmaster attended a meeting at the Youth Employment Office concerning an Introduction to Industry course for school leavers, who at this date could still leave at Easter. In May nine boys from 4.1 attended the course at the Youth Employment Office. In 1962 another nine, in 1963 and 1964 eight, attended similar courses and by the late 1960s the courses were taking place at the Darlington Technical College.

Miss Armstrong, the newly appointed head teacher at the girls' school, attended a conference relating to an Introduction to Industry course for girls in December 1963 which was also attended by Mr Heworth HMI, Mr Pritchard, the YEO, Miss Walters, Deputy YEO, the Reverend Smith, Industrial Chaplain, and Mrs Vickery, the Personnel Officer at Paton and Baldwins.

In 1964, on 30 June and 1 July, a school leavers' conference titled 'Pathway to the Future' took place at Darlington College of Further Education 'and was attended by 50 girls with Miss Hope, Miss McLeish and the Head. It was organised by the Youth Employment Officer, and the Personnel Officer from Paton and Baldwin's was in the chair.' Attendances by smaller numbers of selected girls at similar conferences were recorded for subsequent years.

A further development in careers guidance was the introduction of careers conventions, where a host of employers' representatives and those from further education were brought together in one or other of the schools for parents and pupils to visit and seek advice. The first of these was held for both the boys and girls in the girls' school hall on 27 January 1964, the second in January 1965. Pupils and parents attended between 7 and 9 p.m.

The initiative to encourage pupils to continue their education beyond the age of 16 included arranging for those already remaining in school for a fifth-year examination course to visit the careers conventions held at the grammar school, and in May 1965 it was noted that the head and fourteen boys from the GCE class visited the grammar school to discuss further education.

As late as January 1967 a careers convention was held at the College of Technology for all girls in the town and in February Miss Armstrong recorded a school leavers' convention, titled 'What Next?' and held in the youth centre, which was attended by girls in 4PG and 4PW in the charge of Miss Brewster. The Reverend Roland Goodwin was chairman and visiting speakers included Mr G. Pritchard, Dr N. Markham and representatives from firms and employees. Miss Armstrong noted that this was a very successful day and referred to it as 'Our first Careers Convention'; supporting the impression that society still accepted there were jobs for girls, and no doubt other jobs for the boys.

A variety of events demonstrated that employment opportunities were available in engineering and technology: in May 1961 there was a Commonwealth Technical Training Week and on 31 May a party of boys visited an engineering exhibition in the Bondgate Hall. In June parties of boys visited exhibitions relating to the event in St

Cuthbert's Hall, Darlington College of Further Education and on Feetham's Field.

In May 1967 two fourth-year forms visited the Industrial Exhibition held at the North Road Works as part of the town's centenary celebrations, evidence that there were still employment prospects in heavy industry at this time. Opportunities for employment in manufacturing were illustrated by the visit to the schools on the afternoon of 3 October 1967 of personnel officers from four local factories in order to talk to leavers.

Teachers on the staff during the last days of the secondary modern schools

Known subject teachers at the boys' school 1967:

S. J. Thornhill – mathematics

A. L. Walker – woodwork

A. R. Foord – metalwork

K. A. Wilkinson – woodwork and metalwork

B. F. Sheppard – music

Mrs W. Doran – temporary

W. Andrews – English

J. H. Jackson – religious knowledge

D. G. Whiteside – history

T. W. Murphy – geography

J. Minikin – maths Newsom groups

C. H. Parkinson – art

J. C. Carling – PE

R. L. Shotton – HoD English

R. W. Charlton – technical drawing

F. L. Mercer – science

I. A. Simpson

R. L. Binns – deputy head

D. N. Heaton

J. Browerbank

D. S. Hogg – French

G. Bramham BSc

Known subject teachers at the girls' school 1967:

Miss K. A. McLeish – English

Miss C. I. Hope – deputy head

Miss Brewster, Mr R. Cummins – graded post history

Miss S. Dodd – graded post English

Miss C. M. Giles – PE, games

Mrs D. D. Watson

Mrs Clarke – mathematics

Mrs Spurr – religious knowledge

Miss E. M. Fairless

Miss Richardson BA

Mr Mather – graded post geography

Mrs Wylie – English

Mrs M. G. Brown – graded post music

Miss D. Lonergan – art and PE

Mrs Thornton – English, geography, grooming

Mrs Forster – English

Miss J. Robinson – science and geography

Mrs Doran – needlework

Mrs Lockett – part-time mathematics

Mrs L. E. Forrest BA – history

Mrs Lunley – graded post English

Mrs Paterson – housecraft & child care

Housecraft staff: Miss Dover, Miss D. Manfield, Miss E. P. Jackson

Preparations for the opening of the comprehensive school

A diary of events leading up to the opening of the Eastbourne Comprehensive School 1964–67

October 1964: Head Teacher visited Red House Comprehensive School, Sunderland.

1.6.65: Dep ed Officer, Mr Ross in school to discuss remodelling of the premises.

28.6.65: Head to education Office to meet architects Re; remodelling of the school.

2.7.65: Architects met the head in school.

13.4.67: Miss Armstrong and Mr Foxon met Mr Fletcher (Architect) and Mr Lomax (Clerk of Works) with reference to the start of the contractors remodelling of the School.

April 1967: Contractors moved into the site to begin the remodelling of the School. Hundens Lane Entrance closed.

17.4.67: Contactors Messrs. Stephenson of Bishop Auckland began to enter the site to seal off the boundary for the construction of the new block of rooms.

19.5.67: The headmaster attended a weekend course on comprehensive education at Leeds University.

15.9.67: Special governors' meeting held in the evening to discuss the conservative proposals to amend the Peter Plan. A resolution was passed rejecting the proposals.

5.12.67: Miss Armstrong and Mr Foxon had a meeting with the CEO to discuss senior posts in the new comprehensive school, in particular Senior Master/Mistress.

7.12.67: After School meeting of heads of departments and graded post holders to discuss the question of horizontal and vertical division of the new large pupil intake.

14.12.67: Mr Foord visited the Education Office to discuss with Mr Ross and the architects the layout of the two metalwork rooms in the new school.

As early as 10 October 1963 a governors' meeting, relating to both departments, was held in the boys' school and the CEO's plan for the reorganisation of secondary education in Darlington was discussed. The seeds of change were sown but it would take almost another five years before the change actually took place.

The plan, eventually to become known as 'The Peter Plan' was put before the Darlington Education Committee on Thursday 12 September 1963.

The diary of events leading up to the opening of the Eastbourne Comprehensive School, below, indicates some of the stages in the delivery of the plan.

During the spring term of 1968 members of staff were making exchange visits with teachers in the high school for observation etc.

March 1968: Course on Comprehensive Education and the Curriculum held at Branksome School.

2.4.68: Headmaster attended a course on comprehensive education at Cambridge.

3.4.68: Parents evening for Third Year Boys and Girls to outline courses and plans for the new school.

1.5.68: Joint meeting of the Boys' and Girls' staffs addressed by Mr Foxon, giving plans already made for the new school, namely: Houses, Mixed Ability Groups, Setting, new uniform and Fourth year alternative courses.

27.6.68: Parents' evening

Parents of pupils due to enter the school in the following September, boys and girls, invited to a meeting in the Girls' Hall addressed by Mr Foxon and Miss Armstrong.

12.7.68: Mr Foxon and Miss Armstrong met the CEO, the architects and members of their staffs to discuss problems connected with the opening of the combined school in September.

Final days of the girls' school

The Earl's Orchard residential course originally arranged for the week of 22 July was cancelled due to staffing problems arising from the coming reorganisation of the school.

On 24 July 1968 the final prize-giving ceremony was an internal affair when Miss Richardson presented the prizes (the oldest member of staff and about to retire). The head teacher and Miss Richardson addressed the school.

The final house assemblies were held on the 25th and on the 26th the final school assembly was held and a presentation made to Miss Richardson by the head girl. Miss Armstrong wrote: 'I gave my Final Address to the Girls' School – 4 p.m. the Eastbourne Girls' School ceased to exist.'

During the afternoon of 26 July 1968 the pupils 'were mixed into their new tutor groups and sent to the rooms they were to occupy after the summer holiday, with their respective form tutors as far as was possible'.

There is a distinct impression that the coming loss of independence was strongly felt by the girls' school staff (or, at least, the senior staff) and that there was a significant regret being expressed at the closure of the girls' department, a suggestion that something important was being lost, which was not expressed in the boys' log. Although never vigorously and openly expressed, this underlying something was often implied by Miss C. I. Hope (who was eventually to become the deputy head of the comprehensive school).

Final days of the boys' school

The entries in the boys' school log were once again briefer than those written by the women head teachers, and routine was seen to continue as much as possible.

The entry for 18 July 1968 merely states that form 4.3 visited the Railway Plant Ltd in the charge of Mr Minikin and on the following day 4.1 visited the Waterworks. In the evening of that day there was a meeting for boys and their parents in the group visiting the Continent with the school.

On 22 July at break in the morning there was a meeting of house masters, and it was reported 'the school closed early at 3.35 p.m. for individual house staff meetings'.

The school sports were finally held on the 24th after two postponements due to wet weather.

The last log entry for the boys' school stated: 'The School closed at the end of the last day as a separate Boys' School. It reopens in September as a combined school with the Girls at the start of the Comprehensive system in Darlington.'

The Comprehensive School
The Birth of the Comprehensive School Ideal

The enterprise of the 1944 Education Act and the philosophy of the new secondary education born out of it hardly advanced from the starting line before division of opinion developed into an emotive controversy. The tripartite system did not satisfy the radicals' deep-felt desire for a utopian social justice. They saw only division: the minority of grammar and perhaps technical pupils achieving the clean authority-commanding posts (while those from the private sector retained their stranglehold on the positions of real power), and the majority of the secondary modern pupils had no choice but to follow their destiny into the lower-paid manual and clerical occupations.

A professional democracy

A leading protagonist in the comprehensive school movement was Robin Pedley, one-time Director of Education of the Exeter University Institute of Education, and in his book *The Comprehensive School*, published in 1963, he comments that England was then an aristocracy, that is, a society in which government is in the hands of the best people. He pointed out that the 'best people' were formerly those born into wealthy aristocratic families but that the situation was changing to one in which those with ability were filling the influential positions, a fact supported by more recent surveys which show the number of grammar school-educated people in managerial and government posts. Such a society has become known as a meritocracy. 'The Englishman of the 1960s,' Pedley said, 'does not believe in equality. What he wants is equal opportunity to be unequal.' He goes on to imply that the acceptance of this state of affairs does nothing to remove class barriers and consequently suggests a democratic form of government as a better way forward. Upon this oversimplified maxim rests the case for one-school-for-all, and much of the underlying philosophy behind many subsequent developments.

Such an oversimplification hardly seems to be worth consideration, but it is this kind of simple, uncluttered statement which is so easily understood and grasped at by those who seek straightforward maxims upon which to build their creed. It lies at the root of much modern thinking on school government, working relationships between senior and assistant staff, teaching styles and child discipline. It places professionally untrained and inexperienced people in positions of authority on school governing bodies. It gives equal weight to the opinions of the newly qualified untried teacher and the long-serving head teacher. It places the child's immature judgements on a par with those of the professionally trained teacher in matters of curriculum and discipline. In short, it dilutes the authority of those who should know and gives it to those who do not know, with the result that decisions are made by compromise and the best solutions to problems lost. If society is to flourish, it must surely accept that all cannot be expert in everything and must rely on the professional expertise of others. Authority needs to be in the hands of those who should have the knowledge, skills and experience to make the best decisions, that is, in the hands of the professionals (whether talking of the traditional professions such as teaching or the wider concept of professionalism where it recognised that other workers, such as fully qualified plumbers and electricians for example, are also professionals). But not only have the pseudo-democratic ideologists succeeded in advancing their cause, the professionals have often let society down because they have been insufficiently professional. What is required is leadership by those with training, knowledge, skills and experience, the professionals, monitored by the elected representatives of the rest of society: a professional democracy.

The all-in-one school

For the extreme radicals in the 1950s and 60s, the development of the all-in-one comprehensive school was the only route by which they could achieve their new idealised classless society. For many educators it was seen as a proper means of ensuring that all pupils received an equal opportunity to develop their true potential, while the existence of the grammar school prevented this. Whether or not the grammar school was doing a good and useful job came to be of little consequence. Grammar schools served an elite group and had to go!

In the meantime, however, grammar schools continued along their pre-determined course, providing an academic education for those who could pass what was fast becoming known as the Eleven-plus Examination. Although the pass rate varied from one education authority to another, usually about 20 per cent of an age group was selected for a grammar school education. The significance lies in the fact that the remainder were not selected and came to be seen as failures, and this real or imaginary social rejection was greatly emphasised by those promoting their cause, until popular opinion hailed it as fact. It was implied that the 80 per cent not selected suffered permanent damage because of this apparent failure at the tender age of eleven. Pedley's emotive language refers to the 'forced segregation of children in separate schools, with the awful implications of daily, publicly hammering home a child's officially assessed inferiority', sentiments which I do not believe to be true and which I certainly never experienced when growing up among a group of some dozen or so youngsters, only two of whom attended grammar schools. But, by the time the enthusiasts had got their way, the poor youngsters had no alternative but to believe what they were told!

The division of children into different schools requires some form of selection to bring about their distribution and people came to doubt the accuracy or suitability of the techniques being used for this purpose. Some pupils selected for grammar schools were later found to be quite unsuited to the academic courses provided. Others, those from homes where books were in short supply, where language used was oversimplified and stereotyped, were not selected and yet eventually showed themselves to be capable of high academic achievement. Pedley commented on what must surely be accepted as the obvious: 'The idea that there are two or three types of child, suitable for two or three types of school, is incredibly crude and naïve.'

But selection continued with the cultural or language anomaly being at least partially answered by the development of non-verbal intelligence tests, where candidates are given the opportunity to demonstrate their thinking abilities by comprehending relationships shown in complex diagrams and pictures rather than words or numbers.

But opponents were not going to have that! They argued that there was little evidence to show that intelligence tests forecast academic success, in spite of the fact that such tests were first validated by correlating pupils' scores with marks gained on traditional school tests. In other words, the tests were designed so that those who did well on traditional school tests also did well on intelligence tests. The perusal of different children's scores on the intelligence tests would therefore be expected to give some indication of the likely performance of these youngsters in school subjects. Furthermore, the fact that some of those selected failed in the later years of the grammar school overlooked other relevant factors such as personality and home pressures.

Education authorities did, however, develop 11-plus selection procedures which attempted to answer all of the criticisms. The objection that the results of attainment and intelligence tests taken on one particular day could be distorted by the child's circumstances or mood at the time was answered by consulting teachers' records and holding interviews with parents and children before the final decision was made.

But for some, any form of testing became a social evil, seen only as permanently dividing those who shall succeed in life from those who shall fail, when instead they should be seen as a means of guiding each along routes leading to different personal successes. Indeed, it was fast becoming taboo to suggest that some people do not have the ability or abilities that others do! That is, in spite of the general acceptance that some people are more athletic than others, some have great musical ability and some considerable artistic talent, it becomes unacceptable to suggest that some are less able to comprehend intellectual matters than others. Failure in all of the special aptitudes is happily explained in terms of people not having that particular ability, and it does not matter one iota, but to suggest that children have different levels of academic ability brings forth a storm of protest with explanations given in terms of a myriad of social inadequacies which can be rectified if only the social conditions are perfected: a notion which seems to have its origins in the misconception that all are born with identical nervous systems having origins in the same genes.

Because those attending the grammar schools appeared to obtain the jobs that were better paid and had more favourable working conditions, while the majority were not selected for these schools there would be overwhelming support from parents for a system which appeared to give all children access to the grammar school style of education, whether it was appropriate or not. The system was, of course, the comprehensive school: demand for its introduction could not fail as the majority of parents saw it as a safer option for a their children to gain entry to a good school, that is, in so far as their children were not certain to pass the 11-plus. Educators saw it as a more just application of resources which ensured a more equal opportunity for all.

The situation in Darlington

There was a proposal for the reorganisation of the secondary schools in Darlington soon after the end of World War II, when it was suggested that there should be nine bi-lateral schools, that is, either grammar/technical or secondary modern/technical. The idea was that the existing technical school should be closed and technical-biased courses introduced and extended into all of the secondary schools. There would be single-sex secondary modern/technical schools at Eastbourne, Haughton and Branksome. The Girls' High School and Queen Elizabeth Boys' Grammar School would become grammar/technical schools.

The Albert Road Boys' Department and North Road Girls would be replaced by two single-sex schools at Haughton, the first of which was opened in 1958, taking both boys and girls and halving the numbers of pupils at the two older schools. Central Secondary School and Reid Street Girls' Department would be closed with the opening of two new schools at Branksome. The first opened, again taking boys and girls, in September 1963. The Reid Street Girls' premises would be used by the adjacent primary school; Central School would become co-educational and housed in the Northgate Building which had been Darlington College of Further Education (re-housed in the new building opened in the early 1960s) and previously used by the technical school. At this time single-sex schools were to be retained, a question around which opinions were divided.

In 1959 there was a proposal to open the new Branksome School as a comprehensive school, with the proviso that there would be an option for those of appropriate ability to choose to attend the grammar or high schools. There was local opposition to any scheme which would lead to the loss of the two grammar schools.

The Peter Plan

The front page of the *Northern Echo* for Tuesday 12 September 1963 announced a 'Revolutionary education plan for Darlington'; referring to a report prepared by the CEO, Mr D. Peter, and seen by him as a proposal to be thoroughly examined through wide consultations with interested parties. The major groups expected to be involved were the Teachers Advisory Committee, the teachers' associations (their trade unions), school governors, and the schools themselves (presumably involving teachers and parents).

The pillars of the proposals were the abolition of selection for secondary schools and the establishing of co-education throughout the town: the report being the result of the Education Committee's discussion on introducing modern-language teaching into all of the secondary schools; the planning of selection of pupils for entry into the secondary school at Haughton; consideration of the question of selection of pupils entering all of the secondary schools; and the overall provision of secondary education in Darlington.

The discussion on the desire to introduce modern-language courses into all of the secondary modern schools argued that there were insufficient able pupils in each of the schools to make the courses viable. That is, groups would be small and require the expensive use of specialist teachers working with few pupils. Added to this problem was the shortage of appropriately qualified teachers.

Under the new proposals it was expected that all of the schools would be able to provide a broader curriculum.

The plan envisaged new schools being built at Blackwell Grange and Longfield Road. The Eastbourne Schools, Haughton (the new secondary school opened in 1958 with a second proposed for inclusion in the 1964–65 building programme) and Branksome would serve their respective geographical areas, with Central (or a new school built to replace it). The Longfield School was due to open in 1967.

The historic site of the boys' grammar school would be retained as a part of a new further education campus, including the Darlington Teacher Training College and the Darlington College of Further Education, and changes to its provision were seen as steps in the progressive development of a better education system for Darlington. The idea was born that it should become a sixth-form centre, taking a larger number of students and breaking from the traditional division into arts and sciences courses to provide a greater choice for young people.

The Girls' High School was to become one of the seven or eight co-educational secondary schools, each serving their local geographical areas; that is, they would be neighbourhood schools, all providing courses leading to the GCE 'O' level and the new CSE examinations. The two schools at Eastbourne would continue, although the Director's personal view was that single-sex schools were an unnatural segregation of boys and girls at a time when they were growing towards adulthood. Also, at this time, the Eastbourne premises were recognised as being inadequate for modern (1960s) requirements and could either be amalgamated (and presumably be upgraded) or be accommodated in new buildings.

This was the start of considerable debate, in which polarised views were enthusiastically advanced, lasting until 1965 when the plan was approved by the council.

Arguments for and against the Peter Plan reported in the *Northern Despatch*

From the National Association of Schoolmasters

The NAS promoted the idea that there should be six mixed secondary technical schools, that the boys' grammar and girls' high schools should be retained, and that there should be more posts of special responsibility available for the staff of the technical schools. They also suggested that more vocationally biased subjects, such as rural science, building and plumbing (for boys), nursing, physiotherapy and typing (for girls), should be provided in these schools.

The Association was generally in favour of retaining the 11-plus selection examination, arguing that it allowed for the integration of pupils into the grammar schools; meaning the early introduction to an academic discipline which they did not see as present or necessary in other types of school. It also pointed out the shortage of specialist teachers as a further reason for retaining grammar schools. However, one member advanced the idea that there should be three comprehensive schools in order to move the stresses associated with selection at the age of 11, presumably for those who wished to take this route.

They also called for smaller classes in all state schools, claiming that this would eliminate the private sector.

From the Joint Four Group for teachers in secondary schools

Largely having members working in the grammar and high schools, the Group was concerned that the social mixing of able youngsters from different backgrounds in an environment with a strong academic discipline would be lost, thus reducing social mobility.

From the National Association of Headteachers

Representing their members in Darlington, they supported the Peter Plan given that certain requirements were met. They were in favour of the abolition of the 11-plus although they expressed the opinion that this could depress teaching standards in the primary schools, presumably seeing the demands created by the 11-plus as a strong motivating force in academic teaching.

They felt that purpose-built accommodation would be required to meet the demands of the Plan, and that, with the current shortage of teachers, more teachers of appropriate quality, particularly for the 'high flyers', would be required. They further pointed out that the grammar schools' smaller classes enabled pupils to compete favourably with those from the private sector, and to maintain this position more teachers would be required to keep more classes smaller than they were in many schools at the time. They also said that, in addition, more teachers were going to be required to cater for the increase in numbers due to the raising of the school-leaving age.

On the question of social mixing of pupils they referred to catchment areas, schools serving particular areas of the town, and pointed out that they would have to be constructed in such a way as to produce the desired mix. They felt that, for the more able pupils, the comprehensive system would produce less social mixing than the grammar schools.

A selection of observations from readers' letters

One correspondent, 'Save the Children of Darlington', was clearly against consulting the teachers, putting faith in the professionalism of the CEO to make necessary decisions.

Readers' letters frequently reflected the views expressed by the teachers, sometimes raising allied topics but also new points of interest.

Someone referred to as 'In perspective of Darlington' was concerned that there would a levelling down of educational standards which would affect the economic development of the town. In order to avoid this he or she said that there would need to be enough top-quality teachers to staff all the schools and enough money to provide the equivalent of grammar school resources in all schools, as well as the staffing of small classes in the sixth-form college.

Someone claiming to give a socialist's point of view said that true comprehensive schools would require between 1,500 and 2,000 pupils, the suggested plan being comprised of bi-lateral schools, secondary modern schools with only one academic class in each year group. The writer also suggested the provision of three comprehensive schools, with the facility to develop sixth forms, but with the retention of the grammar schools to provide a system of choice for parents.

Ted Fletcher, writing in February 1964 as the Labour candidate in the current election, said there was an overwhelming case for the support of the Peter Plan, believing that it would bring equality to education and equality of opportunity. He said selection at 11-plus was disgraceful and that Labour would fight injustice, abolish poverty and establish a socialist system.

On 6 February 1964 the Education Committee's recommendations were to be ratified by the full council. The outcome was that there should be six 11–15 or 16 mixed secondary schools with transfer for sixth form studies to the suitably adapted Queen Elizabeth Grammar School. The Girl's High School was to become one of the six schools and it was recommended that the Eastbourne Schools be remodelled as another of the mixed secondary schools.

Councillor James Whelan, in February 1964, voted in favour of the Peter Plan because he was in favour of doing away with the 11-plus, and the Plan would raise the standards of education in the town. He was, however, not in favour of doing away with the grammar schools because he felt parents should have the opportunity of opting out of comprehensive education, and he was also opposed to the enforcement of catchment areas because this also denied parents choice.

'Disgusted Socialist' said he had listened to the recent council debate and concluded that although the Labour Group had already accepted the Plan they had not answered the critics and that there should be further discussion.

'Oliver Twisted' claimed that the Plan had been wrongly accepted, a plan which he said would do 'disservice' to the working class, a plan full of privilege: the West End of the town, with an eight-form entry at

Hummersknott, would have half of its classes which could be treated as a grammar school intake.

'Look before you leap' claimed the Plan would not provide comprehensive education.

'Mum of Three' made the point that children are not all equal and the able should not be denied a grammar school education. 'Esau' pointed out that the 25 per cent then educated in the grammar schools would be divided to become a minority in several schools, particularly in the north and east of the town. He or she also pointed out the GCE 'O' level courses were already provided in the non-grammar schools and that the rest would see no difference in their education as result of reorganisation.

'Progress of Middleton St George' saw the new scheme as being child centred and an advantage, doing away with the 11-plus, which would change the nature of both primary and secondary education, and improve the teaching of many previously seen as neglected talent. Resulting from my own experience as a student teacher in a secondary modern school, seeing talent being neglected, I chose to start my career in the new purpose-built comprehensive schools of inner London, one of which had 2,300 pupils, including the sixth form.

A senior science master at the Queen Elizabeth Grammar School was concerned at the apparent loss of his school and what he felt would be the drop in 'O' level standards due to the dispersal of examination teaching throughout all of the Darlington secondary schools. He also claimed that the scheme was an expensive experiment, abolishing the 11-plus and thus taking away the child's right to an impersonal selection best achieved through examination and not the judgements of the pupil's teachers.

A brief but meaningful comment was made by 'Interested of Darlington': keep the grammar schools and implement the Newsom Report.

The views of Alderman James Skinner, Chairman of the Education Committee
Councillor James, better known as Jim, Skinner, being the Chairman of the Education Committee, had the major task of bringing about the acceptance of the Peter Plan. He held the view that the scheme would widen the opportunities of all children, giving them a fair and equal chance to succeed. He spoke of the segregation of 11-year-olds as unsound both socially and educationally, but experience was to

show that the elimination of social segregation was not achieved in the neighbourhood schools eventually established. In any case, there is a significant majority of people who only want a sound general education for their children, giving them a kind of general knowledge as a basis for solving their immediate problems in life and specialist training in skills and knowledge leading them into a sound money-earning career. The detail in these requirements will be different for different young people.

In addition, Alderman Stephenson rightly recognised that all do not have the same abilities and that consequently some form of selection is necessary. He saw the Plan as postponing selection until the age of 16 and the legislation being made for a majority, presumably at the expense of a significant minority.

In 1965 there was a suggestion that the CEO was never requested to prepare a full report of secondary school reorganisation and Councillor Skinner had to spell out the sequence of events. In the Education minute of July 1963 it was resolved that 'the CEO be asked to prepare a report for consideration by the Committee at a subsequent meeting on the selection for and the organisation of secondary education'. The first report was considered by the Education Committee on 12 September 1963 and a further report requested. This was considered on 27 January 1964.

In answer to criticisms Councillor Skinner wrote in the *Northern Despatch* on 21 January 1965: 'I want all of our children to be given the opportunity of climbing many ladders and progress at their own pace.' He again raised the undesirability of the anxiety caused by the 11-plus selection process and saw the Peter Plan offering the same opportunities to all pupils.

The conclusion to the debate

The outcome of all the arguments was, on 4 June 1965, the acceptance by the council of the Peter Plan. The 11-plus examination would be abolished by 1968; secondary schools would take pupils between the ages of 11-plus and 16 and no longer be separate for boys and girls. The Queen Elizabeth Grammar School would become a sixth-form college, entry to which was seen as the same as that for entry to the existing sixth forms, four to five 'O' levels, including English language, mathematics and possibly a foreign language, with evidence of the student being capable of passing two or three other subjects at 'O' or 'A' level. It was assumed that the college would be concerned with students wishing to continue their education at a university.

There was also the comment that the new comprehensive schools should not be organised around the academic element of the intake, raising the issue of mixed-ability teaching groups. It was argued that mixing both able and less able learners benefited both. With regard to the larger sizes of the new schools, making them impersonal, the introduction of pastoral-style house systems was proposed.

On the question of mixed-ability teaching, on the one hand it was seen that all, but particularly the academic child, would not benefit unless there were sufficient suitably qualified and experienced teachers for all of the schools. It was also suggested that the absence of sixth-form work in the 11–16 schools would deter highly qualified teachers from wishing to work in those schools, and perhaps surprisingly, it was suggested that three-year-trained teachers would be adequate for the task.

The Foundation of the Eastbourne Mixed Comprehensive School

The Eastbourne Mixed Comprehensive School opened on 9 September 1968, formed by the bringing together of the pupils and members of staff from the previously long-established separate secondary modern girls' and boys' schools occupying adjoining buildings.

This is the log entry for the first day at the Eastbourne Mixed Comprehensive School, 9 September 1968, written by the head teacher, Mr F. Foxon:

> The school opened today as a single school formed by the combination of the former Boys' and Girls' School, and with the first unselected first year intake of boys and girls. 415 boys and 359 girls returned and from Darlington Primary Schools we admitted 151 boys and 127 girls. With 10 casual admissions the total roll was 1062 (574 boys and 488 girls).
>
> The Headmaster was Mr H. F. Foxon MA and Miss V. J. Armstrong Deputy Head. The staff in addition consisted of 46 full-time permanent staff, 1 full-time supply teacher and 5 part-time teachers. There were 28 men and 25 women assistants. Twenty-two of the men and 17 of the women were already on the staffs of the former schools and 8 women and 6 men were newcomers.
>
> The School was organised into Houses, Bolton (in charge of Miss C. I. Hope, Senior Mistress/Housemistress), Durham (Mr R. Binns Senior Master/Housemaster), Richmond

(Mr R. L. Shotton, Housemaster) and Witton (Miss A. Brewster, Housemistress). Each House comprised 9 Mixed Tutor groups, two in each of the first four years and one each in the 5th year (which comprised 47 boys and 25 girls).

On 9 September there was an introductory day with staff only, the first-year intake of 280 pupils and the fifth year coming on the following day. The whole school assembled for the first time on 11 September when Mr Foxon noted the staff room was not ready for use and the teachers had to use the youth annexe.

A staff meeting was held after school on 17 September to review the new situation and another on 1 October when the agenda included homework, head boy and head girl, movement in the school, a tutor-group period in place of assemblies, and discipline. The first head boy and girl were Paul Wray and Nadine Bell.

Immense changes

Beneath the skeletal veneer of the log book entries, putting together what they say and experience gained on the job, it is apparent that the change from two single-sex schools to a larger mixed school brought immense changes. There was the increase in size of the building, not just the two buildings put together but with the added new three-storey block: the reality being a larger area to move around and to supervise. There were at least twice as many colleagues; twice as many people to get to know; interaction and communication becoming more difficult. A group of fifty or more is too large, and in any case, spread throughout the larger building, will inevitably break up into smaller cells inhabiting departmental areas. The small-group, informal face-to-face exchange of ideas and concerns among the whole staff, possible in the smaller schools, was lost.

There was also the sudden increase in the number of pupils: they could not so easily know each other or all of the teachers, experiencing a loss of belonging to a previously evolved community, and having no established mutual respect. Boys and girls were suddenly together in the same classes, a very significant factor in a situation where there had been a long tradition of separate boys' and girls' schools more or less isolated from each other. Old friendship groups had possibly been disturbed and new ones had to be discovered and tested.

The interaction of more teachers with more pupils means that the chance of them getting to know and understand those in their care becomes more difficult. In terms of discipline, there are more places for the mischief makers to hide and a good chance that supervising teachers (once outside their own classroom) would not recognise the culprits. More importantly, they would not know and understand how the individuals normally behave and react to others, and consequently not so easily be in a position to give an immediate and appropriate response to behaviour in any given situation.

Not only had the pupils been boys among men and girls among women but the men and women themselves had become entrenched in the attributes seen as more appropriate to their gender.

With communication necessary but difficult, and with new problems arising, there was a mushrooming of meetings to attend: more staff meetings, heads of department meetings, heads of house meetings, liaison meeting between the academic and pastoral staff, formal meetings in the larger departments. This was time consuming but the necessary formality also eroded the intimate feeling of belonging. The school somehow became less friendly, more of a large business complex than a school. After all, the new unit required the interaction of more than a thousand people.

The teachers

The head teacher of the new comprehensive school, Mr H. F. Foxon MA, was first appointed to the staff of the Eastbourne Boys' School in 1946 and therefore worked in the school during the headship of Mr Welford, becoming chief assistant master in 1952 and in 1955 moving to the headship of Albert Road Secondary Boys' School. He returned as head teacher, replacing Mr Welford on his retirement, in 1960, consequently having had long experience of work in boys' secondary modern schools.

The deputy head, Miss V. I. Armstrong, had become head teacher of the girls' school on the retirement of Miss Fenby in 1963. Both the head and deputy head of the new school, established in the ways of the successful but very separate boys' and girls' schools, therefore found themselves in an entirely new situation, being required to implement, manage and develop a new concept in education.

A large proportion of the teachers were therefore also, to various degrees, dependent upon their length of service, established in the ways of single-sex secondary modern schools. The system of awarding posts of special responsibility was well established by this time, also placing some well-established teachers in senior positions in the comprehensive school.

Other senior staff were Miss C. M. Mc Leish, a long-serving teacher in the girls' school, who became head of the English department; Miss C. A. Giles, who had joined the girls' school in 1952, became head of the physical education department; Mr B. F. Sheppard, at the boys' school since 1953, became head of music; Mr D. G. Whiteside, head of history in the boys' school from 1959, became head of social studies; Mr S. J. Thornhill, appointed to the boys' school in 1948 and later head of mathematics, became head of maths in the new school; and Mr T. W. Murphy, who joined the boys' school in 1960, was placed in charge of geography.

Among the new staff joining the comprehensive school in 1968 were: Miss W. E. Acres, English and drama; Miss J. Tennant; Mrs M. Arran; Mr J. Cousins, woodwork; Miss C. J. Hales; and Miss Barraclough. Miss S. E. Dring had married to become Mrs Scott.

There can be no doubt that the reorganisation caused great upheaval, being completely alien to some teachers but viewed by others as the way forward into the future. Whatever their views they were to be faced with further uncertainty because on 2 December 1968, after serving for only one term under the comprehensive school arrangements, both Mr Foxon and Miss Armstrong gave notice of their intention to retire on 30 April 1969.

Teachers serving on the staff of Eastbourne Comprehensive School appointed before September 1968 and previously working in the boys' school:

Mr H. F. Foxon MA, chief assistant master August 1946–July 1955, left to take up the post of head at Albert Road Secondary Modern Boys' School

January 1960 appointed head of Eastbourne Boys' Secondary Modern School and remained as head through the conversion to Eastbourne Comprehensive School until his retirement in April 1969, retired after serving a total of 17 years and 1 term

Mr S. J. Thornhill, maths, March 1948–July 1976, retired after 28 years and 1 term

Mr A. R. Foord, metalwork Sept 1951–July 1974, retired after 23 years

Mr B. F. Sheppard, music, August 1953

Mrs W. E Doran, part-time and temporary, 1953–July 1973 Retired after some 20 years

Mr W. Andrews, English and library, September 1957

Mr D. G. Whiteside, history, September 1959–April 1973, 12 years and 2 terms

Mr T. W. Murphy, geography, August 1960

Mr J. Minikin, maths, August 1960

Mr C. H. Parkinson, art, May 1960–August 1978, retired after 18 years and 1 term

Mr J. C. Carling. PE. September 1960

Mr R. L. Shotton, HoD English, January 1963–July 1970, 6 years

Mr R. W. Charlton, January 1964

Mr F. L. Mercer, science, August 1964–December 1973, 9 years and 1 term

Mr B. Jefferson, January 1965

Mr I. A. Simpson, August 1965

Mr R. L. Binns, deputy head, August 1965

Mr D. N. Heaton, history, August 1966–April 1974, 7 years and 2 terms, to Central School

Mr D. S. Hogg, French, January 1967

Mr G. Bramham BSc, January 1968

Mr J. Cousins, woodwork, January 1968

Teachers serving on the staff of Eastbourne Comprehensive School appointed before September 1968 and previously working in the girls' school:

Miss V. I. Armstrong, deputy head, April 1963–April 1969, retired after 6 years

Miss Dover, 28 August 1939–24 July 1970, 29 years

Miss K. A. McLeish BA, English, temporary 8 November 1943, permanent 1 May 1945–July 1976, retired after 32 years and 2 terms

Miss D. M. Manfield, domestic science, 4 September 1950–July 1983, retired after 33 years

Miss C. M. Giles, PE, 1 September 1952–1981, retired after 29 years

Miss A. Brewster, 1 September 1958–July 1969, but on secondment 1967–68, and joined Longfield School in 1969.

Miss C. I. Hope, 2 September 1963–December 1978, retired after 15 years and 1 term

Mrs Clarke nee Hunter, mathematics, 2 September 1963

Mrs Forster, full-time supply, 4 September 1967

Mrs Ellwood, supply, needlework, 25 April 1965–July 1965

Miss S. Dodd, graded post English, 30 August 1966

Miss W. Robinson, religious knowledge

Mr Mather, graded post geography, 4 September 1967

Mrs Brown, music, 7 May 1962

Miss E. P. Jackson, housecraft, 31 August 1965

Mrs Doran, part-time temporary, needlework, 30 August 1966–July 1973, retired

Mrs Paterson, part-time housecraft & child care, 30 August 1966

Mrs Lockey, maths, 4 September 1967

Mr Tarelli, 9 January 1968–July 1970, to work in Holland after 1 year 2 terms

Mrs Toogood, religious knowledge supply, April 1968

A period of consolidation – head teacher Mr P. Griffin

Mr P. Griffin, an experienced head teacher, became head of the Eastbourne Comprehensive School and Miss C. I. Hope was appointed deputy head in 1969. In addition Mr R. Binns, senior master, having gained promotion, was replaced by Mr R. N. Wrigley in September 1971. Consequently a new senior management team was in place, a team dedicated to the comprehensive ideal.

With the coming of the new head, an enthusiast for the comprehensive ideal including mixed-ability teaching, tutors and the pastoral house system, there was a surge in activities expected of staff, for example house parent evenings and other meetings seen in the calendar and weekly diary, which placed greater demands on teachers' time, an obligation rather than personal choice.

The building

The change to comprehensive education brought extensions and modifications to the 1930s building, the major part of which, by 1968, was some thirty years old. With the exception of four classrooms constructed over the cloakrooms at the four corners of the main building, little had changed. The major aesthetic change was in the building style: the decoratively attractive brick facade having the stark plain panel and glass of a rectangular three-storey block thrust against its western end.

In more practical terms, the facilities were considerably upgraded and extended, the most obvious being the imposing, if not particularly attractive, new block, containing five general purpose classrooms, a laboratory, and new toilets on the ground floor. On the first floor two art rooms and two needlework rooms were accessed from a central staircase, and, viewed from the central landing, a large glass-fronted display case was situated between the art rooms. The top floor housed four laboratories with a large preparation room between them. A small service lift enabled packages to be raised from the ground to the upper floor: it was perhaps not surprising that some pupils did during its lifetime succeed in sending a small boy up by this means!

The old boys' school gymnasium was converted into two music teaching rooms and practice rooms for instrumental music, the position behind the school hall and away from other rooms being well suited to isolation of the sounds of music and singing which would could disturb other lessons.

The loss of the sports accommodation was compensated for and added to by the provision of the new gymnasium and swimming pool, sited to the north-west of the old, and upgraded, girls' gymnasium.

The boys' school workshop block, containing one metalwork and one woodwork room, was increased in size by an extension to the north containing a large general purpose area and two more workshops.

The two halls remained, neither large enough to accommodate the whole school, making it necessary for any occasions where the whole was to assemble together to be held in other outside premises.

The two libraries of the old schools, situated over the flanks of the central arch, could not easily be combined and were subsequently used for separate lending and reference purposes.

The pupils

By 1968 the majority of pupils entering the school at 11-plus came from three primary schools Dodmire: Heathfield and Firthmoor; a smaller number from St John's Church of England School; and a few from a variety of others. The comprehensive school was, consequently, a neighbourhood school.

Dodmire School served the part of the Eastbourne area largely comprised of owner-occupied houses constructed in and before the 1930s. Heathfield School included in its catchment area the post-war housing west of McMullen Road and north of Yarm Road. Of the families living in these areas a significant proportion were caring, responsible working-class people, very happy to send their children to the Eastbourne School. Indeed Robert Hattersley, in his unpublished thesis, suggested that just over 99 per cent of pupils entering the school during the first three years of the comprehensive intake had given Eastbourne as their first choice.

The importance of applying for entry into the local secondary school, given parental satisfaction with the education which they perceived it provided, is significant. There was also the long-established tradition that the parents themselves had attended the boys' or girls' schools and were very supportive of their good reputation.

Firthmoor School served the large Firthmoor council estate, where it was recognised there was a high proportion of underprivileged families, many with personal problems, which consequently were at least in part brought into the school and included problems of behaviour.

School size

The size of the new school is another of the variables requiring the adjustment of routine procedures. The close informal association of relatively few teachers in a smaller area became a more formal organisation in extensive premises: not only were there the two original school buildings to move around but also the new extensions. Into this enlarged space were put almost 1,100 children. Formerly 550 pupils were free to move about in a smaller space; in the new school 1,100 now spread themselves over a much larger area.

In the smaller schools the head and staff stood a far better chance of knowing the behaviour problems associated with some 500 pupils than was possible when the pupil numbers doubled. Pastoral oversight of pupils in the secondary modern schools was a recognised responsibility of the form teacher who, originally, taught the form for a large part of the week. Some teachers always had junior forms and others took charge of senior classes. As the forms were streamed, the lower forms not only held children of low academic ability but, more significantly, a high proportion with behaviour problems – there arose the question of whether teachers should always work with the able or less able, or should they rotate through the whole range of streams?

A different type of house system

In the comprehensive school one of the first tasks was to tackle the size problem by placing pupils into one of four houses – Bolton, Durham, Richmond and Witton, named after castles and avoiding the use of the separate boys' and girls' systems. Although the separate schools did have houses they were mainly intended for competitive and social events, each form having members of each of the houses. The new system was intended to play a greater part in pastoral care, each house being placed in the charge of a house master or mistress who would keep the child's records, liaise with parents and exercise discipline. The heads of house were allocated their own offices and, in order to carry out their pastoral duties, had more lesson time free from class teaching than the academic staff.

Children remained in the same tutor group and, where possible, remained with the same group teacher for the whole of their time in the school. Brothers and sisters were placed in the same house with a view to maintaining family groups. The traditional *forms* became known as *tutor groups*. It was even suggested that heads of house should be given the status equivalent to that of the head in a small school, a situation open to criticism from the senior academic staff.

Corporal punishment

In the boys' school all staff had the delegated authority to use corporal punishment; a form of punishment available in the girls' school but only rarely used, a thorough dressing down apparently usually being sufficient to reduce a wrongdoer to tears. In the comprehensive school the punishment was only delegated to the heads of house, a senior woman standing in for a male colleague in cases where it was felt a girl should receive such punishment. The situation could be seen as a first step in the move to abolish the punishment altogether, and at the time caused resentment among some senior teachers, who felt their authority had been eroded.

School uniform and essential equipment

Pupils were expected to dress in school uniform. Boys and girls wore a navy blue blazer with the school badge on the pocket (but sold separately and therefore capable of being sewn onto an appropriate blazer purchased according to the parents' choice). A replica of the school badge, designed by the art master Mr H. Parkinson, was also displayed on the top of the new building. A school tie was an essential part of the uniform, as were black school shoes.

Uniform for girls in the junior school included a blue shift tunic or navy blue box-pleated skirt, and in the senior school a navy blue tailored skirt with four inverted pleats.

Both juniors and seniors were expected to wear a light blue nylon blouse (Trutex) and either a navy blue cardigan or navy blue V-neck pullover. There was the option of wearing a dress of approved pattern in two shades of blue; details of appropriate material and a pattern were provided.

Boys wore blue nylon shirts (Trutex) with a navy blue pullover and grey flannel trousers.

Outdoor wear was expected to be a navy blue duffle coat or gabardine.

For sport the boys were to provide football boots, stockings (blue and gold), a rugby and football jersey and navy blue shorts; for indoors, plimsolls and white shorts, swimming trunks and a towel.

Girls' sportswear included white plimsolls, white socks and navy blue leotards; hockey boots, navy blue shorts and a pale blue blouse; a swimming costume, swimming cap and a towel.

In addition a satchel for books; a pen, pencil and ruler; and a bag for games equipment were to be provided.

Communications

Attempts to solve the problem of communications in the large school consisted of the use of the internal telephone system, channelling of information through the heads of house, the production of a weekly diary of events and internal written notes: all of which emphasised the lack of personal contact between all teachers and led to feelings, on the part of some, that they were not involved in what was happening. There was also the question of efficiency: all staff were not at the end of a telephone line and were therefore not contactable during teaching time; written notes could be mislaid and the diary of events not read.

Calendar for the term and diary of events

In order to keep people informed of what was happening in the school a calendar of events and a diary of events were prepared. Inclusion of information in the former was essential for future planning, the avoidance of clashes in timing and overcrowding (where possible) of particular periods during the year. Their contents give insight into the workings of the school.

The diary of events was prepared and distributed weekly. It was produced in two parts: the confidential section for staff only, and the section for the classroom noticeboard. Teachers were invited to fill in on sheets provided by the heads of house details of events they had organised for insertion in the diary. Tutors were asked to ensure that the noticeboard copy of the diary was displayed on the notice board in the tutor-group room and to call the attention of pupils to any matters which may concern them.

The organisation of the school

Comprehensive reorganisation introduced a number of considerable changes to the education system in the area, changes affecting both staff and pupils.

Previously, the boys' and girls' schools had not only been separate but the separation seemed to emphasise a social climate in which boys and girls shall not meet (although there was some relaxation of this attitude and examples of contrived coming together in the latter years of the secondary modern era). A particular example of the situation is seen in the different opening hours of the two schools: at one time the girls started at 8.50 a.m., the boys at 9.10 a.m.; the girls finished at 3.55 p.m., the boys at 4.10 p.m.. The school times were, however, equated in the last days of the secondary modern schools.

The staff, particularly those having served longest in the schools, had developed strong attachments to their schools' separate, different, and individual ethos.

The start of the school year

At the start of the school year, in order to produce a trouble-free integration of teachers and some 240 pupils new to the school and with the introduction of a new timetable requiring more than a thousand people to be in different places during thirty-five weekly lessons, the arrival of the youngsters was staggered. The first year arrived at 9 a.m., before the hustle and bustle of the entry of the more confident older pupils after morning break. They were ushered into hall 1 where they were allocated to their tutor groups and introduced to their teachers. Those with older brothers and sisters in the school would already expect to be in the same houses as their siblings, an arrangement enabling heads of houses to get to know family groups and for parents to get to know one head of house during the period of their children's education, an important factor in the building of trust and co-operation between family and school.

While maintaining family groupings in one house, the policy of having a full pupil–ability range in each tutor group required a previous knowledge of children new to the school. This was obtained by asking the primary schools to provide lists of pupil grades, on a five-point scale, as assessed through their work with the children during their previous school years. It was apparent that different schools applied the grades differently and consequently a bright child in one school did not necessarily equate with one from another, a difficulty minimised by the personal contact between heads of houses and the primary school teachers. Similarly, children known to have behaviour problems were, where possible, evenly distributed throughout the tutor groups, rather than placing them together in one. Where children were known to

314

react together in their misbehaviour, they were also separated in order to give them the opportunity for a new trouble-free start – a break from any previous undesirable reputation.

Mixed-ability teaching groups

At this time (in the late 1960s and early 1970s) the mixed-ability tutor groups were the main teaching groups in the first three years of the secondary school courses. Exceptions included the extraction of special needs children for support work in English and mathematics, for those taking the additional foreign language, German, in the second and third years; and for setting in mathematics. The setting system provided the facility for placing children of near equal ability and attainment in mathematics in four separate classes across half a year group, which consisted of about 120 pupils. A controversial arrangement was the allowing of individual youngsters to be extracted from other lessons in order to be given tuition in instrumental music. In spite of trying to extract them from different lessons on each occasion, they still missed what could be vital steps in their other classwork.

An interesting event is recorded in the calendar for 16 September: a professional photographer came in to school each year to photograph individual children, firstly for purchase by parents, if required, but also for school records as an aid to recognition and recall in cases of enquiry.

The Christian ethic

The continued significance of the Christian ethic in the school's education is demonstrated by the promotion of such occasions as the Christian Education Movement Conference and Christmas carol services.

The school was clearly accepted as suitable for colleges of education to use for the teaching practice sessions necessary for their students.

Extra-curricular activities

From the weekly diary it can be seen that the traditional voluntarily supervised sporting activities, well established in the secondary modern schools, continued into the comprehensive school years. Sports teams engaged in inter-school competitions which took place out of class time, but there were also practices during the midday break, after school and even before school at 8 a.m. There was an athletics coach and in addition the more recent introductions of tennis, badminton, basketball, gymnastics and golf.

There was a variety of indoor recreational activities such as the chess, table tennis and stamp clubs. The music department held extra classes for guitar and recorder, a violin group, band practice and choir rehearsals. There was a junior country dancing club run by a physical education teacher with connections to the Darlington Schools Music Festival. Work on the pantomime started in September.

There was a photography club and a printing club, an old set of printing equipment being acquired for the purpose and stored under the stairs near hall 2.

There were extra-curricular classes in typewriting, science (largely providing homework facilities), and French oral practice.

The quiz team, bringing kudos to the school by winning the Radio Cleveland inter-schools competition, also met out of class hours. The note from Miss Hope under staff notices in the confidential-to-staff diary, seeking someone to take over the coaching of the quiz team, was perhaps a sign of things to come. A keen staff member leaves, having gained promotion in another school, and there is difficulty in finding someone to take over the responsibility for supervising youngsters out of class time.

Visits to the field studies centre at Earls Orchard continued, taking place during the five days of the normal school week, but requiring teachers to engage in extra-curricular preparations and 24-hour-per-day residential care.

The question of pupils remaining in school after the compulsory leaving age
One measure of the success of going comprehensive was claimed to be the number of pupils remaining in school after reaching the compulsory school-leaving age which, at this time, was still 15. During the two years prior to reorganisation, fifth-year classes in both the boys' and girls' schools were relatively small, round about twenty. In the first two years of the comprehensive school the number staying on had nearly doubled – rather more girls than boys – an apparent success.

Remembering that, with reorganisation, the Eastbourne School was receiving children who would previously have attended the grammar schools, where they were expected to remain until 16 years of age, a proportion then going on to sixth form studies, at least a part of this rise could be expected. Nevertheless, there was also a growing acceptance of the idea that young people should remain in school, take leaving examinations, and thus improve their prospects of gaining employment when they did leave, and employment prospects for 16-year-olds were declining.

Robert Hattersley, as a part of his dissertation compiled during teacher training, completed a survey of opinions among senior pupils and one question put to those in the pre-examination year was whether they wanted to remain in school for another year. Almost 60 per cent said they would, the boys being slightly more inclined to do so than the girls. This adds to the impression that for older pupils to remain in school longer was becoming both desirable and acceptable, not overlooking the fact that the raising of the compulsory school-leaving age was on the horizon. On the other hand, when those already opting to remain in school until 16 were asked whether they thought the compulsory school-leaving age should be 16, only a little more than half agreed, with the girls being slightly more in agreement than the boys.

The pupils also gave the impression that they found the new school more to their liking than the old – perhaps not surprising, being at least in part due to its upgraded accommodation with more facilities; but there was also a greater variety of provision being made for senior pupils, particularly in the choices of subjects.

Further development of the curriculum

The teaching of the traditional range of subjects continued with the introduction of French for all and German for those showing ability in language studies. The head of languages reported difficulties with the teaching of French to the new intake pupils due to their coming from several different schools, some having been taught the subject before and others not having done so.

Choice in the senior school

Giving young people, in contrast to children, the ability to choose what they should study and for the content to be relevant to them was recognised as a significant aspect of their motivation to learn. The comprehensive school paid attention to these factors by providing courses which could be put together from a system of options with the proviso that there would be a compulsory element: compulsory subjects being English, mathematics, religious knowledge and physical education.

The amount of choice was limited by the staff and accommodation available, and was achieved by placing subjects in blocks of time during the week. The pupils were asked to choose eight subjects from three groups, being sure to include at least one from each. They were to grade their preferences in the subjects, the attempt being to ensure that all were given their most highly favoured five out of the eight but without the promise of being given everything they would like.

One block was based upon science subjects and contained physics, chemistry, biology, general science, rural science, human biology, engineering science, ecology and cosmetology; the last four not leading to an examination qualification. The second block was arranged around the practical subjects art and craft, building, child care and nursing, drama, housecraft, metalwork, music, needlecraft, technical drawing, typing and woodwork; all except child care and nursing being examination courses. The third group included the traditional geography and history; French, the only foreign language previously taught in the lower school at that time; religious knowledge; the employment-orientated shorthand and typewriting; and two combined subjects, humanities and social studies, which were the only ones not leading to examinations.

A number of aspects to this pattern of choices are worth noting. There is the facility to follow the traditional grammar school course of five compulsory areas of study, English, mathematics, science, a foreign language and one other to examination level. There is a built-in requirement to take a practical subject or the choice to take practical subjects with, for example, general science. A bias towards commerce could be arranged around shorthand and typewriting. There are non-traditional subjects, not offered as an examination course, in some cases combining elements of otherwise traditional subjects. Music, art/craft and drama are available to those who want to build a course around one of these if they are particularly interested or talented. The reservations are always these: can economically sized groups, available teachers and accommodation be timetabled into what must be a system catering for some 240 pupils in each of the two senior school years?

Pupils were advised to consider the evidence of their abilities and attainments given on their school reports, to discuss their future with their parents and tutor, and to seek advice concerning subject qualifications required if they have a particular career in mind. The system proved attractive, the vast majority of young people saying, during the early years of the introduction of the scheme, that they, not surprisingly, enjoyed being able to choose their subjects.

When considering behaviour, the traditional class groups, the streams, were broken up into groups comprised of people who chose to be there and any two people need not necessarily meet in any two classes: each has an individual timetable, all have a greater responsibility thrust upon them to make sure they know their individual timetable and turn up in the right place at the right time. There is a greater opportunity for those inclined to go missing, and it would eventually be seen that some did!

Education for leisure

A further innovation, in part designed to educate young people in ways of purposefully occupying their leisure time and in part to make school more attractive to those least motivated by traditional schooling, was the timetabled activities programme. Initially, two groups of activities were offered under the headings of indoor and outdoor. Two outdoor groups could choose to take part in canoeing, horse riding, orienteering, and hiking. There were three indoor groups: one occupied the youth centre where the centre's facilities such as darts, table tennis and snooker were made available, and there was the opportunity for dancing. A second group was based on musical activities, where musical instruments could be played or pupils could listen to music of their choice. The third group took part in things related to drama.

It could be said that this programme, in some cases at least, was insufficiently educational; and, in any case, many young people know very well how to occupy themselves in free time. The real question is whether or not such a programme really does motivate youngsters to take up some purposeful activity after leaving school; and there is the strong suspicion that those who do, do not need to be introduced to specific activities in school, and those that do not are not influenced by such opportunities in any case.

Were the extra-curricular activities in the secondary modern schools, such as the boys' camp, the Duke of Edinburgh's Award Scheme, the production of the pantomime, visits to the abbeys and other excursions, as successful or even more successful in bringing young people to engage purposeful pastimes?

Examinations and the reporting of pupils' progress

Towards the end of term, in the autumn and summer, timetabled internal tests or examinations took place and, with the results of continuous assessment throughout the term, marks were reported in terms of grades, on the half-yearly reports.

The report system in secondary modern schools changed very little during the 1945 to 1968 period. Classes were streamed and each class took the examinations set by their class teachers; papers were marked in such a way that points were earned for what was right in the answers, possibly with marks deducted for what was wrong. For convenience marks were either awarded with a possible total of 100 or turned in to percentages. The pupils knew from their marks the proportion of the questions they had answered correctly. One might think this was a good measure of what had been learned.

In addition, the pupils in each class were ranked according to the total marks they earned: producing a clear picture of where each stood in relation to others in the class. The notions of top and bottom of the class were easily understood, and it was known that *top* and *bottom* referred to the class you were in: pupils could be in the top, middle or bottom of the A, B, and C streams. Those at the top of the class could be promoted from bottom and middle streams; and those at the bottom of the class be demoted from top and middle streams. There was a competitive element to learning in all of the classes, and the knowledge of results was well known to promote learning.

Reporting of progress in the comprehensive school

With the introduction of mixed-ability teaching the reporting of marks obtained and positions in the class were no longer appropriate as the same children would always be in the top, middle or bottom of the mixed-ability class where the ability range was much greater than in the streaming system, and the marks achievable by low and middle ability children would always be around the 50 per cent level or below on test papers set for everybody.

The system adopted consisted of the awarding of grades 1 to 5, 1 being the highest over the whole year group for examination results and effort; backed by the argument that the least able child might always get a grade 5 for examinations and tests but could earn a grade 1 for effort. The grades were defined in terms of three being average, 1 and 2 above average and 4 and 5 below. Teachers' supporting remarks were still expected to be written in support of the grades, to be objective and contain useful, constructive advice.

The need for tutors to head reports with pupils' names and other appropriate details, for subject teachers to enter grades and comments, for tutors to make comments on their knowledge of the children's progress in their care, for the heads of house to add their observations and for them to be approved by the head teacher or deputy head, a strict timetable for each stage was imperative. There were no computer-aided strategies available in those days!

External school-leaving examinations for 16-year-olds

As the CSE became established so the Northern Counties Schools Certificate Examination was phased out and records suggest that the GCE courses at the secondary modern schools declined. The extensive timetable, possible timetable clashes between subjects examined by the different examination boards, differences between the content of subject syllabuses set by the different boards, and decisions about which pupils should take which examinations made the idea of having one (the same) examination for all a very attractive proposition. There was also the apparent attraction, for those in favour of mixed-ability teaching, of being able to use common syllabus content for all of the pupils in their classes: apparent, because in reality the CSE was established in such a way as to make available many different work programmes.

Furthermore, the GCE was the established examination taken by the pupils at the boys' grammar and girls' high schools before reorganisation, an examination well known and trusted by employers and in further education. The question arose in the minds of some regarding the standards in the great variety of subject syllabuses in the CSE.

In addition some candidates could be entered for the examinations set by the Guildhall School of Music and Drama, the Associated Board of the Royal School of Music and the Royal Society of Arts.

Examinations taken at other Darlington schools

Those in favour of have GCE or 'O' level courses in Eastbourne also had the knowledge that other Darlington comprehensive schools were entering pupils for these examinations.

Hummersknott, evolving from the Girls' High School, had a selective fifth form, girls who had passed the 11-plus examination and who had been prepared for the 'O' level papers during their time in the upper school. They had to be entered for the 'O' level examinations. But Branksome and to a lesser degree Haughton and Longfield schools also entered some pupils for some subjects at 'O' level, and Central School entered a few.

The Comprehensive School
January 1973–August 1986

I was appointed head teacher of the Eastbourne Mixed Comprehensive School in January 1973, one term into the school year during which all pupils had to remain in school until they reached the new school-leaving age of 16. The early years of my career had been spent in two London purpose-built comprehensive schools, the largest having some 2,300 pupils and over 100 teachers: a deliberate career choice on my part because I felt that the comprehensive school would provide better educational opportunities for the majority of young people who had previously attended the secondary modern schools. Subsequently, I served seven years as the deputy head of the King Edmund School, Rochford, Essex, where, with the head teacher Sam Pollard, I helped to integrate the Great Wakering Secondary School into the existing Rochford School to form a new comprehensive school.

A year or so after my arriving at Eastbourne a team of HMIs, under team leader Mr Chalmers, announced their intention of visiting Eastbourne, requesting a full written report from the head teacher on all aspects of the school: this document provided the factual material subsequently given here.

The head teacher's initial impressions of the Eastbourne School
Immediate contact with senior staff suggested that they held very positive views concerning comprehensive education at Eastbourne. There was a very strong emphasis placed on the value of maintaining the school as a

homogenous whole. The need to maintain this unity appeared to be of primary concern and previous policy had been formulated around this ideal (probably arising out of the need to bring together the staff and children of the two very individual separate boys' and girls' secondary modern schools). For example, although children with weaknesses in the basic subjects could be extracted for remedial teaching, brighter children could not be extracted in order to be given instruction in a second foreign language in case this should be interpreted as a form of selective education. The prefect system was discouraged, being seen as divisive and liable to form an elite. Only one external examination, the CSE, was at first to be taken, but this particular situation changed before the appointment of the present head teacher (as explained in the previous chapter).

An air of self-confidence emanated from those in charge of the house system and from those enthusiastically involved in the mixed-ability teaching programme. The appointment of a new head teacher, however, after a relatively short time and in spite of statements made that no revolutionary changes were to be made, caused feelings of insecurity to develop among these particular teachers. Areas existed where mixed-ability teaching was pursued with enthusiasm, namely in science and social studies (integrated history and geography), but doubts were expressed in other departments.

There was also the feeling among some staff that the house system thrived at the expense of the academic side of the school. A feeling of being 'done down' existed among staff not involved in the upper levels of the pastoral side of the school. Although efforts were being made in certain departments to adapt teaching methods to the needs of children in mixed-ability groups, there was a suggestion of 'status quo' is some subjects and misconceptions in others. Some clearly taught as they had always done while others possibly became too reliant on the project approach and failed to involve themselves sufficiently in class instruction. There was some suggestion of a loss of subject content in the desire to fit subject material to the teaching methods and some danger of losing the structure and detail of a traditional subject discipline in order to satisfy the needs of the new teaching strategy.

Groups of staff, involving large numbers working together, took part in such annual activities as the pantomime, Eastbourne Trophy Day, and school concerts. Various teachers organised excursions, weekend trips and school journeys at home and abroad.

The children appeared respectful but friendly and, in general, businesslike. A certain percentage of scruffy children could easily be detected and evidence of difficulties at home was clearly seen in some cases. School uniform was supported but rather neglected in the upper school. Certain fifth-year pupils presented themselves as untidy and uncouth (possibly those who, before the raising of the school-leaving age, would have left to seek employment), although conversation with them showed they were polite and co-operative.

In conclusion, there appeared a friendly school with its positive enthusiasms and some regrets, a hard-working staff moving forward with perhaps certain unrecognised prejudices.

The basis to the head teacher's policy in 1975

By September 1975, seven years after reorganisation, the school had had three head teachers, two deputy heads, and three senior masters; and although some of the teachers had been in the school for a very long time, providing some continuity, the senior management team, those charged with moving the school forward under the new system, had changed considerably, possibly giving rise to uncertainty among the rest of the staff.

The house system, with its emphasis on the significance of the individual child and contact with parents, proved advantageous; in a school with a significant proportion of children coming from underprivileged families discipline was good. The friendly atmosphere and positive relationships with most parents were advantages to be cherished.

The policy of mixed-ability teaching throughout all years was more difficult to assess and accept. Some teachers were extremely enthusiastic about its benefits but dangers appeared to lie in the watering down of subject material to fit the teaching methods and a consequent failure to extend the quicker and more intensive academic learners. Some heads of department were requesting modifications to the programme in the final year in order to bring potential 'O' level candidates in line with the more intensive demands of this external examination. The request came in particular due to the need for 'O' level pupils to have a greater depth of knowledge and skills in order to write more complex answers than those required in the CSE.

The size of the school

In 1973 the school-leaving age was raised to 16 and at Eastbourne School the number of pupils on roll at the start of the school year in 1973 would have been about 1,260: 1,120 in the first four years of an eight-form-entry school and 140 staying on into the fifth year.

NB The sessions taught by part-time teachers are added together to give the equivalent of full-time teachers.

Date	No of pupils on roll	Total no. of teachers including head	Full-time	Part-time	Observations
March 1973	1125		57	6	Also attached to the school: youth tutor, French assistant and music teachers
June 1973	1098		56	7	
November 1973	1254	63	61	5	
February 1974	1258	64	61	5	
June 1974		63	60	5	
November 1974	1258	63.3	61	4	One county teacher for remedial work and one county staff to cover a vacancy in RE
July 1975	1174				The additional (0.75) teacher for remedial work continued as did the Youth Tutor and Instrumental staff
September 1975	1224	63.7	60	6	
March 1976	1209	63.7	60	6	
June 1976	1167	63.7	60	6	
1977		63			Some concern expressed over the fall in pupil numbers
October 1979	1139	63	60	7	
March 1980	1135	63	58	8	Plans were being made to close Central School

Date	No of pupils on roll	Total no. of teachers including head	Full-time	Part-time	Observations
September 1982	1260				After a year or two of falling rolls, numbers rose due to the ex-Central Pupils joining the school
September 1985	1141	63			Fall in pupil numbers evident
September 1986	1085	60			Total number of teachers decreasing

In March 1973 there were 1,125 pupils on roll and by June the number had reduced to 1,098. A considerable proportion of the families therefore were happy for their children to leave school as soon as they reached the age to do so. The exact reasons for this are not known but it can be assumed that they did not see sufficient value in their children remaining in education; they needed the young members of the family to be in the work situation, being less of a burden on the family budget and adding to the overall income; and the young people themselves wanted to be out of the school situation.

Consequently, there was an element of the population of the senior school that, given the choice, would sooner not be there: most, however, conformed to the new requirements without a fuss, but with a minority likely to show signs of rebellion.

The school understood this situation and made arrangements to cater for the whole range of youngsters involved by developing the careers and activities programme in the upper school.

By September 1975 the roll had already declined to 1,224 and in 1977 concern was being expressed over the looming problem of fewer pupils meaning fewer teachers. A necessary cutback in the number of teachers gives rise to problems because the loss of a teacher means the loss of a complete teacher in *one subject area* as secondary school teachers are mostly subject specialists.

The problem of the number of children needing remedial help with their learning in the basic subjects was partly answered by the appointment of an extra county teacher for three-quarters of a week's teaching load.

The youth tutor taught for a small part of the week in the upper school, the aim of the exercise being to encourage young people to become involved in the activities provided by the youth centre (on the school site) outside school hours and after leaving school.

In the early 1980s the falling rolls situation at Eastbourne was eased temporarily by the LEA's decision to close Central School in response to the overall decline in pupil numbers in the Darlington area. But by 1985 the September roll had fallen to 1,141 and by 1986, with the anticipated loss of a nine-form-entry year group passing through the school during the previous 5 years, to 1,085.

The pupils – the intake of first-year boys and girls

The majority of the children entering the school at 11-plus came from one of three primary schools, a smaller number from a fourth and a few from a variety of others.

Number of first-year pupils on roll on the first day of the autumn term:

1972	Boys 132	Girls 123	Total 255
1973	Boys 134	Girls 119	Total 253
1974	Boys 128	Girls 124	Total 252
1975	Boys 112	Girls 130	Total 242

Dodmire, the oldest of the feeder schools, served an area (and still does) of Darlington where properties were built in the 1930s largely for owner occupation, becoming a long-term catchment area for the Eastbourne Secondary Schools. Equally, an area located closer to the main line railway and to the south of Yarm Road was also largely one of owner occupation, the children attending Eastbourne Schools. This population formed the traditional core of the school, with several generations of the same families building a very favourable, sympathetic, trusting, and supportive relationship between the home and the staff in general.

Heathfield, a much newer school constructed on the boundary between the older housing and a new post-war development of largely owner-occupied properties, also presented many families which supported the school but, in some cases, without the long-standing family connections. St John's Church of England School was housed in a new building, replacing the old premises on Yarm Road, and was similar in its traditions to Dodmire School. It is interesting to note that most of the active members of the Parents' Association came from those with children in these three schools.

The Firthmoor School served the post-war development of the Firthmoor Council Estate, which, although housing many supportive families including that of one of the school governors, was also known to include some of the town's most severely underprivileged and troubled people.

In contrast, the Abbey and Mowden schools, situated in the south-west of the town, noted for its higher proportion of more affluent and professional families, for the most part did not send children to Eastbourne. Consequently, the Hummersknott School, evolved from the Girl's High School, and having the Abbey and Mowden primary schools as its feeder schools, more easily gained the reputation of the school to which many parents wished to send their children, even moving into the area for this purpose. On the other hand, Eastbourne was in the position of having to struggle to build and retain such a reputation.

Liaison with primary schools
The transfer of children from primary school to secondary was seen to be a traumatic event in their lives, perhaps too much so. Individual differences, so often submerged in the day-to-day organisation of large numbers of youngsters, determine that some will indeed be nervous of the change from small school, where they were the biggest and having the prestige of being most senior, to that where monsters the size of adults ruled the playground (perhaps). There was also the threat of being thrown into the prickly bushes in the vicinity of the walled field, a real threat until the ground staff were requested to remove the offending vegetation, which was an inheritance from the area's pre-school days.

Some children were mildly concerned about change, others more excited than concerned, and a few, those for whom school was of little relevance to their lives, could not have cared less. Those disinclined to settle, in later years, seemed to influence the others, so that transfer became rather more an exercise of imposing discipline than settling in the timid.

Nevertheless, it was always the policy of the school to make the transfer as easy as possible for everyone. The process started with staff, heads of house, deputy head, senior master and the head teacher liaising with the head and staffs of the primary schools in the January before the relevant September. There were a number of objectives: to obtain from the primary school class teachers observations on the individual children in their care, achievements of the bright ones who needed encouragement, notes on those needing special help to improve their knowledge and skills in the basic subjects, behaviour and health problems to watch out for, and difficulties to follow up; to obtain lists of grades for the children to be used in the compiling of mixed-ability tutor groups; and to be presented to the groups of children concerned so that they at least gained an initial picture of teachers they would meet in the new school.

In 1981, with a recognised standard intake of 240 pupils to make eight classes, it was discovered that there were more parents seeking admission for their children to the school than in the previous eight years. The demand for places had always been high, the school being seen by parents living within the catchment area as a good place for their children to be. As early as 1973, in discussion with the then CEO in Darlington, it was said that there were more applicants than places, the head teacher accepting that it was the Education Authority's responsibility to settle the question of who gained entry but requesting that thought be given to the proportion of those from underprivileged families being sent to the school in relation to that of the other Darlington secondary schools. In order to be an ideal comprehensive school there should not be an over large proportion of pupils from any one social or achieving group.

Following the discovery that the different primary schools judged the standards of achievement of their pupils differently, the school introduced its own standardised testing programme. The significance of differences being in the difficulties produced when compiling the teaching groups when a grade A, or for that matter any other grade, did not indicate equivalent attainment or ability in the different primary schools.

Early in the new school year, for instance from 4 to 7 p.m. on 17 September 1980, the opportunity would be given to parents of new first-year children to arrange for an appointment to see tutors and heads of house in order to discuss any problems that may have arisen.

Opportunities for parents to meet staff

Parents were encouraged to come into school at any time, by appointment if possible, to meet their children's head of house: many did so, as was demonstrated by the examples given later, but there was also a major programme of parents' evenings for them to discuss their children's progress throughout their time in the school.

A particularly significant stage was in the child's third year, when careers advice was given through the careers conventions, attainments discussed during evening consultations, and choices of subjects to be taken in the fourth year made. For example, parents with children from two houses would be invited in for one evening and from the other two on another, to enable them to see all of the subject teachers and heads of department as appropriate.

There is a telling diary entry for 6 February 1979: 'Third Year Parents' Evening, times changed from 7–9 p.m. to 4–6 p.m. due to caretakers' industrial action closing schools at 6 p.m.'

Another from 16 January 1979 reads: 'Meeting for parents of fourth-year pupils with subject teachers at 7 p.m.' These meetings have been a regular feature of the school calendar for many years and the matter is mentioned here because some teachers' associations were questioning the length of the school working day.

And on 25 November 1982: 'Parents Evening cancelled due to industrial action by teachers.'

By 1982 the policy had been introduced of encouraging parents to meet the head teacher at least three times during the child's life in school: before entry from primary school, at the time of selecting options for senior school courses, and at the fifth-year pre-mock-examination stage. It was seen as particularly important to identify to both pupils and parents the apparent ability (as shown by the standardised testing programme) of the young people, with a view to encouraging them to develop their true potential, and significant that the head should be seen to be involved in this exercise. At this time, it had been demonstrated that a number of academically able children were not achieving to the best of their ability for personality (not social) reasons.

From time to time the school held open evenings during which parents could tour the school and see the work completed by the pupils. On 18 October 1973 the school was open between 7 and 9 p.m. when all departments organised displays and demonstrations. About 289 parents attended from a pupil roll of about 1,250 and the venture was felt to be well worthwhile by both staff and visitors. However, on 21 May 1980 an exhibition of art, needlework, woodwork and metalwork projects completed during CSE courses was held between 6 and 8.30 p.m. On this occasion there were twenty-two visitors; five of these were fifth-year pupils and in addition five staff visited: a sign of the times, perhaps!

Some unexpected meetings with parents

Shortly before morning break abusive shouting was heard disturbing the peace in the entrance hall: a rather short, excited middle-aged lady was waving her arms about near the reception window and rudely demanding to see the head of house. Among the gush of language there seemed to be the accusation that her child was being victimised. A first requirement was an essential calming exercise otherwise we would get absolutely nowhere. With staff doing more listening than talking, allowing much of the annoyance to exhaust itself, the lady eventually quietened sufficiently to listen a little: but she did not want to see the head teacher, continuing to demand the presence of the head of house. The office staff had already made contact with the teacher in question and he eventually appeared. Tactfully, as it was now break time and eager young eyes watched events with interest, we gently moved the group to the medical room where the parent accused the head of house of saying that her daughter was absent from school when she was, quite properly, buying shoes accompanied by her mother.

The head of house pointed out that he was not accusing the pupil of being absent Wednesday, when he knew she was buying shoes, but was concerned about other absences, particularly an absence on Tuesday.

The parent was immediately deflated: 'Don't know nothing about that,' she reflected. 'She wasn't with 'er boy friend, 'cos I saw 'im! She must 'ave been skiving.'

The lady was by this time quiet and being perfectly reasonable, and we were able to move into the head's study, where, I explained, we could be more comfortable.

The child was also called in and asked to tell her us where she was on Tuesday.

'I've told yer once,' she growled at the head of house, 'I was skiving!' She was asked to tell her mother exactly where she was.

'I've bloody-well told yer once and I'm not telling yer again,' she growled, rising from her chair, stomping out of the room and slamming the door behind her.

There was a moment's quiet while we all reflected upon the incident and then the parent said: 'Do you think Hurworth school would take her?' Hurworth was another Darlington school. There was further pause, the mother silently debating the situation with herself.

'No they wouldn't would they,' she stated rather than questioned, slowly and wearily pulling herself to her feet and making for the door. 'I'll try to get her back tomorrow,' she explained; and left pushing a pram containing a small baby crying from neglect, and explaining further: 'That's me other daughter's baby; 'er husband's inside, she's on the streets, but he don't care!'

We watched the mother slowly walk away down the drive, eventually fetching cups of coffee and retiring to my office to take a moment to return to normality.

It was not the last visit to the school made by this parent but, with luck, someone would see her approaching, calling a senior member of staff to greet her and take her into a vacant office where she could be seated and offered a cup of tea.

On another occasion I was working in my office, which was situated opposite reception and near to the front door, when there was someone very loudly demanding to see the 'bloody headmaster'. There being no doubt who was required and being at least a little annoyed myself by such a rowdy approach, I flung open my door and announced, 'I'm the bloody headmaster, who wants him?'

An inappropriate response, perhaps, but it was one that worked. The gentleman immediately calmed down and we were able to discuss his difficulty quite amiably: so much so, that the event is remembered but complaint lost!

One father came breathlessly into the entrance hall as I was about to go out: he had run all the way from a neighbouring estate and was gasping out something to do with finding his son sitting on a dustbin outside his house in the middle of the afternoon. Basically, the argument seemed to be that we had not exercised our responsibility of caring for his 13-year-old son, letting him out of school unsupervised and at an unexpected time. I pointed out that we were not a prison, and, in those days, the premises were extensive and had open access at all of the extremities as well as from the front: without locked rooms and chains we could be not be sure that a determined youngster could not truant from a disliked lesson if he chose to do so.

A telephone call was taken in the physical education department at 5.30 p.m. one late afternoon and the head of department reported the following day that a very bad-tempered lady had asked for the head or deputy head. Neither being available at the particular time the lady said she was going to throw her daughter's books on the fire because she did not want her to do any homework. I met her face to face next day when she burst into my room dragging her daughter by the arm and carrying a handful of exercise books.

I invited the lady to take a seat but was greeted with: 'There's no need for that. I'm not staying.' She then emptied a bag of torn-up exercise books across the desk and floor. She then left. I called after her, wishing to discuss the matter but received no reply. In an effort to bring her back I told her I could not have her child in the school without discussing the matter, but she was well on her way, taking the child with her.

Discussions with the Education Welfare Officer, during which it was understood that the lady in question was the problem and not the child, it was agreed that the girl should return to school. Parent–school liaison continued with intermittent outbursts but the child was a bright and conscientious pupil, eventually going on to obtain a good collection of 'O' level passes and maintaining contact with the head of house for some time after leaving school.

The parent had been a problem since the child entered the school, cutting the child's school uniform, refusing to accept the school's homework policy and refusing to sign any forms (except those relating to social security). There was constant liaison with Social Services and the school welfare officer frequently visited the home. At one stage the child came to school in complete uniform but two months later the mother would not let her child wear it.

The Parents' Association

Certainly, from the early days of the comprehensive school, through the 1970s and into the 80s, there was always a strong and active group of parents who ran the Parents' Association, although the group was a small minority. In the 1980s, at the request of the parents, the Parent–Teachers Association was formed, with the intention of bringing parents and teachers together in a social environment as well as in the more formal consultation meetings.

In the 1970s there was a particular member of the committee who had the know-how, experience and necessary qualifications to organise and run well-attended firework displays. These, like the pantomime and concerts, were valuable occasions during which members of the community could socialise with school staff, but, like the non-timetabled events organised by teachers, these events were lost once the parent and his family moved on in life.

Regular business meetings were held, including the Annual General Meeting, but attended only by the conscientious few. There were well-attended summer and autumn fetes, with one log book note on a cancellation: 'Summer Fete cancelled due to uncertainties arising from the NAS/UWT work to rule and caretakers' strike.' Dances were held, such as that for St Valentine's Day between 7.30 and 11.30 p.m. on 12 February 1983 and regular ceilidhs in the school hall.

In the 1980s a group of parents even organised and ran December discos in the school for third-year pupils between 7 and 9 p.m.

A log entry for 18 January 1979 refers to the Parent–Teachers Association meeting held at 7.30 p.m: 'A small group of very busy and active parents involved in a comprehensive programme of events but support from parents in general is poor: some 50 attended out of a total family population of 1100.'

So, most people were perhaps not interested. Should they be? It has already been noted that a high proportion of families were content to let their children leave school as soon as possible; the school catchment area included areas of disadvantaged and problem families and the proportion of pupils with learning difficulties was high. Such evidence caused the school to look more closely at the proportion of children who may be coming from underprivileged homes.

Survey of the number of children coming from underprivileged families

The heads of house at Eastbourne were quick to voice their opinion that some 20 per cent of the pupils came from underprivileged homes and for this reason a confidential survey was conducted of pupils in their last year, and of those in the penultimate year of compulsory schooling over the three years since the raising of the school-leaving age, using data known to the staff through their pastoral duties.

Between 19 and 24 per cent of the intake had families in which the father's influence could be taken as inadequate; the figures for the mother, between 10 and 14 per cent, are clearly lower but significant. Absenteeism was clearly a problem, with between 20 and 28 per cent of pupils, or some quarter of the year group, in year five being involved. The number in the fourth year is lower but it is not known whether this increased when the pupils moved into year five. The figures for truancy and lateness also suggest there was a significant number who did not view their schooling as a priority.

Survey of underprivileged families – figures given as a percentage of cases in the whole year group								
	1973–74		1974–75		1975–76		1975–76**	
Pupil in care of Local Authority	1		1				2	
Pupil living with foster parent	1		1		1			
Number of children in the family *								
Relating to the father – died	4	Total 20	1	Total 21	5	Total 22	4	Total 19
left home	6		6		11		7	
ill/infirm	3		2		2		1	
unco-operative	1		4		1		1	
inadequate	3		6		1		4	
elderly*								
unemployed	3		2		2		2	
Relating to the mother – died	2	Total 11	1	Total 14	2	Total 12	2	Total 11
left home	3		1		2		1	
ill/infirm	1		1		3		2	

Survey of underprivileged families – figures given as a percentage of cases in the whole year group								
unco-operative		Total	4	Total	1	Total	2	Total
inadequate	5	11	7	14	4	12	4	11
elderly*								
employed*								
Record of absenteeism	20		18		21		11	
Record of truancy	9		17		16		6	
Record of lateness	7		19		16		5	
Record of aggressive behaviour	3		7		8		7	
Frequently out of school dress/uniform*								
Has appeared before the juvenile court	11		9		5		3	
Very low learning ability	11		16		11		7	

* Items thought to have been appropriate but finally not recoreded

** The last column refers to pupils in their penultimate year

Problem pupils

The survey also included information on the number of young people who may cause disciplinary problems for the school: those displaying aggressive and/or delinquent behaviour.

As there had been a decline of 14 per cent of the total intake coming from the Dodmire and Heathfield schools, and an increase of 5 per cent from Firthmoor, concern was expressed that in future years the number of pupils in the school from underprivileged homes and having behaviour problems would increase. As such characteristics of a school become general public knowledge, and they surely do, the positive picture of the education being provided declines, and families without problems seek to send their children elsewhere.

By 1973 young people were obliged to remain in school until they were sixteen; many would probably have preferred to go out to work but settled to what they were expected to do. Conversely, there have always been a few who have presented problems because of their antisocial behaviour; their aggression, shown in their attitude, use of unacceptable language and tendency to become violent, and very probably leading them into conflict with the law. These young people were now expected to remain in school, bringing increasing pressure upon schools to find out reasons for their apparent antagonism and to try to find ways of bringing them into the system. This created a major problem; a problem aggravated by the erosion of the teachers' authority resulting from a more liberal attitude being adopted towards the upbringing and educating of children.

Already, in the early days of the comprehensive school, there was evidence that these young people were causing difficulties for the school. Cloakrooms that had for many years been open had lockable gates fitted to prevent theft, meaning that someone had to be responsible for locking and unlocking them when people needed to leave or retrieve their coats. In January 1975, when the gates were left unlocked, five coats were taken from Durham cloakroom between 9.05 and 11.30 a.m. The seriousness of the matter resulted in the police being called in to school to investigate a case of theft: undesirable but necessary. The coats were recovered.

Examples of youngsters breaking into the premises outside school hours were evidence of those with behaviour problems directing their hostility towards the school. In March 1975 a senior pupil was reported by his head of house as being unmanageable. A few evenings later, with a pupil from another school, he broke in to the premises, setting off fire extinguishers, tearing paper and distributing it throughout the corridors, breaking furniture and pouring washing-up liquid into video recorders. The disruption was such that the school had to be confined to the assembly halls while the mess was cleaned up.

In May 1977 a storage shed was set on fire outside school hours.

Unacceptable behaviour of older pupils on the way to and from school also increased. There was an incident involving one pupil and the proprietor of a mobile shop which gave rise to the situation in which the school was not permitted to take disciplinary action against the culprit because the police were involved in the case and the youngster could not be placed in the position of being punished twice for the same offence.

On the last day of one spring term a group of fifth-year boys were involved in dangerous egg-throwing incidents on their way home, the eggs being thrown at and through windows of nearby houses resulting in the residents calling the police. Charges were brought against the boys and they appeared in court. According to reports in the local press the magistrates saw the incident as no more than a schoolboy prank but this was not the view of the residents who had witnessed the unpleasant threatening and aggressive behaviour of uncouth youths who did not resemble schoolchildren in any way whatsoever. The school recognised the youths concerned as difficult and delinquent pupils who contained their behaviour while they were on school premises, but was powerless to act on incidents outside school – especially when some parents took the attitude that such goings-on were nothing to do with the school.

A different kind of incident involved an injury to a child playing netball in the centre playground at 3.15 one afternoon, when a yellow car driven by a youth, with another youth as passenger, drove at speed through the centre arch. The pupil had stepped backwards to be caught by the wheel of the car causing swelling and bruising. A doctor conducting medicals on the premises was able to examine the injury. The parents were called and the child taken to hospital by ambulance. Luckily, the injury was not serious. The police were informed but, in spite of the offending vehicle being known by many in the area, and almost certainly driven by an ex-pupil, it was never found. When asked what they could do about the incident, and knowing the LEA would prosecute if the car driver was traced, the response was more or less 'nothing'. Rather cheekily but with serious intention, the police were asked about the hypothetical situation in which a child had been killed rather than injured; they implied that would be a different matter – that would be considered murder!

On one occasion the school was asked for confidential reports on about seventeen senior pupils who were being investigated in relation to their allegedly being involved in the theft of motor vehicles.

A survey of the number of pupils in the school thought to have Special Educational Needs (SEN)

Although the number of problem pupils in the school varied from one year to another, there was always a sufficient number for this to impinge on the ethos of school as a whole and subsequent to the survey of the number of pupils coming from underprivileged families, a further study was made in 1985 of pupils who the school felt needed to be considered as having Special Educational Needs (SEN). Copies of the report summarising the findings were presented to the governing body and sent to the Deputy Director of Education. It was emphasised that the number of pupils with slow-learning and or remedial-language problems was particularly significant. Linked with these pupils, often the same children in fact, were those with behaviour problems and the school had to deal with an increasing number of children with behaviour difficulties. The report demonstrated that approximately 36 per cent of the pupils in the school were in need of special support.

The survey covered four year groups – the first to fourth years 1984–85 – and the following categories were defined:

1. Attendance problems

   a) Non-attenders, where the EWO and Court were involved

   b) Travelling families – who left the area for months at a time – sometimes as genuine travellers – sometimes the child merely seeming to be 'away'

   c) Children kept at home to help out

   d) Medical absences – sometimes phobias

   e) Truants – a number of boys who could not be kept in school as they would not stay unless constantly and closely supervised by a teacher

2. Medical problems – where some special individual support was desirable or essential

3. Problems involving remedial education – genuine slow-learning or retardation problems

4. Those pupils already known to the educational psychologist

5. Social problems recognised by the head of year (formerly head of House)

6. Disturbed, disruptive or delinquent pupils

The percentage of pupils from each year group fitting the defined categories was found to be as follows:

	Catergories of SEN					
Year Groups	1	2	3	4	5	6
4th Year	12	4	18	13	7	16
3rd Year	13	7	22	11	7	8
2nd Year	12	8	25	13	12	12
1st Year	3	9	25	12	10	8

The average number of pupils with some SEN, as defined above, was 11.34 per tutor group or 38.69 per cent. That is, on average each tutor group of between 29 and 30 pupils has eleven or more children with some special educational need. Some 38–39 per cent of the school's pupils required some form of special educational support.

Conclusion
The school desperately needed help if it was not merely to go on struggling to contain a difficult situation and it was suggested the following assistance was required:

1. An educational psychologist to work full-time with Eastbourne

2. A full-time social worker be attached to the school (in consultation with the District Controller Social Services; a situation was achieved where a particular social worker liaised regularly once each week with the school)

3. Two posts to be created for teachers who would have special responsibility for teaching children with emotional and behavioural problems: these posts to be over and above the present establishment

4. Two teacher-counsellors to be appointed, again extra to the present establishment

5. Resources to be made available for the development of an education-industry training project through which a more appropriate curriculum could be developed for the large majority of the children in years 4 and 5.

School discipline

While recognising the difficulties posed by the maladjusted minority it must be emphasised that the majority of pupils at Eastbourne were pleasant, co-operative young people involved in the many activities offered by the school.

The aims of the school policy on discipline were to maintain a disciplined and properly controlled school in which the atmosphere was one of cheerful co-operation; and to educate young people towards a self-discipline which would provide everyone with a maximum amount of freedom compatible with life in the adult world.

In the notes for the guidance of staff it was emphasised that discipline is the responsibility of all teachers and that they must expect and demand respect from the pupils, including respect for the building. In addition, discipline, a relaxed yet controlled behaviour where respect brings a personal freedom which does not impinge upon the freedom of others, is the result of the interaction of different personalities, and successful school discipline results from mutual respect between pupils and teachers.

Uniformity of standards was asked for, and it was explained that significant differences in what was expected caused confusion (and also gave excuses for non-compliance) – in particular, where the pupil comes from a disturbed or insecure home.

Many experienced teachers may well have felt insulted by being given notes on how to maintain discipline, including rules for the successful management of a classroom full of lively youngsters, but it was nevertheless thought essential that advice be circulated to all in order for those feeling the need to have access to it.

Things to watch out for

As adults in charge of children we must always be on the lookout for any lowering of standards and be ready to correct these in a firm but pleasant manner.

1. Expect courtesy from all children – good manners should be encouraged at all times.

2. Children should be expected to speak correctly to staff and each other – in a pleasant tone and without rudely interrupting others.

Hence the need for hand raising in the classroom.

3. Orderly behaviour must be promoted in the classroom at all times (including break times).

4. Members of staff should feel a responsibility for all children, not only the ones in their own class. They should also prevent unruly behaviour about the school.

5. They should also keep a watchful eye on staircases and in corridors. Staff should supervise the dismissal of their classes and be prepared to move to the classroom door to ensure order prevails outside. In general children should walk quietly in single file. Although silence is not expected, responsible behaviour resulting in purposeful movement is required.

Comment

Under the watchful eye of Miss Fenby such notes would hardly have been required. There were the rules, less liberal than those above, and their application is what happened, teachers knowing that it was their job to keep order, and doing so. There have always been young, new and inexperienced teachers joining their first school and it was understood that they would be expected to follow the rules and be told how to do so if they did not.

Times changed. There were those who decided that their job was to teach in their classroom and not much else. Once one or two teachers take up this attitude, the job of maintaining order becomes more difficult for the rest. Some who were conscientious felt that others were not pulling their weight and began to adopt the attitude of 'why should I do their job for them?'

Simple rules of classroom management must be applied at all times.

1. Staff need to be in position, ready to receive pupils, whenever possible.

2. Children should not be left standing in corridors.

3. Whenever a teacher enters a classroom he or she should have clear plans in mind concerning the work to be done during the lesson. All lessons should be prepared. This task becomes easier with length of teaching experience.

4. Books, worksheets, visual aids etc. should be prepared before the lesson begins and be ready for the pupils as soon as required. Pupils who are kept waiting with nothing to do are more likely to cause trouble than when kept busy.

5. When lessons are well prepared and the children are busy the teacher can give maximum supervision to the class and correct the child who tries to disturb the routine before he or she can attract the attention of any admirers.

6. Expect children to be quiet and attentive when an adult enters the room. Expect them to be ready to start the lesson when you are ready.

7. Talking while the teacher is giving class instruction or when other children are answering questions, should not be tolerated.

8. Insist on hands being raised rather than voices.

9. Expect to be addressed by name, or sir, or madam in the correct tone. (The correct tone is perhaps more important than the words used!)

10. Always position yourself in the classroom so that you can see all of the children. In turn, do not allow movement around the classroom, which allows a child to hide from your supervision.

The early recognition of the child who is trying to disturb routine and his or her firm but pleasant correction is the foundation for the growth of mutual respect between teacher and pupils.

All teachers appointed to schools have to be qualified and registered, so it would be expected that having followed a training course, they would know all of the above. Yet, it was not a lone occasion when I observed a struggling new recruit standing with her back to the class, children hiding behind any obstacle at hand and near chaos existing in the room.

In addition to the inexperienced, unintentional defaulter, however, some educational theorists have actually opposed such rules as being too autocratic. Perhaps, therefore, some new teachers came out of college having taken on board the so-called democratic freedoms and felt their senior colleagues to be old fashioned, insisting on imposing the new way of doing things.

Whatever the reasons, much of what worked and should have been done was not done.

Concerning the recognition of the child about to disrupt the good order in the room, there is an almost personal skill involved. It is concerned with being able to assess the personality of the child in an instant and to react appropriately to the different personalities in the class. Some people have this skill; some can be taught it. Others, no matter what help they are offered, never manage to understand its significance or learn to use it.

Awards and punishments

The argument about the relative merits of using awards and punishments to motivate youngsters to behave properly and perform well in their studies is another of the aspects of teaching which often evoke the expression of emotional and dogmatic views. At Eastbourne the philosophy was to use both, the latter only when absolutely necessary: a system set out in the notes for guidance of staff.

A. The general indiscipline of an individual child

Minor breaches of discipline, e.g. talking in class, occasional lateness, shouting in the building, cheekiness, should be dealt with by the teacher concerned. Whenever possible, members of staff should deal with problems themselves. This strengthens their position in the eyes of the pupils.

Punishments will follow the pattern:

1. A verbal reprimand. (Given time and time again! In particular, look out for the child who always 'forgets' the correct behaviour, but always responds to the verbal warning. To be too harsh on such a child will cause him or her to over react and hostility between teacher and child develops.)

2. A written apology – to be well written (within the ability range of the child) before being accepted.

3. A written explanation of the conduct or an essay on a suitable subject (again bearing in mind the ability of the child concerned).

4. Additional work on the lines of the lesson.

Without doubt, the successful use of the verbal reprimand is the key to good classroom relationships. Written exercises invariably give the teacher more work – chasing up the child who believes that he is out of mind when out of sight! [And some teachers began to believe that the setting of such extra work was outside their job description in any case! Going a step further, some teachers were beginning to adopt the attitude that when they failed to get the required response by use of the verbal reprimand, the problem should become someone else's.]

5. The Report Slip System

In a school where all are working together in order to obtain certain standards, communications are very significant. In the large school written communications are essential. [Once again, the loss of the informal meetings of staff are shown to be more difficult because of the larger size of the school; and teachers being requested to write things down – another job where there was no need for one under the former regime. Teachers were asked to complete a Report Slip whenever something particularly good or bad happened.]

When the report is bad, the slip should be taken to the child's tutor, who would consult with the Head of House and investigate the matter. [Here is the need for a formal seeking out of a colleague in large extensive premises, it not always being possible to guarantee that the person will be in the staff room at break times, or that you will be able to get there in any case.]

When the report is good, the slip is to be taken to the tutor and Head of House by the child itself.

In all cases of persistent indiscipline or serious misbehaviour a report slip had to be sent via the tutor to the Head of House.

The tutor and Head of House would then consult and take appropriate action. This may well include calling the child's parent to come to school and discuss the matter.

[The intention here is fine but, again, the informal contact is lost. It may well be that a brief discussion with a colleague will enable the teacher to resolve the matter instead of turning the situation into some long-drawn-out exercise. There is also the underlying temptation to pass on difficulties to another when they are better dealt with oneself: there is a tendency here to encourage the notion that disciplinary matters are someone else's responsibility, not an inevitable attitude but one to be guarded against.]

B. Difficult pupils

If the Report Slip system works properly, all difficult pupils should be quickly recognised by the Heads of House. It is most important in these cases that a careful record is kept of actual examples of difficult behaviour involving the child.

If the worst situation arises, where it is felt as a team that things are getting out of hand concerning a particular pupil, and all have done all that they can together to solve the problem, it is essential that there is a long record of bad behaviour (real events) and the attempts made to find solutions to the problems in relation to that child. Some parents need to be convinced that their child is not as angelic as they thought! If ever it is required to seek the support of the governors and Education Office on such a matter it is also reasonable for them to expect us to provide a clear case for their action.

[This is evidence of the changing attitude of many parents towards the authority of the school, the head teacher and teachers. Where once there was unquestionable trust and respect, with the new liberal attitudes adopted towards behaviour and the introduction of the ideal of participatory democracy in which everyone's opinion is of equal value, this trust was lost and the notion evolved that every act of alleged bad behaviour should be proven, no longer taking the word of those in authority as the right one. This situation revolved around the time-consuming and long-winded attempts to produce justice through discussions between staff, meetings with parents and case conferences involving outside agencies. Not the way to bring about a correction in the behaviour of the young who require the application of an instant sanction and an immediate fresh start.]

C. The general indiscipline of a whole class during lesson time

If the whole class is unruly it is usually because the teacher has misjudged the situation in some way and this is, in general, due to inexperience, recognising that all can make mistakes sometimes. It is important to remember that experience in one school is not always going to guarantee immediate success in another. It is the knowledge of the personalities of particular children which is important – as well as the general techniques of classroom management.

A teacher must be certain that he or she is providing plenty of work, at the appropriate level, to occupy all of the children and should consult the appropriate Head of Department for help with lesson preparation. [In the fashionable mixed-ability teaching situation, this is a more onerous task than when dealing with groups of equal ability because it is necessary to have prepared and have at hand a whole variety of work in various formats, for maintaining the enthusiasm and interest of all.]

It is possible to mishandle a class and thus provoke them when meaning to do exactly the opposite. Again, the Head of Department should be able to help.

[This advice was intended to be helpful for the newly qualified but there was a tendency among some to see no problem with their handling of the situation, all difficulties arising from the particularly bad behaviour of the children, which was nothing to with them.]

D. Difficult classes

It must be recognised that, even with mixed-ability teaching groups, where it may be thought that the most difficult pupils tend to be dispersed, sometimes a particular group will come together and react together to produce difficult situations. Under these circumstances, several teachers will be reporting the group and the Head of House (in the case of the tutor group) or Head of Department (in the case of a set or option group) may feel that it is necessary to take some action in order to separate members of a troublesome clique. This should be done in consultation with the head teacher.

The cane

There is no doubt that corporal punishment was a sanction applied to those demonstrating serious misbehaviour in the boys' school, and many former pupils have expressed the view that the punishment was deserved, did them no harm and acted as a deterrent. In the girls' school it was the autocratic Fenby regime which very largely maintained discipline. At the time boys were expected to be boys and to become men; girls were girls, different from boys, and expected to become young ladies. This reminder of difference may seem facetious but it is necessary to recognise that things have changed and were changing during the 1960s, 70s and 80s. Many differences between male and female have been minimised and in schools, now largely having mixed populations, boys and girls are expected to be treated the same.

In addition, the lobby against corporal punishment gained influence and the use of the sanction in state schools was eventually banned. It was in April 1984 that the County NASUWT (National Association of Schoolmasters Union of Women Teachers) member on the staff of Eastbourne was out of school to attend discussions at County Hall on the question of corporal punishment: the European Court had recently ruled that a parent should have the right to choose whether or not their child should be subjected to this punishment, and it was necessary to consider what alternative punishments were to be available for use when necessary.

Detention

Most schools had in place a system for detaining pupils after class hours as a sanction against misbehaviour and Eastbourne was no exception, stating in its notes for the guidance of staff how the system should be applied:

> All detentions must be seen to be reasonable, in particular, making sure that no child is sent away from school late or alone during the dark half of the year.

If detention is given –

i. In order not to cause anxiety to parents, detainees should be given one day's notice of detention.

ii. No child should be detained for longer than one half-hour.

iii. During detention a useful piece of work should normally be given.

iv. In cases where detention clashes with other school activities, the teacher giving the detention should consult the Deputy Head or Senior Master who will liaise with all the teachers concerned, including the Head of House, in order to reach an agreement satisfactory to all.

v. Mass detention i.e. the detention of classes, groups of classes or large sections of classes is inadvisable. If any member of staff feels that this might usefully be done in particular circumstances the Head of Department and Head of House concerned should be consulted first. In such cases the Head of Department and Head of House should inform the Deputy Head, who will inform the Head Teacher if this is thought to be necessary.

vi. Members of staff are responsible for seeing children whom they detain off the school premises.

House detention

The Heads of House hold detention classes for persistent latecomers and troublesome children. It is for the Head of House to decide who should be detained, although all staff should discuss, with the Head of House, the possibility of troublesome pupils being detained.

Observations

The arrangements for detention are cumbersome, there being too much additional work required from teachers generated by the need to consult others – although it is clearly essential in some (but not all) cases. Again, authority is taken away from the class teacher by the imposition of too many restrictions, encouraging the feeling that someone else should solve one's own disciplinary problems. Within the present day, and indeed the long-developing climate of mistrust and accusations of child abuse, there has also arisen the necessity of ensuring that a teacher is not left vulnerable by being alone with small groups of challenging youngsters.

Involvement of parents

Where there is persistent misbehaviour (lateness, failure to do homework and classroom disturbance, for instance) the parents must be brought into school to discuss the problems relating to their child.

Each class teacher is a tutor within the house system and should therefore become informed about the pupils in his or her group. The tutor should be in constant liaison with the head of house and it should be the head of house who invites the parents to school. However, other staff should then be invited to meet parents with whom they are having particular difficulties, if appropriate.

Disruptive pupils and the avoidance of provocation.

Disruptive pupils are disruptive because they do not have the relative stability of the normal child – they have not been taught or, due to some personality problem, have not adopted the normal accepted forms of behaviour. They react wrongly (in unacceptable ways) to situations or overreact to events. They are known for their confrontations with other children and staff. They vary in their reactions from day to day, depending on what has happened to them at home, on their way to school, or in the playground. They go through school from one crisis to another.

It is the job of the school to do all it can to help these children, involving as many outside agencies as appropriate or possible, and ensuring that the majority of the children do not suffer seriously as a result of the maladjustments of the few.

In cases of maladjustment of this kind the teacher has the extremely difficult job of combining tolerance with an expectation of certain standards. It is the balance that is obtained that, in turn, enables the child to live with us or explode!

At Eastbourne it was claimed that many difficult or problem children did fit into the normal classroom environment for most of the time due to the patient and sympathetic way in which the teachers worked with them. There existed a friendly school which, in general, lacked harshness, yet maintained a good discipline.

This does not mean that each of us will never arrive at some crisis point with one or other of the problem children. When this happens, heads of department, heads of house, the senior master, deputy head and head (in general, one at a time!) need to provide an escape route for the problem, but one which is accepted as being within the normal framework of school discipline.

The house point system

It is important that rewards should be available for use by the teacher and the house point system provided a useful means of giving some reward for good work, good behaviour, co-operation etc. Again, the system was explained in the notes for guidance:

> There appears to be a wealth of punishments – reprimands, report slips, and some times detention – but it is important to be positive rather than negative in our attitudes to the pupils' behaviour. It is important to be seen to be acknowledging the good in a pupil.
>
> The System can be used in two ways:
>
> i. as a part of the inter-House competition.
>
> ii. as a recognition of personal achievement.
>
> The administration of the system.
>
> i.   Duplicated proformas will be issued to staff each month. To ensure that House Points are not over used, and thus devalued, a limit of 200 per teacher per month will be allocated.
>
> ii. House Points should be awarded to individual children for good behaviour, effort in school work, good standards of work completed, improvement in punctuality, attendance and dress (general turnout), reliability in completing a given task, helpfulness etc.
>
> iii. House Points must be awarded irrespective of the child's natural basic abilities. In other words, the non-reader who struggles through a book which is difficult for him (but easy for others) is worthy of reward. The non-athletic child who puts himself out to play as last man in some team, thus

saving the whole from defeat, is also worthy, although he may never hit or kick a ball.

iv, Pupils must hand in their House Points to their tutor who will record each child's score in a mark book.

v. (a) Once each week at Friday morning registration the Deputy Head of House must collect the House Point Books from the tutors and total the points scored by the House during the previous month and give the House Record to the Deputy Head, who will co-ordinate the scores for the inter-House competition.

(b) Once each month, note all pupils who have scored for 50 or more House Points during the month and submit their names to the Head of House, with a summary of the tasks rewarded.

vi. The two pupils in each Tutor group scoring most House Points in any one term should be reported to the Head Teacher who will arrange to send a letter home in order to congratulate the child and also inform the parents of the child's progress.

vii. House Point totals will be read out in the first Senior and Junior School assemblies each week.

Challenges to good order

Some of the reasons for concern relating to a perceived deterioration of the behaviour of some pupils have already been outlined but further examples of such behaviour serve to illustrate a growing problem.

In January 1974 heads of house expressed their concern about damage being done to the pupils' toilets: walls had been written on with felt-tip pens and spray-paint; basins and pipes broken; and tiles pulled from walls.

The heads of house were asked to carry out the duty of supervision as closely as possible; but dinner time was identified as a major problem as it became a matter of personal choice and not an obligation for teachers to be on duty at this time and the midday supervisors were inadequate; for instance, those on duty sometimes being only all male or all female.

On 5 April 1974, the last day of term, senior pupils were observed 'ganging up' and defying staff on playground duty. The problem started during the morning break and, once again, became a more serious problem at lunchtime. It is worth noting that there were, however, no problems in school during class time. The situation resulted in the review of the arrangements for supervising pupils due to leave school at this time.

In February 1975 heads of house reported some senior pupils becoming unmanageable, referring to incidents of smoking, truanting and refusing punishment. There was a report of one such pupil apparently deliberately burning another boy's wrist and arm when attending the Darlington Technical College.

The situation meant that pupils were having to be excluded or suspended from attendance as they were unmanageable, disruptive and sometimes dangerous: for example in February 1976 a pupil was suspended following aggressive behaviour towards a teacher.

A further problem was the behaviour of pupils on school premises and outside school hours, matters which reflected upon the discipline of the school although beyond its control. On Saturday 14 May 1977 a groundsman's shed was destroyed by fire. It was known who was responsible but, at a time when it had become fashionable for culprits to deny their guilt and the resulting need for schools to prove guilt as though in a court of law, the school was not in a position to punish the culprit.

Responses

The apparent increase in the number of difficult and delinquent children, the eroding of the respect for the position of the teacher as one in authority, the denunciation of traditional sanctions combined with changing attitudes to child discipline, and the lack of co-operation from a number of parents, particularly those with the most difficult children, made it necessary for the school's response to disciplinary matters to change.

Involvement of the police

The refusal of parents to accept the school's judgement and application of punishments, and the increasing tendency for pupils to strongly deny any wrongdoing, requiring the teachers to prove, as though in a court of law, every misdemeanour, has led to the involvement of the police in cases of bullying (now called assault), petty theft and damage to property, even though the incidents took place on school premises and during school hours.

Conversely, some parents are disinclined to permit the school to sort out confrontations between pupils and teachers, too quickly turning to the law themselves: a situation encouraged by legislation.

Immediate action by the police, too quickly taking the word of the child as the truth, may result in the suspension of teachers for trivial lapses in their professional behaviour or, worse still, when they are completely innocent of any wrongdoing whatsoever.

Suspensions and exclusions

Even when the police and/or the law have not become directly involved, the refusal to accept the authority of the school in matters of misbehaviour and the increasing numbers of children displaying apparently uncontrollable behaviour have required schools to remove such children from the classroom and school, in the form of exclusions and suspensions. Children were excluded on a temporary and informal basis for refusing to conform to the school's requirements for two reasons: one was to remove the child from the immediate confrontation situation and the other to encourage a parent to come to school, with the youngster, as soon as reasonably possible to discuss and hopefully resolve the situation quickly.

In the 1970s and 80s schools were in a state of change. No clear-cut actions were uniformly recognised and supported by government and LEAs as appropriate to replace the traditional procedures: it was a time of uncertainty.

Gradually, as teachers grew more restless and their trade unions started to take action, systems began to evolve.

Situations developed where teachers sometimes refused to teach a child, and where this was apparent and a youngster declared as impossible to work with in the normal school environment, the offender would be suspended from attendance as a best solution under the circumstances. The term 'disruptive pupil' came to be used to describe such youngsters.

Much time was consumed dealing with these matters. Suspensions were referred to the governing body for their consideration: they may have upheld the head teacher's judgement, requiring certain conditions to be met for the suspension to be lifted, or possibly disagreed with the school, issuing instructions that the child should be immediately readmitted.

One September the governors' consideration of the suspension of a pupil did result in the suspension being lifted in spite of unfavourable observations from head teacher, staff representative on the governing body and the educational psychologist. It was encouraging to see the professional response from the staff in the face of such an unexpected judgement. The staff were asked to treat the pupil, as near as possible, just as they would treat any other child and if they felt he was becoming 'high', excitable, would they please report this to the head of house. If anyone felt they were facing a situation which they could not control would they please send for the head, deputy head, or head of house, depending upon their availability.

In April 1974 there was an incident involving a class moving from one room to another resulting in rowdy behaviour, during which a teacher came out of a classroom in order to calm the situation. There was cause for two boys to be called into the teacher's classroom in order to be reprimanded separately from the class as a whole, during which one of the boys objected to being spoken to and actually struck the teacher.

The boy concerned was immediately isolated from all other pupils, being placed in the area of the administrative offices, and was then taken home by the school welfare (attendance) officer with a letter to the parent indicating that the child had been suspended for the rest of term and requiring the father to come to school as soon as possible to meet the head teacher.

Letters detailing the situation were sent to the chairman of governors and area administrative officer.

In this instance the father came in to school at 2 p.m. on the same day: he accepted that his child was entirely wrong in what he had done and agreed with the school's action of having him out of school during the last days of the term. It was also agreed that the child would be brought to school on the first day of the new term with the purpose of investigating how reintegration should be completed.

The teachers who taught the pupil were all asked for their observations on the child's progress and for their views on any reintegration procedure. It was the mother who brought the youngster into school on the first day of the new term and she gave her support concerning what was expected of the child. A modified timetable was arranged; lunch break was to be taken at home; and it was made clear that any further misbehaviour would result in a more permanent suspension. This situation was amicably resolved, others were not.

Where it was deemed to be appropriate, a case conference involving the head teacher, educational psychologist and senior education adviser would be arranged to consider what should be done.

For instance, on one occasion the team met to consider the case of an aggressive, disruptive fourth-year pupil (possibly one of twenty or so in school at the time) when it was accepted that although little real assistance was available the school would try to encourage the pupil's mother to allow him to attend the Child Guidance Clinic, but with no confidence of being successful.

There was little one could do with disruptive and delinquent pupils: the basic principle of care without discipline does not work. This family had its boys running wild, clearly out of control; the father had left home, and the mother was inadequate, anxious and unable to exert discipline.

In the case of one delinquent pupil an arrangement was made for the parent to meet the probation officer and head teacher in the school, but, although they waited for one hour beyond the appointed time, the parent did not turn up.

Visit by probation officers

In November 1979, in an effort to obtain the best outcome from a difficult situation for both the school and all pupils in general, one probation officer arrived one morning at 9.30 a.m. and another at 10.30 a.m. The particular pupils in this case were beyond control at home and, for most of the time, in school (except when they chose to co-operate). Discussion took place in order to co-ordinate their supervision. However, little help was obtained from the probation department: one gentleman regretted earlier times when he considered he had more authority but agreed to do what he could; the other officer merely indicated he could do very little. Everyone parted feeling that supervision of offenders was seriously inadequate. The pupils resumed school until such time as they refused to behave correctly and had to be suspended or alternatively until they opted out of the system and merely stayed out of school.

In February of one year it was recorded that a second letter had to be sent to the parent of one disruptive pupil and a third copy was sent to another, the letters requesting the attendance of a parent in order to gain their assurances relating to the behaviour of their children. One gave assurances but was quite incapable of ensuring the child conformed to appropriate standards of behaviour; the other proved to be unco-operative.

The head and chairman of governors met the parents of two pupils with the objective of reintegrating the children into the school. Although readmission was arranged, the chairman commented privately that he saw no real possibility of success.

A different situation arose when a third-year pupil was due to be reintegrated into school after time in the Aycliffe Assessment Centre, where attempts were made to determine the best way to treat the child with a view to bringing about improved and, in this case, non-delinquent behaviour. The staff observations on the child are revealing. His immediate presence in the room, although doing nothing unusual, created an atmosphere of expectancy, each child anticipating that something would occur instigated by the newcomer to the group. Consequently the child's presence created a tension in the class which disrupted the concentration and learning of the other pupils in the group.

Another agreement was reached with the father of a pupil who was previously suspended from attendance and had been reintegrated into class from a one-to-one teaching situation: but this youngster did not wish to be in school and did everything possible to create situations resulting in further exclusion: not a satisfactory answer to the youngster's problems, but the school as a whole is of greater importance than one pupil.

At the end of January a teacher from Redworth Hall Special School and an educational psychologist came into school with reference to the admission of a maladjusted pupil to normal school. A programme of reintegration was agreed with the understanding that the pupil would be returned to Redworth if his behaviour was unsatisfactory.

The father of another pupil was seen with reference to the repeated disruptive behaviour of his child. It had previously been ascertained that he had told the child to be disruptive in order to be excluded!

Another suspension, involving a child's behaviour outside school premises but on the way to and from school, became a major incident. The parent engaged legal advice and argued that the child could not be suspended from attendance; the LEA argued that the child could not be punished twice for the same offence and, as the matter had been taken to court, the school should readmit the pupil without prejudice; and a large proportion of the staff, with the backing of their trade unions, refused to teach the youngster: a situation taking up much time and energy which should have been spent ensuring the smooth running of the school for the vast majority of well-behaved, conscientious young people.

Eventually the LEA established the Special Unit at Spennymoor, where suspended disruptive pupils could be sent, following case conferences and agreement between the parties involved, to be taught in small groups by specialist staff.

Sometimes the child was kept in school but isolated from the other children to work on a special timetable in a one-to-one situation under the supervision of a county unattached teacher with special responsibility for working with such children.

The involvement of social workers

As some disruptive children have problems which bring them into contact with Social Services, it was considered that regular liaison with members of the department would be beneficial to both school and young people.

In 1977 a meeting was held with the Social Services Department with regard to the initiation of a scheme for social workers to be school based, and eventually the school received a visit from 'school-based social workers', but they turned out not to be school based at all! If the school needed to contact them it should do so via Social Services HQ, but only in relation to pupils from one particular part of the school catchment area!

When a social worker called with reference to a child no longer on the school roll and thought to be at risk, wanting the pupil to resume normal school, it was concluded that the school could not meet the special educational needs of the youngster.

The teachers

By 1968, at the time of the foundation of the comprehensive school, the relatively simple system of head teacher, first assistant, and assistants had long been replaced by one involving posts of special responsibility. From a situation in which there was one clearly defined head teacher, one senior teacher as assistant to the head and all others merely distinguished in rank by their length of service and experience, there was by the early 1970s a clear hierarchical division of teachers according to their defined additional extra responsibilities. No longer did age and length of service necessarily equate with seniority: younger teachers could apply for and achieve promotion and additional remuneration by taking on the responsibilities of running a department or in other areas of school administration – areas not always recognised as significant by those who had not achieved promotion but leading to a scramble for upgrading by those who felt they deserved it.

In the early days of the comprehensive school the senior teachers were the head teacher (male), the deputy head (female), and senior or second master. Both titles and job descriptions were modified during subsequent years to answer the demands of the changing school.

At the time of the appointment of Mr R. V. Bryant as head teacher, the third head at the school since it became comprehensive, the deputy head had served the school for about nine years, the first four in the girls' school; but the senior master had only taken up his post in 1971 (and left to take up a headship in December 1973): in addition, the deputy head had acted as head teacher during the previous term, giving the school an unsettled senior management team for the first four-plus years in its new form and extended premises.

Another seven teachers had been at Eastbourne for between nineteen and twenty-nine years, much of their time spent in the separate boys' and girls' secondary modern schools where the ethos was different and reluctant students could leave school to enter work from the fourth year. It was in 1973 that the compulsory school-leaving age was raised, producing a compulsory fifth-year population for the first time.

Fifteen men and women joined the secondary modern schools as relatively young and inexperienced teachers at various times during the period 1960 to 1968, and consequently needed to adjust from the old to new regimes. Some regretted the passing of the traditional styles of discipline and staff relationships, although being promoted into head-of-department positions in the comprehensive school.

The staffing situation in 1973–1974

Some five new and, again, relatively inexperienced teachers had been appointed during 1972; sixteen more new teachers, many coming to their first school, joined in 1973. A significant number of teachers were appointed to the staff from the LEA pool, that is they had applied to the authority and not the school, the authority allocating them to schools as vacancies arose, a situation having the disadvantage of denying the head teacher full control over who would be appointed.

Several teachers came from the Darlington Teacher Training College, which, due to there being too many people qualifying as teachers, was one of those to close, its final term being in the summer of 1978. Its buildings became the home of the Darlington Arts Centre.

Eight more new staff joined the school in January 1974 including the replacement for the senior master, two new heads of department, and one to be second in the English department: these were good appointments but there were also two for one term only and another described simply as temporary. This suggests that vacancies could not be filled properly, and the failure to find teachers who would be coming into the school to give their full attention to the job for a reasonable length of time would have a detrimental effect on the education of the children, no matter how small a disturbance this may seem.

Four more appointments were made in April and another seven in September. Once again these were mainly short-term appointments with one temporary. On the positive side were the newcomers in the technical studies, previously the craft department.

The staffing situation throughout the period 1975–1985

In 1975 a new head of house was appointed, bringing in an experienced teacher, but there were still two temporary appointments, one 'county unattached staff' being an experienced teacher but only used to temporarily fill vacancies which could not be properly covered by the appointment of a regular teacher, and one person in the English department. Several of the newcomers were new to the profession.

Two further temporary appointments were made in 1976, one of which was later made permanent. Significant changes came to the mathematics department in September following the retirement of a long-serving member of staff and his immediate replacement; otherwise the staffing situation remained unchanged for the first time in many years.

The more stable situation continued during the next two years although four new teachers took up posts of responsibility in 1977, and another in 1978. The problem associated with the necessary appointment of temporary staff continued.

TUTOR GROUPS AND ROOMS 1974–1975.
STAFF.

(Blue) BOLTON HOUSE.	ROOM.	(Green) DURHAM HOUSE	ROOM.
Mr. Charlton Hd/House		Mr. Clark Hd/House	
5B Mr. Hogg (Dep:)	111............	5D Mr. Fox-Roberts	124.........
5B1 Mr. Ruston	116............	5D1 Mr. Dawson	Mus.2.....
4B Mr. Fay	128............	4D Mrs. Todd	112.........
4B1 Mrs. Stephenson	106............	4D1 Mr. Rosindell	121.........
3B Mr. Marshall	28............	3D Mrs. Newton	120.........
3B1 Mrs. Scott	127............	3D1 Mrs. Brown	108.........

TUTOR GROUPS AND ROOMS 1974 – 1975.
STAFF.

(Blue) BOLTON HOUSE.	ROOM.	(Green) DURHAM HOUSE	ROOM.
2B Mrs. Johnstone	13............	2D Mr. Holford	109.........
2B1 Miss Ritchie	N/W 1........	2D1 Mr. Routledge	Lib.2..........
1B Mr. Alderson	Lib 1............	1D Mr. Murphy	126..........
1B1 Mr. Coles	117............	1D1 Mr. Neenan	107..........
Mr. Parkinson	....	Miss Manfield	....
Mr. Andrew	....	Mrs. Topham	....
Miss Giles	....	Mr. Nunn (Dept:)	....
Mrs. Jolly (P/Time)	....	Mrs. Robb (P/Time)	....

(Amber) WITTON HOUSE.	ROOM.	(Red) RICHMOND HOUSE	ROOM.
Mr. Carling		Mr. Minikin Hd/House	
5W Mr. Hodgson	11............	5R Miss Mcleish	56.........
5W1 Mr. French	201............	5R1 Mr. Cousins (Dep:)	Mus.1.......
5WA Mr. Thornhill	32............	4R Mrs. Pegg	51.........
4W Mr. Roberts	Terr...........	4R1 Mr. Kay	129.........
4W1 Mrs. Frise	204............	3R Mr. Boyle	133.........
3W Mr. Walker	202............	3R1 Mr. Atkinson	M.W2........
3W1 Mrs. Knight	6............	2R Mr. Maull	130.........
2W Miss Pounder	10............	2R1 Mr. Bladen	113.........
2W1 Miss Webber	29............	1R Mrs. Forster	50.........
1W Mrs. Clarke	31............	1R1 Mrs. Midcalf	125.........
1W1 Mrs. Whiteside	12............	1RA Miss Acres	59.........

In 1979 eleven new teachers were appointed, including a new deputy head, a head of the art department and one teacher with responsibilities in English. Four of these left after one year, one stayed for one term and one for two terms. There were three temporary appointments, including one covering a teacher on secondment for one year.

In January 1980 three posts of special responsibility were filled but one of the teachers only remained on the staff for two terms, hardly enough time to become established. There were three part-time teachers appointed for one term only.

Of the eight new appointments made in September four were temporary. It was also at this time that an appointment was made to fill the second master's position, vacated the previous December.

In January 1981, in spite of the claim that there was a surplus of teachers, it had not been possible to find replacements for the graduate scientists who left before Christmas. There were insufficient well-qualified teachers while there was a surplus of those of mediocre ability and qualifications. There were married women wishing to return to teaching part-time who were very good but could not offer the shortage subjects and who were offered temporary appointments while further searches were made for the required specialists.

One lady called for interview, seeking part-time teaching, decided she was not interested in working at Eastbourne.

In April interviews were held for the vacant science posts and an appointment made to cover the vacancy in chemistry, but not until the following September, leaving the department with inadequate staffing for another term.

Although the qualifications of the chemistry candidates were found to be adequate this was not the case in physics: there were no appropriate applicants. The person eventually appointed had taught before joining the police force but his physics qualifications were barely adequate. It was made an informal condition of appointment that the teacher would read for additional qualifications in physics while in post.

Teachers are not all saints

On a day at about this time a parent called to see the head teacher with reference to her son, claiming that a teacher had grabbed and pulled the boy's hair after an incident of name calling, also alleging that the teacher had said, 'How would you like me to rearrange your face for you?' An immediate apology, expressing the regret that any parent should find it necessary to have to come to school on such a matter, was given, with the additional promise that an investigation would be carried out into the alleged incident.

The teacher concerned was interviewed by the head teacher and admitted grabbing the boy as one of only two boys who could have been responsible for the name calling, and apologised for the loss of temper, although denying making the alleged remark, saying: 'I am not sure what I said, but it was nothing like that!'

A formal verbal warning was given to this teacher with the strong instruction that in cases where there is a likelihood of the teacher wanting to hit a child, the teacher should stand back and attempt to cool the situation, possibly sending the child to wait outside the classroom until the teacher is ready to pursue the matter.

A phone call from a parent alleging a teacher had struck her son across the face called for an investigation, at the time the sole responsibility of the head teacher. The head of house spoke to the teacher in the first instance and was greeted with the response that the details of the incident could not be recalled, but there certainly was no question of the child being hit about the face; it was rather a matter of a boy hitting the teacher (a different boy!).

Further investigation revealed that a class was not under the proper control of the teacher in charge: difficult boys had provoked a disturbance which had not been satisfactorily handled. Both boys and two girls had been sent out of the classroom, one of the girls claiming she had been told to go for a walk, denied by the teacher.

When interviewed by the head teacher, the excuse was, once again, that the details of the event could not be recalled but the child may have caused a loss of temper on the part of the teacher and was sent to stand outside the classroom, certainly not intending to suggest any child should go for a walk. The teacher claimed that the boy concerned had been out of order, responding to a reprimand with words something like 'I don't give two damns' and further hostile comments.

As the situation was clearly one in which the teacher had lost control and a child had been struck, a verbal warning and advice were given. The teacher must not touch a child, let alone hit it. In cases where frustration produces anger in the teacher he or she must stand back and allow time for matters to calm down. When giving instructions, language and the content of what is said must give no excuse for any misunderstanding of what the child is meant to do.

Such incidents would, today, lead to the teacher's immediate suspension with allegations of an assault by a teacher upon a child or young person being made to the police. The matter would be taken extremely seriously, with insufficient thought being given to the provocation brought about by the behaviour of the child. It may well be the case, of course, that the teacher is unable to gain and keep the respect of a particular class. It can be asked whether the event is an isolated incident, or does the teacher have difficulties with all or most classes, in which case it would seem that retraining or a complete change of occupation is advisable.

If the child is known to be troublesome and any contact does not result in significant injury, the matter would be more sensibly resolved by having it considered by a school disciplinary committee on which would serve a number of the senior staff and members of the governing body. It should be understood that a disturbed child seeing a teacher apparently punished for an action which he (the child) knows he provoked, makes the disciplining of the youngster more difficult for everybody and does nothing to bring about the improvement in his or her bad behaviour.

Conversely, it was difficult to bring about the discipline of teachers when necessary and there was one occasion where, after repeated warnings given to one teacher, that teacher's union brought about the cancellation of those warnings, giving the teacher a 'clean sheet' as it were, when it was generally known that the disciplinary action had been justified.

It has to be said, however, that there is no excuse for any excessive, inappropriate behaviour being exerted on a pupil by any teacher.

Staffing from 1982 onwards

Although there were few newcomers to the staff in 1982, one was redeployed from the closing Central School and another, once again, was temporary cover provided by a county unattached teacher.

Fourteen newcomers arrived in 1983 and, yet again, seven were temporary appointments only. Another was redeployed from another school, but not because it was closing: this was a time of falling rolls and cutbacks in the financing of education and to avoid making people redundant they were required to move from overstaffed schools to fill vacancies elsewhere.

Thirteen teachers were appointed to commence in September 1984 but three of these were well-qualified and experienced former part-time staff becoming full-time, a pleasing development. Ten of the posts were associated with special responsibilities and consequently attracted established teachers rather than those starting out on their careers.

One of the temporary staff covered for one on maternity leave.

It was in 1984 that the following note was handed to the head teacher:

> The child X has decided to be insolent again, when asked for her report book she told me she didn't know where it was and she didn't care. She also refused, at first, to sit in the place I had allotted to her in this classroom. She then told me she was sick of teachers telling her what to do, then spent most of her time grinning like a Cheshire cat.
>
> According to the philosophy of the school, I am supposed to find something in my lesson content that will keep her engrossed in the subject. That having failed, I am supposed to keep her in detention in or out of school hours, failing that I am supposed to send her to the head.

Staff responsibilities 1970s–80s
The deputy head

1. General oversight of the whole school and all matters relating to the smooth running of the school as deputy to the head teacher.

2. Settling in and supervision of all new staff – in particular, probationary staff.

3. Liaison with Colleges and Departments of Education including the supervision of students in conjunction with Heads of Department.

4. Control of expenditure along lines laid down by the head teacher, including oversight of requisitions submitted by Heads of Department.

5. Allocation of stock and oversight of department stock records.

6. Supervision of the School Fund Account.

7. Oversight and planning of school functions in conjunction with the Senior Master.

8. Administration in relation to the awarding of school prizes.

9. Oversight of girls' welfare and discipline in conjunction with the Heads of House.

10. Liaison with primary schools and allocation of all new entrants to Tutor Groups.

In addition, the deputy head in 1973, who had acted as the head of the school for one term, had taken on responsibility for making the school timetable, a responsibility which remained with the deputy head throughout the 1970s and into the mid '80s, according to the policies laid down by the head teacher following consultations with the staff, particularly heads of departments.

Unfortunate, in many ways, was the appointment of a male deputy head following the retirement of Miss C. I. Hope, leading to a senior team entirely comprising men in a mixed secondary school.

The second master (later called the senior master or second deputy)

1. Construction of the timetable and all amendments to the timetable according to school policy defined by the head teacher and following consultation with the staff: a duty assumed by the deputy by 1973.

2. Day-to-day running of the school, including arrangements for the cover of absent staff and timetable arrangements for examinations.

3. Liaison with the Co-ordinator for the Senior School in matters relating to internal and external examinations, timetabling of 4th Year Option sets and the academic progress of pupils.

4. Liaison with and assistance to the Deputy Head in the planning of school functions.

5. Oversight of boys' welfare and discipline in conjunction with Heads of House.

The co-ordinator for the senior school (later title senior master)

1. All administration related to pupils' examinations, and liaison with Heads of Department, Heads of House and parents concerning pupils' entries.

2. Oversight of pupils' progress on their fourth and fifth year courses, and appropriate liaison with Heads of Department and Heads of House.

3. All arrangements for the 4th Year Option sets, starting with pupil assessments in the 3rd year.

4. Liaison with Heads of Department and Heads of House concerning pupils' choices in the third year and meeting parents when necessary.

5. Liaison with the Second Master concerning the availability of staff and possible timetable combinations appropriate to the make-up of the new 4th year sets.

6. Liaison with the College of Technology in relation to Link Courses and the supervision of pupils' welfare and discipline (including dress) while on Link courses.

A further emphasis, although unintentional and unavoidable, was given to this position of male dominance by the eventual appointment of a second deputy head (male) and the renaming of the senior school co-ordinator post as senior master. Senior women teachers with appropriate qualifications and experience could not be attracted to apply for the posts when advertised. Also, with the coming of misplaced equality legislation, it was no longer possible to advertise specifically for senior mistress (or senior master, if applicable) or a woman deputy head.

Pastoral posts

Resulting from the perceived large size of the comprehensive school and the understanding that the catchment area of Eastbourne contained a significant number of children coming from underprivileged homes, the house system was established to play a major pastoral role as well as fostering the various house competitions.

The heads of house

1. Welfare, discipline, including dress of pupils in the House.

2. Keeping of pupils' records, oversight of the pupils' progress in school work and appropriate liaison with Heads of Department, the Co-ordinator for the Senior School and subject teachers.

3. Promoting and maintaining contacts with parents.

4. Liaison with all outside welfare organisations which have contact with pupils in the school.

5. Careers advice and Liaison with the Careers Advisory Officer and other careers contacts. Responsibility for the careers programmes in the 4th and 5th Years and for the Careers convention for 3rd year pupils and parents.

6. Supervision and encouragement of House Tutors and activities in tutorial periods.

7. Supervision and allocation of staff duties.

8. Encouragement and oversight of House social activities.

9. Supervision and control of House Tutor Group attendance registers including follow-up of poor attenders, lates and truants.

10. House assemblies.

11. House meal arrangements.

12. Appointment, training and oversight of House Prefects.

13. Preparation of leavers' testimonials.

14. General oversight of the fabric of House rooms and cloakrooms.

15. Inter-house competitions.

NB Communications

Heads of House are responsible for communicating information to their staff by means of regular meetings and written memos and from staff to head teacher by written memos or minutes.

Deputy heads of house

1. To deputise in all House matters in the absence of the Head of House.

2. To take a share in the leading of Houses' Assemblies.

3. To take responsibility for settling the Houses in School Assemblies – in conjunction with the Head of House.

4 To help with the supervision and organisation of the House meals system.

5. To assist with the general oversight and fabric of the House rooms and cloakrooms.

6. To be responsible for the House Point System.

7. To co-ordinate the House sporting activities.

8. To assist with communications.

9. To be responsible for the training, counselling, and administration of the House Prefects.

The responsibilities of the heads of house as defined in the initial years of the comprehensive school were intended to place the pastoral staff in positions of considerable authority, almost, as it were, as heads of their own schools within the school: a scheme which did not entirely work. Although responsibilities were clearly laid down, they did not always seem to be carried out effectively, probably due to a two-way interaction of heads of houses with other staff. Many long-experienced staff who had taught and held positions of seniority, solely on length of service, in the secondary modern schools and were accustomed to referring only to the more senior head teacher, found it difficult to adjust to the concept of younger, apparently less experienced teachers being in apparently more senior positions of authority over themselves. Conversely, these teachers in their turn possibly found it difficult to exert authority if and when necessary. This was particularly awkward if teachers were reluctant to carry out those duties associated with the supervision of the school premises beyond the walls of their teaching room.

House tutors

All staff with responsibility for a tutor group are house tutors and staff not allocated a particular group may always be called upon to act as tutor to a group where the regular teacher is absent.

Clearly the success of the house system depends upon all tutors working conscientiously within this area of responsibility.

Heads of house have the responsibility of supervising and helping tutors.

1. Pastoral care of every child in the group. Including control and guidance in behaviour, dress and standards of work.

2. Provision of the detailed information for the Head of House to build up a full picture of the child.

3. Knowledge of each child's background and familiarity with the child's files and records so that appropriate discipline and help can be provided for each individual.

4. Conscientious completion of appropriate reports and records throughout the year. Any information relating to home difficulties, problems of health, behaviour, and work should be noted and the Head of House informed. Where difficulties or other events are likely to influence the child's behaviour in classes, subject teachers should be informed of the problem and close liaison be maintained between them and the House tutor.

5. Supervision and care of exercise books and furnishings and investigating any loss or damage with the help of the Head of House, if necessary.

6. Development of a good businesslike and friendly attitude towards the school including active participation in activities and clubs.

7. Attendance registers – recording absences and lates, and reporting offenders to the Head of House.

8. Arrangement of a homework timetable in consultation with subject teachers and in line with school policy.

9. Liaison with all other staff as appropriate, keeping the Head of House informed of all matters arising and consulting with him or her as necessary.

10. Full use should be made of Tutor Group periods. Some activities for these sessions are:

Calling pupils' attention to significant matters arising in the Diary of Events,

Checking homework, work standards, standards of dress and House Point sheets,

Discussion of matters arising for possible report to the School Council,

Discussion and counselling of group and individual problems,

Arrangements for a form of morning assembly.

As far as the tutors were concerned, some teachers found the formality of the new house system to be an imposition. If the situation is examined more carefully, there is with the change of educational provision in the new schools an apparent, if not realistic, change in the responsibilities associated with the classroom teacher. Before reorganisation the assistant teacher knew that his or her job was first to maintain good behaviour in the classroom; to teach one's subject to the best of one's ability, adapting teaching methods to motivate children of different abilities, to mark and correct children's work; to prepare, set and mark tests and internal examinations for your classes; to complete school reports for parents; to prepare older pupils for public examinations; if you were also a form teacher, that is in charge of a class during registration and assembly time, to keep the register correctly and neatly up to date; and to take an interest in the children in your care in so far as this was necessary for the purpose of carrying out your other duties. All of these things understood and accepted as the usual duties of a teacher, to be carried out under the direction of the head teacher, in a small school in which intercommunication was for the most part informal.

Some teachers were able and happy to get to know their pupils more closely; others were unable to do this and probably did not want to do so in any case. There is the saying from some unknown member of the profession that he taught mathematics, not children!

The job was changing. There suddenly appeared a formal statement of responsibilities, and among these the requirement to be more involved with the child's welfare. No longer was a sympathetic acknowledgment of a youngster's personal circumstances sufficient, coupled with one's own personal view of what one should be concerned about: there was now the duty to observe and report on health, home circumstances and behaviour; to record and report to others one's observations; and to enter into discussions with others on these matters.

For some the formal stipulation of what they had always done was an insult to their professionalism; to newcomers, whose attitudes were different to those entering the profession in earlier years, the duties, of welfare in particular, were nothing to with them – they taught a subject.

Heads of department

1. Preparation of syllabus and modification as required to keep up-to-date.

   A written programme of work for each year should be available for inspection and one up-to-date copy handed to the head teacher.

2. Interpretation of the syllabus with guidance as to possible teaching methods and materials available.

3. Leadership of the subject team of teachers in such matters as evaluation of work being done, instigation or trial of new teaching techniques and help with class control.

4. Oversight of subject teacher record books appropriate to the department.

5. Oversight of college students in the appropriate subject under the guidance of the Deputy Head.

6. Assessment of each child in attainment and application and appropriate liaison with Heads of House and Co-ordinator of the Senior School.

7. Assistance to the Head Teacher in the selection of new staff.

8. Control of all stock, text-books, equipment, instruments and apparatus in the care of the department; including the keeping of an appropriate stock book and stock distribution records under the guidance of the Deputy Head. In the case of books issued to individual children

there should be a record which shows precisely the title and number of each book issued to each child.

9. Expenditure of money allocated to the department under the guidance of the Deputy Head.

10. Liaison with the Remedial department.

11. Liaison with other departments, as appropriate, in order to promote purposeful correlation in courses of study.

12. Determination (in consultation with the Head Teacher) of the responsibilities of any other person in the department who holds a special responsibility allowance.

NB Communications

Heads of Department are responsible for communicating information to their staff by means of regular meetings and written memos and from staff to the head teacher through meetings and written minutes.

The formality of the head of department's duties had gradually developed with the introduction of the payment of extra money for posts of special responsibility but even so, under the new regime, more formality was expected: there were to be meetings with staff and minutes kept, taking up time outside normal pupil-contact hours.

The class teacher was involved in such meetings – and in the meetings which came to be required by the heads of house. Heads of house and heads of department attended regular and frequent meetings with the head teacher and other senior staff.

Time which was once one's own in which to volunteer to get involved, or not depending upon one's own circumstances and interests, had been formally taken and turned into an obligation. The freedom of the professional was being eroded.

Participatory democracy

During the 1960s there was a growth in the movement seeking to have workers' representatives involved in management decisions and for clients to have more say in the decisions made by professionals. In schools there were efforts on the part of some teachers to have staff committees involved in the decision making previously the province of the head teacher, in spite of there already being in existence regular staff meetings in which policies were discussed and staff views considered. In turn the growing strength of the teacher unions encouraged the development of a negotiation situation in which elected school union representatives were expected to bring the views of their members to the head teacher. Not only did this hide the individual teacher's views behind the majority trade-union view but also fragmented the staff into those in different unions or no union at all.

Some LEAs encouraged the involvement of trade-union representatives in decision making at both the education committee stage and in individual management of the school by head teachers.

In the 1980s, the government of the day decided to give elected representatives of both teachers and parents seats on the governing body. This matter was separate to that of trade-union representation but, as the majority of the members of the governing body were elected members of the local council, the teachers and parents had little influence on the making of decisions, except in so far as they could express their points of view and depending upon the political governors' willingness to listen.

The motivation for these developments grew out of the ideal that people should be given the opportunity to have a greater say in matters affecting them; creating a participatory democracy. The problem with this idea is that the majority of people would sooner trust those appointed to run our various institutions to do so in an efficient and just fashion while they can be left free to carry out their own responsibilities without the additional burden of being involved in time-consuming discussions in committees.

In addition, resulting from the preference of the majority to expect others to run things for them, a minority of activists tend to fill the elected representatives' posts, promoting the enthusiasm and views of pressure groups; a situation which can apply to those advancing themselves as candidates in any form of democratic elections.

Teachers' strikes 1977–1985

In the 1970s there developed a spell of unrest in the teaching profession with strikes disrupting the education of young people: the stated reason being the schoolteachers' unions' claim to be seeking better pay and working conditions for their members.

It was at this time, as a reaction to the disruption in schools, a group of teachers founded the Professional Association of Teachers (now known as Voice, the union for education professionals) the only teachers' trade union whose members do not go on strike, believing that a better way of resolving disagreements is by negotiation and arbitration. Appointed to Eastbourne in 1973 I (with Colin Leicester) was one of the two founders of this new-style trade union, a significant factor in the working relationships between some activists in the traditional trade unions and the head.

In early October 1977 the Darlington Secretary of the NASUWT, a member of the staff of Eastbourne School, made one of his many regular visits to County Hall, it was presumed to raise concerns relating to reduction of the staff of the school from head plus 64 to head plus 63, due the reduction in the number of pupils on roll. It was the LEA's job to determine, according to a recognised formula relating to the number of pupils on roll, the number of teachers a school should have; and it is the head teacher's responsibility to deploy these teachers.

On 21 October, the first 'formal' notification of an NASUWT grievance and impending action was received via a telephone call from County Hall, followed by a letter. Sanctions imposed by the union were due to commence after the mid-term holiday and were to include the refusal by members to cover for staff absent for more than three days. The grievance, however, was reported to be the union's dissatisfaction with the distribution of the teaching load, in particular with the non-teaching time allocated to heads of house and other senior staff.

On 2 November the head sent a letter to the school representative of the union requesting details of their grievance as there had been no information sent to the head teacher from the union direct.

On 11 November in a conversation between the school representative of the union and the head it was suggested by the union that there was no requirement to be on duty before the bell sounds: in other words there was supposed to be no responsibility on the part of union members to supervise the children on school premises for the period of ten minutes before the bell.

The head replied in writing later in the day stating that he had been concerned about the supervision of the pupils in school before morning and afternoon sessions for some considerable time (a fact which must have been known to members of the NASUWT at the time because of the head's frequent reinforcement of the need for teachers to be on duty around the school as well as in their classrooms). Nevertheless, the head called the attention of the NASUWT to the opinion expressed by G. R. Barrell in *Teachers and the Law* that the generally accepted practice, which was not legally binding unless required by the LEA's regulations or the head teacher carrying out his or her responsibilities according to the rules of management or articles of government of the school, was for teachers to have responsibility for the children for between ten and fifteen minutes before the start of school. This situation had always been accepted and the duty maintained from the earliest days of the school and it was therefore quite reasonable for at least some staff to be on duty throughout the school before the children entered the premises. It was emphasised that with some 1,200 young people all on the move at the same time, some adult supervision was necessary. The Director of Education for Durham County Council supported this view in a letter to the head teacher.

The note in the school log book at the time expressed the head teacher's view that the action of the trade union and its alleged grievance was an attempt to overrule or take on the responsibilities of the head teacher and to modify certain working arrangements to suit themselves without paying due regard to their professional responsibilities, particularly in relation to the safety of the children in their care. In addition, activists were seeking minor irritations on the part of some of their members, which could and should have been raised with the head and discussed in staff meetings (as indeed, they were), to use in their campaign.

On 14 November the newly appointed Senior Education Adviser for Durham County Education Authority came into school to speak with the Darlington and Eastbourne School NASUWT representatives, the subject of the discussions not being made known to the head teacher.

The following day the head received a letter from the union representative indicating that no consultations had taken place between the head and the union in relation to the matter in dispute.

With hindsight and examining papers some thirty years later the suggestion was true in so far as there had been no discussions with that minority of the staff which belonged to the NASUWT in isolation from the rest of the staff, a practice which would fragment the staff and was undesirable.

The head teacher responded to the letter by reminding the union representative that a matter, relating to internal school policy, had been taken by them to their union officials and LEA officers outside school and sanctions imposed on the school. It was pointed out that by this stage the union had imposed these sanctions because its members were dissatisfied with the allocation of non-teaching time. The matter had been mentioned previously but no formal interview requested to discuss the question and the head expressed his view that he found their behaviour distasteful and was reluctant to negotiate while sanctions were imposed. In addition it was said that if the sanctions were lifted with effect from 2 November the head would be willing to meet the school and area representative at 9.30 a.m. on that day to discuss the matter.

A further development followed discussions with senior staff, an assistant director and senior adviser from Durham, and the decision was taken to place the matter on the agenda of the staff meeting to be held on Tuesday 29 November: Item 1 – The supposed imbalance between the teaching loads of senior and other staff.

Early in the morning of 25 November the school union representative met the head teacher in the corridor and returned the slips of his members who were refusing to cover for absent staff and asked if the head would withdraw the first item from the next staff meeting agenda. The request was firmly refused, the head indicating his annoyance, emphasising his view that the matter, influencing all of the staff, must be discussed at a full staff meeting. The representative's view was that his members would probably refuse to attend the staff meeting.

The head subsequently approached each of the individual union members refusing to cover for absent colleagues, asking them to reaffirm their position and indicating his annoyance with the union for refusing to attend the staff meeting. This action brought a complaint from the union's full-time representative to the LEA that the head had been harassing and intimidating his members!

The individual teachers' view seemed to be dominated by the need to carry out a union instruction although this may be distasteful to them.

The head clarified the position relating to the staff meeting by inviting both the school and area union representatives concerned to his room later in the day. As there was no willingness on their part to withdraw sanctions the position remained unchanged.

The letter from the NASUWT national official resulted in another letter from the LEA to the head asking for his views on the subject. He responded by stating that he found the stance taken by the union in Eastbourne as quite incredible, pointing out that this was the second time they had taken an internal school matter to their area headquarters and to the county education officials without informing him and consequently the head's response was that he had no knowledge of the complaint whatsoever. He also stated that he felt he could no longer speak person to person with any member of the NASUWT in the school as the meaning of his words and actions may be distorted and misinterpreted. He also said that, under the circumstances, he felt he would now find it very difficult to provide the union members with an honest reference or testimonial, since, if any confidentiality was broken in any way and for any reason, his words may well once again be misinterpreted and the meaning distorted.

Monday 3 April 1978, the start of the summer term: a letter was received by the head teacher from the NASUWT representative in which it was stated that sanctions in the school had been lifted while pay and conditions problems were being negotiated at national level. Having satisfied the requirement that those sanctions be lifted before the head would discuss their grievances on school business the representative now requested that a meeting take place.

As an aside, the representative had also said that in any case they did not think they were going to get anywhere with the school issues.

The prime objective changed to the request that the head meet union representatives from time to time in order to discuss matters raised by their members and as it was agreed that representatives of all the teachers' unions should be involved, this was agreed.

The school was able to get on with its normal routine undisturbed, until those who thought that strike action produced positive advances for union members once again disrupted the education service. On Monday 22 January 1979 the school was closed due to a NUPE (National Union of Public Employees) strike: caretakers were not on duty and the kitchen staff not in school. It was a one-day token strike and after discussion schools were closed by the LEA in an effort to maintain goodwill – expecting normal school to resume on Tuesday.

In February there was further industrial action by manual workers: school caretakers in Darlington were to withdraw their services, on the instructions of their trade union, from Monday 5 February. Consequently it was expected that normal school would not be possible from this date until further notice and further instructions and advice would be issued by the Director of Education as soon as possible.

On 6 February the third-year parents' evening times were changed from 7–9 p.m. to 4–6 p.m. in anticipation of the caretakers closing school premises at 6 p.m.

On 7 February all primary and secondary heads in Darlington were summoned to a meeting with the Director at the teachers' centre at which it was decided that the head teachers would not open their schools next week because they:

1. Did not want to subject teaching staffs to picketing because of their (the head teachers') decision to open schools;
2. If they did open, picketing and the withdrawal of goodwill would be continued after a national agreement was reached (from a statement made by representatives of the caretakers' union);
3. Manual workers would be withdrawn from residential schools which would then be closed.

At this stage therefore, the Authority decided to investigate possibilities of getting other people to open the schools, put on heating and complete other necessary duties. If this was arranged it was expected that teachers would go to work as usual presumably crossing picket lines to do so. If the move to find others to open the schools failed, the LEA said that it would have to decide what alternatives may be available to them.

Following a further meeting with the Director the school was closed to pupils, with only staff attending on 12 and 13 February to carry out preparation work. It is interesting that overnight on 12 February there was a break-in to the plant room and swimming pool: perhaps someone was taking the opportunity to come in when they thought the premises would be unsupervised.

By 14 February arrangements had been made for the partial opening of the school: fifth years were then able to attend to follow their normal timetable, and first to fourth years to attend for two hours only on Wednesdays and Fridays, between 9 and 11 a.m., to collect and hand in work completed at home.

A digression to consider the weather

In order to reassure those who have recently experienced what they perceive as some kind of unusual disaster, a winter with heavy snow and freezing temperatures lasting for more than a week or so, there is plenty of evidence to tell us such events do come along from time to time.

On 14 February 1979, as well as contending with a caretakers' strike, it was reported that there were very strong winds and heavy snowfall across north-east England again. The road from Darlington to Barnard Castle was difficult, that to Bowes was closed, and in north-east Durham a 'whiteout' caused by blowing snow reduced visibility to almost nil.

February 15 was described as the worst winter's day in Darlington since 1947! Snow fell late the previous evening and overnight giving an even spread of about nine inches in the town, with drifts of eighteen inches. Heavy, prolonged snow showers continued throughout the morning filling indentations made by cars and pedestrians. The road from Darlington to Barnard Castle was closed, and in Cleveland, business premises advised by the police to close at 3 p.m.

Only fifth-year pupils, staff, and staff from feeder primary schools were in school and most of these were sent home after lunch. Eleven of the Eastbourne teachers had been unable to get to school. Mr Forrest, from Danby, in the North York moors, dug himself out only to be sent back home by the police when he reached the main road. Mrs Hughes was cut off on Bowes Moor in the Pennines.

On 16 February the school was open for years 1 to 4 from 9 till 11 a.m., the fifth year following their normal timetable, which included mock examinations. There had been light snowfall overnight and some of the teachers were still unable to get to school, particularly from Barnard Castle, Bowes and the higher parts of County Durham.

On Monday 19 February the school was open for fifth years only: major roads were now clear although minor roads were still difficult or closed. Distant staff had returned to duty, including Mrs Hughes from Bowes Moor, where troops had cleared the road.

On Monday 19 March the school was again closed due to the weather following a broadcast directive from County Hall. There had been heavy snowfall throughout a 100-mile belt across northern England and Scotland. Many roads throughout Durham had been closed. Some nine inches of snow was reported to have fallen overnight on the previous Friday and Saturday, laying on that which had fallen previously and then frozen. Further falls during Saturday and Sunday produced depths of up to eighteen inches, with deeper drifts in places.

Further industrial action by schoolteachers

There is evidence of more disruption in May 1979 in a letter written to parents by the head teacher on the first of the month.

> Dear Parent,
>
> I have today been informed by the members of the Assistant Masters and Mistresses Association that they will be absent from school during the afternoon of Wednesday 2nd May.
>
> This means that there may not be a teacher available to teach your child during Wednesday afternoon. However, school will be open as normal for most of the pupils.
>
> Pupils coming to school and finding no teacher present should settle down in class and complete private study. There is no reason why secondary school pupils should not do this although some do from time to time take advantage of a teacher's absence from the room.
>
> In view of the fact that your child may be in an unsupervised class at this time you may wish to keep him or her at home after dinner. The absence will be approved if you so decide.
>
> NB All examination work will continue as usual and all candidates due to take papers at this time must attend in the usual way.

Twelve teachers were in fact absent on this occasion.

Monday 7 May was the Bank Holiday closure. But, due to further impending action on the part of another trade union, another letter was sent home to parents before the holiday:

> Members of the National Association of School Masters/ Union of Women teachers are withdrawing from all activities at lunchtime, taking no part in evening or weekend extra-curricular activities and working five hours per day from Tuesday 8th May 1979. Members of the National Union of Teachers have already withdrawn from lunch time and after school activities.

Resulting from the imposing of these various sanctions, the following arrangements will be necessary from Tuesday 8th May.

The following classes will be sent home at 3.10 pm each day until further notice.

Mondays: classes timetabled as follows for periods 7 and 81B/B1 boys only – Second Year Bolton boys metalwork group – 2 RW Maths set using room 117 – 3D and 3D1 3RW Physics group using room 201 – 3RW Biology group using 7 4BD English set using 106 or library 1 – 4 RW Maths using 113 – 4RW Maths using 13.

Examination arrangements continue as previously notified.

Similar arrangements were made for other days of the week. Nineteen teachers were involved in this action.

Yet another letter was sent to parents on 9 May:

Trade Union Activities by Teachers

I regret that I have to inform you that no teachers will be on duty in school at lunch time from Thursday 10th May. I cannot therefore guarantee the safety of pupils in school at this time and cannot accept responsibility for them on school premises.

Until further notice, school will close at 12.05 pm and reopen at 1.15 pm. Pupils should leave the buildings and grounds after the morning session.

Sanctions were lifted with effect from Thursday 14 May and the following letter sent home:

I am pleased to inform you that school is able to return to normal working from tomorrow Thursday 24th May.

The afternoon session will finish for all children at 3.55 pm.

A lunch will be served although no choice of meal will be available until after the holiday.

I should be grateful if you would impress upon your child the need for good behaviour both in the dining rooms and outside during the dinner time.

The next diary entry made on 26 March 1982 reads: 'Teachers' Dispute ends – school meals resumed Monday 31 March. Union rep to County Hall. Threat of further industrial action later!' Later seems to have been 2 November when the county secretary and assistant county secretary NASUWT, both on the staff of Eastbourne school, attended a meeting at County Hall, Durham to discuss 'No cover for absent staff provision' and industrial action resulting from the same.

Industrial action certainly continued because a note dated 4 November refers to the school musical evening being cancelled due to both the NUT and NASUWT refusing to cover for absent staff, attend meetings and parents' evenings, supervise the school at lunchtimes and other duties which they saw as Authority instigated. In reality the application of sanctions appeared to be that the staff only did what they fancied doing!

On 17 November 1982 a letter was sent to parents because the teachers' sanctions were to be increased:

> As I am sure you will know, teachers in County Durham have been involved in industrial action: this action is now being increased and I must inform you of arrangements which may consequently become necessary.
>
> 1. Dinner times
> Dinner time supervision will be decreased and you may wish to have your child at home during this time. Depending upon how matters develop, I may have to decrease the availability of, or close down, meals.
>
> 2. Cover for absent teachers
> When a teacher is absent and the absence is unexpected a class may be left without a teacher for a lesson. I think that this is a safer arrangement than sending such groups out of school. Of course, someone will always be in the vicinity in the case of emergency. Pupils should work quietly on any exercise which is available: there should always be reading and revision work at hand.
> When a teacher's absence is expected it may be necessary to ask certain classes to come to school at a later time than usual and also send certain classes home early. In such cases parents will be notified of such arrangements in writing.

I am sure that I can rely on your co-operation in these matters. It is most important that pupils should behave in a responsible way at all times.

On 1 December pupils were given a letter to take home indicating that some should come in late and that some would be sent home early as cover for absent teachers would not be available due to the operation of sanctions: the start of what you might call shift work!

In late February 1983 there was an escalation of the teachers' dispute, when the NUT started strike action in three schools with the expectation that three more would be involved from 24 February. The LEA subsequently reached an agreement with the NUT and teachers were therefore expected to be working normally. Apparently, pay deducted since the start of the term was to be returned but deductions made before Christmas were to stand; in addition cover for absent staff, in general, would be made available after three days.

The LEA had also had a meeting with representatives of the NASUWT and it later transpired that they were displeased with the agreement reached with the NUT: they wanted all of their money back, arguing that teachers cannot be fined for doing their job. Staff did strike but worked in the staff room! The union must have argued that they were within their rights to fail to carry out normal cover duties for absent colleagues! It does so often seem that the NASUWT wished to define its own members' responsibilities in school – the Authority being expected to agree to their demands and have no say in the running of things themselves.

The dispute continued: schools receiving notification from the Authority that the NASUWT would leave work at the end of the morning session on 7 March and return the following day. This was the beginning of a series of sanctions with the union promising to give head teachers twenty-four hours' notice of their intentions. It was left to head teachers to make their own necessary arrangements but it was stated that as many pupils were to be retained in school as could be properly supervised and taught. If children had to be sent home or miss schooling their parents had to be given written notice. Head teachers were expected to keep a record of members of staff taking action so that appropriate salary deductions could be made.

There was the written observation that 'The Authority much regrets that the NASUWT, having refused to accept the terms agreed with the NUT, should now take action which can only once more adversely affect the education of Durham school children'.

This was my comment in the school log book:

> When will people in our society realise that any militant action taken now hurts one's fellows and interferes with their rights more than its hurts the 'boss' or 'paymaster'? A better way to settle disputes must be found! Already other bodies of people, apart from those teachers who have joined the Professional Association of Teachers, are working towards this objective. The Professional Association of Nursery Nurses has been launched. Various representatives of the caring professions have held an initial meeting and have approached PAT for guidance. Even railway workers are taking up this idea.

Nearly thirty years later the reader must wonder how far society has managed to adopt this attitude.

On Monday 7 March there was a meeting of secondary school head teachers with the Director. One point made, from a group now resigned to the disruption in their schools, was the hope that the Authority would not give in to the NASUWT because to do this would suggest that a trade union can take any action it likes without thought for anyone and without the fear of sanctions being brought against it.

Disruption by NASUWT continued through April.

Adding to the problems created for schools by the teachers' unions was the fact that the 1980s was a time of government cutbacks.

As one of the grievances was cover for absent staff, it is perhaps ironic that at Eastbourne there were at one time three representatives of teachers' unions and one or two councillors who were frequently out of school on business other than that associated with specific matters relating directly to the school. Although it can be argued that teachers need to be members of a union and that there need to be officers to whom they can turn in times of need and who they can rely on to represent them when applicable, it is difficult to rationalise the view that anyone can be heavily engaged in union business during pupil-contact time and be a fully active classroom teacher.

At Eastbourne, as well as having the county representative of his union frequently out of school, there was the school staff union representative out, not only on educational matters but also frequently delegated by his union to attend non-educational meetings. Furthermore, would-be union representatives chose to be out of school on training courses for such positions (which could easily have been held at weekends or during holidays, as they were in the case of other unions).

On one occasion a union representative brought a grievance procedure against the head teacher because he disagreed with the question put to a candidate at interview: Do you think that a person who is out of school so much can do a pastoral job?

Another objection arose when the head spoke to a probationary teacher and, among other things, advised that a less extreme hair style and form of dress would help to overcome her problem with unidentifiable adolescent boys making lewd comments about her in the corridors. The teacher was quite happy with the observation but the union representative was not!

By February 1985 sanctions were again being applied against schools when the NUT refused to cover for absent colleagues. Teachers involved had to be reported to the Authority as instructed and pupils were sent home when a teacher was not available. Most came and went responsibly as though working shifts, but some took advantage of the situation, making the sending home an excuse for truancy; and some parents refused to send their children to school for what they claimed to be part-time teaching.

The situation was excellent for those who saw little value in education or who saw other activities as more important.

In June 1985 the NASUWT was engaged in what was described as selective strike action, consisting of the withdrawal of members for short periods at a time. The result of this action was of course that pupils were out of school for longer than the defined time, both with genuine reasons based upon travel home and by taking advantage of the situation, choosing not to attend.

It is difficult to understand what this action was supposed to achieve. It was directed at pupils and consequently parents who seemed to make little objection except where a midday lunch was at risk or where the child was imposed upon the home when parents found this inconvenient. The real principles of education do not seem to enter into the matter. Strike action continued throughout June.

The frustration felt by head teachers was illustrated when on 8 October 1985 they attended a meeting at County Hall to discuss industrial activity in schools. The meeting did not seem to have any great impact: head teachers somehow resigned or 'punch drunk' to the action which was preventing them from developing any future policy. Withdrawal of so-called 'goodwill' seemed to mean that teachers did not attend meetings and refused to co-operate with any management-instigated activities. There was the threat to refuse to co-operate over matters relating to the new General Certificate of Secondary Education (GCSE) which was to replace CSE and GCE from 1988 onwards.

The actions related to the failure to settle the 1985 pay award and at the time the NUT-dominated Burnham Committee spent many months prolonging argument. Since the NUT was about to lose its majority, a settlement involving agreement to talk about teachers' contractual duties and appropriate salary structures was becoming more likely. Nevertheless it is clear that both the NUT and NASUWT wanted an ongoing dispute up to the time of the next general election – apparently content to use the disruption of the education of children and young people for their purposes.

Industrial action by the NASUWT continued in the form of selective strike action, refusal to cover for absent colleagues, refusal to do any work outside class pupil-contact hours. The three latter sanctions were also imposed by both the NUT and AMMA (Assistant Masters and Mistresses Association) and this action was continued for many months.

School routine and organisation

In any school, not being like any other institution, having many immature young people in the care of relatively few adults, organisation of routine is of prime significance. In a large school it is of major importance and, although not the largest by any means, Eastbourne Comprehensive School was large enough. To lay down clear guidelines for day-to-day routine is a start.

Annual events

Large-scale events, such as the former boys' school annual camp and girls' outing to the abbeys, became part of a tradition, a demonstration of stability, and an indication of what the school could do. With the passing of the years between 1936 and 1973, change had been inevitable but the significance of continuity and of the whole school being involved in some significantly large activity, whether it was in the form of some outdoor physical pursuit, drama or music, remained an important element in maintaining the school ethos.

On 19 January 1973, during the mid-term holiday, the school staged a concert in the Darlington Civic Theatre. Final rehearsals, involving large numbers of pupils in the choir, orchestra and band, took place during the morning with the performance during the evening from 7.30 till 9.30 p.m. The table of staff duties on this occasion demonstrates the work necessary on their part as well the effort put in by the young people.

The following staff were involved:

> Staff in charge of music: Mr Sheppard, Mr Price, Mrs Jolly
>
> Business Manager: Mr Wrigley
>
> Stage Manager: Mr Minikin
>
> Assisting at rehearsals and behind the scenes during the evening: Miss Hope,
>
> Mrs Hamilton, Mr G. Clark, Miss McLeish, Mr Carling, Mrs P. Scott, Mrs J. Clarke,
>
> Mr W. Foster, Mr Maull, Mr Wright, Miss Giles, Mr Hogg.

In addition, whereas the autocratic regimes of the smaller schools made life easier, the changed social climate, not least the attitude to pupil discipline, produced a contradictory state of affairs: larger schools need a more rigid organisation than small ones but the climate of opinion, as schools grew in size, was for more freedom of expression, not less.

Morning school assembly was either house assemblies or junior and senior school assemblies, there being no place on the premises for the whole school to meet together. The two former secondary school halls plus the dining halls and sometimes the gymnasium could be used.

Other annual productions, pantomimes and concerts for example, also required the support of a large number of teachers.

> Staff support required for pantomimes and musical evenings
>
> Business manager: to arrange seating, printing and sale of tickets and programmes, accounts

Producers: drama and music

Member in charge and team members for preparation of costumes

Scenery painting team when appropriate

Supervision of front door and premises, including car parking

Teachers to take classes of colleagues engaged in rehearsals

Special administrative arrangements required during performance preparation:

Provision of alternative rooms for any classes normally timetabled to use the hall

Provision for the withdrawal of pupils participating in rehearsals from normal classes during the week of the performance

Setting out of seating in the hall and balcony

(Main seating area – ground floor – two blocks of seats: one 8 by 15 and one 7 by 15, with gangways on each side and at the centre and space in front of the stage for the orchestra)

Checking of fire exits and lighting of signs

The timetable for the school day

Staff on duty from 8.50 a.m.

Bell for entry of pupils. Pupils move straight to tutor group rooms 9.00 a.m.

Registration – register to be closed at 9.10 a.m.

Lates: pupils should be marked late if they enter the room after 9.05 a.m.

Latecomers are also recorded at the gate and are late if arriving after 9.00 a.m.

Unexplained absence and repeated lateness should be reported to the head of house

Move to assemblies 9.11 a.m. to arrive before 9.15 a.m.

Assembly period 9.15 a.m. till 9.30 a.m.

Period 1 – 9.30 a.m. till 10.05 a.m.

Movement of classes should be direct from the assembly to lesson 1

Note: A class register should be kept and the roll checked each lesson

Unexplained absences should be reported to the appropriate head of house using the absentee report slips

Period 2 – 10.05 a.m. till 10.40 a.m.

Break – 10.40 a.m. till 10.55 a.m.

Period 3 – 10.55 a.m. till 11.30 a.m.

Period 4 – 11.30 a.m. till 12.05 p.m.

Lunch break – 12.05 p.m. till 1.15 p.m.

Staff on duty from 1.05 p.m.

Bell for entry of pupils 1.15 p.m. Pupils move straight to tutor group rooms

Registration – register to be closed at 1.25 p.m.

Lates: pupils should be marked late if they enter the room after 1.20 p.m.

Latecomers are also recorded at the gate and are late if arriving after 1.15 p.m.

Unexplained absence and repeated lateness should be reported to the head of house

Period 5 – 1.20 p.m. till 1.55 p.m.

Period 6 – 1.55 p.m. till 2.30 p.m.

Break – 2.30 p.m. till 2.45 p.m.

Period 7 – 2.45 p.m. till 3.20 p.m.

Period 8 – 3.20 p.m. till 3.55 p.m.

Clearance of the school

At the end of the day, each member of staff has the responsibility for seeing children out of their teaching room and overseeing the clearing of the corridor area outside their room.

In general, this does mean that all staff should remain in their teaching areas for the period 3.55 till 4.05 p.m.

Heads of house supervise the cloakroom areas 3.55 p.m. till 4.05 p.m.

Senior Staff supervise the front of the school 3.55 p.m. till 4.05 p.m.

Sporting events

The traditional pattern of athletics meetings and swimming galas continued. Inter-house athletics meetings were held during the summer term in the walled field (the old hospital site where the surrounding wall had been retained to provide an excellent arena site). Those not representing their teams in the events were taken onto the field as spectators, sometimes organised to carry chairs, particularly the old wooden units, to provide some seating.

The best of the performers took part in the Darlington Area Sports but there was no longer a half-day holiday from school work for the rest of the pupils. As physical education teachers were required to help run the town event, their classes, left in school, had to be supervised by other staff.

The best from all Darlington schools represented the town in the Durham Schools Championships and the best of these represented Durham in the English Schools National Championships.

Similarly, inter-house and Darlington schools swimming galas continued to be held, with spectators in attendance, until the old Town Baths were closed and demolished at the time of the opening of the Dolphin Centre, where the pool was not provided with adequate spectator seating – the loss of a valued facility.

The small pool constructed on the school site at the time of comprehensive school reorganisation provided adequate accommodation for class swimming instruction, and in the handling of canoes, but was not at all suitable for the whole-school galas, involving both competitors and supporters: teaching participation in team competitions and support for those representing their house teams. Attempts were made to have galas for year groups without spectators – fine for the minority taking part but of little value to the remainder.

Sponsored swims also took place in the school pool, raising money for various charities. Sponsored runs, such as that held during the afternoon of 15 October 1981 when the whole school was on the field, took place from time to time.

The annual cross country run, for both girls and boys, took place in the spring term, largely held on the school fields for reasons of safety and supervision.

In addition the school organised several town cross country competitions on Saturdays, the neighbouring Cummins Engineering Works sponsoring the event and their representative, Mr Gledhill, presenting the medals.

The Trophy Day, initiated and organised by Mr Carling, continued to take place on a Saturday during the summer.

Games teams continued the tradition of representing their school in inter-school matches but the note of a meeting between the head, heads of house, and physical education staff as early as March 1973 indicates a change in attitude on the part of a significant number of able youngsters. No longer was it seen as an honour to represent your school in any teams: the staff complained that first-class competitors were refusing to take part in inter-house and inter-school matches, and that the unacceptable behaviour of some who did take part was difficult to admonish because they also merely responded to correction by refusing to take part.

Minority activities

Such annual events as that of April 1977, when two pupils went to Howtown on a canoeing course and another fifteen went with the school's swimming instructor to Derwent Reservoir Sailing Centre for one week, were a valuable addition to the physical education curriculum.

When a school is fortunate enough to have a member of its teaching staff both well qualified and enthusiastic about a particular physical activity the range of pupil involvement can be extended. Such was the case for both boys and girls at Eastbourne in gymnastics. For instance in December 1973, girls in the gymnastic team attended the National Gymnastics Championships, coming fourth out of twelve, and the individual pupil Angela Newton in the fifth year came fifth out of sixty.

The Duke of Edinburgh's Award Scheme continued to run in conjunction with the youth centre.

School journeys and field excursions

House Excursion Day took place during the summer term in the 1970s, following the pattern of that in 1973 when Bolton House travelled to Scarborough and Flamingo Park; Durham House groups went to

Edinburgh and the Lake District; Richmond to Staithes, Runswick Bay, Port Mulgrave and Holy Island; and Witton to Swaledale.

The senior staff, eight full-time teachers and four part-time, remained in school with 220 pupils not on the excursions. The participation rate for the excursions was therefore about 80 per cent.

In addition three science staff took the opportunity to take a fourth-year group on a seashore field study trip to Bradwell Bay.

Various other field trips, allied to timetabled subject projects such as those given below, also took place throughout the 1970s and 80s.

Saturday 22 June 1977: A physical education group accompanied by two staff and their respective husband and wife visited Wembley.

Saturday 20 April to Saturday 29th April 1977: Mr Weare, Mr Fox-Roberts and Mrs Cross took a party to the Ingleton Youth Hostel for a geography field trip.

4 July 1989: A fourth-year group in charge of Miss Lamb and Mr Anderson visited a farm as part of their school studies.

By the 1980s House Excursion Day had become Activities Day, when the different year groups took part in excursions to different places of interest.

Each year, a party made up of pupils from all Darlington schools journeyed abroad to a skiing resort to take part in a sport for which there was little opportunity at home. Prior to the visit a film show for parents of the participating young people was arranged to give an idea of what was to be expected on the journey.

There is a log book entry for 12 February 1983 stating that during the period of teacher sanctions, when routine parents' evening meetings could not be held due to lack of co-operation of staff, there was nevertheless a meeting of parents of children going on the skiing trip to Innsbruck.

The journey took place in school time and therefore it was not accepted that it should be purely recreational and in addition the arrangement required one or more teachers from participating schools to accompany the youngsters – more teachers absent from their routine teaching duties, more absences, more cover required from colleagues

As a part of its cultural programme Darlington was (and still is) twinned with Amiens in France and out of this partnership has grown the annual exchange of school parties between the two countries. Eastbourne pupils regularly sent pupils to stay in the homes of French pupils, in return hosting them on their visit to Darlington. For example in 1974 the exchange party travelled to France for the period Friday 15 March to Monday 8 April when they followed a programme involving time in class and on excursions. The French children made their return visit from Friday 10 May till Monday 3 June.

On 16 October 1981 Mr Brand and Miss Wade departed for France in charge of twenty Eastbourne pupils who would be staying in the family homes of French children attending the Collège D'Enseignement Secondaire, Amiens. On this occasion it had also been arranged for Darlington head teachers to visit their partner schools and Mr Bryant stayed with M et Mme Floquet, the head and deputy head of the French school. The accommodation was interesting as the school was provided with on-site flats for both the head and deputy head, and their families. In the case of the Floquets, being a married couple, they only occupied one of the flats and the visiting head had a bedroom in the other but had meals with the family.

Each morning M Floquet, having partaken of *petite déjeuner*, would proceed to the entrance hall, with large fluffy-haired dog at his heels, put on his coat and scarf, proceed down one flight of stairs to his office, remove the coat and scarf and set to work. Some days he would venture out to the gate adjacent to the flat to supervise the entrance of the pupils; at other times it was the turn of the deputy.

Some children arrived at 8.00 a.m. on the Saturday morning with a second batch coming in at 9 a.m.; all behaved like youngsters anywhere, ambling out of buses, parking cycles, in pairs or small groups, some shouting after friends, running and dodging about. A group of boys were caught attempting to catapult missiles with elastic bands, promptly confiscated, with a severe reprimand by Madame.

The morning was spent in school and it was quickly understood that there was a distinct division of provision into academic and vocational courses; the school having a special centre attached to it for pupils deemed non-academic. After a staff lunch which lasted for some three hours, the adults involved in the exchange attended a conference at which the French education system was described: again the selection of pupils between academic and non-academic courses was explained although it was also said that there had been a recent change of attitude at national level and that mixed-ability teaching groups were to be introduced into the first year of secondary education.

On the following day M Floquet took Mr Bryant to a residential school for maladjusted girls where a colleague was the head teacher: the term 'maladjusted' better understood today as meaning those with behaviour problems. Clearly, at a time when the UK was closing such establishments, with the intention to 'treat' such children in the community, the more traditional approach was still being used in France.

An incident occurred during this year's exchange: one of the English children somehow became involved with two host families, the pupil's attitude towards the problem not helping efforts to resolve the situation with necessary tact.

The end of term
The most settled, pleasant and well-remembered end of term each year was probably the one before the Christmas holiday. At this stage in the school year the potential leavers were not anticipating their leaving and not adopting what they saw as the leaving traditions; those taking public examinations, in spite of 'mocks' approaching in January, knew that they still had time for more studying before the summer; and it was Christmas time. The customs associated with the Christian festival, albeit in some ways parting from its strictly theological interpretation, were celebrated with enthusiasm.

The end of the autumn term, the approach of the Christmas holidays, was probably the busiest and most rewarding of term ends, involving the performances of the pantomime, house parties, discos and carol services, all being a part of the school's traditional activities.

On 16 December 1980 the whole school was brought together for a carol service, using the Beehive Ballroom at Paton and Baldwins.

In December 1982 the service, again for the whole school, was held in the Dolphin Centre, using the large hall with banks of seats on three sides. This was one of the few buildings that could take 1,260 pupils but the atmosphere was not ideal. Although the service proved to be a cross between a service and a concert, with pupils deciding to clap all of the readers and performances by the school band, and staff possibly initiating such a response, the event was most worthwhile due simply to the complete involvement of everyone.

It was at the review of this year's service that the need was raised to consider how to maintain the involvement of and yet cater for the increasing number of pupils who followed different faiths from the traditional Christian ethos.

Lunchtimes

The opening time for school was for many years 9 a.m., with a lengthy lunch break for children to go to and from home, and a closure at 4 p.m. with the development of the school meals service and the increase in the number of parents, mothers in particular, going out to work, more and more of the pupils, in theory, remained in school for the lunchtime break – in theory, because many preferred to wander off premises to local shops, returning during the break at times that suited them. Their supervision became a tricky problem.

Eastbourne had purpose-built kitchens and dining halls at the east and west extremities of the original building. Children took their meals in their house groups in two sittings: the first commenced at the end of morning school, at 12.05, and the second thirty minutes later. Bolton and Witton were served in the dining hall at the domestic science end of the building and Durham and Richmond in the dining hall at the workshop end.

In 1975 staff wishing to have a school meal took it during their house sitting and if they supervised the children in the dining rooms or took a lunchtime club, they were entitled to a free meal. The presence of teachers in the dining halls was an invaluable aid to maintaining order but this situation was to change with their withdrawal from compulsory involvement in any supervision of children during the lunch break.

At this date, 1975, six midday supervisory assistants were employed by the LEA to supervise the school at lunchtimes; clearly completely inadequate: teaching staff performing such duties, in the large premises, required the deployment of twelve staff.

There was therefore a loss of teacher–pupil contact in the social environment of the dining room, the loss of an arrangement originally intended to support the pastoral aspect of the house system.

Developments in supervision of school meals

In September 1982 the cafeteria system was introduced in kitchens 1 and 2 with staff volunteers helping with supervision. They did not like the system and linked with the voluntary nature of the duty and intermittent union sanctions, staff did not in general give their assistance. Consequently, the standard of pupil behaviour was often very poor.

By November the majority of the staff, having the option of not taking part in the supervision of the school meals, had opted out of all midday supervision. A few still did oversee the children in the dining rooms but did little or nothing about children's behaviour around the school. Midday assistants were of limited value, often, due to their lack of experience in dealing with large numbers of unknown children, provoking poor behaviour rather than calming things, where no problem existed, and quite unable to control the 'wild' ones. It was to the credit of the vast majority of children that nothing serious occurred.

On 26 November a meeting with the Director was held at County Hall and attended by all head teachers, LEA advisers and area officers in order to introduce a new scheme designed to take supervision away from teachers and to place it in the hands of supervisory assistants under the direction of the head teacher.

At Eastbourne we decided to continue with our current arrangement, with no staff assistance except for two deputies, and to appoint assistants carefully during the coming weeks – attempting to find the right kind of person, one who would be able to control the pupils.

I had no great faith in the scheme: many teachers find great difficulty when trying to control large numbers of pupils in the relatively free out-of-classroom situation! Non-teachers may well find the task impossible. But we did try to make it work!

Open school

When 'open school' was declared the pupils were allowed to be in the building during break times. During spells of rain, significant cold, snow and fog for example, heads of house, in consultation with the head teacher or deputy, decided the school was open, when pupils may go to their open school room.

The open school room was usually the tutor-group room but certain rooms, for example the laboratories and workshops, could not, for reasons of safety, be used for this purpose and groups displaced from them were allocated other rooms by the head of house. Each room had a notice clearly displayed to show which pupils should be in it during open school.

The prefect system

The concept and something of the philosophy of the prefect system as viewed by the staff are included here, which also demonstrates the confusion of ideals arising out of the one-school-for-all policy.

The idea of a prefect system existing in a comprehensive school was foreign to the understanding of some of its strongest supporters. It is, however, proper that young people should take some part in the running of their school and a significant part of this responsibility lies in the supervision of the school at break times.

After much discussion with the heads of house and staff it was decided that such a system should be organised in Eastbourne. Initial trials highlighted a number of problems, such as difficulties arising from different houses following different routines and from the question of the selection (or no selection) of pupils to take office. More discussion followed, the following matters being questioned.

All senior pupils should be given the opportunity to accept and experience responsibility, and the fact that they do not all respond in a very positive way should not mean that they are deprived of the opportunity.

The establishing of groups which may be seen as forming an elite is not in keeping with the philosophy of the comprehensive school.

The rejection of some pupils, particularly in the fifth year, could produce the nucleus around which difficult or disaffected pupils could come together to produce a problem group.

Conversely the need for some form of selection was considered necessary as prefects have to be seen as supporters of the standards expected of all pupils, particularly the younger ones. Their behaviour and dress should be in keeping with these standards. Senior pupils who are badly behaved and poorly dressed could not be placed in a position of authority over others. Failure to take this matter into account could encourage the notion that 'if they can get away with it, so can I' and 'why should my standards be any better than theirs?' It was also considered that a situation could be reached in which a tough couldn't-care-less attitude is adopted by the majority in order not to be seen by one's peers as an odd one out and become the focus of bullying.

Consequently, if selection is necessary, how should it be achieved? Should all fifth-year pupils initially become prefects and subsequently individuals be removed for unreliability, lack of co-operation, scruffy turnout and so on? It was argued that on reaching the fourth year, pupils have already proved whether or not they are able and willing to uphold the expected standards, and during their fourth year still have the opportunity to achieve these standards before the suitability of their becoming prefects is considered. It was concluded they would have to be judged on how they presented themselves at the time of selection.

If a few are rejected they will be a minority and may adopt the characteristics of the disaffected. If half the year group is selected, and therefore half rejected, perhaps the notions of elitism and rejection will be minimised. It was, at the time, emphasised that the chosen must not be regarded as an elite group and it was said that this would be achieved through the method of selection and how they were treated when appointed. Certain qualities would be looked for in the behaviour of the prefects. The ability to get one's peers to do what is required in a firm but pleasant way was one; another the ability to get along well with one's peers – prefects should be good mixers, not, presumably, isolated from the majority. Teachers' pets (it was said, if we have any) should not be prefects and those not selected should be considered for other responsibilities such as games captains, or couriers for the head of house.

The system eventually adopted was that each house selected twenty prefects, in general twelve boys and twelve girls, providing four teams; each team being on duty on the house duty day. The deputy head of house was given the responsibility for training, counselling and organising the house prefects and was expected to hold a formal meeting with them once each week. The members of the team registered with the deputy head of house on the duty day so that absentees could be covered and duty positions checked. Emphasis was placed on training to avoid confrontations with difficult pupils. Duty positions coincided with those of the house duty staff; in other words the prefects assisted the staff and, of course, the teachers supported the prefects. As far as possible, the same prefects and teachers worked together throughout the year.

The arrangement was later changed, resulting from differences among the routines of the four houses and looseness in organisation, to one where the pupils were school (not house) prefects under the supervision of the senior master or deputy head. There was still a strong feeling of the need to avoid the development of what some saw as an elite group.

Indeed some senior pupils displayed a minor dissatisfaction with the system when on 19 October 1979 a group of fifth years decided to strike regarding the subject of prefects' privileges (given to them as some small reward for carrying out their duties). The decision to leave them in the rain by the youth centre for the afternoon may seem unjust but an immediate investigation proved that the 'strike' was instigated and followed by the least reasonable of pupils. Some of the more conscientious pupils did go out at break time to see what was going on but returned to lessons after judging the demonstration to be inappropriate.

Perhaps the strikers had learnt something from their teachers: indeed how can senior pupils be expected to turn out for duty when some teachers are seen as reluctant to do so?

Education in the senior years of the school

It is frequently said that older pupils become disaffected with school because the curriculum they are offered is inappropriate. An in-school survey suggested that this could have applied to about one fifth of those in the upper school at Eastbourne in the first half of the 1970s, but it is worthwhile pointing out that it did not seem to apply to the other four fifths.

Senior school courses and choices offered at Eastbourne in the early 1970s

The mixed-ability tutor groups in which the younger pupils were taught during the first three years were broken up in the senior school as courses and choices were developed to cater for their wide range of interests and abilities.

In February of each year a careers convention for those in the third year of secondary education was held during one school day when representatives from various forms of employment and further education came into school to give a general talk on their particular expertise to groups of between twenty and thirty youngsters. The groups were rotated through the selection of speakers so that all had the opportunity of hearing about each of the different areas. A teacher accompanied each group, questions were invited and discussion between tutor groups and their tutors was expected to continue during tutor-group periods.

During the evening of the same day parents, with their children, were invited to come into halls 1 and 2 to meet, face to face, representatives from industry, commerce and further education, to ask questions and discuss the requirements of the various employment and further-education opportunities.

Some weeks later, after the issue of the mid-year school report, a parents' evening was held for those with pupils in the third year to come in and talk with subject teachers, tutors and heads of house, to seek advice on their child's abilities and attainments with a view to making choices of subjects to be taken in the following year. Pupils were also expected to discuss their potential choices with their subject teachers.

Following these consultations an option form, with explanatory notes, was issued to the parents of each child for their completion and return. Some restrictions were built into the choices in order to avoid the complete loss of an all-round balanced education, as some, given the freedom to do so, would take only practical subjects, or those they saw as easy, completely avoiding the need for academic learning. This is a particularly difficult situation in the non-selective school as some children have high academic ability and should follow this route while others need a more practical approach to their learning, but the offering of choice may enable individuals to take inappropriate subjects, even after all of the consultations and guidance which have taken place.

The objective was to place each child on an individual course best suited to its potential and attainments. While mixed-ability groups were still timetabled there was provision for setting to take place in the last year in order to provide appropriate preparation for those taking 'O' level examinations, and to separate those who encourage each other into bad behaviour. Using sets or setting involves the rearrangement of pupils within a group of classes according to their abilities and attainments in a specific subject.

Up to 1973 both the fourth and fifth years took English, mathematics, careers and activities, physical education and games, religious education and five subjects chosen from the options scheme. It was decided this format placed too great an emphasis on non-examination subjects, and the choice of only five other subjects narrowed the educational provision, in particular for the most able. From September 1973 it was made possible for six optional subjects to be chosen. This increased the possible number of examination subjects, increasing the qualification opportunities for all, particularly for the brightest pupils, and increasing the school's overall examination results: this already being an element of a school's publically perceived success – like it or not. There were no official league tables published at the time, but examination results were made known and inevitably compared with other schools. Poor examination results could quite easily result in some parents diverting their children to another school where the prospects looked better.

Notes for the guidance of parents helping their children choose their fourth-year courses for the year 1976–77 included the four groups of subjects below with the advice that a soundly based course of general education should include one subject from each group.

Foreign languages: French, German, Latin, French studies

Sciences: physics, chemistry, biology, general science, human biology, rural science

Humanities: geography, history, humanities, religious education, music

Practical subjects: woodwork, metalwork, technical drawing, housecraft, needlework, art/craft, building, motor engineering, physical education, surveying

Each of the subjects could be studied to CSE level and most were also available to 'O' level. The additional point made was that it was expected that all pupils would study the subjects of their choice with a view to taking public examinations but the final choice of entries was not made until the fifth year.

Option Choices offered in 1975–76 – notes for guidance accompanying the form:

Commerce Subjects

Clearly, if commerce subjects are taken, it is very easy to fill up a child's timetable without paying attention to the need to continue a sound basic education. Therefore care must be taken:

1. Not to take too many commerce subjects.
2. To choose commerce subjects which sensibly go together e.g. Commerce and typewriting (consult the Commerce Department).

NB Due to the shortage of accommodation typewriting cannot be taken on its own as a practical subject.

Practical Subjects

It is similarly very easy to overload a timetable with practical subjects. For those aiming at entry into the Sixth Form College, in order to follow a course involving 'A' level subjects with possible later entry into University or College of Education, one is adequate, and more than one could seriously limit the choice of academic subjects.

Those pupils wishing to follow a course with a practical bias should consider the combination of subjects chosen – particularly in the technical studies department, where woodwork and metalwork *and* technical drawing could easily fill a large part of the week. A sensible combination would be metalwork and technical drawing or woodwork and technical drawing.

The surveying course consists of land surveying and levelling leading to CSE or 'O' level qualifications. Pupils choosing this subject should have a good or average attainment in mathematics and drawing.

Foreign Languages

In general, no more than two foreign languages should be taken as the inclusion of a third could result in specialisation at too early an age.

French Studies is a course which is designed to give the child a working background to the language and culture.

Pupils working towards an academic Sixth Form Course should take French and/or German.

Sciences

Three sciences also lead to specialisation and the exclusion of other important areas of study.

Pupils taking either physics or chemistry require a reasonably good standard of mathematics. If in doubt about the level of attainment reached by your child, please consult the science and mathematics department.

General Science is the subject best suited to non-specialists and cannot be taken with other science subjects in the GCE examination.

Both Biology and Human Biology cannot be taken.

Both Biology and Rural Science should not be taken.

The struggle to cater for a wide range of interest and attainment

The notes accompanying the option form illustrate the intention of the school to cater for all ranges of ability and harness the interests of the pupils; and to do this while encouraging each to choose the course most appropriate to their abilities and aspirations.

There was also an attempt to provide additional motivation for those least happy with having to remain in school by the introduction of additional subjects having a less academic but vocational bias. This was achieved by the introduction of Link Courses, where pupils completed a part of their senior school learning at Darlington Technical College. There was however some debate and indeed controversy regarding which pupils should be allowed to attend a Link Course. From the school's point of view, a major aspect of the scheme was to cater for the youngster who learnt best through practical experience in a more adult environment: in many cases the young person who had, until the raising of the compulsory school-leaving age, been happy to leave and take up employment. Among these were those with poor attendance records and those displaying behaviour difficulties.

Those with records of poor attendance were to be given the chance of learning in a different setting from school, but the question always in mind was: would they attend the college? No two difficult pupils were intentionally placed in the same college class, and those displaying significant misbehaviour while attending were returned to and retained in school. Those with the most serious behavioural problems were not sent out of school but kept at Eastbourne where they could be more closely supervised and not be on the loose going to and from the college at various times. Nevertheless there was always the perception on the part of some college staff that the school sent them the pupils they did not want.

A more acceptable student was the one already taking a school-based course, including a variety of technical subjects, who would very likely continue in education at the college after reaching the age of sixteen. But *they* did not need the extra incentives to encourage them in their learning.

> Link Courses taking place at the College of Technology [previously known as Darlington Technical College] 1973–74:
>
> Fifth year engineering workshops: Monday 9.15 to 11.45 – 40 pupils
>
> Motor vehicle course: Thursday 1.30 to 4.00 – 34 pupils; Friday 9.15 to 11.45 – 15 pupils
>
> Building construction: Friday 9.15 to 11.45 – 10 pupils
>
> Fourth year engineering workshops: Thu 9.15 to 11.45 – 20 pupils
>
> Motor vehicle course: Tuesday 1.30 to 4.00 – 34 pupils; Friday 9.15 to 11.45 – 15 pupils
>
> Building construction: Thursday 1.30 to 4.00 – 15 pupils

Throughout the 1970s and early 80s, Eastbourne had four workshops and a project area as well as a technical drawing room: all of these were fully used in an attempt to provide courses with a perceived vocational element – necessary in any school in order to cater for the more practical-minded young person, but absolutely essential where the intake included more than the average number of such learners.

The school did not at this time have a workshop technician who would have been available to prepare wood and metal materials and carry out maintenance on tools and machines.

The careers and activities programme

A further aspect of the work in the senior part of the school, where, in particular with the raising of the school-leaving age, the pupils were now young adults, was the careers and activities part of the timetable. This took place during one afternoon each week.

The careers programme included talks on a range of employment areas, visits to a selection of business establishments and education for life classes. The young people were continuously provided with information relating to career and further-education prospects and requirements during their final two years of compulsory schooling.

In activities, pupils could choose one of a great variety of physical activities – for example, archery, swimming, walking, orienteering, skating and table tennis – or community service.

An afternoon free from the traditional classroom discipline was intended to help make school life more attractive to the majority and more tolerable to the minority who would rather be elsewhere. The community service project was designed to give young people the opportunity to become involved in community projects such as the renovation of old railway stations or school furniture: the idea of giving a service to others was encouraged.

Conversely, the ability to choose almost any type of physical activity, or no activity at all, was based on the notion that young people should not be forced into taking part in the traditional sporting disciplines, but instead develop an interest in something they could pursue in their increasing leisure time after leaving school. This was fine up to a point but possibly overlooked the fact that to get real satisfaction out of anything, you need to apply a disciplined effort. There is a strong case for positive learning and training to be included in the scheme.

The religious education aspect of the programme followed the trend displayed in the nationally growing decline in adherence to the teachings of the Christian Church and allied worship.

The community service project
A significant part of the activities programme was the school's community service project, giving the young people a realistic introduction to caring for others in the community and bringing the positive aspects of school and young people to the notice of the people in the neighbourhood.

The scheme operated in each of the two senior year groups, then referred to as the fourth and fifth years, participants being volunteers and of all abilities and attainments. Mrs P. Knight, the teacher in charge of the project, reported that although all were expected to keep a log book of their work, people should not expect to see first-class, extremely well-written reports from all of them – the project should be judged by seeing what the youngsters were actually doing on the job.

Those taking part did so for periods of six months at a time, one group on for the first half-year, another for the second. Some thirty to forty went out into the neighbourhood to work with the elderly and disabled, carefully placed and supervised by two members of staff. The supervision was necessarily from a distance and on a random drop-in basis, the young people therefore being left on their own with the people they visited, having to behave properly, take full responsibility for their actions and even to show initiative. They knew, of course, that the teachers would ask for a report on their visit from the clients – and it was encouraging to know that hundreds of letters were received by the school praising the pleasant, cheerful and helpful way the youngsters behaved.

The jobs they did were not what you might think young people automatically rushed to complete: gardening, washing windows, shopping and housework, for example. It was even reported that some collected the pensions for those too unwell or disabled to get out, showing a remarkable degree of trust placed on the shoulders of the young people. Of course, such relationships developed over time; the remarkable fact is that they did so, lasting beyond school hours. One group of boys returned during their holidays to carry out garden tidying. Two boys built up a friendship with the elderly person they visited, taking her a cream cake, and even baking a few cakes for her themselves on one occasion.

Others went in pairs to work in schools, old folks' homes and the Memorial Hospital. Two ran the WRVS buffet in the casualty department, serving tea and snacks; three girls went to The Lawns, the then new Eastbourne old people's home, ironing, preparing food, and even assisting with the bathing of patients. Two assisted the staff at the Hundens Nursery School, two attended Dodmire infants, where they did simple art work and took small groups for story time. Three fifth-year girls attended the Hundens Day Hospital where they helped patients recovering from illness to regain their confidence. Two organised the WRVS trolley service at the Gladstone Street Old People's Home, setting things up, visiting the various rooms to serve sweets, lemonade and biscuits. Many of these tasks required the exercise of patience and tact.

Another aspect of the project's contact with the elderly was their invitation to the dress rehearsal of the school pantomime at Christmas. Some 100 people – some in wheelchairs, some brought by ambulance, others coming in buses – were given a free show, with refreshments provided. A similar event was the special performance of the school's summer concert.

The benefits of the scheme to the young participants, to the elderly and disabled, to the community and to the ethos of the school were remarkable, the project so valuable, yet, today, we may wonder whether it would be possible to run such a programme due to health and safety requirements, costly insurance and a climate of blaming others when accidents happen.

Examinations

As both 'O' level and CSE continued as two separate but overlapping examinations – with 'O' level seen as more demanding than CSE; generating problems associated with different subjects, syllabuses, and examination timetables – the school endeavoured to guide pupils towards the courses and qualifications best suited to their individual abilities and interests. Those considered borderline candidates, on a good day capable of an 'O' level pass but more confident of gaining a grade 1 CSE, were often entered for both examinations.

The results during the years 1973–82 demonstrate the degree of examination success achieved by the school, one of the factors which has become significant in the present-day assessment of a school's overall standard when measured against government-defined criteria.

The significance of choosing five subjects at 'O' level or grade 1 CSE as a base line is that it relates to the five-subject pass criteria of the pre 'O' level grammar school examination when candidates had to pass five subjects, including mathematics, a science, a foreign language and two others, in order to gain a certificate. Fail in any one of those and no qualification was awarded.

Things have since changed a great deal, and the challenge of earning five passes during the years 1973–1982 was clearly less demanding than in the older examination: there was less restriction on the subjects which could be taken to make up the group of five.

A first conclusion when looking at the success (or otherwise) of Eastbourne in the search for good examination results is that it certainly did not have a large number of pupils, somewhere between thirteen and thirty-nine each year, reaching the approximate old grammar school standard; but, without some objective comparison with national figures, it cannot be decided whether or not this is a particularly good or bad result. It would be the introduction by government of tables comparing the results of all schools that would attempt to answer the question.

Looking at Eastbourne as it was, in the 1970s and 80s, a variable worthy of note is the staying-on rate of the pupils when they could still leave full-time education before the time for taking the CSE and 'O' level examinations. The number leaving at Easter between 1973 and 1982 varied between ten and thirty-nine, with a general trend of fewer leaving in later years than previously, but a sizeable proportion in fact chose not to take part in the school-leaving examination system, saying something about the ambitions of a good proportion of the youngsters. Perhaps they were able but did not want to take examinations or perhaps their school attainments suggested they could not reach the required standards to make any attempt worthwhile.

If, for the sake of discussion, it is said that not enough pupils were reaching the defined standard, the obvious subsequent question is, why not? So what are the variables which determine success?

One, easily grasped at, is that the teaching was not good enough: not good enough over almost ten years? Strangely, the pass rates change. In 1973, when the pass rate was 8.3 per cent, the year group concerned was the second of the comprehensive intakes, that is, supposedly comprised of the full range of ability. In 1979, the most successful year, it was 12.3 per cent; and at its worst in 1974, 5.2 per cent, the year group being the third intake of the comprehensive school. These variations do not look as though they are the result of changes in teaching. They are more likely due to the nature of the intake, that is, the number of more able children in the year group. As, during the academic year 1975–76, there was also a strong feeling expressed by the staff that the academic standards were falling, that each new intake was worse than the last, something had to be done to make an objective assessment of the situation.

The programme of standardised testing

In order to assess the academic make-up of the pupil intake to any school it is necessary to find a means of comparing it with national standards, and this requires the use of tests which have been given to large numbers of children in each age group coming from a large number of schools. When the scores are examined, they range from a few scoring very high or very low marks with the vast majority falling in the middle. When the tests are given to a specific group in any other school the score obtained by each child can be compared with this distribution, and be shown to fall in the high, low or middle groups: simply put, the child can then be said to score above or below average, or average.

The school decided to use the Cognitive Abilities Test published by Thomas Nelson Ltd., a group of three tests thought to measure three areas of ability which had been shown to play a significant part in an individual's thinking, reasoning or problem solving, the abilities found to correlate with success in learning in the school situation.

Three areas of ability, verbal, quantitative, and non-verbal, were measured by each of three tests. The verbal test is language based and correlates with the ability to reason using words. The quantitative test uses numbers instead of words and scores have been shown to correlate with attainment in mathematics and sciences. The non-verbal test enables the child to use shapes and patterns instead of either words or numbers, taking out the element of learning already achieved by the pupil and consequently thought to avoid some aspects of the child's previous experiences, those related to social background, and thus measuring a basic ability.

The actual marks obtained were translated into grades 1 to 9, 1 being low and 9 high. The idealised number of pupils which would be in each grade if the school had a perfect distribution of pupils through the ability range (as defined by the normal curve of distribution) is given and this is compared with the actual figures obtained from the test results from pupils in six sample year groups.

The six year groups were tested during the period 1978 to 1980, four when the pupils were in their first year at the school, one when in their second year and one in their third year. The results were analysed in 1980, by which time the eldest had become fifth-year pupils and the younger groups correspondingly moved into older age groups. The observations therefore refer to the groups as they were in 1980.

The Chi-square test, a statistical method used to demonstrate the significance of actual scores, was applied to the distributions to determine the level of the significance of the difference between the actual and ideal distributions.

It was accepted that low scores on any or all of the tests were only those attained on one occasion and should not be taken as unalterable, assuming that improvement is possible if further investigation can identify a child's specific learning difficulties and strategies be found to combat its problems. Where a child has low scores on each of the tests, it is likely that remedial teaching will be most difficult and will need to be concerned with very basic concepts associated with learning in early childhood – such things as the differences and similarities between shapes, the understanding of spatial relationships and so on. For instance, a child with low scores on all tests should be more thoroughly tested for signs of impaired perception.

Where a child achieves high scores on both the non-verbal and quantitative tests but poor results in the verbal section, an intensive remedial course in English, or language, could be expected to bring improvement.

Questions asked

How does the distribution of pupils' scores for each of the three tests and each year group compare with the normal or expected distribution? Are they worse than, the same as or better than expected, when compared with a national sample?

Are the distributions different on each of the three tests? If so, how are they different? What is the meaning of the differences?

The non-verbal reasoning results, free from language and number, were taken as an indication of the ability to think and reason, to work things out, as it were, in a medium largely free from school- and cultural-taught English and mathematics. These scores may be taken as some kind of indicator of the level of a relatively raw ability. In old-fashioned terms the non-verbal reasoning test would have been used to obtain a non-verbal intelligence quotient (IQ), a culture-free IQ. The quantitative reasoning test is clearly based upon mathematical ideas and should correlate with mathematical attainment. The results give some indication of the year groups' ability in mathematical work compared with a national sample. Similarly, the verbal reasoning test is loaded with language and good test results require a high level of ability in the use of the English language.

How do the scores compare in the six different year groups. Are the intake groups becoming worse? Is the oldest the most able, the second rather worse, the next worse still and the youngest worst of all?

Are there specific problems indicated by the test results? Is the school overloaded with very poor-ability children? Is there a shortage of the most able pupils? Is there a problem of backwardness in mathematics or English?

Do the boys perform significantly differently from the girls?

Observations on the scores of the oldest three years tested
The scores on the non-verbal test show that the two fifth-year groups are not significantly different from a normal distribution. In other words, on a test which excluded cultural and taught mathematical and language material, the distribution of pupils by ability followed an idealised normal pattern.

On the other hand the fourth year did show a significant difference and an inspection of the individual scores show that this is due to seventeen pupils more than expected obtaining the above-average grade 7 and three more than expected obtaining the very good grade 8. Some twelve pupils less than expected scored the average grade 5.

In conclusion, in the fifth years, the distribution of natural reasoning ability coincided with the normal idealised pattern. There is no evidence to suggest this ability is worse in the subsequent year groups. In the fourth-year group there is evidence to suggest that the school obtained more children than expected having good natural (possibly relatively untrained) ability.

The scores from the quantitative reasoning test do show significant differences from the normal distribution pattern and this is due to a considerably higher number of children than expected scoring high grades 7 and 9. Conversely, the scores of few children fell into the other grades, although there were subtle differences from year to year. The oldest of the fifth years had more children than expected in the very low grade 2 and low average grade 4. The other fifth year has far more than expected in the average grade five, while a lower number of pupils appear in grades 4 and 6.

Each intake therefore appeared to have more than the expected number of brighter children in quantitative reasoning and there is no evidence to show a decline in standards in subsequent intakes.

The scores from the verbal reasoning test show differences but these are only highly significant in the results of the younger of the two fifth-year groups. The differences in each case were found to be due to the number of pupils more than expected obtaining scores in the low average category 4, below average grade 3 and low category 2. This finding pointed to a problem: the number of children doing poorly on a verbal-type test.

The test scores demonstrate improvement rather than decline across the three most senior groups in the school at the time, but all three year groups demonstrate a problem associated with the numbers of children obtaining poor results in verbal reasoning and it is to be expected that this disadvantage would be reflected in all academic subjects.

Observations on the scores of the youngest three years tested

The group scores in non-verbal reasoning showed that the third year did not differ significantly from the norm while the other two years did. The examination of the figures for the second year showed the difference to be due largely to more pupils than expected obtaining the grade 7 or top grade 9. Conversely there were fewer scoring average grades 4 and 5. It is however significant that the expected number of pupils obtained the lowest grades 1, 2, and 3.

In the first year the differences were caused by the variation in top and average scores. Again there was the expected number of pupils gaining the lowest grades. There were more than expected gaining the top grade but fewer with the second grade 8. There were fewer than expected scoring the average grade 5 but twenty-one more than expected in category 4.

It is clear that the differing numbers of pupils falling into the different categories in the different years show subtle changes in the distribution across the ability range. The third-year scores fitted the normal distribution. The extra pupils in the second year scoring high grades with fewer in the average band suggest that the intake will prove to be a good one because it contains more able children. There was a similar distribution in the second-year group but the overall number of bright pupils was not greater than expected compared with a normal distribution. There were, however, many more pupils than expected scoring low average scores while the lowest categories, grades 1, 2 and 3, have the expected number of pupils according to a normal or average distribution. The first year was certainly not as good as the second year (in terms of the number of able pupils) and appears worse than the third year (due to the number of pupils in the low average group).

Scores in the quantitative reasoning test show significant differences from the normal distribution: the differences explained in terms of there being more children than expected gaining the highest grades. In general, the numbers in the lowest grade are at the expected levels. In quantitative reasoning, therefore, all three years have more pupils scoring the high grades than expected while the numbers in the low grades follow the normal pattern.

The scores on the verbal reasoning test follow the normal distribution in the third year, a difference of low significance in the second year, but a highly significant difference in the first year. Even in the third year the figures show more pupils scoring lower grades than expected: in particular, there are a large number of pupils in this year group with very low scores in verbal reasoning. In the second year there were few in the lowest category but more than expected with grades 2 and 3. Again, more pupils score the low average grade 4 than expected. In the first year twenty-two more pupils than would be expected score low average grade 4 and there are five more pupils than expected obtaining grade 3.

The pattern observed throughout the six years suggests that the school has the expected number of low-ability children but far more than expected in the low average and below average groups.

There was a noticeable problem in all years due to the significant number of pupils scoring low grades in verbal reasoning, the ability having greatest influence on academic learning.

The third year has the problem plus a larger than expected number of pupils in the low grade. The second year appears to be an able group but still has a more than expected number of pupils with low average or below average ability. There is an expected number of pupils in the higher categories. The first year has the largest number in the low average categories and the influence of this large group is enhanced by the lack of pupils scoring the highest grades: there were seventeen less than expected in categories 7 and 8.

Retardation in verbal reasoning

Following the identification of the numbers of pupils scoring lower than expected scores in verbal reasoning a closer examination of individual scores was made.

For the purpose of this investigation, 'retardation' is defined as 'the difference between the non-verbal reasoning and verbal reasoning scores' for each child. A difference of only one point was taken to be of little significance and therefore disregarded.

Approximately 20 per cent of the pupils in each year were shown to have a retardation of two or more points on the nine-point scale.

Taking this difference between verbal and non-verbal reasoning as important, because of the link between verbal reasoning and academic learning, approximately one in five of the pupils at the Eastbourne school displayed this characteristic, which would suggest learning via the traditional academic-style classroom teaching, for them, would present a learning difficulty.

One in five pupils presents this learning difficulty: six pupils in a mixed-ability group of thirty.

In all of the year groups, except for the fifth year in 1979–80 where the reverse was the case, a large proportion of those with this learning difficulty were boys.

The fifth year for 1979–80 had most pupils out of the six years tested showing this problem, possibly supporting the staff view that this particular intake was a relatively poor year. Yet the absolute number of pupils displaying the problem, fifty, is only between three and four above the average for the six years. Once again this is the only year in which the problem is not greater among the boys than the girls.

When the public examination results for the year 1978–79 and 79–80 are compared, in the first group thirty-nine gained 5 or more passes at the 'O' level CSE 1 grade, while in the second there were only twenty-two, a significant difference and certainly supporting the teachers' view that in the upper school there was evidence of the decline in the overall academic ability of the intake.

Another measure which was considered in the search for the relative 'goodness' of an intake was the ratio of high-ability to low-ability pupils. High-ability pupils were defined as those scoring 7 or higher grades and low-ability pupils those scoring 3 or lower on each of the three tests. A child scoring two 7s and one 6, for instance, or at the other end of the scale, two 2s and a 4 did not satisfy the definitions of high or low ability in this study and were not included in the figures given. The study listed boys and girls separately and gave the number of pupils as a percentage of the intake. The actual number of pupils in each of the year groups is used to produce the ratio of high to low ability. Clearly, the higher the figure obtained, the more high- and fewer low-ability pupils there are in the group.

There is little significant evidence to conclude that there are more low-ability boys than girls or vice versa. Although there are differences from year to year between the number of boys and girls scoring high grades, sometimes there are more girls and other times more boys.

Response to lack of employment available to 16-year-old school leavers

Arising from the unemployment situation and the lack of jobs for 16-year-old school leavers, the government, through the Manpower Services Commission (MSC), set up a two-year Youth Training Scheme for Easter school leavers. An objective was to ensure that young people would be trained so that they would enter the labour market with qualifications appropriate to employment needs.

The question arising is that of how 'appropriateness' can be defined when it is extremely difficult to determine accurately the true present needs of industry and commerce and even more difficult to look into the future.

Other developments which are supposed to help with this 'appropriate training' are the expansion of adult training; a significant increase in the Training Vocational Educational Initiative in secondary schools; a review of vocational qualifications (with the setting up of a national council to oversee, co-ordinate etc.); a review of the funding of training; improvement of labour-market intelligence; further co-operation with LEAs in the planning of non-advanced vocational training and an extension of the MSC responsibilities in the University Grants Committee.

Clearly more vocation-based training was established through the MSC and over the heads of education authorities and the Department of Education and Science. The approach was certainly one of by-passing traditional educational channels. The education budget was being decreased while MSC funds increased, with the result that the MSC could control what would or would not happen.

Certainly in Eastbourne, with the pupil intake only containing a small number (a proportion of about 7 per cent) of academic pupils, alternative programmes and teaching strategies were required in order to provide more appropriate learning designed to motivate and hold the interest of young people who learn best through real-life experience. But precisely what is appropriate education is still unknown. In the pupils' eyes, appropriate education will be that which gives them access to purposeful, rewarding occupations in the adult world.

Again, employment cannot adequately be provided by inventing jobs which do not have real purpose. Such occupations do not satisfy man's need to occupy a useful place in life – to be needed – to feel wanted. In addition our industry must compete with that elsewhere which is serviced by abundant cheap labour. The products of cheap labour are inexpensive compared with our own where labour demands a reasonable standard of living. Our industry therefore prices itself out of the world markets or reduces labour costs by cutting down on the use of manpower and using techno-robotics to do the work. Both increase unemployment and our response has been to give young people more education – of sorts.

A revolutionary rethinking of concepts of employment, payment of salary/wage, leisure, voluntary work and purposeful occupation is essential before we can ascertain appropriate education and training objectives.

In the 1980s some 22 per cent of young people in the north-east entered further education, compared with some 44 per cent in London.

The Youth Training Scheme (YTS)

On Monday 18 April 1983 the head teacher attended a day conference on the Youth Training Scheme: Implications for Schools and Further Education.

The first lecture was a political tub-thumping talk from some lady, neither a Mrs nor a Miss but a Ms (pronounced something like Mus), on the evil ways of the government at the time in office. The second lecture was a talk from an officer of the Cleveland LEA on their particular youth schemes – so significant that I had already lost the substance of what was said by the end of the day. The third lecture, given by a government minister, proved to be a typical report delivered in ministerial language of the government's wonderful plans, with a secretary noting word-perfect everything the minister said.

After a good and very civilised lunch, away from the hordes associated with midday in schools, a mutual moans session registered one fact: all four schemes submitted to the MSC, in conjunction with their new Technical Education Initiative from the north-east, had been rejected as apparently not good enough!

Initiatives at the time resulted in the setting up of schemes where money was made available by government through the MSC who, in turn, determined the satisfactory nature or otherwise of LEA plans before any finance was awarded.

This government strategy of advancing its preferred projects by only offering financial support to those of which it approved has become a growing element in the state control of education by all governments from the late 1980s onwards.

Finance of MSC-approved schemes also provided cover for staff absent on courses, giving further control over what should and should not constitute in-service training for teachers.

A scheme for Eastbourne pupils was eventually approved, young people taking part in work experience and training.

Some evidence relating to the employment and further education of Eastbourne pupils is given in the Youth Employment Officer's summaries for 1974 and 1975:

> Of 54 boys able to leave at Easter 1974 seven were reported as intending to enter the Sixth Form College and presumably remained in school to take examinations. Of the 82 summer leavers another seven went on to attend the Sixth Form but a further five chose to go to the Darlington College of Technology, perhaps seeing the College as a more adult alternative to what they may have perceived as a school situation. In any case, only 19 out of a year group of 136 chose to continue in education. A total of 77 were taken on by local employers as apprentices or trainees. Their occupations were in the building trade (joinery, plumbing, electrical work, plastering, brick laying, and painting and decorating); the motor industry (sales, vehicle maintenance and repairs); food industries (butchering, baking, and cooking); and engineering (described as heating and servicing engineers). A few were employed in junior occupations such as bank clerk, warehouse assistant, porter, farm labourer, storekeeper and rather vaguely as an 'assistant'. Seven joined the army as junior soldiers.
>
> Of the forty-seven girls eligible to leave school at Easter, seven intended to go on to the Sixth Form College and

another two to the College of Technology. Of sixty-nine summer leavers, eight went to the Sixth Form and ten to the College of Technology. One took a course at a private secretarial college. Rather more girls than boys, 28, therefore entered further education.

A significant destination for the girls was the two clothing/textile manufacturers in the Town (Paton and Baldwins and Alexander Ltd) who employed 21 of the Eastbourne leavers for 1974.

Another area of employment for the girls was as shop assistants, some twenty-two being employed locally. Office work attracted sixteen girls, nursing (including allied office work and working in children's nurseries) only four, and three became apprentice hairdressers (while some may have entered this profession via a Technical College course).

Among the minority occupations were positions in other factories, those described as 'supernumeraries' employed by Darlington Corporation, a cleaner, one employed 'washing up', and one as a packer on a poultry farm.

In 1975 eight boys intended to enter the Sixth Form College but only two showed interest in the College of Technology. Twenty-three girls went to the sixth form and one to the College of Technology.

Forty boys obtained apprenticeships in a variety of occupations such as joinery, baking, butchery, bricklaying, spray painting, electrical work, sheet metal work, plumbing and heat engineering. Four became shop assistants, four worked in warehouses, one went to be a gardener, and seven were described as labourers.

A disturbing feature was that eight were described as 'registered as unemployed'. They could not find work and presumably could see no place for themselves in further education: they were apparently starting a new life without a positive purposeful and wage-earning occupation.

Alexander's took on twelve girls this year but there is no indication that Paton and Baldwins employed any. Eighteen girls found employment in office work, eleven became shop assistants, five obtained apprenticeships as hairdressers.

Fifteen girls were registered as unemployed.

The Comprehensive School August 1986–2007
A Time of Change and Uncertainty

During the 14 years 1986–2000, there were three head teachers in overall charge of the school: from August 1986 till March 1995, Mr R. Dingle; from April till July 1995, Mr P. Bellairs, acting head teacher; and from September 1995 to 2000, Mr R. Appleton. Mr Dingle served for rather more than eight years, long enough to become established and maintaining the period of stability at the school. Subsequently Mr Appleton served for about five years. And, during the whole of this period Mr Bellairs, for the most part, held the post of senior deputy, serving from before Mr Dingle's appointment and until after Mr Appleton's departure. The senior team appears to have been secure.

In addition other senior posts were occupied by long-serving members of staff; for instance, on the academic side, Mr C. French, head of science, and Mr Minikin, senior teacher in the pastoral area.

The size of the school and consequently the teaching force as a whole declined: figures given for 1992–94 illustrate the size of the change. In September 1992 the school roll was 754 and the new intake 149; in September 1993 the roll was 737 and the new intake 134; in 1994, 680 and 103 respectively.

The original and usual size of the school had been an eight-form entry; that is each year group having eight classes of thirty pupils each. Each year group would have a nominal 240 pupils. Five year groups would total 1,200. Consequently, by the 1990s, the school had declined to almost half its original size.

Such changes raise several questions. Is the smaller number of pupils, in terms of behaviour, easier to manage? This must be considered in terms of the nature of the intake: the proportion of bright children, the number of those with learning difficulties, and possibly more significant, the proportion of pupils with behaviour difficulties.

If the staff size decreases by 50 per cent, does this mean that, with specialist class teaching, the number of subjects offered in the curriculum has to decrease? Do more teachers have to teach more than one subject? Is the specialist teacher therefore less of a requirement, being replaced by teachers of general subjects? If so, and teachers in the secondary schools prefer to specialise, does this create a staffing problem?

If the building is designed for 1,200 pupils, and the school population falls to about 600, there will be unused space. The solution in terms of general-purpose classrooms may seem fairly simple. Close half of them. But for specialist teaching there are specialist rooms. Close half of these? The rooms will be grouped in specialist areas, most noticeable in the original girls' home economics accommodation and the boy's workshops. It is therefore interesting to see how this fitting of pupils to space was managed and to ask what if any influence this had on the ethos of the school.

For the first nine years, most of the established practices of the earlier comprehensive school continued but change and uncertainty were nevertheless to become significant factors in its development. Among these were the innovations introduced by government, variously perceived by teachers as unhelpful, unnecessary, sometimes educationally unsound and taking time from their direct work with children and students.

Head teachers were apparently given greater authority over the running of their schools through the Local Management of Schools initiative, taking control of decisions previously the responsibility of the LEA. But in other ways, head teachers were losing their authority, becoming less focussed on the day-to-day education of youngsters and more concerned with managing the buildings in which the education was taking place. Having responsibility for the school buildings meant, for example, when window panes were smashed by accident or intent the head's duty was not only to find and discipline the culprit but to find a glazier, check out his credentials, check that the work is satisfactorily done and ensure that he is justly paid. Furthermore, authority did not rest with the head teacher but became that of the governing body.

In the latter four-plus years of the 1986–2000 period the management of the premises, in some ways, worked against the improvement in educational facilities for the children and young people. The fine character of the impressively designed building was modified, debased and eventually destroyed.

The demands, coming in part from the government directives concerning what, and how, things should be done, and from difficulties arising from the ever-growing problems associated with increasing numbers of pupils with special educational needs, placed a greater burden on the staff. The greater burden in turn caused frustration, giving rise to irritation and fragmentation.

Uncertainty was fostered by rumours concerning the future of the school: discussions were taking place with regard to Darlington returning to its position of being a unitary authority. The head recorded after one meeting with the leader of the council that he felt the future prospects for the school looked bleak, although in March 1995 the governors were given assurances that there were no plans to close the school. But, of course, rumour was sufficient to breed insecurity. Under such threats the head teacher would surely also be concerned about his own position and, possibly, be unsettled to the extent of seeking a post with a more stable future.

The premises

Apart from the problems associated with fitting a smaller school into a larger building, there was the obvious aging of the building itself to be considered. For instance, as reported on 22 September 1992 and 19 May 1993, there were frequent episodes of the top corridor of the main building being awash with water. The glass roof of the corridor and the abundance of small windows facing outwards were excellent for providing a bright passageway from one end of the building to the other; but the frequency with which lead flashing was removed by thieves allowed rain water to inundate the floor. The problem for the head was whether or not this hazard could be rectified before the arrival of the children: clearly, with the building closed during the weekends, and the consequent discovery of the problem at, say, 7 a.m. on Monday, there was not a great deal of time to dry the place; impossible if it was still raining heavily.

A major cause of resentment was the unreliable heating system: for instance on 27 September 1993 a heating valve broke, leaving the rooms by the staff room, at the time still located to the left of the central arch when facing the front of the building, cold and teachers took classes into the hall. There was clearly irritation on the part of the staff as the head reported that the hall was actually colder than the classrooms, and one member of staff 'spoke to the *Northern Echo*' about what was seen as a continuing and unresolved problem.

The irritability is explained further by the head's remarks of 1 October 1993 when he received a complaint from a member of staff that the classroom was too cold when the temperature was 18.3 °C. Another teacher working in one of the laboratories found the room too hot at 26.3 °C. More complaints were received from the modern languages department on 4 October when temperatures were found to be 18.4 and 18.5 °C. Clearly something was wrong and the energy budget had already been over spent by £1,500. On 2 November 1993 consultations were held at County Hall with a view to finding a solution to the problem.

At about the same time, a new medical room was opened at the school and I ask why this was necessary, the school having had a perfectly adequate medical suite from the time of the remodelling and extensions made for the comprehensive school in the 1960s.

The resource base

The staff room in the original comprehensive school, positioned on the ground floor adjacent to the central arch, became the resource base, an innovation filmed by the BBC on 1 February 1994. It was a large space converted from the merger of two classrooms in the girls' school with perimeter seating, a marking and preparation area at one end, and provision of a small kitchen area for making tea or coffee. It was intended as a central meeting place for all the staff, helping to bring together the teachers from the previously separate boys' and girls' departments. The smaller staff was provided with an alternative at the head of the stairs on the first floor in what was originally the library of the girls' school. With the arrival of new technology the old room was set out with computers, copying facilities and other aids as a staff preparation area. By May 1994 staff raised concerns about management of the base, and in June the head met with a member of staff to discuss the matter.

In February 1995 the shrinkage of the school is reflected in the discussions at the governors' meeting relating to the closure of kitchen 1. As the school had grown from its pre-war conception and the development of the school meals service, two kitchens and two dining rooms had been built at the east and west extremities of the site. By the mid 1990s only one set was required.

Security

The original Eastbourne secondary schools were built across an extensive site, enclosed at the front by the housing developments of the 1920s and 30s, in such roads as the Mead, Crossway and Fairway, but to the east, west and north the buildings looked out across largely open fields. The school playing fields extended from the walled field westwards to Hunden's Lane, a valuable resource for the promotion of physical activities. With changes in society between 1936 and 2000 this advantage became a problem: open access meant being open to trouble-making intruders.

There were the dog walkers who could see no hazard to games players from the deposits left by their much-loved and innocent animals. But this was a minor problem when compared to the costs incurred by the intrusions of thieves and vandals. A series of reports from the first half of the 1990s are a vivid description of happenings and actions taken to remedy the situation.

One of several burglaries was reported on 13 December 1992, and another on 29 June 1993, when intruders in a car came on premises, not for the first time – a matter reported to the police. Such occurrences eventually resulted in the bricking up of the central archway. A raisable barrier was fitted in the 1980s but this was clearly seen as insufficient: necessity dictated the complete closure by bricking up the arch, destroying an attractive feature of building's facade. Even the brickwork itself appeared crude and out of place.

In July 1993 the private security firm Steadfast was employed for thirteen weeks to protect the building and at the end of summer holiday at 3.35 a.m. the firm discovered and dealt with small fire in the animal house started by vandals. There was a further report, in January

1994, that the animal house was broken into and signs of drug use were seen. The matter was reported to the police.

On 24 January 1994, over the weekend, there was a report of 'more' windows being broken, an indication of a growing problem explained in the additional comment: 'windows broken on Sundays of the last three weekends.'

On 7 February 1994 there was a request from the local Neighbourhood Watch asking for the school gates to be locked. But only after the horse had bolted because in June the previous year, brass handles from the outside of doors were stolen during a weekend!

An outcome of the increasing damage done to the property both outside and during school hours was the determination of the governors to order the installation of closed-circuit television. The work was completed by October 1994 and no break-ins or broken windows were reported in the subsequent three weeks. (As an aside, it was reported that a pupil stole one of the cameras!)

So, by necessity, a once open, imposing and welcoming frontage was coming to look like some secretive, highly unwelcoming military base.

Internally the building was also having its character changed. The loss of a library to staff accommodation and the opening of the resource base was the beginning of a modification required to improve security and adapt a rambling structure to fit a smaller population.

The grounds

The extensive grounds were both an asset and a liability, the liability being the keeping safe of property open to intruders. Apart from relatively harmless debris left on the site, with the spread of drug use there was evidence of hazardous materials being left lying about.

While the annual inter-house athletics championships had been held for many years in the walled field, by the late 1980s suggestions were made that there should be a modern, properly surfaced athletics track situated on the east of the town (there already being one at Longfield School in the north-west) and that the grounds of the Eastbourne School would be a suitable location. However, it was not until April 1995 that there was formal proposal for the installation of an all-weather hockey/soccer pitch and athletics track in the area. The proposal included the requirement that the facilities should be for both school and community use.

Between the late 1980s and 2007 a significant proportion of the Eastbourne School grounds, formerly for its sole use, were lost. As the Hundens Hospital site became available for housing development, so Durham County Council sold off the area of Eastbourne's playing fields adjacent to it. The land between the new houses and the school became the new sports complex, with its athletics track and all-weather surface area, in keeping with the use of space by the community. A further area, situated between the Mead and the school, was excluded from the grounds to become public open space.

For much of its later life the greatly reduced area of the Eastbourne School property was enclosed by a ring fence installed between 1995 and 2002, giving the once open and extensive site a cramped and constricted appearance, the imposing frontage lost behind a green-painted, zigzagging structure more suited to a factory site than a school.

Following the construction of the ring fence, the purpose-built domestic science rooms and flat, purpose-built kitchen and dining hall, were outside the boundaries of the school property. A visitor being shown around the school by two pupils in 2007 was told that they did not know what those buildings were; they were no longer part of the school. A part had been taken for inclusion in the Eastbourne Sports Complex and the remainder used as a special unit for excluded pupils.

At one stage, the flat became the base for an inclusion centre, a place to which pupils excluded from normal school could be sent, attending different school hours and being isolated from other pupils. It was also a base in which parents of the excluded pupils could be interviewed. This was during Mr Appleton's headship.

This was a tragic loss: older pupils, or students as they should be called, need work experience. The old domestic science area could have been modernised and used as a major area for hotel management, cookery and other courses in the upper school. Continuing domestic courses in cooking etc. could have been developed as a mini mock-up of a hotel, giving maturing youngsters an adult-orientated commercial environment in which such curriculum studies as office and reception skills, property maintenance, cooking and restaurant experience, grounds maintenance and so on could be taught – all requiring the back-up from the academic departments teaching languages and communication, mathematics, computer skills and much else.

Why was it not done? Simply because of the lack of the necessary commitment to the provision of resources, finance and staffing.

There was in the school in 2007, occupying a room in the old boys' dining/kitchen area, an equipped commercial kitchen. It remained unused because of its isolation from a necessary commercial environment and inability to attract appropriate staff to run it.

Eastbourne Sports Complex

The long-standing sporting tradition of Eastbourne and the government scheme in which schools had to bid for money to develop innovative projects brought about the school's intention to apply for Sports College status jointly with Longfield School, a plan which could not be agreed and which was finally abandoned. It was Longfield School which was eventually to gain Sports College status, leaving Eastbourne with nothing and more confusion.

The development of the Eastbourne Sports Complex plan went as far as having appointed a director of physical education, six physical education teachers and the development of a GCSE course.

The loss of other PE and games facilities

The swimming pool went out of use in 2003, when it was said the development of a leak was too expensive to repair. There were also already thoughts of building a new school which would make the Authority reluctant to spend money on the old premises.

As well as losing the swimming pool the PE department was deprived of the use of the old gym, located behind the old girls' hall and the hall, when these areas were converted into school meals, dining and catering facilities around about 2001. This was also due to the sports complex being giving the domestic science block and adjacent dining hall and school meals kitchen. The loss of the girls' hall was a disadvantage as far as the PE department was concerned; the enclosure of both hall balconies denied the school space to bring pupils together in large groups.

The large gymnasium was the major indoor sports accommodation and its loss would, apart from anything else, limit wet-weather physical activity. Gradually, the intrusion of water damaged the facilities, finally rising up through the floor.

The break-up and lack of development of the workshops

The argument relating to the loss of the domestic science unit can also be applied to the workshops. Originally being one woodwork and one metalwork room, these were enlarged at the time of comprehensive reorganisation to include an extra woodwork and extra metalwork room joined to the original workshops by an enclosed general purpose area. The latter was part used in the comprehensive years for automobile maintenance. In a nearby classroom was the technical drawing room which could have been fitted with the necessary computer technology for drawing and design.

The change to craft design technology created a watering down of the focus on the original basic craft subjects (cookery, needlework, art, woodwork, metalwork and technical drawing) and the imposition of a mish-mash sampling of new and old with no real value being gained from any. Photography was a new minority subject.

The desire to introduce more workplace-orientated courses would be excellent but such courses need workplace environments and staff. Many different environments and many different staff, the latter being impossible to recruit due to the restrictions of pupil–teacher ratios and the need to cover only part-time timetables.

With the shrinkage of the school the workshops were reduced to their original size, old fashioned in both appearance and resources. The domestic science–cookery accommodation was by this date also housed in this area. The psychological advantage of older youngsters being able to work in a perceived more adult environment had not only failed to be developed but had in actual fact been reduced to a pre-1936 level.

The loss of the music suite

The area behind the old boys' hall, remodelled from its purpose as a gymnasium and changing rooms as a music suite with two classrooms and music practice rooms for the comprehensive school, was taken out of use. Music was transferred to the large classroom adjacent to the exit to the workshops, the comprehensive school technical drawing room. Clearly, adjacent classrooms were no longer insulated from the inevitable sounds of music practice.

Windows

At the time of its opening, the building was lit by daylight through large areas of glass; many small panes mounted together in large frames along classroom and external corridor walls. These were being vandalised from outside and sometimes from inside (the latter certainly during school hours). Inside at the rear, larger areas of similarly made small frames let in light from the playgrounds to the upper and lower corridors.

In turn, the classroom walls facing onto the corridors were also large areas of small-paned glass windows. The place had the atmosphere of bright open airiness.

This concept of openness changed to one of blocking out the external world by the boarding up in 2003 of most of the corridor windows. With an enclosing railing fence, closed-circuit television cameras and boarded-up windows the school surely took on the ambience of a prison.

To call it prison-like is perhaps rather harsh. The carpeted floor and bright colours, newly painted for use of the Church of England Academy before it moved to its new premises, were surely a brave effort to greatly improve what had become a rather neglected-looking building. Nevertheless, the exclusion of daylight presents a somewhat claustrophobic impression – but a fashion seen in more modern buildings.

The school halls, two of course from the days of separate boys' and girls' schools, plus the dining rooms, were used by the comprehensive school for house and year assemblies. With the much-reduced population and withdrawal into a smaller area, one hall remained for social and business gatherings while the other was largely used as a dining room.

The enclosed area at the back of the boys' hall was previously an open balcony, with a projection room above at the rear. The girls' hall was the same. Clearly their use for seating, converted into offices, says something about the changing priorities in education. Why were so many offices required when the school was decreasing in size? There were four offices for heads of house in the comprehensive school, with similar accommodation for the head teacher, and deputies.

It is clear that a major problem influencing the development of the school from the later 1990s onwards was the obvious running down of the Eastbourne site by the local authority. There is a threat of closure, a hint of something new being required, but nothing straightforward and clear cut, bringing years of uncertainty.

The staff

The sub-surface threat of closure cultivated insecurity among the staff; coming at a time when government initiatives were also bringing unsettling change.

Leadership

Head teachers faced with the need to reduce the size of the staff due to falling rolls, the uncertainties generated by the unclear intentions of the LEA relating to the future of the school, and the need to assimilate advances in education practice initiated by the national government were placed in an unenviable position.

The Durham County Council Education Authority, as a result of local government reorganisation, took responsibility for Darlington's schools in 1974. Some twenty years later there was talk of Darlington returning to the status of unitary authority, raising questions about the commitment of Durham to the future development of Eastbourne. It was on 27 January 1993 that the head teacher attended a meeting with Darlington's Chief Executive Officer relating to the unitary authority situation, with a further meeting on 8 July. In September 1994 the head teacher met the leader of the council and reported his opinion that the future survival of Eastbourne School was bleak! That was some twelve years before the final closure of the school: a twelve-year period of uncertainty was initiated, a period influencing the stability of the educational provision of a very large number of young people. In March 1995 the Durham Director of Education assured the Eastbourne School governors that there were no plans to close a school in Darlington but in April Darlington announced the composition of a working party for education within the new unitary authority, another sign of anticipated and unsettling change.

There began a period during which the length of service of consecutive head teachers declined. Mr Dingle held the position longest, from 1986 till 1995. After one term with Mr Bellairs as acting head, Mr Appleton took responsibility until his departure in the year 2000. There followed seven years during which the senior leadership frequently changed and was confused.

Ms Pemberton, a deputy at the school, became acting head (October 2002) and subsequently head, and eventually advanced the idea of a Church of England-sponsored academy formed from a merger of Hurworth and Eastbourne.

Mr Henderson (from Hummersknott) became executive head when Eastbourne was placed in a federation with Hummersknott School in November 2002, the school having been placed in Special Measures following an Ofsted inspection by HMIs. When placed in Special Measures a school is said to be failing to provide an acceptable standard of education; leadership is inadequate as is the management of the school. This judgement is moderated by HMI and must be confirmed. At Eastbourne, Special Measures lasted a little more than two years.

Subsequently, Mr Farrar from Hurworth became executive head when Eastbourne entered into a federation with Hurworth as plans were suggested for a merger of the two schools, with a new building to be built on the Tommy Cook playing field site near the Yarm Road–McMullen Road roundabout.

Hurworth parents initiated a strong opposition to the merger plans and Mr Farrar's position, as head of Hurworth and potential head of the new school, became impossible due to the conflict of interests.

Mr Ruston, a senior, long-serving member of staff was persuaded to take the position of acting head when Mr Farrar left. An external consultant was also appointed at this time with the responsibility of helping to bring the school up to an acceptable standard.

Mrs E. Richardson became head from September 2006 to August 2007 (although contracted to serve for three years), leaving at the time of the final closure of Eastbourne prior to the transfer of pupils and staff to the Church of England Academy, which opened in the Eastbourne building the following September.

As senior appointments were of short duration, bringing frequent changes of policy, this must have fostered even greater uncertainty in the staff.

At one end of session there were twenty-two staff changes, some 50 per cent of the teachers leaving. Children were even questioning teachers about how long they intended to stay in the school!

In July 1995 six teachers left the school: Mr C. Cernik left the profession after serving as deputy head from 1 January 1993, only in office for two years and two terms; Mrs J. Frise retired after working with special needs pupils for some twenty years and Miss G. Wade took up a post at Beaumont School after spending a decade or so at Eastbourne. Two experienced teachers were therefore lost and one other from the senior management team.

The six teachers were replaced by five, of whom three were newly qualified and one on a temporary contract.

Difficulties with finding appropriate teachers

Any sign of difficulties in a school, particularly relating to the school's future, causes serving teachers to seek posts in more stable and obviously thriving establishments and deters external staff seeking promotion from applying for posts in the school.

As early as October 1992 and certainly continuing in 1994, due to the decrease in the size of the school, staff were being made redundant, another breeder of uncertainty. There is therefore, in Eastbourne at this time, the inadequate staffing of a school with significant problems.

Problems of recruitment are illustrated by the following recorded situations. On 9 May 1995 the Personnel Subcommittee of the governors decided no suitable candidates had applied for the post of head of modern languages and there were too few applicants from which to appoint a head of communications. These were both posts with extra responsibilities requiring experienced teachers seeking promotion and additional remuneration. At about the same time necessary economies led to the appointment of two classroom assistants in place of one fully qualified and experienced teacher. In July 1995 two candidates were called for interview: one did not turn up, the other withdrew at lunchtime, apparently after seeing the school in action, not satisfied with what was on offer.

Signs of stress among the staff

As early as September 1994, the new school year having hardly started, the head teacher felt it necessary to record that a member of staff had left the school saying simply that he or she could not cope with the demands of the job. This teacher was certainly suffering stress and found the stress too great a burden to tolerate a moment longer.

Another indicator of teachers possibly suffering from stress is the level of absences and there are instances of the head teacher finding it necessary comment on this question. Five out of forty-two were ill on one occasion. There is no suggestion that the teachers were not genuinely ill but the hint that under less stressful conditions people make the extra effort to attend. The absence of such a high proportion of the staff is in itself a cause of extra stress, the classes of absent colleagues having to be taken by others. The head also found it necessary to comment on the significant level of absence among teachers during December 1993.

One reason for staff absence was the policy of sending teachers on courses during term time. During September 1992, for instance, teachers were out of school throughout the term. Even if temporary teachers could be appointed to cover such absences, the fact that the regular teacher was not present brought disturbance to routine. Work may have been set by the regular teacher, but he or she was not there to supervise it – incomers are not necessarily able to do this, not being involved in the ongoing programmes of work.

Another disturbance was caused by the absence of a county union representative on the staff, called to County Hall on union business. Although it may be argued that a union representative, or steward as they are called in industrial environments, should be able to attend meetings, schools are not workshops or offices. It may be possible to be absent from an office and catch up on work at another time, and a colleague may be brought in to operate a machine; it is not such a straightforward situation when dealing with classes of thirty young personalities, where unchanging pupil–teacher relationships are a significant part of the learning process. In addition, school union representatives also had time during term to go on union training courses, which seems to be unnecessary as such non-teaching duties should be carried on out of class-contact time.

A further hint of problems was the frequency of allegations being made by parents against staff, suggesting a lack of earned respect being present, a pupil-control problem perhaps, and where interpersonal relationships are not as they should be, giving rise to a state of stress.

There were formal complaints and formal responses which do not bode well for the ethos of the school. For instance, on one occasion the Discipline Subcommittee of the governors issued a formal warning to a member of staff. The teacher appealed, probably with trade-union support, but the judgement made by the governors was not rescinded.

Certainly, by the mid 1990s, there were sufficient incidents concerning the wrong responses from teachers towards pupils to suggest that a proportion of the staff were finding pupil control difficult: for instance there was a complaint from a parent alleging the manhandling of a child by a teacher; a report of a teacher hitting a child; an incident in which it was claimed a teacher threw a paint pot, hitting a pupil on the head; and another of a teacher hitting a pupil.

On another occasion a teacher was counselled after slapping lower-school pupils. There was a report suggesting that a teacher left after being challenged by the head with regard to his or her attitude towards pupils. There was the case of a teacher being suspended after kicking a child.

The governors and the Director of Education were involved in the resolving of these disciplinary matters. In one instance the teacher did not turn up when a disciplinary meeting was held but at other times it was a parent, having accused a teacher of some inappropriate behaviour towards his child, who did not turn up at a meeting called to resolve the matter.

Although any teacher may, through utter frustration, and in a time of stress, use inappropriate methods to try to correct a child's misbehaviour, training and the enacting of school procedures should make transgressions rare occurrences. Where they occur with any degree of frequency the incidents must be a sign of incompetence on the part of the teacher, the extreme uncontrollable behaviour of the child or group of children, or a lack of appropriate support for the newly qualified or appointed teacher. Such extraordinary events need extraordinary remedies, and these are not always forthcoming.

Having been the head teacher at the school for a considerable period of time I venture to repeat that it was known that the school catered for a high proportion of underprivileged children, many having special educational needs, and behind these needs could be very significant behavioural problems. With experienced teachers leaving the school and newly qualified people filling the vacancies there would be every chance that situations like those above would arise. When a school is in this position, it requires a very generous pupil–teacher ratio and a great deal of extra help from people specialising in the treatment of educational and behavioural disorders.

Failure in this area will place all of the teachers under stress, difficulties in one area overflowing to cause difficulties elsewhere, which in turn will reflect on the ethos of the school. In others words, where children and young people (and adults also but with subtle differences) find their learning environment is disrupted, they also will tend to become disruptive.

Trade-union actions

There is clear evidence that during the period 1936 to 2007 the more professional attitudes associated with teacher trade unionism became more militant. Although most teachers were concerned with being left to get on with their job, some were too ready to adopt the confrontational approach to management–teacher negotiations. Since the days of Fenby–Welford, when management was equated with autocratic headship, the social climate has changed to invite more assistant-teacher involvement in decision making. The uncertainties and stressful situations at Eastbourne further encouraged some to assume the only approach was the confrontational method, with some too keen to seek union intervention in cases of disagreement over unforeseen and accidental occurrences. Unco-operative attitudes seemed to manifest themselves. Consequently inter-staff relationships suffered, creating more stress.

Such events as that when all union representatives complained to the head about the deputy head instructing a senior teacher to require staff to cover for absent teachers, and when the NASUWT found it necessary to refuse to teach a pupil returned to school after a period of exclusion, should not have arisen.

The influence of government initiatives

The actions of consecutive governments over some thirty years eroded teachers' professionalism and undermined their confidence. The combination of appraisal, Standard Assessment Tests, Ofsted inspections and the publication of league tables listing so-called failing schools led to the public humiliation of teachers unfortunate enough to find themselves in such schools, dampening their enthusiasm, career prospects and willingness to co-operate with leadership.

Appraisal

Recognising that *a few* teachers were seriously failing in their responsibilities and a *vast majority seemed* to be producing only average results with most of their pupils and students, the government sought ways of making them, the teachers, more accountable for their performances. One response was the introduction of the compromise method for checking standards: appraisal.

Instead of relying on outside, independent inspectors to check and respond to head teachers' judgements relating to their staff, a system was introduced to formalise the assessment of teachers through a practice of mutual assessment: one teacher apparently sitting in judgement over another without themselves holding a position of sufficient authority.

At Eastbourne the immediate question was: who should appraise me? Firstly, schoolteachers are trained to be in charge of groups of thirty or more personalities for all of their working day; they are expected to get in there and get on with it. So who can come along and tell them they can do better? In business one's immediate senior, manager or supervisor is clearly placed in the hierarchy. But who is this in the school situation: the head of academic department? Teachers would, in general, see their department head as one of their team, one responsible for the objective academic matters such as providing the syllabus, ordering appropriate available resources and allocating equipment, but not necessarily in a position to assess and pass judgement on their unique teaching ability. This would be accepted in the case of the newly qualified but questioned for the long-serving teacher, who may be, in terms of service, better qualified to counsel, advise and mentor than the head of department. So there was the immediately unsettling situation of there having to be someone, who you consider no better qualified than yourself, who could apparently sit in judgement over your teaching ability.

Arising out of this matter was the question as to what should happen in cases of a clash of personality?

At Eastbourne, debate resolved that the appraisers would come from the senior management team and that individuals should be free to choose which team member would appraise them. Result: some of the team were in great demand and others were not.

The exercise of course was seen to be a part of the need for teachers to be seen as accountable; but is a mutually satisfactory chat about one's standard of work a waste of time?

A procedure that should be followed was agreed: there would be an initial meeting, two visits to classes being taught, discussion of matters arising, and the writing of a final report. In the case where a teacher's lesson was seen to be unsatisfactory the teacher attended a debriefing during which targets were set, and improvements looked for outlined.

The general conclusion was that more non-teaching work had been generated, and teachers were placed in a stressful situation unnecessarily. After all everyone knows who are the 'best' teachers and it should be the head teacher and inspectors who are responsible for identifying, assessing, counselling, and, if necessary, disciplining those who are failing.

The question as to who appraises the appraisers is not answered. It may be that the senior management team appraised each other, as it appears did the head teachers.

Mushrooming of meetings

As the fashion for consulting staff took hold so the pressure on staff time increased and at least some teachers felt they were taken away from extra-curricular activities as a result. Priority was apparently given to attending meetings.

One of the meetings was the regular staff meeting and some comments made by the head teacher record just a few telling stories. Staff morale was said to be low and pupil indiscipline mentioned, indicating two ongoing problems. The head recorded one meeting with an exclamation mark: 'staff meeting held!' One entry said the staff considered the curriculum for the following year. One wonders what this meant: a consultation, perhaps, relating to limitations being imposed by, on the one hand, the demands of the National Curriculum and on the other, the decline in available resources. Again, repeating concerns relating to standards of pupil behaviour, a summer term meeting was concerned with pupil attendance and how to improve it.

Standard Assessment Tests (SATs)

Another innovation in the quest for raising standards was the government insistence that children should be assessed on standardised tests at several stages during their school careers. So far so good. A situation akin to that introduced into the Eastbourne Comprehensive School some years previously, when, incidentally, some of the staff felt that the system was devised to test them rather than assess the standards and progress of the young people.

In the school system the individual and group test results were kept confidential to the teachers, parents and pupils on a need-to-know basis. Individual scores were used to monitor individuals and to identify weaknesses where remedial teaching could be to advantage. Group scores were used to compare the levels of attainment of classes and to assess how teaching strategies were being applied to ensure that the school's performance was not below that expected when measured against objectively determined external rational standards.

The government scheme, on the other hand, was to publish the test results in league tables showing how each school compared to every other. Disaster! The league tables were not the disaster; it has already been seen that Eastbourne needed to know how its results and standards compared with other schools. The publishing of league tables nationally, by definition, identified schools at the bottom. To the non-educational professional and general public the system identified and broadcast, labelled, schools which, according to the unexplained test results, were failing.

The results of such a policy are that parents and young people see themselves as failures. Parents with young children immediately start proceedings to avoid having their children sent to such a school; some parents immediately request a transfer of their children out of such a school. The teachers also become restless and seek posts elsewhere, the most able, experienced and best qualified finding the exit easiest. Outside, teachers avoid applying for posts in the school they see advertised as a failure – they would need to be saints to want to work there.

So, government policy caused Eastbourne additional problems, and the staff, in particular, to suffer further stress. The school was left with an intake in which the proportion of underprivileged pupils and those with learning and behavioural problems increased, in a situation where it was more difficult for the school to recruit sufficient well-qualified, experienced specialist staff. It was also at this time that government policy led to pastoral staff being appointed who would be free from class teaching. Unfortunately, the policy included lower pay and the recruitment of non-teachers. Those in Eastbourne were two ex-personal assistants, two teaching assistants and one student mentor.

It is not surprising that there was considerable teacher union opposition to the SATS project. The head recorded, in October 1992 that the pilot project in some schools had been a dsaster. But by May 1993 preparations, including the briefing of the staff, were being made at Eastbourne for the tests to begin, but arrangements were not proceeding without problems. In March 1993 the head teacher found it necessary to formally direct members of the NASUWT to take part in

Key Stage 3 SATs in line with national policy. The union representative in the school responded with the union policy, refusing to take part. On 7 June the head teacher recorded that SATs could not go ahead but on 8 June informed the staff of arrangements for the invigilation of SATs.

Key Stage 3 SATS were cancelled by the governors in March 1994 and the tests only began at Eastbourne on 5 May 1995.

Ofsted

The earlier scheme by which schools were inspected by HMIs was replaced by the Office for Standards in Education, Children's Services and Skills (Ofsted) in 1984, being reorganised in 1992, with the stated aim of standardising and improving education. But instead, it may be regarded as introducing a bureaucratic system of trying to assure accountability which is threatening rather than testing and supportive. Attached to the publication of its reports and of league tables, the change has brought about a climate of threat and stress.

It was claimed that the original purpose of HMIs in education had been lost by the 1980s. For instance, the Schools Council assumed greater significance in curriculum development and in the advising of government. Previously it had been the HMIs, a body seen to have authority and status, and more knowledgeable than the teachers themselves, who were respected for their overseeing and maintaining of standards. The working of the system is well demonstrated in the earlier chapters of this book. An inspector was regarded as a well-qualified and experienced member of the education services, albeit sometimes criticised for being remote from the classroom.

The result of the imposition of Ofsted was the establishment of a system in which the inspectors were less respected, but inspections more frequent and more threatening. Results were published, open to lay people when they should have been for professionals only – a misconceived system in which parents and others should have access to a school's performance. Indeed, parents should have access, but via the professional report, with full explanations of judgements and efforts made to amend failings, available on a need-to-know basis. The system in place merely exposes schools to sensational criticisms by the uninformed.

Among other factors, such as the failure of the local authority to reach agreement on the future development of the school, wrong decisions such as the rolling lunchtime and break scheme caused confusion and added to disorder.

Local Management of Schools

One major change during the second half of the 1980s was the introduction of the Local Management of Schools (LMS), which was intended to give schools a greater degree of control over the way in which resources were allocated – as opposed to control resting with the LEAs. In reality the scheme put in the hands of the schools the task of buying in all services, from specialist educational services to those associated with property maintenance. This immediately removes the bulk purchase of services by one group, local government, and replaces it by a number of smaller organisations, the schools, trying to buy in smaller quantities – not necessarily a cost-cutting exercise and in some cases not even a realistic possibility. This is particularly the case in areas of specialist educational assistance such as the psychological service: who will run such a service, the local authority? A private company?

Of greater significance is the fact that the traditional head teacher, concentrating on educational matters such as the curriculum, internal school organisation, examinations and pupil behaviour, has to give a larger amount of time to those matters which are not solely educational. He or she will have much larger financial problems to face. The school secretary becomes a bursar and personal assistant to the head teacher.

Side by side with these considerations comes the position of the school governors: from the days when they were the LEA to those where they become members of an influential committee not necessarily having any professional educational knowledge whatsoever, and very likely having party-political allegiance.

The governors' growth in responsibilities and influence in the running of the school contrasted with their decreasing personal close involvement in the actual life of the school compared with, for instance, the Fenby–Welford years when they played such a full and meaningful part in school functions such as galas and prize-givings (awards days). During the 1990s they were rarely if ever in school unless on committee business. The chairman is recorded as visiting once.

The lack of knowledge and experience of governors was recognised and so governor training courses were introduced in what appears to be a wasteful situation in which lay people are taught to do the professionals' job. The head regularly and frequently recorded spending time at meetings concerned with governor training, and organised governor training sessions himself.

So what were the governors' functions?

The whole governing body met once each term to consider routine business with extra meetings as required. Much of their work was completed in the subcommittees of the governing body and they give some indication of what they were required to do.

Of major importance was the Finance Committee. The procedure was for the head to request submissions of requirements from the heads of departments and to build these into his proposed budget, initially overseen by the LEA. The budget was then put to the governors' Finance Subcommittee for acceptance. It is recorded in July 1993 that the committee set the budget at £45,000 and in the following November allocated £2,500 to the science department and £300 to D & T (design and technology).

There was the Personnel Subcommittee concerned with all matters relating to the workforce, including the shortlisting of applicants for teaching posts in the school – non-professionals appointing professionals. In July 1994 they were reported as reviewing staff pay.

There was a Building Subcommittee, reminding us that the head and governors had taken on responsibilities for the building previously in the hands of the local authority. As an example of what was being done, in July 1993 the head attended a meeting relating to the contract for the cleaning of the school.

In keeping with the desire to enable parents to raise any concerns they may have about the school the governors invited parents to an annual parents' meeting. The need and desirability for such a meeting can be questioned. Firstly, the original pastoral care arrangements made by the school gave parents access to a head of house or year at any reasonable time. In addition, there were meetings for parents of new entrants, for those with pupils about to enter the senior school, examination progress meetings and annual general progress meetings. These meetings were well attended and an indication of some individual parent–teacher meetings is given elsewhere.

An indication of the popularity of the governors' meetings for parents is given by two attendances: in December 1992 six parents attended and in 1993 only four.

Opting out

Following the introduction of LMS, came Opting Out of LEA control. More independence perhaps, but certainly more work. Schools became responsible for arranging contracts for all services formerly the responsibility of education administrators at the area or county office.

Organisation of the school

It has already been noted that the school was, by the 1990s, much smaller than during all of the previous years, but the pupils, fewer in number, were coming from the same catchment area as in the past, in part serving an area of council properties housing some of the most underprivileged families.

There is an interesting comment recorded by the head teacher on 3 December 1992 when he says he convened a meeting relating to the 'state of Firthmoor'. It can be assumed that he was referring to the Firthmoor School but the comment was not specific. It was, however, generally known that it was from Firthmoor, in spite of there being many normal families living there, that Eastbourne received most of its problem pupils – most but not all.

New entrants' days

The policy of a careful introduction of new primary school children to the secondary school continued with allocating a whole day in July to an induction programme for pupils from the contributory primary schools. If numbers were sufficiently high, two days would be used, bringing one group of children on each day.

With an intake of about 120 youngsters each year, a simple arrangement would place 30 in each of four classes for each of the five years catered for up the age of 16. However, teaching groups would vary from subject to subject and from year to year according to the demands arising from the need to cater for those with learning difficulties, practical subjects and in the upper school, the variety of subjects taken in public examinations.

Attendance, registration and SIMS

Throughout most of the years subsequent to the raising of the school-leaving age from 14 there has been a greater problem of some children not attending school. As teachers have always been required to keep a register of pupil attendance, there has always been a method of recording whether a pupil is present at the start of the morning and afternoon sessions, but with the arrival of the much larger schools and comprehensive education, it has become necessary to check that pupils are present in each and every lesson. In turn this has become an extra task for the classroom teacher who is anxious to get on with the job of teaching and sees registration as a mere administrative task.

To ease the burden but enforce attendance, through the thorough and regular checks on absentees throughout the day, a new registration of attendance system was introduced in the mid 1990s. The staff were briefed on the workings of the system in July 1994, and each teacher given what one described as a 'funny box' into which they typed those absent from every lesson or traditional registration period for which they were responsible. Results were automatically transmitted to a central point, where a senior teacher investigated absentees. For those requiring it, there was a printout of the results. Nevertheless, it was claimed that the system was open to errors and also the temptation to make things look better than they actually were. The significance being that government initiatives demanded that a school improve its attendance figures, and reports of high levels of truancy and absenteeism added to the criticisms aimed at a school with a high proportion of youngsters coming from problem families.

One strategy for dealing with absentees is reported in March and again in June 1994, when meetings of the Attendance and Behaviour Clinic were held under the chairmanship of the head teacher, during which parents and children were counselled in an effort to improve matters.

Discipline

School discipline, good, bad or indifferent, is the outcome of the interaction of hundreds of very different immature individuals with each other and the mutual interaction between each of these unique individuals and the lesser number of teachers. The outcomes, the natures of these interactions, determine the ethos of the school.

Seeking evidence of the factors which lie behind the nature of interactions is therefore essential in the understanding of how school discipline works.

At Eastbourne the repeated emphasis of the influence of a high proportion of individuals with learning and behaviour problems cannot be ignored but there are other factors, for instance in the evidence recorded by the head teacher in 1994. The School Council, made up of pupil representatives from each class, actually complained that teachers were not doing their duties, an interesting and very significant factor which teachers would want to deny. So is there other evidence that *some* teachers were not carrying out their responsibilities? If some are failing in this respect a greater burden is placed on those that are conscientious in this matter, and weakness seen by the pupils in some teachers leads the least self-disciplined immature youngsters to transgress even more than they would otherwise do.

On one occasion in a September, early in the school year, when everyone should be fresh from the long summer holiday, the head found pupils locked in the gym at break time. Another time there was a fight in the gym area, where pupils had been left changing when staff had apparently gone to lunch. On the third day of the new school year seven pupils were discovered in the loft, presumably accessed through one of the projection rooms reached by stairs from one of the halls on the first floor. During one lunchtime paper was set alight in Durham Toilets, that is toilets located in the school building and allocated for use to the pupils in Durham House. These are indicators of a lack of supervision, the latter highlighting the difficulties arising during lunchtimes when teachers chose not to be on duty, leaving non-professionals in charge.

There is evidence of abnormal behaviour from pupils. One such event ended in the exclusion of the pupil after he had deliberately put his head through a window pane, breaking the glass and cutting his face when in a temper, an aggressive reaction to events. A pupil attacked another member of a group with an iron ball causing a skull fracture and although the child claimed the attack was an accident this was not seen as a true explanation and he was excluded after consideration by senior staff. The NASUWT refused to teach a pupil known to have attempted suicide, the knowledge of the exceptional event resulting in the calling of an emergency case conference.

In 1993 a lady teacher was hit by girl pupil and in January 1997 a pupil was excluded following misbehaviour in front of the deputy head. Both of these events demonstrate an unusual absence of respect for authority observed in youngsters having behaviour problems.

A great deal of time had to be taken up dealing with problem children, including attending case conferences and calling parents into school for a face-to-face discussion about their child's behaviour. For instance, one parent was seen about his son's behaviour, which included being caught on camera spraying graffiti on the front porch. Also, the exclusion of a pupil required a meeting to discuss the case, including discussion with the appropriate governors' subcommittee.

Exclusions

Repeated and/or serious misbehaviour could result in the indefinite exclusion of the pupil from school. Such situations had to be reported to the governors, who would consider the parents' and school's views on the situation at a meeting of the Disciplinary Subcommittee. It was not always the case that the committee would support the school's decision to suspend the child. A noteworthy example was when the governors upheld an exclusion following a long series of incidents involving a child. One was when the youngster broke a light bulb in the swimming pool.

Exclusions were not only subject to ratification by the governors but also by the LEA, which could then decide to support the exclusion or not as the case may be.

The curriculum

From the time of Mr Dingle the academic organisation of the school was based on faculties: that is where subjects are grouped under faculty titles, with a head of faculty in charge. But, no matter what the organisation, the curriculum was dominated by the requirements of the National Curriculum, first established by Kenneth Baker during the Thatcher government and variously added to or subtracted from according to the political enthusiasm of the moment. In addition, the upper school programme was dominated by the requirements of the 16-plus GCSE. In addition, as already noted, with the shrinking size of the school population limitations would have been imposed by availability of staff and specialist accommodation.

Whatever conclusions may be reached from the knowledge available it must be recorded that in November 1992 the school achieved the National Curriculum Award and on the 26th of the month the school closed at 2 p.m. for the reception organised as a part of this achievement.

Such questions as the desirability of streaming, setting or mixed ability continued and in the 1990s there was considerable time spent on curriculum models, that is different patterns for what things were taught, and how. It is pertinent to recall the head teacher's observation following the staff discussion of the various plans put to them. He said the staff were only interested in the plan which gave them less contact time with classes. This is a pity but probably arising from the demands made upon teachers by the government imposition of bureaucratic procedures that they felt were of little real educational value but had been made a part of their duty.

The computer age had arrived, at first there being a specialised computer room, which in the early 1990s was also used by visiting primary school groups. For instance, it was reported that on 23 May 1995 a group of junior school pupils used the computer room throughout the afternoon. Such restricted availability was eventually superseded by the provision of individual computers in almost all teaching rooms.

The requirement of religious study and worship remained largely unchanged but the actual carrying out of the requirement was losing its momentum. School policy on the subject was considered in a presentation to the staff in 1994, when school and house assemblies continued to be held. A note states that years 7 and 8 attended a carol service at St Cuthbert's Church in 1994. Years 7 and 8 were the two junior secondary school years and one must wonder whether the senior pupils attended such a service. Certainly, group singing of hymns became less attractive.

For the senior school there was a continuous liaison with the Technical College with a view to providing more work-based courses for those pupils finding the school environment somewhat hostile. Visits were arranged, such as those in the summer of 1995, when a third of year group 10 at one time visited the college to be introduced to opportunities in further education.

Work experience for pupils in year 10 continued throughout this period. All pupils were given the opportunity to take part in the programme, which lasted for two weeks and took place at the end of the summer term.

Extra-curricular activities

Established extra-curricular activities continued. The annual pantomime certainly continued to be produced during the early part of this period, with performances on several evenings and one for special groups, such as that for pupils from the junior schools. With the decreasing size of the school such productions must surely have become more difficult to stage due to staff shortages, the loss of those experienced in the work involved and the overwhelming requirements of bureaucracy – and perhaps due to the withdrawal of at least some goodwill by teachers suffering low morale. There is also the observation that there was a decline in the numbers of senior pupils taking part due to their involvement in examination work – a pity, because they could be the leaders in such enterprises, giving much to younger pupils, gaining self esteem from their involvement and adding to the positive ethos of the school as a whole.

There are reports of pupils winning individual and team prizes in public-speaking competitions. On the social side of life were discos, and even, on at least one occasion, a dinner-dance for pupils in year 11.

In the early part of the period the timetable continued to be suspended for the organisation of Activities Week.

Examinations and the reporting of progress

Sixteen-plus school examinations and internal tests or examinations continued to be held. In the area of public examinations it was inevitable that, in a school with a high proportion of pupils with special needs, the results appearing in the national league tables were never going to be very high and it is this area of achievement, or lack of it, that became one aspect of the school being seen to fail. The fact that those who could achieved their optimum results meant very little in the world of league tables.

School reports were by this time records of achievement, designed to record all positive achievements of each pupil, including not only those based on academic subjects but also on sporting and social activities.

The parents

A core of very supportive parents had always been a part of Eastbourne School and this was still true during the 1990s. The Parent–Teachers Association ran bingo sessions, quiz nights, fashion shows, and car boot sales for example, raising much-appreciated money for the school fund.

The school did all it could to bring parents into the school to discuss their children's progress, behaviour when necessary, and to explain new developments and actions. For instance, in March 1993 there was a parents' evening, which used an appointments scheme for face-to-face meetings between parents and subject teachers. These meetings were regular and occurred after the issue of reports or records of achievement. There was also at this time a meeting concerning the problem of bullying. In June parents were invited to have explained the school uniform policy and for the school to receive any concerns they may have had. Parents of new primary school entrants were always invited to a meeting before the new school year and another to review how well the children had settled into the new environment. For most parents and for much of the time liaison was very good.

A final word

On a latter day in the history of the school the head teacher kindly took me round the school. It was my first visit to the whole school in some twenty years, having only attended special functions in the main school hall. I left feeling depressed. What had been a thriving and well-respected school was clearly, by this time, suffering serious problems. I was dismayed to see the domestic science, home economics or whatever modern terminology may have titled the area, outside the school premises, the surroundings to the flat looking somewhat neglected and abandoned.

I had already entered by the main gate, with some of the cherry trees still standing and flowering but the facade of the imposing brick building, with its entrance porticos and stone enhancements, broken by the poorly placed ring fence and crudely bricked-up central archway. Some trees had clearly disappeared; the workshops were still there but looking neglected and the two boys with whom I had been left after seeing the head teacher knowing nothing of their history. At the rear, looking into the old boys' and girls' playgrounds, the scene was not inviting – all of the windows were covered in, looking boarded up, and the upper-floor corridors' external woodwork painted a drab blue.

Inside, the corridors were enclosed, one might say claustrophobic, all windows, once giving natural light, having had their glass replaced by opaque wooden panels, painted in a ubiquitous cream. The classrooms were similarly treated, most of their corridor windows turned into walls, creating the impression of unfriendliness, any visitors being unwelcome. One classroom in particular, extremely well decorated by colourful visual aids, was to me overpowering, completely enclosed from the outside world.

The halls had lost their balconies, making them, of course, smaller, but also adding to this overall impression of enclosure, as though no one was to overlook any other.

One staircase, with its quality green-tiled lower wall, leading to the upper floor and entrance to what was once a hall balcony, had been caged in by a metal frame. I wondered if this was for health and safety or security reasons. Certainly, during some fifty or more years, no child had ever been forced, accidentally fallen or chosen to practice dangerous climbing skills over the handrails.

The swimming pool, in which thousands of children had learned to swim, and some even leaned the skills need to handle canoes in preparation for their visits to outdoor sports centres, was empty, with debris at its bottom.

The sports hall, a modern provision in the sixties, looked unkempt, but clearly was still used as an examination hall for the senior school examinations.

The corridor entrance to the 'new' or 'science' block invited the visitor to enter the tunnel of love, presumably a student project which, in my personal view, was not appropriate. I thought it crude and as a piece of art, not particularly attractive.

I did not meet many young people. There were the two boys who guided me through corridors I had known so well, first-year pupils, well dressed in school uniforms. One spoke well, the other remained silent, perhaps in awe of the elderly gentleman they were escorting. One boy, when I was still with the head teacher, rushed noisily by, neither stopping nor paying any attention to two adults. He was asked what he was doing, turned round and shouted some unintelligible objection to being challenged. Miss Fenby would have exploded with rage! Three senior girls, arm in arm, almost danced, noisily engaged in some apparently hilarious conversation, along the corridor. They would have immediately been stopped, been seriously silenced, if they had met

Miss Hope, the deputy head in my day. Their excuse for absence from class was that one seemed to have had an injured thumb, and the immediate response should have been: why are three of you needed to deal with one thumb? Without waiting for a reply, two would be sent straight back to class, and a discreet follow-up made to see why the teacher had allowed them out of the room in the first place.

We hurried along one corridor where I heard the high-pitched agonised voice of another teacher trying to be heard over the cacophony of youthful yells, screeches and laughter – something amiss there! We reached another room, which we entered, and my guide briefly spoke with the teacher in charge. The class was clearly one of the older, non-intellectual young folk, variously draped over classroom chairs and clearly waiting for the day school ended. One bold young lady, alert and interested in the new arrival, me, loudly called out, without considering she could possibly be interrupting an expected introduction: 'Who's yer friend then?' I was introduced, and it transpired that the parents of these young people were in the school when I was head teacher. The conversation was brief; we were soon on our way back to reception, the visit over.

The school closed in September 2007 and the pupils transferred to the new Church of England Academy, but for two years occupied the renovated Eastbourne building.